Superhumanity

Superhumanity: Design of the Self

Nick Axel, Beatriz Colomina,
Nikolaus Hirsch, Anton Vidokle,
Mark Wigley, Editors

e-flux Architecture
University of Minnesota Press
The Graham Foundation

Contents

Introduction

Superhumanity is first and foremost a question, a self-question, even a radical questioning of the self. It is not a species, a thing, a condition, or a phenomenon. It is not supercharged humans extended by shiny technologies and ideologies—as if the creature with a cell phone in its hand is existentially different from the creature holding a stone axe. Rather, it is an all-too-human questioning of the very category "human."

The 3rd Istanbul Design Biennial of 2017—"ARE WE HUMAN?: The Design Of The Species: 2 Seconds, 2 Days, 2 Years, 200 Years, 200,000 Years"—made the following proposition: "Design is always design of the human." Design, then, is the very means by which that question is asked. The Biennial explored the radical implications of the thought that we have always been continuously reshaped by the artifacts that we have shaped. If the penetration of design into life is any measure to go by, perhaps we have never been more human than we are today. As the Biennial manifesto points out:

> The average day involves the experience of thousands of layers of design that reach to outer space but also reach deep into our bodies and brains. We literally live inside design, like the spider lives inside the web constructed from inside its own body. But

> unlike the spider, we have spawned countless overlapping and interacting webs. Even the planet itself has been completely encrusted by design as a geological layer. There is no longer an outside to the world of design. Design has become the world.[1]

To recognize oneself as human might be the strangest act of all, yet it is a position whose assumption, in spite of whatever complications it may bring, we take to be of utmost urgency. Superhumanity, a project by e-flux Architecture, seeks to reposition the idea of a form of life by exploring the intimate relationship between the concepts of "design" and "the human." What, then—rather than who—is it that is capable of asking such questions? In asking about the lives we inhabit, about the ones both once and soon to be designed, we point to the sites, and the techniques, to design others. Wielding the weapon of design, the fifty contributors to Superhumanity took the concept of the "self" as a privileged site to analyze, debate, and speculate upon these and other questions from a diversity of viewpoints.

In "The Obligation to Self-Design," Boris Groys traces a possible genealogy of design from the design of the soul to the design of the body and the emergence of "self-design":

> With the death of God, design became the medium of the soul, the revelation of the subject hidden inside the human body. Thus design took on an ethical dimension it had not had previously. In design, ethics became aesthetics; it became form. Where religion once was, design has emerged. The modern subject now has a new obligation: the obligation to self-design, an aesthetic presentation as ethical subject.[2]

Far from its origins as a luxury of leisure time only the aristocracy could afford, the self has become fully integrated into the core of contemporary economic systems and social structures. It is the very medium through which interpersonal exchange takes place, be it of a commercial, romantic, or violent nature. You must have a self, know your self, and be your self, for otherwise, well, what are you? And how can you possibly expect, not to mention hope, to become? The self and platforms for its careful design dominate contemporary mediascapes, from avatars and surrogate identities with virtual plastic surgery to digital streams of consciousness that disappear before they can become memories, incessantly hungry feeds that devour one's voice like screaming into a black hole, endless personal museums for the exhibition of one's tastes and interests, and profiles never quite perfect enough, always in need of further attention.

Yet the field of design has radically expanded, "from carefully crafted individual looks and online identities, to the surrounding galaxies of personal devices, new materials, interfaces, networks, systems, infrastructures, data, chemicals, organisms, and genetic codes," as the manifesto of the Biennial puts it. Well beyond what we typically think of as either media or the social, the self today has nearly limitless potential for its own design. But to return to the words of Groys, "the ultimate problem of design concerns not how I design the world outside, but how I design myself—or, rather, how I deal with the way in which the world designs me." With reference to the utilitarian art of Russian Constructivism that sought to use design as a way to transcend the individual and manifest the collective soul, Groys ultimately identifies the "design of life as a whole" as the very means of realizing a political project. Reading Groys in reverse, we could say that the self cannot help but live as a project, understood as political design. The self is a trap that we are born into and sink further down with every day that passes, but its design might just be its only means of escape.

The notion of "self-design" is a provocation. It is a call to challenge any assumptions we may have about both the "self" and "design," again and again, now and tomorrow, so that we might be able to catch a fleeting glimpse of what it might mean to be human. For humanity has, and always will have, a design problem. A problem of whose future is sculpted by design. Of the shape of its user. Its actual interface.

The human is this question of arranging physical, chemical, electromagnetic, and genetic apparatuses in time and space. How long a finger is needed to reach the trigger, or stroke another animal? How far must it extend in space? Elevated from humble materiality to a metaphysical program, the collective constellation of these design extensions is the humanist project. But what happens when that program is itself extended beyond its own limits?

Superhumanity emerged from this crack. It names the fetishes of humanism when costumed in the inherited clothes of an older body politic. Clothes that don't fit, can't fit, and when we voice our discomfort in protest, the response is our total destruction. The political environment currently boiling over makes it necessary to materialize the superhuman so that we may, one day, finally recognize ourselves as human.

History, as we know, proceeds by its bad side, and the battle for the design of the twenty-first century has just begun. Freedoms, institutions, and alliances are under assault by populism, nationalism, and fascism, with no sign of deceleration in the near future. The machine currently in power can learn—it has proven itself capable of that—but it cannot think for itself. Its thought is driven by feedback. It is caught in a loop, yet not the type of loop that draws circles over itself, but rather one that spirals out of control.

The question of extension asks again: Are we human? Yet the question is, and always has been, what do we mean by "we"? The superhuman is the horror of our inescapable potential, of the error to which we are fundamentally prone. But it is also an acknowledgement that whatever the human has been is not all that it can become in the days and decades ahead. Hearts on fire, brains on ice, we race against the inevitable. Until then.

Nick Axel, Beatriz Colomina, Nikolaus Hirsch,
Anton Vidokle, Mark Wigley

1 Beatriz Colomina and Mark Wigley, *Bis Insan Miyiz? / Are We Human?: Design of the Species: 2 Seconds 2 Days 2 Years 200 Years 200,000 Years* (IKSV: Istanbul Foundation for Culture and Art, Istanbul, 2016).

2 Boris Groys, "The Obligation to Self-Design," *e-flux Journal* 0 (2008).

Self-Design, or Productive Narcissism

Boris Groys

Our culture is commonly described as being narcissistic. And narcissism is understood as a total concentration on oneself, as a lack of interest in society. However, it is difficult to say that the mythological Narcissus is interested exclusively in himself. Obviously he is not interested in satisfying his desires, which he ascetically rejects. But neither is he interested in an "inner," "subjective" vision accessible exclusively to his own contemplation, isolating him from others. Rather, he is enchanted by the reflection of his body in the lake presenting itself as an "objective," profane image—produced by Nature and potentially accessible to everyone. It would be wrong to say that Narcissus is uninterested in others, in society. Rather, he completely identifies his own perspective with an "objective" social perspective. And so he assumes that others will be also fascinated by his own worldly image. As a member of Greek culture, he knows that he shares the aesthetic taste of other Greeks.

The contemporary Narcissus, however, cannot be so certain of his own taste. Today we are unable to like ourselves if we are not liked by the society in which we live. And in our society we have to become active if we want to be the objects of others' admiration. Contemporary subjects cannot only rely on the looks they were born with: they must practice self-design, and produce their own image with the goal of becoming liked by society. Even those whose activities are limited to taking selfies must still actively distribute them to get the "likes" they want. But self-design does not stop here. We also produce aesthetically relevant things and/or surround ourselves with things we believe to be impressive and seductive. And we act publicly—even sacrificing oneself in the name of a public good—in order to be admired by others.

Alexandre Kojève believed that the desire to be desired is specifically human—that it is precisely what makes us human, what distinguishes us from animals. The animal, "natural" desire always negates the object of desire: if I am hungry, I eat bread, and thus destroy the bread. If I am thirsty I destroy water by drinking it. But there is also the anthropogenic desire—not for particular things but for being desired: "Thus, in the relationship between man and woman, for example, Desire is human only if one desires not the body but the desire of the other."[1] It is this anthropogenic desire that initiates and moves history: "human history is the history of desired Desires."[2] Kojève describes history as being moved by heroes pushed to sacrifice themselves in the name of humankind by this specifically human desire: the desire for recognition, for becoming an object of society's admiration and love. The desire for desire produces self-consciousness and even the "self" as such, but it is also what turns the subject into an object—ultimately, a dead object. Kojève writes: "Without this fight to the death for pure prestige, there would never have been human beings on Earth."[3] The subject of the desire for desire is not "natural" because it is ready to sacrifice all natural needs and even "natural" existence for an abstract Idea of recognition. By renouncing everything natural, this subject becomes historical, insofar as it is constituted by the desire for historical recognition. Thus, this subject becomes dependent on the historical conditions of recognition: on the existence of mankind. None are as interested in the survival and well-being of society as the contemporary Narcissus.

This interest is characteristically modern, secular, atheistic. As long as God was considered to be alive, the design of the soul was more important than the design of the body. The subject wanted their soul to be loved or at least recognized by God. The desire for admiration by others, by society, was regarded as a sin because it substituted "worldly" recognition for the only true spiritual recognition—external values for inner values. Thus, the relationship of the subject to society was ethical: one did something good for society to please God—not society itself. The death of God signified the disappearance of the divine viewer of the soul, the viewer for whom the soul had been designed for centuries. In the secular age, God was replaced by society, and thus, instead of an ethical relationship, our relationship to society became erotic. Suddenly, the only possible manifestation of human subjectivity became its design: the look of the clothes in which humans appear, the everyday things with which they surround themselves, the spaces they inhabit, and so forth. Where religion once was, design emerged.

As a result, design has transformed society itself into an exhibition space in which individuals appear as both artists and self-produced works of art. Modern design thus avoids Kant's famous distinction between disinterested aesthetic contemplation and the use of things guided by interests. For a long time after Kant, disinterested contemplation was considered superior to a practical attitude, as a higher, if not the highest, manifestation of the human spirit. But already by the end of the nineteenth century, the *vita contemplativa* was thoroughly discredited and the *vita activa* was elevated to the true task of humankind. At least since Guy Debord's *Society of the Spectacle*, design has been accused of seducing people into weakening their activity, vitality, and energy—of making them passive consumers who lack will, who are manipulated by omnipresent advertising to become victims of capital. The apparent cure for this trance was a shock-like encounter with the "real" capable of rescuing people from their contemplative passivity and moving them to action, to the only thing that promises an experience of truth as living intensity. The only debate that remained was over the question of whether such an encounter with the real was still possible, or whether the real has definitively disappeared behind its designed surface.

After History: Alexandre Kojève as a Photographer, 2012, BAK, basis voor actuele kunst, Utrecht, installation view with postcards and itineraries. Photo: Victor Nieuwenhuijs.

However, the subject of self-design clearly has a vital interest in the image on offer to the outside world. This subject is therefore not passive, but active and productive. Where it was once both a privilege and a burden for the chosen few, in our time self-design has become the mass cultural practice par excellence. The internet is a place for self-presentation—from Facebook to YouTube to Instagram—but likewise in the "real," or let's say "analog" world, one is expected to be responsible for the image they present to the gaze of others. The subject of self-design is therefore not only interested in their own existence, but also in that of mankind, their only possible spectator. Like a lover's interest in the existence of a partner to find love and be loved by, the subject of self-design is interested in the existence of society to find and receive recognition and admiration. This interest is intense because mankind is, as we know, vulnerable and mortal. The desire for the other's desire is permanently haunted by the possibility of mankind's final disappearance—the physical death of human spectators after the metaphysical death of God.

This anxiety concerning mankind's ultimate fate was powerfully expressed by Jean-François Lyotard in his 1987 essay "Can Thought Go On Without a Body?" Lyotard begins his essay with a reference to the scientific prediction that the sun will explode in 4.5 billion years. He writes that this prediction

> is the sole serious question to face humanity today. In comparison everything else seems insignificant. Wars, conflicts, political tensions, shift in opinion, philosophical debates, even passions—everything is dead already if this infinite reserve from which you draw now your energy ... dies out with the Sun.[4]

The death of mankind seems distant, but it already poisons us and makes our efforts senseless. Scientists have proven that there are weak waves produced by the Big Bang that still come to us. So one can assume that there are informational waves from the sun's explosion in 4.5 billion years that already reach us and make our souls tremble. Humankind can replace God as the ultimate spectator of our self-design only if we become immortal. Thus the real challenge is to create new hardware that can replace the human body, finding a new medium on which to write human software, i.e. thought. According to Lyotard, the possibility of such a rewriting is given by the fact that "technology wasn't invented by us humans."[5] The development of technology is a cosmic process in which humans are only episodically involved. By shifting the focus from software (attitudes, opinions, ideologies) to hardware (organism, machine, their combinations, cosmic processes, and events), Lyotard opened the way to thinking the post- or transhuman.

However, from its beginning, the practice of self-design prefigured the problematic of the post- and transhuman condition. Self-design means rewriting inner, psychological, political attitudes or economic interests on external media: self-design creates a second, artificial body that potentially replaces and survives that of the human. Indeed, when somebody dies, the things they chose and used remain available. If the person was famous, a museum may keep these things as a substitute for the absent body. Thus, the use of things is a form of self-design: things are not only tools for practical life but also manifestations of their user's soul. In fact, as heirs to palaces and churches, art museums were originally design museums.

Of course, one does not only use things; one also produces them. These things—artworks, books, films, photos, etc.—circulate and are dispersed globally. This dispersal is even more obvious with the internet, where not only famous people but all people are able to rewrite their personality. Yet if one does a search for a particular name on the internet, the thousands of results that come up do not build any unity. Thus, one feels that these secondary, self-designed, artificial bodies are already in a state of slow-motion explosion, reminding one of the final scene of Antonioni's *Zabriski Point*. The eternal struggle between Apollo and Dionysus as described by Nietzsche leads here to a strange result: the self-designed body is dismembered, dispersed, and decentered, but still maintains a virtual unity.[6] This virtual unity, however, is not accessible to the human gaze. Only surveillance and search programs like Google can analyze the internet in its entirety and thus identify the secondary bodies of living and dead persons. Here, a machine is recognized by a machine, and an algorithm by another algorithm. Maybe the internet prefigures the condition Lyotard envisioned: mankind's persistence in a state of explosion.

1 Alexandre Kojève, *Introduction to the Reading of Hegel*, trans. James H. Nichols (Ithaca: Cornell University Press, 1980), 5.
2 Ibid, 6–7.
3 Ibid., 6.
4 Jean-François Lyotard, *Inhuman. Reflections on Time*, trans. Geoffrey Bennington and Rachel Bowlby (London: Polity Press, 1989), 9.
5 Ibid., 12.
6 Friedrich Nietzsche, *The Birth of Tragedy* (1872).

No You're Not

Keller Easterling

It is probably a mistake to elevate those attributes of *Homo sapiens*' nervous system that long for the right answer, the unified field, the elementary particle, or the universal truth. These beliefs are present not only in formalized philosophies, religions, and political regimes of the human, but at the heart of the human's daily activities. Some cerebral constructs—the most immaterial and ephemeral of all the body's inventions—ossify into cast-iron closed loops of logical thinking that demand to be "the one and only." A dictator, professor, spiritual leader, parent, or coworker all practice daily meditations or tireless litigations about the reasons why they are right. Almost everything else in the soft assemblies of most organisms works by endless iteration, multiplication, or trial and error. Yet this stray symptom of stubborn self-regard holds sway over the entire organism, causing it to constantly circle a very limited repertoire of behaviors. Observing the fact that there do not seem to be other creatures who sit, with fins and flagellates limp, transfixed in thought about something like dialectic and telos, humans even make the mistake of thinking that this restrictive habit of mind is a gift that sets them above the rest.

Since superiority cannot abide contradiction, the whole assembly also often oscillates between a closed loop—the circulation of flattering and compatible evidence—and a binary fight—the vilification of nonconforming evidence. Fighting is essential to being right. There is no growth or ideation without argument or debate. There is no literature without conflict. Bombastic arguments must naturally ask for successive rather than coexistent thoughts or practices. They must wipe away the incumbent and establish the new and transcendent. The root of the problem—the desire to be right—is treated as the progressive answer to the problem. The new right answer kills the old right answer, and the very habits of mind that help to incite violence are deployed in an impossible attempt to alleviate it. Essentially there is very little difference in spirit or intent between an avant-garde of ideas and an avant-garde of combat formation. Whether taking the form of intellectual sparring or all-out war, these are the grisly histories of the "humanities."

True to the disposition of the closed loop, the argument that is inescapable will, structurally, always be correct. In a recent book about winning arguments, a human named Stanley Fish quotes an exchange from Monty Python's sketch "The Argument Clinic." Michael Palin, who has come to the clinic to pay for an argument, says, "Argument is an intellectual process. Contradiction is just the automatic gainsaying of anything the other person says." John Cleese replies, "It is NOT!" Unwittingly adding to the comedy, Fish uses the exchange to prove that *he* himself was right all along about the ubiquity of argument.[1] He and so many others, as if perpetually saying "there you are, you see," will always be human and always be right. And culture continues to congratulate itself on its ability to debate or deploy the logics of reasonable thinking to arrive at proofs that demonstrate the right answer.

Beyond the daily preoccupations of individuals, the loop and the binary are scalable. Whole populations of people and huge territories captivated by some universal belief or totalizing regime of control can move in lockstep to demonstrate that they are right. Muscles and fists harden into weapons. Demonstrating all reasonable outcomes of aggression or consumption, statistics, data, and game theory support rationalizing wars and markets. Global infrastructure platforms historically portray themselves as ultimate, transcendent, and redemptive; it was as true for railroads as it is now for digital technologies that treat data as the only information of consequence in a world that is Turing complete. It is not just ISIS teenagers who, gun and sledgehammer in hand, long for their own caliphate.

From the ancients to the moderns, those who have so suggestively attempted to break the spell of the loop and the binary with other powers of *Homo sapiens* are often drawn back into its vortex. With faith in corporeal agency, polytheism, and democracy, the ancients, still often regarded as a pinnacle of culture, offered only a suggestive start in uncovering the organism's power. Or, to escape the "iron cage" of rationalized culture, we choose an ideology that is even more right. Perhaps a Marxist position will duel with the market until it arrives at a utopian ultimate, one that will fail only because of a lack of purity. Deleuze and Guattari provide another vivid example of philosophers so learned that they are capable of pointing to things outside their philosophy—to animals, everyday practices, and colloquial expressions. "Many people have a tree growing in their heads, but the brain itself is much more a grass than a tree," they write. Yet in trying to break free, they nevertheless deploy habits of mind that sometimes drift toward monism and binary opposition. "So much getting even, for epistemology is not innocent."[2] And isn't the loop and binary securely locked in place when an attempt to escape the humanities calls itself "radical" or "posthuman?" Again, the logic that humans have prized thrives on it own self-perpetuating negation.

But while difficult to express within rational structures of thought, humans are always escaping the cage and exceeding the bounds of the human. The world is run on irrationality and comedy that often will not compute within our philosophies. Many things change not because of logical proof or a reasonable plan but because of irrational desires, and the most rationalized game theory can be outwitted with a simple series of lies. For philosophers, these powers are often treated like witchcraft or some other unknowable, magical quest, even though they are just another kind of knowledge that is often manifest in ephemeral, even practical, activities. This is the knowledge of use—of "knowing how" *in addition to* "knowing that."[3] These are the powers of Marx's "mystical" dancing table, which many have said should be made to stand still. But maybe these powers are really more like Gabriel Tarde's social "contagions," the lifeblood of economies of exchange. They are persuasions rather than arguments that start nowhere and move across populations. Perhaps many of the world's most puzzling problems—problems that resist rational explanation—reside in this outlying territory.

The most dangerous human bullies and sociopaths are perhaps so sturdy because they not only have an abiding faith in the loop and the binary, but also a crafty talent for wielding irrationality and fiction. They never tire of a circular argument and engage, almost involuntarily and until their last breath, in a "did / did not" or an "is / is not" exchange. Not only will they not back down; they are eager to deliver an offensive strike. They are happy in the loop because they *are* the loop. They are the "one and only," and any contradiction is not only expelled but also tracked down and destroyed. Still, the most successful bullies *also* know about the contagion of persuasion and how to manipulate it. They know that telling one lie activates and strengthens rational behavior because it calls on the necessity of rational behavior to sort out and restore truth, yet the presence of many lies begins to build up the Teflon coating on which rationality slips and slides. This is the power of religious leaders, politicians, and celebrities. Their siren song can cause people to stand in single file and walk over a cliff. Like a drunk who tries especially hard to walk as if sober and composed, as each follower falls, they will tell you that they are more right, even more rational, than others not in line. Trump supporters and ISIS recruits, acting as if they alone have access to the facts, condescend to litigate the details of their project for the less reasonable or the ill-informed. The familiar human desire to occupy a superior platform perfectly camouflages the power to seduce and hustle. So, armed only with rationality or a desire to win the argument, it is nearly impossible to derail or interrupt this seduction or oppression, whether from a schoolyard menace, a petty administrator, or an authoritarian leader of our modern "democracies."

Opposition to a bully is doomed to circle the human tautology about being right, but offering an expanded repertoire of behaviors is a power that can baffle philosophies by exceeding competition, rationality, and righteous self-regard. These powers are so familiar that they may be almost imperceptible, or perhaps they are only difficult to express within familiar forms of discourse. In order to exist *beyond* the human, they *include* the human rather than negate it. They are "more than human" and sometimes beyond the skin and the self.[4] While often treated as paranormal to the reasonable human, everyone possesses the capacity to exercise these powers—to wander away from dominant constructs and outwit their persistent violence.

Design is an excellent arena in which to observe the relentlessly human as well as the possibilities of the *more than human*. Within the narrow framework of the human, design can be about the total extension of rationality into the surrounding environment with universal systems of proportion or geometry that make claims to "natural laws." While it is easy to think of a historical *Gesamtkunstwerk* reflecting these design ideologies, contemporary digital environments are also locked around totalizing dreams and the very limited powers of a nervous system oversaturated with optics and default sexuality. But design can also be about extending other powers of that nervous system. There are so many underexploited faculties of voice, skin, skeleton, and muscles in interplay with other solids, photons, and waves. The *more than human* doesn't negate human design; it only multiplies those designs in a larger field so that there are always many instead of only one.

Beyond the design of things is the design of the medium in which they are suspended, and beyond the design of a totalizing medium is the design of an iterative medium. The right answer is doomed to be right only for an instant before its superiority is challenged. But just as navigating a river is indeterminate, time-released designs offer an unfolding, indeterminate set of changes that continually redirect away from the loop and the binary. That indeterminacy is not marginal or weak—just agile enough to respond to the moment when it is outmaneuvered. So in addition to the design of master plans, we should see the design of reagents, mixtures, interdependencies, chemistries, chain reactions, and ratchets. These designs offer no correct answer or homeostatic balance, but if there are dispositions of violence embodied in space, are there not also dispositions that ease or neutralize tension and violence? The documents that architects present in the future might not be snapshots of perfect moments, but specifications for linkage and interdependency that remain in place to counterbalance and *imbalance* each other.

Designing the *more than human* is a little bit like playing pool. The balls on the table are a topology, a network of sequenced relationships. There is no single target at which to aim but rather a stretchy network of hard and absorptive surfaces. The player who sees only one fixed sequence will sink fewer balls, reduce the potentials of the table, and lose. Rarely are the cue ball and its target geometrically aligned with the hole, so the majority of shots involve the expertise of indirect contact and ricochet. The game is played like a chain reaction, with multiple branching possibilities that change after every shot. And yet with every shot, the most constructive thing that can be done is to increase the chances for more shots—generate more branches in the network of possibilities, more information. There is no need to call each shot, and it is better to keep the spectators guessing. Then there is also the matter of touch, which can't easily be described, but only understood by doing it. Pool is only a reminder of all the things that can change when a body, with all of its sentience and force fields, brushes against the air. It can be a matter of deliberate speed and impact, coming from hands through the cue stick and out to the ball. But sometimes it is a matter of English—the spin placed on the cue ball that is later transferred to another. English is an advanced technique that can't be predicted, but it can be exploited. It is less about the intention of the shooter and more about something between the moving solids outside the human skin. The player who can continue to set up potentials and options can play the table longer. It is something like being too smart to be right.

1 Stanley Fish, *Winning Arguments: What Works and Doesn't Work in Politics, the Bedroom, the Courtroom, and the Classroom* (New York: Harper Collins, 2016).

2 Gilles Deleuze and Felix Guattari, *A Thousand Plateaus: Capitalism and Schizophrenia* (Minneapolis: University of Minnesota Press, 1987), 15, 53.

3 Gilbert Ryle, *The Concept of Mind* (Chicago: University of Chicago Press, 1949), 27–33.

4 Jane Bennett, "Systems and Things: A Response to Graham Harman and Timothy Morton," *New Literary History* 34, no. 2 (Spring 2013): 225.

Prescribing Reflection

Brooke Holmes

The idea of self-design is a paradox. Or, to put it more accurately, the idea of self-design will be a paradox if the self involved is understood as either too unified or too heterogeneous. If you want the concept to work, you need to articulate the self into an agent capable of taking on the verb "to design," a target for her labor, and a relatively coherent object that emerges at the end. Even so, paradox lingers. The self that emerges should merge back into the very agent who is doing the designing. Does self-design mean just going in circles?

If we follow Michel Foucault, the answer is no—for the process just described is nothing other than the formation of the subject. In the introduction to the second volume of the *History of Sexuality*, he explains that he has had to add a new axis of analysis to his genealogy of sexuality, absent from the first volume published six years earlier—namely, the modes of relating to the self, the "arts of existence," through which individuals come to recognize themselves as *subjects* of sexuality.[1] That is, it is through turning back on the self that the subject comes to recognize herself as such. The site where this pivot is accomplished is what Foucault calls "ethical substance." Together with the individual who initiates the action and the subject who emerges, ethical substance results from decomposing the "self" into the components of a process that, in essence, creates its own author.

In "The Obligation to Self-Design," Boris Groys argues that for much of Western history, the ethical substance on which individuals expended their design efforts was the soul, beautified for the benefit of an immortal gaze.[2] It is only after Friedrich Nietzsche proclaimed the death of God that attention turned towards external avatars of the soul—designed objects and the body itself—which made the design of the modern self at once ethical and political. The right to judge thus shifted from God to an ethico-political community that comes to issue an obligation to self-design. By contrast, Foucault's genealogy seeks the hermeneutics of the subject in Greek antiquity, to which he turned after determining that he could not tell the history of sexuality from the vantage point of the nineteenth century alone. And whereas Groys emphasizes an imperative imposed from without on a modern subject who pays a high cost for noncompliance, Foucault locates agency within the subject herself, whose care for the self (*souci de soi*) constitutes a form of freedom.

These accounts appear diametrically opposed. But without downplaying their divergence, it's not hard to map the difference of perspective between Foucault and Groys onto their respective strategies of historicization. Groys adopts a dystopian tone that clothes the modern and postmodern subject in a perennially grey suit, while the last two published volumes of the *History of Sexuality* are pretty sunny. With respect to tone, then, both genealogies, taken as stories we tell about modernity, complement one another as much as they seem to contrast. (Nietzsche, tellingly, is a common denominator for both Groys and Foucault.) Ruptured from its past, modernity is born into a state of melancholy and alienation that either calls us back to the Greeks as origin and lost model, or demands an antidote tailored to the historically unprecedented state of the species.

The point I want to make here at the outset is simply that turning to the Greeks in stories about the self is as constitutive of modernity as is the diagnosis of radical novelty. By this I don't mean that either of these moves are pure gesture, but rather that these templates are freighted and entangled. Beneath genealogies of the self are genealogies of those genealogies. If recognition of these layers risks regression or paralysis, it also holds out the promise of more complexity, nuance, and self-awareness in narratives about "the West," a not-entirely-fictional construct that is as powerful and vexed today as ever. I emphasize this point in particular because I agree with Foucault that it's worth going back to the Greeks as a strategy for clarifying aspects of a contemporary problem that Groys rightly diagnoses as an obligation to self-design, yet this strategy requires resisting the impulse to valorize or dismiss classical antiquity too quickly. My aim here is to provide a brief revisionary account of a historical moment when the components of a self-constituting reflexive process—a variant on self-design—are first articulated around body and soul—two terms that have had a thriving afterlife in a range of intellectual traditions of thinking the self, traditions that continue to shape our terms for tackling the problem of the self in the present. I'm especially interested in examining, from an angle oblique to the present, how the imperative to design the self emerges out of what begins as a medical approach to human nature, which is to say an approach that is both materialist and therapeutic. Understanding mechanisms that strengthen obligations to shape the self can be a way of understanding what disrupts them, too.

Let me begin with the body, for the physical body (*sōma*) is the first object of *technē*, and as such, the first ethical substance. The language of *technē* proliferates in the fifth and fourth centuries BCE, and the practices and form of knowledge to which it gravitates are those of medicine. Indeed, medicine amasses cultural authority in this period precisely because of its claims to be a *technē*—a science of recognizing and manipulating regularities in things. Situated within the broader "inquiry into nature" of Presocratic philosophy, physicians and medical writers recast health and disease not as conditions subject to divine or daemonic agents but as states of an object; the biological body has a nature, they claimed, one that is legible but also largely hidden, and thus it is subject to expert interpretation. Legibility and obscurity are equally important to what is happening here. Under the terms of traditional religion, the domain of the unseen is populated by gods and daemons who act effortlessly on humans but represent radical otherness. Yet with the rise of Hippocratic medicine, the daemonic domain of the unseen migrates inside, creating a discontinuity between the person and an interior that is not just hidden from view but largely unavailable to consciousness. Much of what happens within a human being, as a result, goes on undetected even by the embodied person until the shock of the symptom. Moreover, even when events within the body are perceived, they cannot be managed directly by an "I," for the stuffs and forces at work inside a human being—primarily the wildly dynamic fluids called humors—resemble in many respects those which are out in the world, and given that they have their own natures, they play by their own rules. The interior therefore has to be manipulated indirectly, through forms of practice such as food and drugs. To manage the forces at work in the depths of the body, you need to know the rules: you need the *technē* of medicine. By tracing, first, the springs of suffering and eventually all aspects of human nature to impersonal forces acting within the unseen and mostly unfelt depths of the person, Greek physicians ushered the biological body into visibility for the first time in the West. The biological body, so often taken for granted as a timeless given (even in the *History of Sexuality*), is born as an object of *technē*.

So what then of the soul? In countless accounts of the birth of the subject in Greek antiquity, most notably Bruno Snell's midcentury classic *The Discovery of the Mind*, soul is discovered in a stroke of genius, leaving body to gather up the mortal and material remnants of the human.[3] There are indeed a few tantalizing fragments that suggest a rising interest in the soul in the sixth and fifth centuries BCE (the word *psychē* in Homer, for instance, denotes a wisp that hovers over the corpse at the moment of death), and soul makes a few appearances in the medical writings of the Hippocratic Corpus as the locus of cognition and perception. But the soul really only comes into its own towards the end of the fifth century BCE as an object of care that is often explicitly modeled on the body as a subject of medicine. Indeed, in the fragments of Democritus and the early Socratic dialogues of Plato, we see the soul being put forth as a more worthy recipient of attention than the body precisely because, as the seat of reason, it holds a more secure claim to being the true self, the proper ethical substance.

Behind the pitting of soul against body we can detect attempts to wrest cultural power away from medicine for the newer practice of philosophy. In the third book of the *Republic*, for example, Socrates openly laments the surfeit of physicians in Athens and what he calls "the excessive care of the body" consuming the elites and distracting them from the care of the soul.[4] Socrates's critique of the care of the body indirectly confirms medicine's ambitions in this period. If medicine's explicit object was the nature of the body, this was because the body had come to be seen as holding the secret to human nature. Yet like modern-day philosophers who insist on the autonomy of mind or consciousness, Plato resists the idea that the logic of the biological body exhausts what it is to be human—hence the need for new therapeutic techniques that target the psychic forces that cause us to suffer, generate excessive desires, and form false beliefs. Yet the language of technique belies medicine's contamination of ethical philosophy at its origins. The soul's pathologies, like those of the body, arise from forces that lie within it and are strengthened unwittingly by the subject herself. The very failure of human beings to grasp the reasons why they suffer or even notice that their natures have grown perverted necessitates a philosophical form of *technē.* The relationship to the self is mediated by objective knowledge of what kind of thing the soul is and therefore how to manage it, the kind of knowledge sought in Plato's dialogues.

Yet the fact that there is a need to cultivate a relation of the self to the self, that ethics *demands* such a relation, owes much to medicine. One of the reverberating consequences arising from the conceptualization of the physical body is the split it introduces within the human being, a form of self-alienation that calls out to be bridged. Such alienation is exaggerated by the very form of the physician-patient relationship; through the clinical relationship, knowledge of the body, on the one hand, and embodiment, on the other, are allocated to different positions. At the same time, by exaggerating the difference between these two positions, the relationship between physician and patient sharply articulates what will become self-reflexivity into its component parts; it cuts the self into the parts needed for reflexivity. In short, the "I" who acquires technical knowledge in order to maintain health or cure disease does not coincide with the "I" who is being acted upon.

The contribution of medicine to practices of self-reflexivity is not only formal but also material. For as Socrates's reference to elites monitoring their bodies for the slightest symptom indicates, by the late fifth century BCE medical knowledge was thought to be something everyone should acquire—not to the level of the doctor's expertise, but enough so that one can regulate their own body through regimen (e.g., diet, exercise, sexual practice) and hold their own in conversations with doctors. The "should" is strongly felt. At least among elites, the care of the self—of the body and, certainly by the time of the imperial period, also of the soul—came to be seen as an ethical obligation—the essence of what it meant to be master in one's own home.

But why should the relation to the self become an ethical obligation at all? The kernel of the process lies in the impulse to make sense of suffering, and to control it. The impulse isn't always operative, of course; there are conditions, cultural and contingent, under which we are prepared to accept suffering as inevitable or senseless or part of the human condition. Nevertheless, it is by all indications a strong impulse. Under a magico-religious model, suffering was usually traced to some offense given to a god or daemon. It is sometimes said that Hippocratic medicine banished morality from disease. But this is to underestimate the strength of our need to make sense and to control. What medical accounts do in the fifth century BCE, in shifting disease into the body, is swap an impersonal model of causality for an agent-based one. The thing about a god is that once they form the intention to harm, the act of harming is itself uncomplicated. After all, gods are ontologically distinguished in part by being exceedingly efficacious actors. You don't get between Apollo and his arrow. By contrast, disease on naturalizing models is, above all, a process, triggered by an external factor (a change in weather, a type of food), then carried out, step by step, one after the other, within the cavity of the body. The power to hurt that was once symbolized by the hand of a god has to build up over a series of micro-events before it appears to be unleashed in the symptom, which really just marks the point at which a snowballing power crosses a threshold into consciousness, after which it may very well be too late to stop. The task of medicine is to intervene earlier. We can see, against such a backdrop, why prophylaxis becomes increasingly important—why the author of a text on regimen dating to about 400 BCE is triumphant at having discovered what he calls "pre-symptoms" of disease. Think of his discovery as a conceptual precursor to the mammogram.

We expect women today to have mammograms because the technology is there. It is true that there was nothing like the current battery of technologies available in ancient Greece. But this observation misses the fact that it matters surprisingly little to an ethics of self-care whether the techniques are effective: what matters is that they are believed to be. Once medicine is conceptualized as a *technē*, the space that the Greek ethical philosophers came to designate as "up to us" opens up considerably. It is "in our power to change pathological states of the body—in fact, to turn them towards the better," writes Galen in the second century CE.[5] If things could have been otherwise, if suffering could have been averted, someone or something can be blamed. The responsibility for things going wrong is like a free radical in naturalized accounts of disease. The obvious culprit is either the body or the things inside it, which in so much early medical writing seem predisposed to disruption. But the body is too impersonal, too strange to absorb responsibility or blame. Blame therefore attaches to the agent most proximate to the object-body—the embodied person. Doctors did get blamed, too, but an ethical responsibility for care seems to gravitate most to its subjects. This is because the very capacity to exercise technical agency, even as it reinforces alienation, offers a way to claim the body, one's nature, one's self, as one's own. Once the techniques are there to manage an inherently unruly object, a person can be faulted for not laying claim to that object, for becoming a subject. If the physical body emerges as an object of *technē*, then, we might conclude that it will necessarily bring with it new concepts of vulnerability and flourishing, together with a new ethics of the subject.

Is this a genealogy of self-design? If design is understood narrowly as a twentieth-century phenomenon, then the answer will obviously be no. But insofar as we gloss *technē* as the inquiry into and manipulation of regularities in natures, especially for human ends, then the state of affairs just recounted takes its proper place within a *longue durée* history of design, all the more important because of how important the self is as an early object of *technē*—perhaps the first—in ancient Greece. If I have given considerable attention to *technē* as a means of countering suffering, and in particular, suffering rooted in the body, this is because it is primarily through a therapeutic and materialist lens that human nature and the soul came to be taken up as objects for a wider range of techniques to have order imposed on, and human life subsequently shaped. The tight relationship that we are witnessing in the early twenty-first century between the biotech industry and the means available for self-design suggests it is worth reflecting on the deep roots of self-reflexive techniques in the history of the self. There might be no seamless continuity between antiquity and today, yet I would argue that we are still living out the complexities introduced by the biological body and the forms of dualism and monism to which it gives rise—complexities that come into focus if we defamiliarize the body as an ahistorical given.

Both the therapeutic and materialist roots of self-design can shed light on why self-design seems to come in the form of an ethical imperative. To imagine a *technē* addressed primarily to the achievement of health is to impose a strongly normative model on the self. The norms of nature are a dominant thread in ancient medicine and ethics, offering a standard by which to judge the success of one's techniques. This model focused on incremental processes of opening up spaces for intervention, coded as opportunities to correct and create human nature. Once the opportunities to improve are there, the imperative to act follows.

The opportunity to intervene suggests a final question: Is the imperative to self-design part of a historical process that we should encourage, or move to reorient? There is no easy answer to this question. I would venture only to say that the physical body and the techniques of improvement that the care of human nature encourages are not going away any time soon. The challenge, in my view, is to adopt an inherently paradoxical position, one that neither tries to block the impulse to self-design nor codes all of human life in terms of technical control. How can we aspire to support the flourishing of human nature through our design efforts without casting all suffering as the culpable failure to mastermind every vulnerability, every design flaw in human nature? This is not to deny the fact that there is much culpability for suffering in the world, but rather to complicate a pattern whereby suffering is traced to an error or weakness that could have been corrected, so often, in our culture of individual responsibility (as in antiquity), by the person who suffered the harm.

The total design—of the self, of the human, of the world—is an impossibility, yet the impulse to design is neither inherently bad nor eradicable. How we think about the past—what has happened—and how we think of the future (what could happen) can never be isomorphic. Both orientations are nevertheless essential to thinking the human. As Gilles Deleuze glosses Stoic ethics in *The Logic of Sense*, "either ethics makes no sense at all, or this is what it means and has nothing else to say: not to be unworthy of what happens to us."[6]

1 Michel Foucault, *The History of Sexuality, Vol. 2: The Use of Pleasure*, trans. Robert Hurley (New York: Random House, 1985), 3–13.
2 Boris Groys, "The Obligation to Self-Design," *e-flux Journal* 0 (November 2008).
3 Bruno Snell, *The Discovery of the Mind*, trans. Thomas Rosenmeyer (Oxford: Blackwell, 1953).
4 Plato, *Republic*, 3.407b8-c5.
5 Galen, *On the Natural Faculties*, 2.8.
6 Gilles Deleuze, *The Logic of Sense*, trans. Constantin V. Boundas (New York: Columbia University Press, 1990), 149.

Cardboard for Humanity

Andrew Herscher

Top: Shigeru Ban, *Paper Log House*, Daanbantayan, Cebu, Philippines, constructed after Typhoon Haiyan, 2014. Bottom: Shigeru Ban, *Emergency Shelters at Gihembe Refugee Camp*, Rwanda, 1999.

> Apparently nobody wants to know that contemporary history has created a new kind of human being—the kind that are put in concentration camps by their foes and in internment camps by their friends.
> —Hannah Arendt[1]

Humanitarianism is often posed as a "practice of humanity": an ensemble of forms of care that protect a notionally universal "human." But who or what is the humanitarian human? Might the humanitarian protection of humanity also involve a production of humanity, the fabrication of specific sorts of bodies and lives? And how might the humanitarian human exist in relation to other humans? Humanitarian architecture—architecture designed to respond to "humanitarian emergencies"—offers one way into these and related questions.

Consider Shigeru Ban's renowned "emergency shelters" at the Gihembe Refugee Camp in Rwanda.[2] In 1998, the first year of Gihembe's operation, the United Nations High Commissioner for Refugees (UNHCR) provided incoming refugees with plastic sheets and aluminum poles to use for shelter, but refugees would often cut down trees to use as supports for the plastic sheets and sell the aluminum poles in the adjacent town of Byumba. While this entrepreneurialism provided refugees a rare opportunity to produce value and accumulate capital, it also led to what the UNHCR called "deforestation" around the camp, despite the fact that the building of the camp initiated the process of "deforestation" in the first place.[3] The question was actually who at Gihembe had the right to deforest. In response to this question, Ban created a prototype shelter that used recycled cardboard tubes, which refugees could not sell, in place of aluminum poles to support the plastic sheets.[4] Fifty of these prototypes were erected at Gihembe in 1999.

Following his work in post-earthquake Kobe in 1995, Ban's project at Gihembe extended professional architectural practice to sites and problems hitherto regarded as marginal, and his work was justly celebrated in architectural circles. According to one critic, it was Ban's emergency shelters at Gihembe that "made him famous and particularly admired ... in a field where humanitarian relief work isn't exactly commonplace."[5] Ban subsequently carried out a series of other projects using recycled materials for post-disaster shelter—in the post-typhoon Philippines, post-earthquake Nepal, Japan, and Haiti, and post-hurricane New Orleans—alongside other architectural work in the field's more conventional contexts.

In 2014, Ban was awarded the Pritzker Architecture Prize, typically described as the highest honor an architect can receive. In the announcement of Ban's award, the Pritzker jury made much of Ban's humanitarian work, declaring that Ban "uses the same inventive and resourceful design approach for his extensive humanitarian efforts" as he does in his "elegant, innovative work for private clients."[6] But this claim should be understood differently, with the recognition that, at Gihembe, *the architect's invention and resourcefulness replaced the invention and resourcefulness of refugees*. The architecture that Ban provided at Gihembe may have been minimal, just as in his "elegant, innovative work for private clients," but it was precisely this minimal architecture that limited the capacity of refugees to build their own spaces and their own lives. That precisely this act of limitation is nevertheless read as humanitarian is more than irony; this reading points to a politics of inequity embedded in humanitarian architecture—if not humanitarianism more generally—that mystifies the notion of a common humanity.

And yet, the dominant reading of Ban's project in architectural discourse is much more than a fiction of architecture as an art of equality in which "the same design approach" subtends the shelters of refugees and the refuges of the tax-sheltering class. Just this same fiction testifies to the actual inequality that motivates the staging of fictions of equality, the recruitment of the refugee as the human figure by means of which architecture seeks redemption, and, perhaps most importantly, the relationship between the refugee's performance in architectural narratives of humanitarian intervention and her actual life in the humanitarian space of the refugee camp. I want to suggest, then, that the impact of Ban's emergency shelters at Gihembe lay in the way they furthered the helplessness of refugees, received acclaim for providing assistance to the helpless, and thereby produced the human they were understood to merely assist.

The residents of Gihembe are descendants of Rwandan Tutsis who found sanctuary in the neighboring Belgian Congo when anti-Tutsi violence swept Rwanda between 1959 and 1961.[7] Those refugees subsequently received citizenship in what became Zaire, where many built secure and prosperous lives. But with the collapse of Zaire in the aftermath of the Rwandan Genocide and Civil War, their citizenship was revoked and they were forced to return to Rwanda. Many refugees were forced to turn over all their possessions to Congolese soldiers or militia members as they fled, and therefore arrived in Rwanda with little or nothing of value.[8]

The UNHCR first housed these refugees close to the border between Rwanda and the Democratic Republic of the Congo—Zaire's successor state—in a refugee camp at Mudende. In the months after this camp was established, however, Interahamwe militias launched a series of attacks on it, killing an estimated three thousand refugees. The UNHCR then moved the surviving refugees further from the border, to Gihembe, at the end of 1997, where Ban's prototype emergency shelters were erected about a year later.[9] His shelters accommodated newly arriving refugees at the camp, which from its founding lacked sufficient housing to accommodate all of its residents.

The humanitarian emergency that Ban's shelters responded to—the lack of accommodation for refugees at Gihembe—was conjoined to and supplanted by another emergency that humanitarianism itself was accomplice to: the normalized emergency in which stateless refugees indefinitely occupy refugee camps and depend on humanitarian assistance for their survival.[10] The refugee residents of Gihembe are unable to be repatriated to the Democratic Republic of Congo, where they are considered to be Rwandan; they are unable to be repatriated in Rwanda, where they are considered to be Congolese; and very few of them have been able to secure resettlement in a third country.[11] The refugee camp at Gihembe therefore exists as a permanently temporary space where the threshold conditions of bare life extend indefinitely into the future.[12]

Indeed, it was the *punctual* emergency that Ban's shelters aimed to ameliorate that inaugurated the *protracted* emergency of everyday life in Gihembe—an emergency in which Gihembe's refugees "live in the conditions of the camp that further immobilize, demoralize, and often extend their experiences of brutality on a daily basis."[13] Yet Ban's shelters did not only introduce refugees to Gihembe; through the exchange of valuable aluminum poles for valueless cardboard tubes, those shelters also introduced refugees to the abjection that humanitarian assistance at Gihembe entailed.

Ban's shelters, intended for short-term use, have long since been replaced by more durable houses at Gihembe. Sometimes with the assistance of aid workers, the camp's long-term residents have built themselves houses with wood frames and mud-plaster walls. The wood harvesting that Ban's temporary shelters were designed to forestall has surreptitiously continued to yield building material for these permanently temporary houses.[14] The only part of Ban's emergency shelters that could be recycled for these houses was the part that Ban inherited from the UNHCR's emergency shelters: the plastic sheet, which provides the roof for houses whose residents cannot afford corrugated metal. Many houses lack windows and no house is supplied with water or electricity. Around twelve square meters in size, the houses accommodate families that can include many children—among the only sanctioned objects of production at Gihembe.

The repeated display of images of Ban's emergency shelters in exhibitions and texts about humanitarian architecture from 1999 into the present should be viewed in relation to the protracted emergency in which Gihembe's refugee residents reside. As Ban's shelters appear and reappear amidst professional architecture's conjoined expressions of self-congratulation and guilt, the residents of Gihembe still live in an emergency—no longer crowded under tents, but now crowded into houses. The fact that there are no new architectural images of Gihembe does not mean that Ban's emergency shelters solved the shelter problem (as Ban himself would no doubt admit), but the continuous replay of his initial response undoubtedly obscures the fact that the shelter problem persists.

From 1999 to the present, professional architecture has been preoccupied with punctual responses to punctual emergencies like those that faced incoming refugees to Gihembe. The exemplars of "humanity" that "humanitarian architecture" has recognized and responded to occupy *situations* of abjection and distress amidst wars, disasters, and displacements, rather than the *conditions* of abjection and distress that characterize everyday life for the vast majority of humans on the planet.[15] In fact, what the humanitarian rescue of human beings from situations of abjection and distress has in many cases accomplished is a restoration of those humans to the conditions that made them vulnerable to those situations in the first place. This is why Slavoj Žižek argues that "much more than a refugee, a slum-dweller is a *homo sacer,* the systematically generated 'living dead' of global capitalism. The slum-dweller is a kind of negative of the refugee: a refugee from his own community."[16]

In the fall of 2016, the Museum of Modern Art (MoMA) in New York opened the exhibition "Insecurities: Tracing Displacement and Shelter." "Bringing together works by architects, designers, and artists in a range of mediums and scales that respond to the complex circumstances brought about by forced displacement," the press release announced, "the exhibition focuses on conditions that disrupt conventional images of the built environment as an arbiter of modernity and globalization."[17] While this exhibition might locate itself in the context of recent and contemporary humanitarianism, it can be located in a related, but different context, as well.

In 1986 Shigeru Ban was commissioned by MoMA to design an exhibition in Tokyo of Alvar Aalto's furniture and glass work. In Ban's words, "in order to avoid the expense and the inevitable waste of resources, recycled paper tubing was adopted as alternative material and was used to create ceiling panels, partitions, and display stands. The material explorations in this exhibit design mark the beginning of 'paper architecture.'"[18] Ban famously brought this "paper architecture" to humanitarianism at Gihembe and, in so doing, directed architectural attention to spaces and activities hitherto on the periphery of the discipline. From 1999 to the present, this attention has steadily grown.[19] MoMA's "Insecurities" exhibition marked what might be taken as the full unfolding of this attention—the circulation of paper architecture from MoMA exhibition material, through humanitarian architecture, to a MoMA exhibition on humanitarian architecture. That these sorts of circulations take place is, of course, old news; what is of interest in this case is the way in which the stasis of refugees at Gihembe is on some level sustained by the continuous global circulation of images of temporary architecture that some of these refugees briefly inhabited.

In "The Decline of the Nation-State and the End of the Rights of Man," an essay written in the years following World War II, Hannah Arendt probed the contradictions that statelessness posed to humanitarian and human rights politics. In the course of her analysis, she anticipated what is now the reality of refugee life in places like Gihembe—the way in which the camp became "the only 'country' the world had to offer the stateless."[20] For Arendt, however, it was clear that the fundamental problem of the camp was less architectural than political:

> The first loss which the rightless suffered was the loss of their homes ... This calamity is far from unprecedented; in the long memory of history, forced migrations of individuals or whole groups of people for political or economic reasons look like everyday occurrences. What is unprecedented is not the loss of a home but the impossibility of finding a new one ... It was a problem not of space but of political organization.[21]

To the extent that humanitarian architecture is *only* understood as "a problem of space" in the context of the punctual emergency, Arendt suggests, it will be inadequate both to the punctual emergency that seems to disrupt social order and to the enduring emergency that is that order. To put it differently, one could ask: "Is it possible to design a 'better' refugee camp?"

In a text that was only able to be published because it was given in typescript to Arendt in Marseille, before she and her husband made their way to Lisbon and a ship traveling to New York, Arendt's friend and intellectual colleague Walter Benjamin famously wrote: "The tradition of the oppressed teaches us that the 'state of emergency' in which we live is not the exception but the rule. We must attain to a conception of history that is in keeping with this insight."[22] Read in conjunction with Arendt, and with attention to Gihembe, perhaps it could be said that we must attain a conception of architecture that is in keeping with that insight, too.

Postscript

In 2014, the year in which Ban won the Pritzker Prize, the World Food Program and Visa Inc. selected Gihembe as the site to launch mVISA, a digital humanitarian relief program. One of a proliferating number of similar examples of "voucher humanitarianism" developed through collaborations between humanitarian institutions and the financial services sector, "mVISA is a bank account in the form of a virtual wallet linked to a mobile phone number."[23] The World Food Program distributed mobile phones to heads of households at Gihembe and then, through mVISA, transferred 6,300 RWF ($8.60 USD) per month to them, allowing these funds to be used to make purchases.

According the World Food Program, mVISA's cash transfers "support market behavior"; with the funds they are given, refugees can act as consumers, spending relief money on "food of their choice."[24] If Ban's emergency shelters marked the beginning of refugee life in Gihembe by preventing refugees from acting as producers, then mVISA marks another stage in that life by incorporating refugees as consumers in the financial services industry. Cardboard prevented Gihembe's refugees from architecting their way into consumption; they had to wait until consumption, too, was added to the menu of humanitarian relief.

1 Hannah Arendt, "We Refugees," *The Menorah Journal*, (Winter, 1943).

2 Shigeru Ban Architects, "Paper Emergency Shelters for UNHCR—Byumba Refugee Camp, Rwanda, 1999," shigerubanarchitects.com. This essay focuses as much on readings of this project as the project itself; those readings are the object of the critique that follows.

3 In December 1998, UNHCR reported that, in Rwanda, it "supports the forestry programme that is redressing damage done to the environment by massive shelter programmes and refugee camps. In addition to reforestation programmes, UNHCR has also introduced, in both camps and settlement sites, energy-saving stoves that reduce energy lost by open cooking fires by at least 60 per cent. The use of 'paper poles' for shelter construction is also being investigated." UNHCR, "UNHCR Global Appeal 1999—Rwanda," unhcr.org, December 1, 1998.

4 Ban described the tubes as "paper"; I use the term "cardboard" because it more precisely defines the material of the tubes and also extracts the project from the category of "paper architecture" that Ban uses for projects like the emergency shelters at Gihembe. Both "paper architecture" and "cardboard architecture" have genealogies in architecture; Ban's employment of the former term over the latter might suggest his work be read as a materialization of what otherwise exists as utopian architecture "on paper."

5 Michael Kimmelman, "Shigeru Ban: Building to Last, Just Long Enough," *New York Times*, May 22, 2007.

6 See pritzkerprize.com/2014/announcement.

7 On the prehistory of Gihembe, see René Lemarchand, *The Dynamics of Violence in Central Africa* (Philadelphia: University of Pennsylvania Press, 2009); Gerard Prunier, *Africa's World War: Congo, the Rwandan Genocide, and the Making of a Continental Catastrophe* (New York: Oxford University Press, 2009); and Filip Reyntjens, *The Great African War: Congo and Regional Geopolotics, 1996–2006* (Cambridge: Cambridge University Press, 2009).

8 Michael Wakabi and Gaaki Kigambo, "Congo: Refugee Life and the Cycle of War," *The East*

African, November 9, 2012.

9 Emily A. Lynch, "Mudende: Trauma and Massacre in a Refugee Camp," *Oral History Forum* no. 33 (2013).

10 In Rwandan refugee camps like Gihembe, "nearly every Congolese refugee relied exclusively on UNHCR for basic needs, including food, water, health care, education, and clothing." United States Committee for Refugees and Immigrants, "U.S. Committee for Refugees World Refugee Survey 2003—Rwanda," refworld.org, June 1, 2003.

11 UNHCR Rwanda, "Resettlement: A Life-Changing Journey," unhcr.org, June 2014.

12 See Eric Kabeera, "Life Inside Gihembe Refugee Camp," *New Times,* June 25, 2012.

13 Lynch, "Mudende," 8.

14 On the use of wood for building material at Gihembe, see UNHCR Rwanda, "Environmental Management in Refugee Situations Learning Workshop," humanitarianresponse.info, September 2009.

15 See, for example, Architecture for Humanity, *Design Like You Give a Damn: Architectural Responses to Humanitarian Crises* (New York: Metropolis Books, 2006).

16 Slavoj Žižek, *In Defense of Lost Causes* (New York: Verso, 2009), 425.

17 Museum of Modern Art Department of Communications, "Insecurities Press Announcement," press.moma.org, May 5, 2016.

18 Shigeru Ban Architects, "Alvar Aalto—Tokyo, Japan, 1986," shigerubanarchitects.com.

19 Among its contemporary manifestations was the 2016 Venice Biennale of Architecture; oriented around the theme of "Reporting from the Front," the Biennale attended to architecture's encounter with refugees in the national pavilions of Austria and Germany as well as in a number of other projects.

20 Hannah Arendt, "The Decline of the Nation-State and the End of the Rights of Man," in *The Origins of Totalitarianism* (New York: Meridian, 1958), 284.

21 Ibid., 293–94.

22 Walter Benjamin, "Theses on the Philosophy of History," in *Illuminations,* trans. Harry Zorn (New York: Schocken, 1969), 257. On Arendt and Benjamin, see *Arendt und Benjamin: Texte, Briefe, Dokumente,* eds. Detlev Schöttker and Erdmut Wizisla (Berlin: Suhrkamp, 2006).

23 Ernesto González, "Working With the Private Sector Through Cash-Based Interventions," *Inter Agency Working Group on Disaster Preparedness for East and Central Africa*, humanitarianpartnershipconference.wordpress.com, September 16, 2015. On voucher humanitarianism, see Daniel Bertrand Monk and Andrew Herscher, "The New Universalism: Refuges and Refugees Between Global History and Voucher Humanitarianism," *Grey Room* 61 (2015).

24 John Paul Sesonga, "Rwanda: WFP Introduces Cash Transfers to Refugees in Gihembe Camp," wfp.org, February 19, 2014.

Carceral Architectures

Mabel O. Wilson

> This "space of Otherness" line of nonhomogeneity had then functioned to validate the socio-ontological line now drawn between rational, political Man (Prospero, the settler of European descent) and its irrational Human Others (the categories of Caliban [i.e. subordinated Indians and the enslaved Negroes]).
> —Sylvia Wynter[1]

In 2014, the San Francisco-based Architects/Designers/Planners for Social Responsibility (ADPSR) requested that the American Institute of Architects (AIA) adopt a rule prohibiting architects from designing buildings for the purpose of execution, torture, or solitary confinement. An estimated eighty thousand prisoners currently live in some form of solitary confinement, including those housed in "supermax" prisons designed specifically to segregate. Not only are black and Hispanic men and women disproportionally represented in the prison population, but they are also disproportionally represented among those sentenced to solitary confinement.[2] ADPSR was unequivocal in its stance that spaces purposefully designed to facilitate cruel, inhumane, and degrading acts should not be sanctioned by the profession and are "fundamentally incompatible with professional practice that respects standards of decency and human rights."[3] The AIA declined their request to amend their Code of Ethics (although the organization is currently reconsidering its initial response). Given that architecture is one the least racially diverse professions in the United States—according to the Department of Labor, 80 percent of architects are white—it comes as little surprise that an effort to ban the design of spaces for the unethical treatment of a largely black and brown incarcerated population would fail.[4]

That gap in understanding incarceration's impact on black and Hispanic Americans may have to do in part with who designs prisons, but it is also influenced by architecture's own genealogy in racialized modern discourses of history and science. It's an outcome of how theories of architecture and theories of the racial paradigm of human difference—modern discourses that engage with human needs and modern subjectivity—emerged from Enlightenment and post-Enlightenment thought.

Eighteenth-century debates among European architects on the aesthetic character and historical origins of architecture spurred the abandonment of classical architectural theory. These formative treatises on modern architecture also drew upon epistemic and ontological queries in both natural history and philosophy about the nature of humans, the world, and the cosmos. During this same period, secular forms of knowing the world continued to upend ecclesiastical doctrines. The European—the philosophe, the revolutionary, the citizen, and the architect—believed himself to self-determined and self-conscious. It is an act of self-fashioning that Boris Groys, writing about design modernism at the beginning of the twentieth century, asserts was "the ultimate form of design"; that is, "the design of the subject."[5] As the power and influence of Christianity waned, design became a vehicle for self-realization whereby "the problems of design are only adequately addressed if the subject is asked how it wants to manifest itself, what form it wants to give itself, and how it wants to present itself to the gaze of the Other." What Groys identifies as "self-design" I would argue emerges much earlier in the Enlightenment, when an understanding of personhood is formed by distinguishing the essence of the self not only from others, but also from other things.

Also by design, Europe distinguished itself from its Others, a critical sociopolitical context that Groys's analysis also does not take into account. As different kingdoms throughout the fifteenth and sixteenth centuries launched explorations and colonizing missions to the New World, Africa, and Asia, Europeans began to see themselves and their continent as unique and superior. Religious and lay scholars began to not only differentiate the human species from other animal and plant species, but also observe and rationalize the differences in appearance and behaviors seen in those people encountered on their colonial voyages. For Denise Ferreira Da Silva, "the productive narratives of science and history have consistently contained the others of Europe outside of the subject that emerged in post-Enlightenment Europe."[6] The racial became discursively productive of concepts and representations of human difference, ones that established hierarchies of mental and physical fitness affirming why Europeans were the most capable of advancing world civilization—in other words, why they were most capable of being modern.

Racial difference also became productive of the material conditions of modern life, fueling the unequal distribution of the resources—namely, food and shelter—that sustain it. To expand and entrench their imperial power over Europe's others, Europeans constructed colonial settlements composed of an architectural ensemble of docks, storehouses, government buildings, plantations, and slave quarters. In the colonies, the transatlantic slave trade and the enslavement of Africans—rationalized as inferior and lacking faculties of reason—provided a key labor force to cultivate rice, sugar, and tobacco, particularly during the eighteenth and nineteenth centuries. The wealth gleaned from the movement of slaves, raw materials, and finished goods to market not only filled Europe's treasuries, banks accounts, church coffers, and private fortunes, but also financed a building boom in the metropoles of governmental offices, universities, cathedrals, banks, stock exchanges, factories, and country estates.[7]

With the exception of the Haitian Revolution, the French and Americans failed to put an end to chattel slavery after their respective revolutions, despite the fact that its logic ran against the grain of modern democracy's values of self-determination and natural rights. As self-governing, democratic nations formed—no longer under divine rule of monarchies—new civic architecture needed to be designed and built, including prisons, an integral part of the judicial functions of the new government. But the presence of Europe's Others in the United States—Native Americans, as well as, and more specifically, freed and enslaved blacks—complicated how prisons were designed and utilized, and how the newly constituted democratic values of America clashed with its slave-based economy.

Architectures of Punishment or Penitence

In the first decades of the nineteenth century, the statesmen, natural philosopher, planter, and architect Thomas Jefferson designed a prison for nearby Cumberland County in the Piedmont region of Virginia, where his plantation Monticello was located. In 1823 the prison plans were adapted and built in Nelson County at the request of his friend Joseph Carrington Cabell, whose family owned several plantations in the region. Jefferson's efficient, compact design organized seven cells, including one for solitary confinement, which was to be used for "ill behaved prisoners."[8] Jefferson provided an extensive list of materials—brick for walls, iron for grating, tin for floors, and wood for rafters—along with their quantity, price specifications, and the cost of free labor (the labor of slaves owned by contractors was left unaccounted). Construction details were calculated for security, cleanliness, and durability. Reflecting Michel Foucault's observation that the body served "as object and target of power," Jefferson placed a privy in the corner of each cell that was to be limed daily, along with a stove.[9] With taxonomic precision, the architect labeled the cells according to crime, gender, and race.

The first two cells were designed to hold "White Male and Female Debtors." These two cells to the left and right of the entrance occupied the front of the prison. This area would be the most accessible to public visitors, which indicates that debtors would most likely go free once creditors were satisfied that debts had been paid. The segregation of debtors and criminals likely reflects class differences in the prison's population, as well as the understanding that debt might result from imprudent decisions, but crime was the outcome of deeper moral deficiencies.

Jefferson designated two rooms on the left for "White Male and Female Criminals." Under Virginia common law, men and

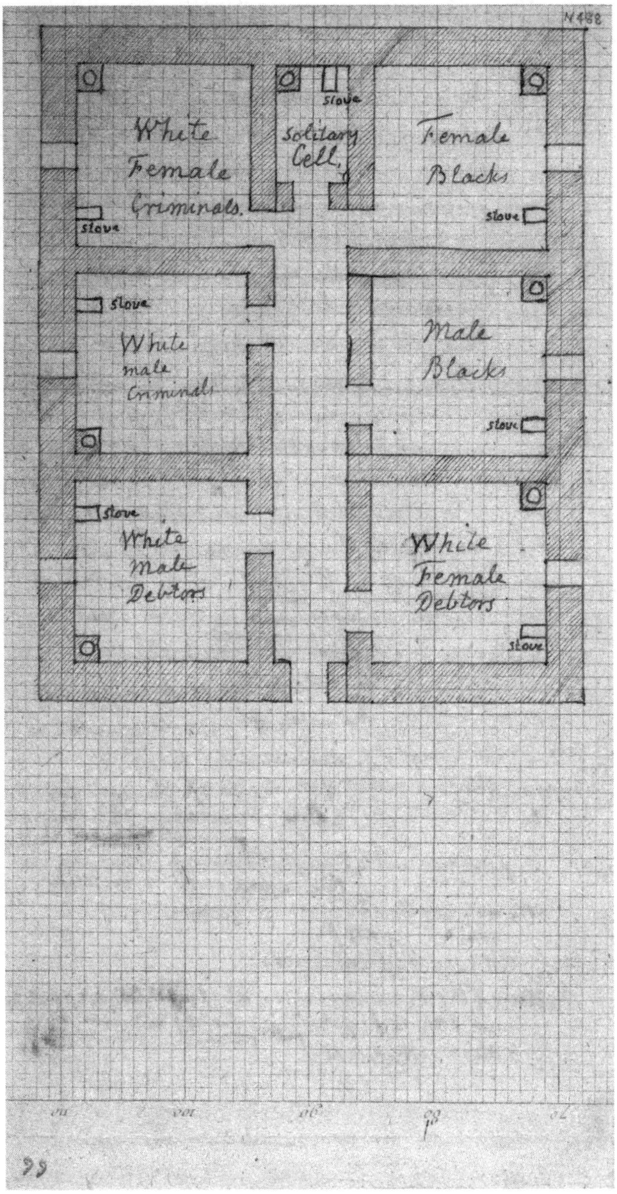

Thomas Jefferson's plan for a prison in Piedmont, Virginia, features segregated cells specifically designed for "solitary confinement and other cells designated 'White Female Criminals,' 'White Male Criminals,' 'White Male Debtors,' 'White Female Debtors,' 'Male Blacks,' and 'Female Blacks'—with a stove and a 'necessary' in each cell." Draft from the Thomas Jefferson papers, undated. Coolidge Collection of Thomas Jefferson Manuscripts, Massachusetts Historical Society.

women could be sentenced for a range of criminal activities. White male criminals could be imprisoned while awaiting trial, punishment, or death, while white women were less likely to be incarcerated for lengthy periods of time. The institution of marriage ensconced white women—wives, mothers, and daughters—in the private realm of domestic regulation, meaning that husbands bore the responsibility for disciplining their morality and protecting their virtue. If white women, particularly thieves and prostitutes, were caught violating the law, the courts often transferred them to the care and guidance of religious or charitable reform organizations, rather than sending them to prison.[10]

In between the two corner cells at the rear of the jail, Jefferson placed a narrow solitary confinement cell. This type of cell was a new invention that was only recently being incorporated into prisons in Great Britain and France, which Jefferson came into contact with and learned from while serving as a diplomat to France shortly after the end of the Revolutionary War. In Paris, Jefferson, working with French architect Charles-Louis Clèrisseau, designed civic buildings for the state of Virginia, including the Virginia State Capitol building, a residence for the governor, and a state prison. Jefferson took interest in the designs for a French solitary confinement prison by architect Pierre Gabriel Bugniet, which Jefferson loosely based his Virginia state prison design. Bugniet's scheme advocated the idea that introspection and reflection could reform immoral behavior.[11] His plan also organized courtyards and windows between cells to facilitate circulation of air to stem sickness.[12] These prospects of moral and physical regeneration fascinated Jefferson, who noted in his autobiography:

> I had heard of a benevolent society, in England, which had been indulged by the government, in an experiment of the effect of labor, in *solitary confinement*, on some of their criminals ... This I sent to the Directors [in charge of constructing Virginia's capital], instead of a plan of a common prison, in hope that it would suggest the idea of labor in solitary confinement, instead of that on the public works.[13]

Jefferson was also aware that northern Quakers advocated solitary confinement as a form of penitence for criminal behavior and activities, which they considered to be more humane and just than the cruel corporeal punishments administered by temperamental sovereigns.[14]

The Negro: Human or Subhuman?

Enlightenment and post-Enlightenment naturalists argued vociferously over the monogenetic or polygenetic origin of humans, speculating on whether Africans, Asians, and Native Americans had developed from the same species as Europeans. Geography and geology proved central to these questions of character and physiognomy. For Immanuel Kant, "Negroes and Whites are not different species of humans (for they belong presumably to one stock), but they are different *races,* for each perpetuates itself in every area, and they generate between them children that are necessarily hybrid, or blendlings (mulattoes)."[15] Whether humans of African descent had the ability to reason, and therefore the moral and intellectual capacity to create anything more than a "primitive" culture, was studied by natural philosophers and historians who largely relied on reports and diaries from colonial voyagers for their research and analysis.[16] Pondering the nature of national character, Kant, for example, observed: "Mr. [David] Hume challenges anyone to cite a single example in which a Negro has shown talents, and asserts among the hundreds of thousands of blacks who are transported elsewhere from their countries, although many of them have even been set free, still not a single one was ever found who presented anything great in art or science or any other praiseworthy quality."[17] Through their comparative analysis of physical and mental traits, climate and geography, most naturalists concluded Africans and Negroes to be an inferior race with little or no capacity to evolve beyond a primitive state no matter where they lived.

The need to set a firm national economic foundation after the war for independence rendered enslaved labor indispensable to rebuilding the nation's wealth. It was also necessary for sustaining the life and livelihoods of its white population. The end of the US Civil War brought constitutional amendments that granted emancipation, citizenship, and legal protection to all, but before this, blacks had toiled under common laws and brutal slave codes that rendered them without rights. Most lived among white Americans whose sociocultural beliefs and practices dehumanized them without reprieve. Any injustice or criminal act upon enslaved blacks was typically resolved outside the judicial system. If they were charged with a crime, trial would take place in front of white judges and be decided upon by all-white juries. As Saidiya Hartman writes about why the rape of enslaved women, for instance, was rarely adjudicated, "the invocation of person and property made issues of consent, will, and agency complicated and ungainly."[18]

In his *Notes on the State of Virginia* (1785) Jefferson expressed his "physical and moral objections" to the Negro based on astute observations of the comportment and character of his more than one hundred slaves at Monticello. The Negro's inability to appreciate beauty except in the most sensual manner, or to create works of true aesthetic value except out of mimicry, provided Jefferson with evidence of their natural mental inferiority. In their faculties of recollection they are equal to whites, observed Jefferson, but the Negroes' ability to reason, to comprehend mathematics and sciences, is certainly inferior. "In their imagination," Jefferson condemned, "they are dull, tasteless, and anomalous."[19]

A proponent of natural rights—that all men are born free—Jefferson had advocated for the incremental emancipation of slaves and for the elimination of the international slave trade early in his political career. But emancipation could only be successful as a national enterprise if blacks, he claimed, once freed, left the United States and immigrated to colonies in the West Indies or Africa. "Why not retain and incorporate blacks into the state?" asked Jefferson in *Notes on the State of Virginia.* Because of "deep rooted prejudices entertained by the whites; ten thousand recollections, by the blacks, of the injuries they have sustained; new provocations; the real distinctions which nature has made."[20] Jefferson's proposition, which paralleled similar movements in England that established Sierra Leone in 1787, would become the foundation for the colonization movement in the United States. The American Colonization Society was founded in 1816, whose members included architect of the US Capitol William Thornton and the son of British architect Benjamin Henry Latrobe. With the foundation of Liberia in 1821 by the United States, integration of blacks into the fabric of the nation was not a desired course of action. The colonization movement, which formed from an alliance between white northern abolitionists and mid-Atlantic slaveholders who held similar views to Jefferson's, tacitly agreed that there was no place for the freed Negro in America's democratic society or within its national boundaries.

We can now return to Jefferson's 1823 design for the county prison and unpack the significance of the two cells reserved on the right for "Black Men and Women." It is notable that Jefferson did not include the labels "debtor" or "criminal" on these cells, which were most likely designed to hold captured slaves who had escaped either from their masters or while in transit westward for sale to till in the frontier territories created from Jefferson's purchase of the Louisiana territory. In other words, these prison cells served as holding cells for private property.

Authorities rarely incarcerated enslaved men and women for criminal activity, but instead implemented harsh measures—beatings or death—for improper and unlawful behavior.[21] Unless the public prosecution of a slave's criminal deed, such as plotting insurrection, murder, or violence against a white person, could function as a deterrent to slave disobedience, disciplining the enslaved body fell under the jurisdiction of their owners, who meted out various forms of punishment for minor infractions. The fabrication and use of iron shackles, collars, bridles, and regular displays of punitive justice at the whipping post within the slave quarters were regimes of violence deployed by slavers, owners, overseers, and slave patrols to subdue a person and maintain lawful and submissive behavior. The black slave body became the site of what Hartman calls the "routinized violence of slavery."[22] Through these means, Southerners made the disciplining of slave populations a private rather than public matter, which was also an attempt to keep the dispute over slavery's inhumanity out of the public space of political debate.

The two "Black" cells would have also held free black men and women who had committed crimes. Fearing freed slaves would become a financial burden, undermine the wages of white workers, pose a criminal threat, or incite slave rebellions, in 1793 Virginia restricted the migration of freed blacks to the state and required that manumitted men and women either register with local authorities or leave the state within a year of their liberation.[23] Failure to migrate would entail forfeiture of their freedom. Any freed black person caught committing a crime would be arrested and, depending on the severity of the crime, possibly sold back into slavery. Freed blacks were given higher penalties and longer sentences for criminal acts. Despite a lack of civil liberties—freedom of movement, higher taxes, and threats of violence and enslavement—many freed blacks chose to remain near enslaved family members.[24] By 1820 some thirty thousand free-people resided in Virginia, while enslaved and freed blacks comprised more than a third of the entire population of the United States.[25]

Virginia, like other Southern states, refused to recognize the humanity and equality of black people. To be of African descent in antebellum Virginia meant one could only live as property in the system of chattel slavery. Certainly, to be free and black was an anomaly. Lacking rights and citizenship and reduced to the status of a possession, blacks were dehumanized under Virginia's law, the very laws which constituted the spaces of everyday life. Jefferson, like many of the ruling planter class, had depended his entire life on enslaved blacks to take care his family's personal needs wherever he travelled and to work his various plantations in Virginia. Through his prison plan for nearby Cumberland and Nelson counties, Jefferson had designed a racialized apparatus of modern incarceration, a typology of captivity and violence that has continued to evolve through the twenty-first century.

From Plantation to Prison

Debates on racial character and physiognomy remained active until the "Sciences of Man," disciplines such as biology, anthropology, and sociology that were invented during the nineteenth century, naturalized earlier concepts of racial difference. Da Silva writes that the "scientists of man attempted to prove what eighteen century naturalists could only describe and the philosophers who framed man could only postulate."[26] By the twentieth century, race and raciality—the productive signifiers of race—had rationalized and naturalized the physical (bodily) and mental (moral) inferiority of Europe's Others as objective fact. The logics of modern planning, development policy, and neoliberal economics justified their continued dehumanization and marginalization in the slum, the ghetto, the favela, the projects, the banlieue, and of course, the prison.

Plantation enclosures directly link to the carceral spaces of prisons. During post-Civil War Reconstruction, Louisiana erected, for example, its new prison on parcels of land from several plantations known as Angola, named for the region of Africa where the plantation's slaves had originated. The plantation's old slave quarter remained in active use at Angola prison, as did the farming operations and the regimes of violence exacted on black convicts, who, like their enslaved ancestors, were also leased out for the profit of the prison's management and the state. The adaptation of Angola plantation to a prison tethers the abuses of slavery to modern incarceration. Today, the eighteen-thousand-acre Louisiana State Penitentiary at Angola, known as "The Farm," operates as the largest maximum security prison in the United States. Sentences to solitary confinement can last for decades in its supermax cellblocks.[27]

The billion-dollar prison-industrial complex, an increasingly privatized, corporate-managed system, continues slavery's vicious dehumanization of black men and women. ADPSR's request to the AIA marks a noble effort to disentangle the architect's expertise from its centuries-long productive engagement with America's inhumane and exploitive carceral system. ADPSR's goal is to restrict architects from profiting by the design of the most violent spaces of the prison-industrial complex. Perhaps then, the profession will recognize that black lives actually do matter.

1 Sylvia Wynter, "Unsettling the Coloniality of Being/Power/Truth/Freedom: Towards the Human, After Man, Its Overrepresentation—An Argument," *The New Centennial Review* 3, no. 3 (Fall 2003): 313–14.
2 New York Advisory Committee on the U.S. Commission on Civil Rights, *The Solitary Confinement of Youth in New York: A Civil Rights Violation* (Washington, DC: US Commission on Civil Rights, 2014), 19.
3 Architects/Designers/Planners for Social Responsibility, "Human Rights & Professional Ethics," adpsr.org.
4 US Bureau of Labor Statistics tabulates data on professions: bls.gov/cps/cpsaat11.htm. Recent statistics on prison construction note that supermax prisons cost two to three times more than other facility types: solitarywatch.com/facts/fact-sheets.
5 Boris Groys, "The Obligation to Self-Design," *e-flux journal* 0 (November 2008).
6 Denise Ferreira Da Silva, *Toward a Global Idea of Race* (Minneapolis: University of Minnesota Press, 2007), xviii.
7 Eric Williams, *Capitalism and Slavery* (Chapel Hill: University of North Carolina Press, 1994). See also Simon Gikandi, *Slavery and the Culture of Taste* (Princeton: Princeton University Press, 2004).
8 Thomas Jefferson, "Miscellaneous Buildings prison (plan), verso, undated," in *Thomas Jefferson Papers*, masshist.org/thomasjeffersonpapers.
9 Michel Foucault, *Discipline and Punish: The Birth of the Prison* (New York: Vintage Books, 1995), 136.
10 Mark E. Kann, *Punishment, Prisons, and Patriarchy: Liberty and Power in the Early American Republic* (New York: New York University Press, 2005), 81.
11 The concept of penitentiaries spread quickly in the United States beginning with the construction of Walnut Street Prison in 1774, established by a group of Quakers led by Benjamin Franklin. Michel Foucault described Walnut Street as an experiment where "life was partitioned according to an absolutely strict time-table, under constant supervision." Foucault, *Discipline and Punish*, 124.
12 Howard C. Rice, Jr., "A French Source of Jefferson's Plan for the Prison at Richmond," *Journal of Society of Architectural Historians* vol. 12, no. 4 (December 1953): 28–30.
13 Thomas Jefferson, *Autobiography of Thomas Jefferson* (Mineola, NY: Dover, 1959), 42.
14 Foucault, *Discipline and Punish*, 124.
15 Immanuel Kant, "On the Different Races of Men," in *Race and the Enlightenment,* ed. Emmanuel Chukwudi Eze (Cambridge: Blackwell, 1997), 40
16 David Bindman, *From Ape to Apollo, Aesthetics and the Idea of Race in the 18th Century* (Ithaca, NY: Cornell University Press, 2002).
17 Immanuel Kant, "On National Characteristics, so far as They Depend upon the Distinct Feeling of the Beautiful and Sublime," in *Race and the Enlightenment*, 55.
18 Saidiya Hartman, *Scenes of Subjection: Terror, Slavery, and Self-Making in Nineteenth Century America* (Oxford: Oxford University Press, 1997), 80.
19 Thomas Jefferson, "Query: Administration of justice and description of the laws," *Notes on the State of Virginia* (1785), avalon.law.yale.edu/18th_century/jeffvir.asp.
20 Ibid.
21 Paul Finkelman, "Slavery in the United States: Persons or Property?," in *The Legal Understanding of Slavery: From the Historical to the Contemporary*, ed. Jean Allain (Oxford: Oxford University Press, 2012), 105–34.
22 Hartman, *Scenes of Subjection*, 4.
23 Ellen D. Katz, "African-American Freedom in Antebellum Cumberland County, Virginia – Freedom: Personal Liberty and Private Law," in *Chicago Kent Law Review* 70, no. 3 (April 1995): 952.
24 Ibid., 952–53.
25 Foucault, *Discipline and Punish*, 232. The total slave population in Virginia in 1820 was 425,153. The number of freed men and women totaled 39,889 making them 9% of the total black population in the state.
26 Ferriera Da Silva, *Toward a Global Idea of Race*, 120.
27 Thomas Beller, "Angola Prison in the Shadow of Slavery," *The New Yorker,* August 19, 2015. See also Amnesty International, "The Angola Three," amnestyusa.org.

Some Sketches on Vertical Geographies

Trevor Paglen

Top: Trevor Paglen, *NSA-Tapped Undersea Cables, North Pacific Ocean*, 2016. Bottom: Author's Field Note: Undersea Work.

I've long thought that conventional understandings of geography were a little too "horizontal." That geographical concepts such as production, uneven development, territory, scale, geopolitics, and the like tended to be theorized on an assumed horizontal plane of human existence makes sense, because the vast majority of human activity does more or less conform to the relatively narrow vertical band on the earth's surface that can support human life. But human infrastructures and activities also inhabit a vertical axis, from deep-sea mining and undersea cables to outer, and even arguably interstellar, space. As others have observed, different topologies of development, politics, urbanism, and the production of space emerge when we begin to consider the vertical dimensions of human world-making.[1]

What follows are some sketches of case studies from my own work that have been personally helpful in considering what a theory of vertical geography might encompass. There is nothing comprehensive here, nor anything actually theorized at all. These are simply some examples of things I think about.

–20,000ft (Undersea Cables)

More than 99 percent of the world's data travels through fiber-optic cables draped across the ocean floor. Undersea cables encircle the globe at depths of 20,000ft (6,000m), connecting continents and providing the backbone of the world's telecommunications infrastructure.

After an aborted attempt in 1857, the first undersea cable connecting North America to the UK was laid in 1858 when the warships Niagra and Agamemnon met in the middle of the Atlantic to splice the two ends of the telegraph cable they had lain from their respective ports. The first transcontinental conversation (which took a day to conduct) was the following:

Repeat, please.
Please send slower for the present.
How?
How do you receive?
Send slower.
Please send slower.
How do you receive?
Please say if you can read this.
Can you read this?
Yes.
How are signals?
Do you receive?

Pease send something. Please send V's and B's.
How are signals?

Within a month, the cable was dead. Other attempts between 1857 and 1866 either failed outright or after short amounts of time. The first reliable cable came online in 1866.[2] As of 2016, there are more than three hundred active undersea cables.

The undersea world of cables and communications is studied and acted upon by an American intelligence agency called the National Underwater Reconnaissance Office (NURO), jointly staffed by the CIA and the Navy.[3] A sister agency to the National Reconnaissance Office (charged with the operations of reconnaissance satellites), the NURO conducts undersea surveying, search operations, oceanographic research, and the installation of undersea infrastructure, including taps on undersea cables. Since its inception in 1969, the NURO has deployed a handful of specialized ships and submarines to conduct its operations, including the USS *Parche*, the Hughes Glomar Explorer, the USS *Halibut*, the NR-1, and the more recent USS *Jimmy Carter*. The National Underwater Reconnaissance Office is a so-called "black" agency, meaning its existence is classified.

The deep-sea geographies of internet cables and telecommunication are, quite literally, a submerged infrastructure that exists far below the altitudes that can support human bodies. On a vertical axis, the depth of undersea communications and reconnaissance activities is only superseded by specialized oil-drilling activities; the ill-fated Deepwater Horizon platform in the Gulf of Mexico drilled the deepest oil well in history at a vertical depth of 35,055ft (10,685m).

0 (Backbone)

Cable landing points are the places where undersea cables come onshore, usually connecting to a building called a cable landing station. The cable landing station is typically a windowless building that supplies power to an undersea cable's amplifiers and repeaters (a typical undersea cable has between three and four thousand volts applied to it). In many cases, the cable landing station also connects the undersea cable to terrestrial "backhaul" cables, which lead to the common internet backbone, with switches, core routers, and other equipment, effectively connecting the undersea cable to the terrestrial internet infrastructure.

Cable landing stations serve as natural "choke points" of the internet, and are therefore of great interest to intelligence agencies like the NSA. Numerous internal NSA documents describe the importance of cable landing stations as surreptitious data-collection sites, often in collaboration with local telecommunications companies, including AT&T ("FAIRVIEW" in internal NSA documents), Verizon ("STORMBREW"), British Telecom ("REMEDY"), Vodafone Cable ("GERONTIC"), etc.

Author's field note: NSA Utah Data Center.

2,500ft (Persistent Surveillance)

Modern aerostats began to see widespread use in the 1980s when the US Customs Service installed the Tethered Aerostat Radar System (TARS) at High Rock, Grand Bahamas and Fort Huachuca, Arizona as part of the Reagan-Era "War on Drugs."[4] These airships were designed to provide radar surveillance of border regions, and have been subsequently deployed throughout the Caribbean and the Southwest at: Cudjoe Key, Florida; Deming, New Mexico; Eagle Pass, Texas; Fort Huachuca, Arizona; Lajas, Puerto Rico; Marfa, Texas; Rio Grande City, Texas; and Yuma, Arizona.

In the aftermath of the US invasions of Afghanistan and Iraq, the US Army contracted Lockheed Martin to develop aerostats that could be used to conduct persistent surveillance over occupied cities. The first Army aerostat was deployed in 2004. In the ensuing years, the Army has ordered and installed dozens of other aerostats over urban centers and war zones. Military aerostats utilize surveillance and sensor payloads such as Gorgon Stare, Kestral, and ARGUS-IS (Autonomous Real-Time Ground Ubiquitous Surveillance Imaging System, which uses 368 cell phone cameras to provide a 1.8 gigapixel video imaging system). ARGUS can continuously monitor a thirty-six-square-mile area and uses automated tracking software to algorithmically track vehicles, pedestrians, and other objects and to conduct automated "pattern-of-life" analyses. Other sensor packages are designed to track cell phone and geolocation metadata, conduct multispectral analysis, synthetic aperture radar imaging, and more.

Inspired by the military's use of persistent surveillance systems over war zones, companies in the US have developed variations intended for domestic law enforcement. The most widely known of these, Persistent Surveillance Systems of Dayton, Ohio, uses modified lightweight aircraft to provide law enforcement with continuous 0.5m resolution video over a sixty-four-square-kilometer area. An export-authorized variation on the military's Kestral system, developed by a company named Logos, was deployed on four aerostats over the Rio de Janeiro Olympics in 2016. "We create a Google Earth view of the city and update it every second," John Marion, president of Logos, told *Popular Mechanics*. "And we store everything, so we can go through it like TiVo."[5]

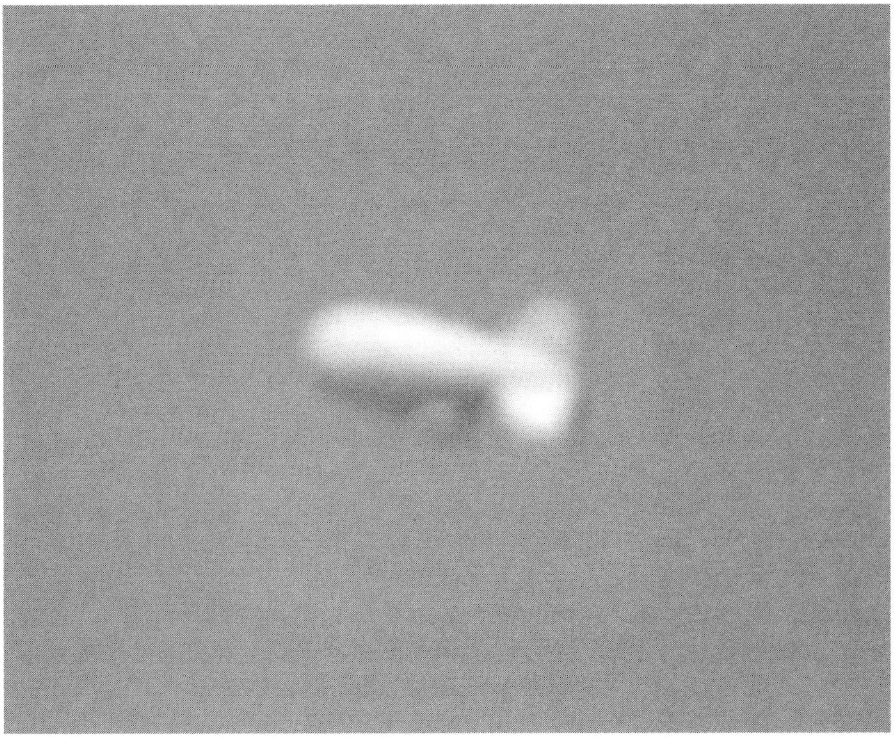

Top: Experimental Aerostat over Utah. (Author's field note).
Bottom: Experimental Aerostat over Utah, detail. (Author's field note).

25,000ft (Predators, Reapers, Sentinels)

Top: Trevor Paglen, *Untitled (Sentinel Drone)*, 2014, C-print, 20 × 25 in.
Bottom: Detail of *Untitled (Sentinel Drone)*, 2014.

260,000ft (Numbers)

In the 1920s, amateur shortwave radio operators discovered something unusual about radio transmissions between 1.3–30Mhz: when radio transmissions at these frequencies encountered ionized air in the upper atmosphere, they were "backscattered," "skipping" back to earth. This meant that shortwave signals could be used for long distance communication and other applications beyond the "line of sight" limitations of most radio transmissions.

Throughout the Cold War and into the present, amateur radio enthusiasts and state entities have taken advantage of skipping in a number of ways, like stations broadcasting propaganda and news or militaries creating "over the horizon" radar systems and developing detection capabilities in otherwise inaccessible regions. Transmitting shortwave is inexpensive, difficult to censor, and ownership of shortwave radios outside the Western world is common. Moreover, much machine-to-machine communication happens over shortwave, especially in applications for synchronizing time across global infrastructures, oceanic air traffic control, and weather reporting.

The most unusual signals skipping between the earth's surface and the ionosphere are arguably the "number stations," which typically consist of a computer-generated voice reading seemingly random sequences of numbers, usually preceded by a signature piece of music or other unique sound to identify itself. Numbers stations are used by intelligence agencies to communicate with agents in the field; the signals' intended recipient is able to decode the signal using a "one-time pad," an encryption technique that is mathematically impossible to decrypt. While number stations were far more pervasive during the Cold War, there are a few still in use. Although finding the source of shortwave broadcasts can be exceptionally difficult, radio enthusiasts have been able to trace some numbers stations to various intelligence installations.

Trevor Paglen, *The Counting Station / Cynthia (Numbers Station near Egelsbach, Germany)*, 2015, C-print, 21 × 24 cm.

160–2,000km (Low Earth Orbit)

One of the most important things to understand about space, explains military space theorist Jim Oberg, is that "space is unearthly" and that "much ordinary 'common sense' doesn't apply. One has to be cautious about making analogies with everyday life."[6] Oberg's point is that objects in orbital space inhabit very different topologies than more familiar infrastructures on the planet's surface. Orbital space isn't even closely analogous to the strategic notion of "high ground" used in terrestrial military theory, but neither is orbital space smooth and undifferentiated, an unmodulated expanse of nothingness. Orbital space is rather a topology characterized by the gravitational interactions of the sun, earth, moon, and outer planets; by irregularities in the earth's surface that translate into gravitational peaks and troughs in orbital space; by magnetic fields, solar radiation pressure, and by stray atmospheric molecules that travel upwards. What's more, the topology of orbital space is strongly influenced by geopolitical and economic policies and conventions of spacefaring nations on the earth below.

Low Earth Orbit (LEO) is generally defined as the orbital region between about 160–2,000km from earth (objects cannot remain in orbit under 160km), and is where the vast majority of earth's satellites are based. LEO is primarily used for remote sensing and imaging satellites, scientific monitoring, and communications infrastructures such as the Iridium system, the most popular satellite phone network. Low Earth Orbits are also the domain of optical and radar-imaging reconnaissance satellites, which take advantage of their closeness to earth to conduct high-resolution photography over vast swaths of land in a short periods of time.

Trevor Paglen, *X-37B/OTV-3 in Gemini (Orbital Test Vehicle, "Space Plane"; USA 240)*, 2013, C-print, 60 × 85 in.

The fact that Low Earth Orbit exists at all is the result of a geopolitical quirk that became a de facto convention. Before the Soviet Union launched Sputnik, no one knew whether a satellite in orbit could be said to violate the territorial integrity of the nations that it overflew. As historian Everett Dolman points out, the Eisenhower administration was secretly elated that the Soviet Union first established the precedent that a satellite in orbit did not violate the sovereignty of the countries that it overflew.[7] Some historians have gone so far as to suggest that the Eisenhower administration deliberately allowed the Soviets to put the first object in orbital space, confident that American spy satellites in development would be able to use the Soviet precedent to overfly and conduct reconnaissance of the Russian interior without resorting to the increasingly dangerous U-2 spy plane program.

Still to this day there is no internationally agreed upon vertical limit of a nation's territory. The highest airships and balloons can operate up to an altitude of about 37km, while the lowest satellites can only operate at approximately 160km. The fact of this practical "grey zone" in which no vehicles typically operate has meant that it's been unnecessary to define an agreed-upon international convention on the limits of vertical sovereignty.

36,000km (Geostationary Orbit)

The "space" in "earth-orbit-space" that has most in common with terrestrial territory is the geostationary-orbit (GEO), a thin gravitational ring only a few kilometers thick and wide, 36,000km directly above the equator. This space is important to the world's militaries, intelligence agencies, and corporations because objects placed in GEO orbit the earth at the exact same rate that the earth itself rotates. An object in geostationary orbit effectively "hovers" over a particular place on the earth's surface, making it an ideal location for communications satellites. Because the ring of space where the geostationary orbit "works" is so thin, and because prime geostationary "slots" are finite, the International Telecommunications Union (ITU) regulates the allocation of space within the geostationary belt.

The geostationary belt of commercial and military communications satellites, data-relay satellites, and television and broadcast satellites—all of which are, in fact, small variations on a basic "communications satellite" design—are a core part of global military and commercial telecommunications systems. Unsurprisingly, the geostationary belt is also home to scads of signals intelligence (SIGINT) satellites designed to vacuum up communications of all sorts emanating from the planet below.

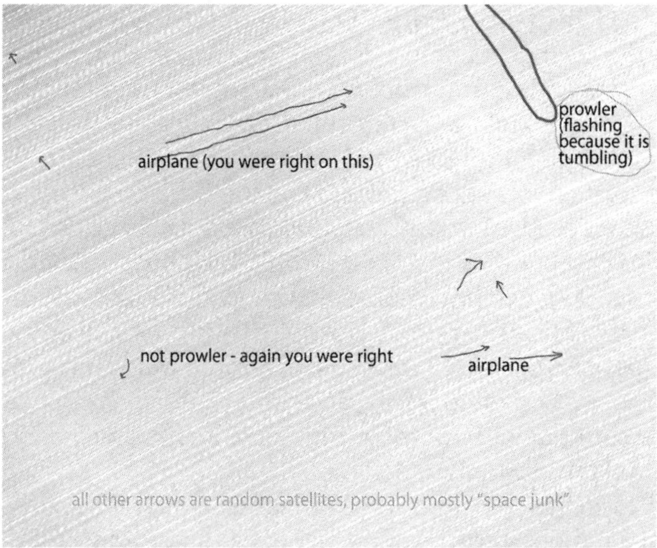

At a distance of 36,000km above earth, geostationary orbit is far more distant than the satellites in Low Earth Orbit (160–2000km). This makes ground-based monitoring of the geostationary belt exceptionally difficult. As the American military began developing technologies and techniques of countersurveillance and covert action, an increasingly significant geopolitical infrastructure has been placed in GEO. Beginning with a classified payload called "PROWLER" in the early 1990s and continuing more recently with spacecraft like "MiTEx" (Micro-Satellite Technology Experiment), the US military has sought to build small, stealthy spacecraft that can wander undetected through the geostationary orbit. The ultimate goal of such satellites appears to be the capability to turn on and off other countries' military and commercial communications infrastructures, and to do it in such a way that the institution being targeted wouldn't be able to attribute the attack to any specific agent or even differentiate between an attack and a mechanical failure.

In the longer term, geostationary spacecraft are not only part of the world's communications backbone, but will invariable be among of humankind's longest-lasting artifacts. Because the belt is so far from earth, GEO spacecraft don't experience orbital decay (which is caused by small quantities of atmospheric molecules that make it into space and induce drag on lower orbiting spacecraft). In an environment absent of erosion, volcanism, rain, winds, and other geomorphic processes, the spacecraft in geostationary orbit could potentially remain there for billions of years into the future, long after humans have gone extinct or evolved into other life-forms as alien to mankind as lobsters.

Author's note on the above work: Prowler.

60ly (Galaxy)

Researchers involved in the Search for Extraterrestrial Intelligence (SETI) understand that their discipline has a paradox at its core, which is that no one knows what an extraterrestrial civilization (ET) is supposed to look like. Thus, scientists periodically ask what human civilization might look like to a civilization in the vicinity of a distant star. It turns out that the earth looks like a kind of cosmic lighthouse, oscillating with a distinct spectral signature of radio peaks and valleys over a twenty-four-hour period.

In 1979, astronomer W. T. "Woody" Sullivan worked with two undergraduates at the University of Washington to publish a now-classic paper entitled "Eavesdropping: The Radio Signature of Earth."[8] Sullivan et al. found that the brightest continuous signals emanating from earth came from military radar systems designed to detect ballistic missiles and track satellites in earth orbit, followed by carrier waves used in conventional television broadcasting. The researchers concluded that since 1957, when significant military radar systems began going online, "the earth has indeed become a very bright planet, in fact easily outshining the sun in certain narrow frequency ranges."

In "Eavesdropping," the astronomers pointed out that earth's galactic footprint now extends to neighboring planets up to about sixty light years away (the distance that military radio waves have travelled since they started going online in the late 1950s). What's more, they pointed out, an alien civilization examining earth's radio signature could deduce "far more ... about our culture than one would at first think." "The very fact that we allow all of this power

Trevor Paglen, *The Fence (Lake Kickapoo, Texas)*, 2010, C-print, 50 × 40 in.

to escape might be taken as a sign of our prodigal nature," the authors surmised, "or even of our lack of an ethic concerning environmental pollution in our galaxy." Moreover, the repeating peaks and valleys of our planet's radio signature might strongly imply the uneven economic development that characterizes human societies, and the political, territorial, and cultural divisions that characterize human civilizations.

From its inception in the 1960s to its closure in 2013, earth's most powerful radio source was a 216.983MHz signal emanating 768kW from Lake Kickapoo, Texas. Colloquially known as "the Fence" or the "Space Fence," the Lake Kickapoo transmitter was used to track satellites overflying the continental United States as part of the military's space surveillance network. Although the Fence was shut down in 2013, it is being replaced with a new transmitter based at Kwajalein Atoll scheduled to go online in 2019.

1 Eyal Weizman, *Hollow Land* (London: Verso, 2007). Stephen Graham and Lucy Hewitt, "Getting off the ground: On the politics of urban verticality," *Progress in Human Geography* 37, no. 1 (2012): 72–92. Benjamin Bratton, "The Black Stack," *e-flux journal* 53 (March 2014).

2 Arthur C. Clarke, *How the World Was One* (New York: Bantam, 1992).

3 Jeffrey Richelson, *The U.S. Intelligence Community – Seventh Edition* (Boulder: Westview Press, 2016); Shelly Sontag and Christopher Drew with Annette Lawrence Drew, *Blind Man's Bluff: The Untold Story of American Submarine Espionage* (New York: Public Affairs, 1998).

4 See archive.is/20120719065800/http://www.af.mil/information/factsheets/factsheet.asp?id=3507.

5 David Hambling, "The All-Seeing Eye That Spies on an Entire City at Once," *Popular Mechanics*, January 12, 2016.

6 Jim Oberg, *Space Power Theory* (US Air Force Academy, 1999).

7 Everett Dolman, *Astropolitik: Classical Geopolitics in the Space Age* (London: Routledge, 2001).

8 See internal.physics.uwa.edu.au/~agm/eme-articles/1979.pdf.

Mass Gestaltung

Zeynep Çelik Alexander

> If we contemplate any natural object, especially any part of animated nature, fully and in all its bearings, we can arrive only at this conclusion: that there is *design* in the mechanical construction, benevolence shown in the living properties, and that good predominates: we shall perceive that the sensibilities of the body have a relation to the qualities of things external, and that delicacy of texture is a necessary consequence of this relation.
> —Charles Bell[1]

Scottish surgeon Charles Bell is remembered today primarily for the discoveries he made in the 1820s about how nerves connect to the spinal cord, but in a little book from 1833 he was not so concerned with the intricacies of the nervous system. Instead, he elaborated at length on "design," a translation of the Italian *disegno*. Yet even while Bell's use of the term "design" cleverly resonated with debates surrounding *disegno e colore* that had preoccupied sixteenth-century Italian painters (the hand, after all, is the organ that draws), it also departed from them. Neither did the kind of "design" that Bell discussed in the book conform to the dichotomy that characterized the intellectual skirmishes in seventeenth-century France over whether art should strive to appeal to the mind or to the senses.[2] Instead, Bell inquired into a more fundamental question that preoccupied philosophers as well as artists: How can we even assume a relationship of correspondence between the mind of the subject and the sensations received from the world that is its object?

Bell's solution to this philosophical conundrum was that the correspondence between the subjective and the objective had been "designed" as such from the outset. One needed only to look around: not only the human anatomy but everything in the universe—from the "heavenly bodies" to "a globule of blood"—had been designed with benevolence.[3] Bell thus concluded: "We cannot resist those proofs of a beginning, or of *design* prevailing everywhere, or of a First Cause."[4] In other words, Bell described the divine author that others might have called the Creator as the "Designer." If Bell's use of the term in the early nineteenth century is any indication, "design"—at least in the broader sense that we use it today—seems to have appeared in the English language with a distinctly theological subtext. As Matthew Craske has noted, in the century preceding Bell's usage of the term, "design" was used in England to describe the perceived machinations of the Catholic Church.[5] Paradoxically, a new culture of well-designed artifacts developed in the eighteenth century, in part as a "bulwark" against the devious schemes of Catholicism. Little surprise, then, that Bell's book had a Protestant subtext. In fact, the text was published as the fourth installment of the *Bridgewater Treatises*, commissioned by Reverend Francis

Henry, Earl of Bridgewater, shortly before his death in order to demonstrate "the Power, Wisdom, and Goodness of God" as manifested in "the variety and formation of God's creatures."[6] The series was an important outlet for the English Natural Theology movement, theorized by the likes of the Anglican William Paley, who, unlike his Catholic counterparts, sought to prove God's existence through an examination of the "book of nature."[7] This was called "argument from design." Much like arguments of "intelligent design" in our day, it asserted that for anyone who knew to look, the evidence of the hand of a benevolent Designer was everywhere.

Because "argument from design" pointedly avoided the textual authority of Scripture, it proved a convenient way of making arguments in the name of God in Protestant parts of Europe throughout the nineteenth century. This was especially the case at mid-century, after the rise of mechanistic and materialist explanations, some of which went so far as to deny any telos—Catholic or otherwise—to the universe.[8] But it was in German-speaking lands that design, with its theological subtext, was transformed into a full-fledged pedagogical program and, as the century progressed, into a distinct epistemological agenda. Like natural theology, the "new pedagogy," as it was called, put its faith in the self-evidence of natural phenomena rather than in texts that required the interpretation of the mind. In the pedagogy of the Swiss Johann Heinrich Pestalozzi and his student Friedrich Froebel, for example, "form" was granted such a central role that it eclipsed the primacy of the "word."[9] "Form," like natural phenomena, was perceived directly, whereas "word," like Scripture in Latin, required translation. In practical terms, this meant that children in Pestalozzi's kindergarten learned to draw angles, squares, and curves before learning to write the alphabet. More relevant here is that Pestalozzi's kindergarteners and natural theologians alike signaled the emergence of an epistemological principle that would gain momentum in the decades to follow. If patterns of forms, otherwise known as *Gestalten*, spoke to the human mind directly without any mediating agents, they could be the basis of another way of knowing, one that rivaled conventional knowledge—that is, propositional knowledge dependent on language, logic, or concepts. This other way of knowing was predicated on a form of cognition that was called *Anschauung*: a presumed direct intimacy with the world through the senses prior to intellectual cogitation.

The historical arc that I have outlined so far from the natural theologian's interest in the divine hand to the hand exercises invented by Pestalozzi for kindergarten children, however, should not be read as an arc of secularization. Religion was as much present at the end of this historical arc as at its beginning. Pestalozzi's pedagogy, after all, dovetailed with the new education system that was being forged by Wilhelm von Humboldt in Prussia, where theology occupied a privileged position among the faculty at the Berlin University.[10] Borrowing heavily from Pietist techniques of rigorous introspection, which made sure that the subject turned inwards as much as outwards, Humboldt formulated a conception of education (arguably Prussia's most important export in the course of the nineteenth century) that merged conceptions of institutional instruction with a techniques of self-cultivation.[11] More strikingly, when Pestalozzi's "new pedagogy" was taken up with renewed fervor after the unification of Germany in 1871, it was done in support of the abortive, yet nonetheless influential *Kulturkampf*, the campaign that the German state conducted against Catholic minorities under the banner of modernization.

It was with the political thrust of this war of modernization—frequently mischaracterized in historiography as a war of secularization—that Pestalozzi's *Anschauung* invaded every level of the education system at the end of the nineteenth century. Crucial in this effort in Germany were the so-called "Falk Laws" of 1872—named after the minister of education of the same name—which, apart from reconfiguring the confessional organization of Prussian schools, removing Catholic clergy from teaching positions, and establishing interconfessional schools, did something less predictable: drawing classes were made mandatory in elementary and secondary schools.[12] In early modern Europe, drawing instruction had been considered part of an aristocrat's education, yet in late-nineteenth-century Germany—as well as in America, France, England, and their colonies—it became the centerpiece of the new attempt to educate the masses.

The battlefield for this war of modernization, then, was not only educational institutions, but more significantly, the soul of individuals. *Kulturkampf* was waged in Germany with a "Protestant ethic," as Max Weber would call it, against a Catholic population portrayed as sentimental, irrational, impressionable, and therefore likely to fall prey to political manipulation.[13] Furthermore, the kind of selfhood identified with women, children, and the uneducated merged with this Catholic self in the Protestant imagination. In 1876, at the height of the *Kulturkampf*, when thousands flocked to the provincial town of Marpingen where three eight-year-olds claimed to have seen the Virgin Mary in the woods, Protestant commentators explained this "disgrace to Reason" in psychological terms.[14] The problem, as they saw it, was that these subjects could not synthesize the indiscriminate sensations coming from the world into coherent cognition. Yet if these subjects were to be reformed, they reasoned, it would have to be through a pedagogy that spoke the language of the sensations—that is, the very threat to the integrity of their souls.

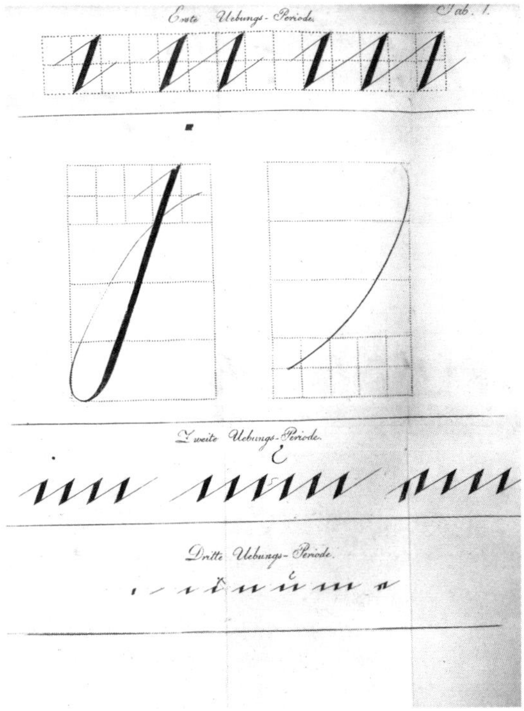

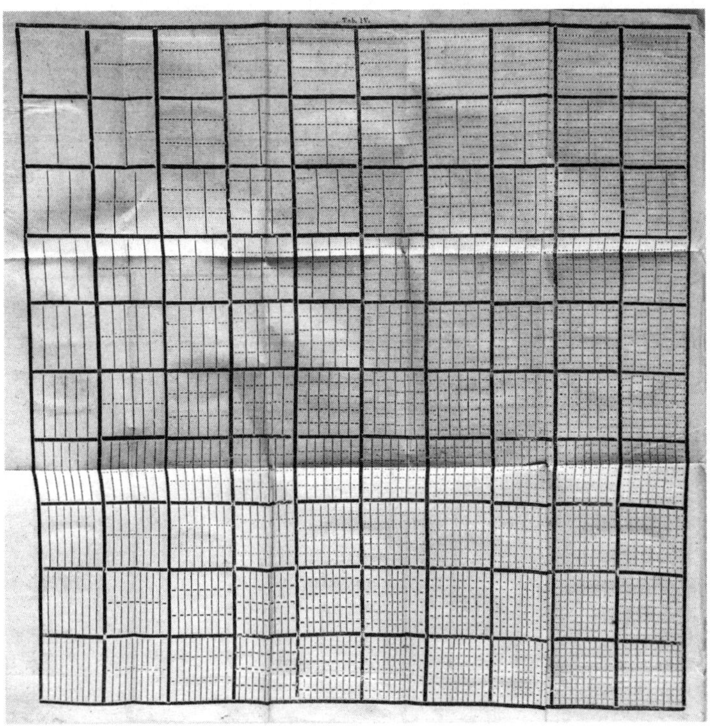

Tables for teaching relationships of dimension, from J. H. Pestalozzi, *Elementar-Buecher* (Hamburg: Friedrich Perthes, 1804). Top: plate X, fig. 1. Bottom: plate X, fig. 3.

This is how an epistemology that privileged *Anschauung* over propositional knowledge became appealing again in late-nineteenth-century Germany. Liberal-minded reformers launched educational programs whose primary purpose was to discipline what was considered the most fundamental of human abilities: the recognition and manipulation of *Gestalten*, which was now proposed as the first step at every level. The new pedagogy assumed that the student had to learn to *look* before she could *read* and learn to *draw* before she could *write*. The so-called "object lesson" (*Anschauungsunterricht*) provided shortcuts in this new pedagogical program: if the German ideal of education had been conventionally achieved through the laborious acquisition of Latin, Greek, and historical knowledge, the "new pedagogy" promised a shorter route to self-realization through the study of forms. This was true even at the level of the university. In response to his disgruntled colleagues' complaints that they could not teach students who were not familiar with the *Divine Comedy*, for example, the art historian Hermann Grimm, teaching at Berlin University, suggested in 1892 that they follow his model and devise a slide lecture that would teach Dante's work speedily through pictures.[15]

Such measures sought to tap into subjects' hidden aesthetic sensibilities and release their creative potential—but not without ensuring that this potential would be simultaneously kept under control. In the case of mandatory drawing classes instituted during the *Kulturkampf,* one such control device turned out to be the grid, which had been a crucial part of the arts at least since the technique of perspective drawing had been codified in the early modern period. In the nineteenth century, however, the grid acquired new valency as an instrument for mass education. One particular technique called "stigmography" started with points arranged in a grid so as to guide not only drawing but all the academic activities of the child, including reading, writing, mathematics, and music.[16] Stigmography offered distinct pedagogical advantages: first, both the grid and the elementary shapes drawn on it were neutral guides that facilitated the work of even the most unskilled teacher and the slowest learner; second, because it was easily repeatable, stigmography relieved the pressures of mass education by reducing the amount of time that the teacher had to dedicate to individual students; and finally, the employment of the grid in the classroom turned all components of the curriculum into *Gestalten*. These patterns taught a hermeneutics of form that compelled students to turn their attention inwards with the goal of organizing their scattered sensations into disciplined self-examination. As letters and numbers were all transformed into forms in the classroom, self-formation and form-making became synonymous.

Much ink has been spilled concerning the indebtedness of modern design education to Pestalozzi, but what goes unmentioned in these accounts is that Pestalozzi's influence made its way into the twentieth century only after passing through the filter of *Kulturkampf*. It was the techniques that were developed for elementary and secondary education after 1871 that became the distinguishing marks of the pedagogy that developed in numerous private art schools at the turn of the twentieth century: a propaedeutic course (which appeared under various names as *Vorkurs*, *Vorlehre*, or *Vorunterricht*), reliance on elementary geometries, the need for such heuristic devices as the grid, the privileging of drawing, etc.[17] Once again, this pedagogical program addressed marginal subjects such as women, who were not admitted to turn-of-the-century art academies.[18] By then most of the Protestant underpinnings of design had disappeared except for one: design (*Gestaltung*) developed at these schools as a process whereby haphazard self-observation was converted into methodical inner perception. Informed as much by Pietist techniques of introspection as by scientific methods of observation and experimentation, design in these schools became a matter of developing strict protocols for self-examination. At the Bauhaus, perhaps the last and certainly the most famous of these art schools, Johannes Itten devised exercises to hone attentive capabilities (observe an object for five minutes; draw it from memory the next day; compare to the original object), Paul Klee transformed grids with the aid of mathematical matrices, and Wassily Kandinsky invented contraptions to manipulate form and color as he lectured his students.

We seem to have forgotten today, however, that even when such techniques were adopted at the Bauhaus, the goal was not specialized art education but general education for the masses. As Walter Gropius, founder and first director of the school, put it in his lecture notes from 1921, artistic work was only the means through which one built oneself (*uns selbst aufbauen*).[19] In this sense, *Bau* in the school's name signified more than architecture. "Academies make a grave mistake by neglecting the formation of the human being," wrote his fellow Bauhäusler Oskar Schlemmer; "Bauhaus is 'building' something quite different from what was planned—human beings."[20] Modern design education, in other words, did not simply train artists for the modern age. Following a long trajectory inherited from the nineteenth century, it proposed formalism as the quintessential educational model for modernity, thus merging the two meanings of *Gestaltung*—the design of forms and the design of the self—into one.[21]

1 Charles Bell, *The Hand, Its Mechanism and Vital Endowments, as Evincing Design* (Philadelphia: Carey, Lea & Blanchard, 1833), 1. Emphasis mine.
2 I am referring to the debates between Poussinists and Rubenists in the seventeenth century.
3 Bell, *The Hand*, 231.
4 Ibid., 221. Emphasis mine.
5 Matthew Craske, "Plan and Control: Design and the Competitive Spirit in Early and Mid-Eighteenth-Century England," *Journal of Design History* 12, no. 3 (1999): 187–216, especially 180–90.
6 See "Notice" in Bell, *The Hand*. The same notice appeared in every volume of the *Bridgewater Treatises*.
7 William Paley, *Natural Theology. With Illustrative Notes by Henry Lord Brougham and Charles Bell. To which are Added Supplementary Dissertations by Charles Bell with Numerous Woodcuts* (London: C. Knight and W. Jackson, 1836). Paradoxically, this outlook was as much inherent in Cuvier's theory of extinction as in Darwin's theory of evolution.
8 For an account of materialist and mechanistic explanations in Germany at this time, see Frederick Gregory, *Scientific Materialism in Nineteenth-Century Germany* (Dordrecht: D. Reidel, 1977).
9 See, for example, Johann Heinrich Pestalozzi, *Sämmtliche Schriften*, vol. 5, *Wie Gertrud ihre Kinder lehrt*: *Ein Versuch den Müttern Anleitung zu geben, ihre Kinder selbst zu unterrichten* (Stuttgart: Gottaschen, 1820).
10 Furthermore, as Marjorie Lamberti has demonstrated, religion never lost its prominence in elementary and secondary education even as late as the Weimar Republic. See Marjorie Lamberti, *State, Society, and Elementary School in Imperial Germany* (New York: Oxford University Press, 1989).
11 Thomas A. Howard, *Protestant Theology and the Making of the Modern German University* (Oxford: Oxford University Press, 2006).
12 Adalbert Falk, "Die Reform der Preussischen Volksschule vom October 15 1872," *Annalen des deutschen Reiches für Gesetzgebung, Verwaltung und Statistik* (Leipzig: Georg Hirth, 1873), 897–940.
13 David Blackbourn, *Populists and Patricians: Essays in Modern German History* (London: Allen & Unwin, 1987); Helmut Walser Smith, *German Nationalism and Religious Conflict: Culture, Ideology, Politics, 1870–1914* (Princeton: Princeton University Press, 1995); and Michael B. Gross, *The War Against Catholicism: Liberalism and the Anti-Catholics Imagination in Nineteenth-Century Germany* (Ann Arbor: University of Michigan Press, 2004).
14 David Blackbourn, *Marpingen: Apparitions of the Virgin Mary in Nineteenth-Century Germany* (New York: Knopf, 1994).
15 Hermann Grimm, "Die Umgestaltung der Universitätsvorlesungen über neuere Kunstgeschichte durch die Anwendung des Skioptikons" (1892–93), *Beiträge zur deutschen Culturgeschichte* (Berlin: Wilhelm Herz, 1897), 298.
16 Franz Carl Hillardt, *Stigmographie. Das Schreiben und Zeichnen nach Punkten. Eine neue Methode* (Kohlmarkt: Mueller, 1846).
17 I am thinking here of Wilhelm von Debschitz and Hermann Obrist's Debschitzschule in Munich (founded in 1902), Henry van de Velde's Kunstgewerbliches Seminar in Weimar (founded in 1902 and converted into the Bauhaus in 1919), the Ažbè Schule (founded 1891), the Lothar von Kunowski Schule (founded 1902), Kandinsky's Phalanx-Schule (founded 1901), August Endell's Formschule in Berlin (founded 1904), etc. For histories of these schools, see *Kunstschulreform 1900–1933*, ed. Hans M. Wingler (Berlin: Gebr. Mann, 1977) and John V. Maciuika, *Before the Bauhaus: Architecture, Politics, and the German State, 1890–1920* (New York: Cambridge University Press, 2005).
18 This was true of most German universities as well. See James C. Albisetti, *Schooling German Girls and Women: Secondary and Higher Education in the Nineteenth Century* (Princeton: Princeton University Press, 1988) and the statistics presented in W. H. R. A. Lexis, *A General View of the History and Organisation of Public Education in the German Empire*, trans. G. J. Tamson (Berlin: A. Asher, 1904).
19 Transcription of Walter Gropius, "Raumkunde," Bauhaus-Archiv Berlin, GS 20, Mappe 21, 1.
20 Oskar Schlemmer to Otto Meyer, letter dated February 3, 1921, *The Letters and Diaries of Oskar Schlemmer*, ed. Tut Schlemmer, trans. Krishna Winston (Evanstan, IL: Northwestern University Press, 1972), 98.
21 Walter Gropius, *Scope of Total Architecture* (New York: Harper and Broth, 1955), 145.

Are They Human?

Eyal Weizman

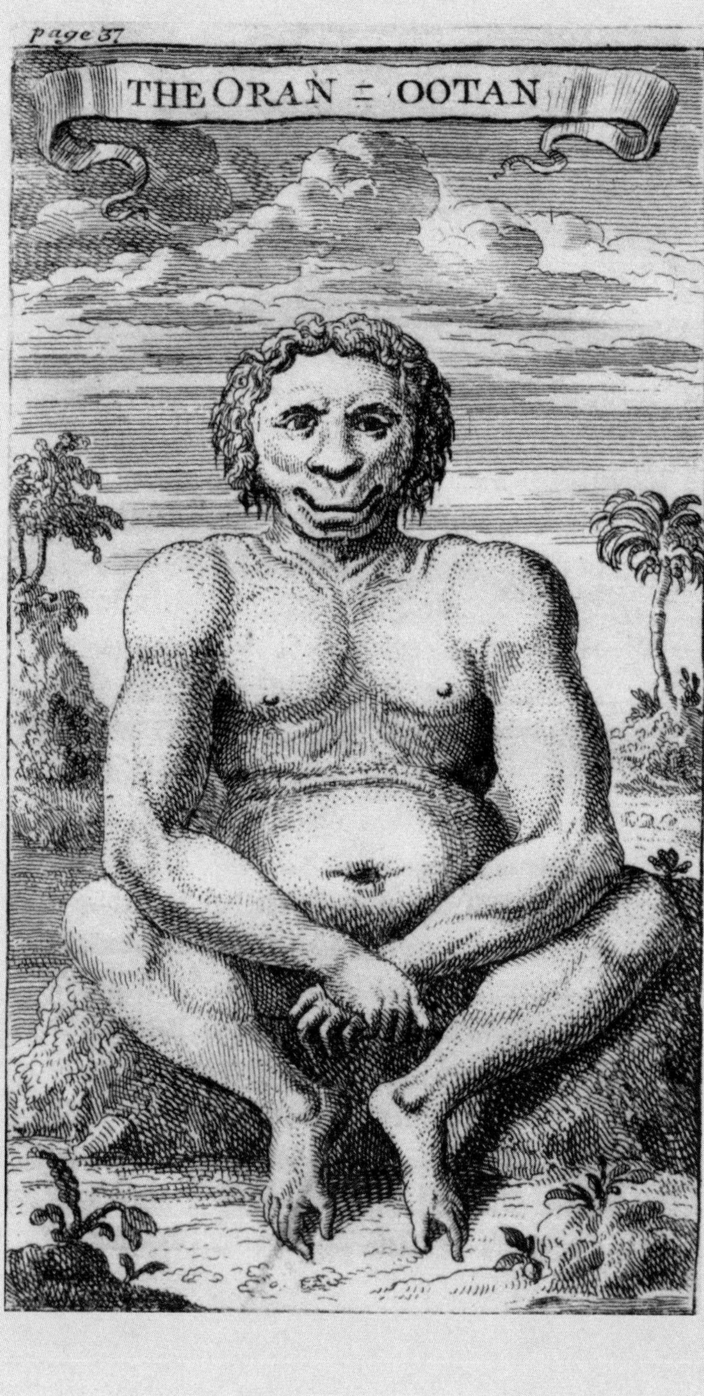

Illustration of an "oran·ootan" by Daniel Beeckman in *A Voyage to and from the Island of Borneo* (1718), 37. Beeckman describes a young Orangutan he bought in Borneo (Kalimantan): "[he] loved strong Liquor; for if our Backs were turned, he would be at the Punch-bowl, and very often would open the Brandy Case, take out a Bottle, drink plentifully, and put it very carefully into its place again ... If at any time I was angry with him, he would sigh, sob, and cry, till he found that I was reconciled to him." From Daniel Beeckman, *A Voyage to and from the Island of Borneo, in the East Indies* (1718).

Throughout the seventeenth and eighteenth centuries—the period when the conceptual framework of the "state of nature" reshaped moral, legal, and political philosophy—European forests were taken down at the fastest rate to date.[1] The great forests largely turned into cropland and fuel prior to wood's replacement by coal as Europe's main source of energy, and the colonial economy's appetite for ships finished off the rest, with merchant ships and gunboats requiring between four and six thousand mature oaks—several hectares of forest—each.

While some pockets of woodland did survive, primarily in the less densely populated terrain of the Alps, the Pyrenees, parts of the Balkans, and other areas of southeastern Europe, the line separating field from forest was shifting at an unprecedented speed, retreating north well past the Baltics to southern Scandinavia, Scotland, and northern Siberia, and south into the northern Balkans. Abraham Bosse's etching for the 1651 frontispiece of Thomas Hobbes's *Leviathan* depicts the figure of the sovereign rising over deforested hills. This is not a coincidence: in the European imagination of the time, the forest line still marked the limit of sovereignty, the areas of productive economy, and thus also the threshold of the law. Sovereignty could only rise over cultivated nature—that is, over a destroyed ecosystem.[2] By the end of the eighteenth century, the forest line has ebbed miles north of Edinburgh. With the exception of David Hume, who settled there, European philosophers using the concept of the "state of nature" to describe an era prior to law and the social contract experienced nothing more than tamed local woodlands, stranded within an ocean of fields.

The hypothetical forest of the "state of nature" was a vast pre-judicial zone, the mythic limit to culture and law. The outlaw and the werewolf, and later the indigenous residents, were human-like creatures that could be killed without the slaying being considered a murder. With the conversion of European forests into fields, cities, and ships, other forests were discovered beyond the oceans Europeans crossed by floating on their own decimated ones. Those that most captured the European imagination of the "state of nature" were found along the equatorial belt in the tropics: Central Africa, Southeast Asia, and Central America. Today we know, from works by Paulo Tavares and others, that these forests, in contrast to their Western perception at the time, were environments cultivated by human civilizations and imbued with their own conceptions of politics and law.[3]

Accounts of these impenetrable forests reached seventeenth- and eighteenth-century Europe by colonial travelers, settlers, traders, and cartographers who had penetrated their dense biomass, unbearable heat, and disease. This second encounter with the forest provoked European philosophers to think about the origins of society, savagery, and human nature. From the perspective of these early moderns, the "state of nature" was now no longer separated from civilization in time—that is, a condition prior to the foundation of society and legal order—but rather coincided with it in space. Existing beyond this shifting boundary was an extraterritorial space, conceived under the imperial and racist framework of *terra nullius* which ignored the social structures and forms of ownership of indigenous people and regarded them as "part of the natural environment."

One of the most challenging things Europeans recorded beyond the receding thresholds of the forests were great apes. Perceived as "intermediate animals," these creatures embodied the confusion of the imperial process of colonization. From then on, as Donna Haraway explained in her groundbreaking *Primate Vision*, apes inhabited the blurry and murky border between animals and humans, nature and culture.[4] During the early Enlightenment, three limit conditions were thus brought into relation with each other: the threshold of the forest—a shifting environmental condition together with its unique climate; the threshold of the law—the political limit of territory and sovereignty; and the threshold of the human—a blurry limit to the human species. Each of the three of these then became, and continue to be, entangled frontiers; shifts made in one challenge all others.

First Encounters

Apes were first described as strange animals, monsters, or satyrs, which were, following medieval iconography, a reflection of man's drives, lust, and sins. Gradually, however, their difference from monkeys started to be appreciated. Apes, like humans, have no tails, and questions regarding their potential humanity started to emerge. Robert Cribb, Helen Gilbert, and Helen Tiffin's masterful *Cultural History of the Orangutan* is full of accounts of confused first encounters between Europeans and tropical apes.[5] The first European description of an orangutan (which in its original Malay means "man of the forest") was recorded by Nicolaes Tulp, a Dutch physician and eventual four-term mayor of Amsterdam, in 1641, and was accompanied by an etching of a friendly and embarrassed-looking female orangutan. The drawing emphasized her more human features, such as her smile and modest posture in covering her sexual organs with the palms of her hands. Along similarly blurry lines, Jacobus Bontius suggested that the "ourang outangs" were the result of intercourse between humans and beasts. And what the Scottish sea captain Alexander Hamilton actually saw when he described an orangutan that "blows his Nose, and throws away the Snot with his Fingers, can kindle a Fire, and blow it with his Mouth. And I saw one broyl a Fish to eat with his boyled Rice," is ultimately unclear.[6] Some travelers thought orang-utans to be one of the strangest and most exotic forest people of Southeast Asia. Others thought that, despite all these points of resemblance, just like other animals orangutans were essentially different from humans in that they lacked a soul.[7]

Though scientists now differentiate between four genera of great apes or hominids, in the eighteenth century the lines of differentiation were erratic.[8] On the one hand, all of the more hairy, human-like creatures were referred to as "orangutans" regardless of whether they originated in Africa or Southeast Asia, and on the other, their relation to humans—this time being prior to the theory of evolution—was uncertain. Apes inhabited the thickness of the line between nature and culture, yet they were more often regarded as closer to beasts than to humans.

All those who argued *for* the orangutan's humanity had to concede that at the very least, compared to the human, the orangutan was imperfect. In the words of American primatologist Robert Yerkes, by being "almost human," apes were perceived to be less than human.[9] There were, of course, other groups considered by Europeans to be imperfectly human as well, like indigenous people and slaves. The interplay of the ape's human proximity and imperfectness extenuated the philosophical, scientific, and juridical problems of the time. Could apes be "perfected"? Taken out of the forest, could they be made to work in fields and cities, even introduced into civilized life? Could they become the subject of laws and rights?

These questions started a debate that ebbed and flowed over the next three hundred years. Contemporary attempts by animal rights activists to extend a form of human-like rights to apes (some of which have been spectacularly successful) are argued on the basis of similarity between the species—on the basis of the anatomical, genetic, and mental proximity of apes to humans. In recent years, primatologists have successfully mapped traits and proven characteristics as complex as mental and emotional consciousness, self-awareness, compassion, and causal and logical reasoning—previously thought to be uniquely human—as existing in these "almost human" creatures. Such similarity has allowed activists to use the vocabulary originally conceived to refer to violence inflicted by humans on humans, such as genocide, incarceration, concentration camps, and torture, to describe the human treatment of animals. Within the animal rights debate, apes were not the only target of activists, yet they functioned as emissaries in crossing the nature/culture divide; once awarded to apes—based on their proximity to humans— rights could be extended to mammals and other sentient beings—based on their proximity to apes.

Climate as the Project of History

Even the most militant of today's environmentalists and climate activists tend to hold a form of perception that has already been largely discarded in other contexts such as human rights and antiwar activism: climate change is regarded as the "collateral damage" of history, such as the unintended byproduct of industrialization. Seen from the point of view of eighteenth century colonial history, however, climate change is an intentional project: colonial administrators did not only seek to take control of and tame the physical reality of newly discovered lands, but to engineer and change the environments, including their cyclical climate patterns. The aim was to, on the one hand, increase precipitation and cool environments in places too hot and dry such as the American west, Australia, and later, after WWI, in "the Orient," and on the other, to reduce humidity in inhospitable tropical environments. The term "climate change" was born not with the recent discovery of the devastating effects of global warming but in the late eighteenth century as a potentially positive consequence of the human husbandry of nature. David Hume, Hugh Williamson, Thomas Jefferson, and Noah Webster all held differing views about the human capacity to—and the relative advantages of—effect climate patterns across the expanding colonial frontier.[10] While there were various techniques for affecting climate change such as draining swamps, digging canals, and constructing towns and cities, practices of afforestation and deforestation were most common. For instance, the American meteorologist James Espy, nicknamed the "Storm King," believed that burning forests would create artificial clouds and irrigate deserts. Planting along desert thresholds, such as the twentieth-century Zionist campaign to "make the desert bloom," was conversely believed to reduce temperature and increase humidity. Despite the fact that an understanding of climate at the scale of the planet did not yet exist, small-scale changes were thought to be capable of causing not just local but long-term change in climate cycle patterns. Once climate change was understood as a potential outcome of human action, the climate—like eventually the planet itself—came to be approached from a managerial, technocratic, and profit-oriented perspective as a design object—as a form of government over nature and man.

Some eighteenth-century thinkers not only believed in the capacity of man to induce changes in the climate, but also the inverse—in the power of the climate to determine changes in humans and their social and political structures. As Thomas Jefferson wrote in one of his more overtly racist paragraphs (as did many other contemporary writers), while the frequent variation of seasonal weather in more northern latitudes necessitated constant adaptation, and thus led to more developed societies with a stronger work ethic, the tropical climate, in which he thought seasons were less distinct, encouraged laziness and promiscuity, and was degenerative to society.[11] From such a perspective, salvation—of both people and environments—was offered only by the redeeming force of labor. Idle forests had to turn into productive fields in the same way that "primitive peoples trapped in ape-like indolence" would find a route to civilization in the forced labor of slavery. Changes in the climate were believed to lead to changes in the human and vice versa: anthropogenic "climate change" meant environmental "human change." Where the climate was to change, so was man.

Rousseau and the Orangutan

In a long footnote to his 1754 *Discourse on the Origin and Basis of Inequality Among Men*, Jean-Jacques Rousseau unexpectedly turns his attention to the orangutan. His hilarious descriptions of the ape are clearly influenced by travelers' accounts from the late seventeenth and early eighteenth century, in that they "fall upon elephants who come to graze in the places where they live and make them so uncomfortable with punches or blows with sticks that they force them to run away screaming." While they are evidently cunning, Rousseau's orangutans also perform all of the other things Europeans attributed to them at the time, including enjoying fire, cooking, and burying their dead. Rousseau also mentions that the orangutan erects in the trees "a kind of roof which keeps them covered from the rain."[12] The perceived sense of discomfort—evidenced by this architecture—reveals a gap, an imperfect connection between the ape and its indigenous environment. Such a gap is typical of humans, but in the perception of the eighteenth century, an animal's relation to its environment must be immediate and perfect. The orangutans were, for Rousseau, human beings at the beginning of the process of civilization, and while never explicitly interpreted as such, the architecture of the orangutan could be seen as one of the first steps in such a process (or, in fact, the first slip on a slippery slope towards it, considering Rousseau's well-known ambivalence about civilization).

Unlike most of his contemporary writers, Rousseau's argument for the humanity of the orangutan was not based on physical and behavioral resemblance, and he did not celebrate the orangutan as an archetypical "noble savage." Rather, he was impressed that the ape shared a certain elasticity with humans: the capacity to learn, improve, and perfect one's self to make a "civil man above his original state."[13] Yet if the threshold of the human is indeed elastic, it is elastic in all directions: once you can "become human" you can also, depending on conditions, possibility, and of course value systems, slide back across the border again and "become animal."[14] The model Rousseau found for crossing back over the line of the human was several reports of "wild childrens," abandoned in the forest beyond the outlying villages of Europe, who managed to survive by "becoming animals." Rousseau mentioned a report about one such *enfant sauvage* found in 1694 in particular: the child "did not give any sign of reason, walked on this hands and legs, had no language, and formed sounds which bore no resemblance to those of a man," yet was reportedly taught to speak quickly and readied "to (re)enter human society."[15]

Left: Drawing next to the entry "Orangutan," in Comte de Buffon, *Histoire naturelle, générale et particuliere*, 1770; Vol. 6, Plate 42, 172. Buffon's orangutan empathically stands upright against the backdrop of deforested land. The stick he is holding in his hand has still some live leaves on it. It is a branch therefore recently cut from a tree; the ape has just steped out beyond the forest line and entered agrarian economy of the fields. Center: "Orangs in their Native Woods," plate from Richard Lydekker, *The Royal Natural History*, Vol. 1 (London: Frederick Warne, 1893–94), 47. By the end of the eighteenth century, scientific research had "dehumanized" the orangutan. In this nineteenth-century depiction, one detail significantly changed: the orangutan still holds a branch in its hand, but here it is still connected to a tree; the orangutan is back in the forest. Right: An orangutan nest in Tanjung Puting National Park, South Kalimantan, Indonesia. Photo: Forensic Architecture, 2016. The architecture of this nest demonstrates an important synthesis of left and center: branches are used as tools, but remain connected to the tree. The ape has fractured, bent, and tied them together to form the basic structure of a nest.

The Dehumanization of Nature

Rousseau wrote at a time when barely half a dozen great apes had been scientifically examined. In 1777, two decades after Rousseau's *Discourse* was published, a so-called "orangutan war" erupted in the Netherlands. It started when a young ape brought from Borneo died. "War" is perhaps an overstatement, but the incident did involve a sharp exchange between two groups rallying around opposing figures: a taxidermist named Arnout Vosmaer, who had begun to prepare the body of the dead orangutan for display (in an upright position), and anatomist Petrus Camper, who wanted to dissect it for scientific purposes. After Camper's better connections in the Dutch court were sufficient to get hold of the remains—which were already partly prepared for stuffing—his skeletal analysis identified that, contrary to contemporary pictorial representations, walking upright was anatomically impossible.

Yet beyond posture, the crucial element Camper searched for was the human source of language, which in the eighteenth century was thought to be the voice.[16] Camper dissected, opened up, and carefully documented the ape's throat, and finally proclaimed the orangutan's larynx—the organ housing the vocal cords essential for sound production and phonation—foreclosed to the possibility of anything resembling human speech.[17] Without a human-like larynx, he concluded that the orangutan could not become human. The threshold between man and animal, previously blurry and elastic, had thus become fixed in a position where it stood for the following centuries. The dehumanization of the ape was one step taken—among many during the turn of the nineteenth century—away from the anthropocentric perspective of nature.

Camper's exclusion of the orangutan from humanity took place at an important fold in history: it coincided with the destruction of the ancien régime—a period bracketed by two important markers by which the ideology of humanism was ratified, the American *Declaration of Independence* and France's revolutionary assembly's *Declaration of the Rights of Man and of the Citizen*—and the beginning of the geological era of the Anthropocene. (The era of the human could seemingly only begin once the question of *what a human is* was decided.)[18] These declarations had an ambivalent relation to the question of who or what a human is. On the one hand, both relied on a conception of humanity that is apparently clear and unchangeable—all men are "born and remain" what they are, their rights "inalienable" and "self-evident" rather than, for example, having to evolve into rights (and out of them).[19] Taken by their word, the declarations' definition of the human seems static and eternal. However, as Thomas Keenan, following historian Lynn Hunt, shows, the declarations' ongoing dissemination and influence was precisely due to the fact that they did not define or fix what they meant by "human."[20] Yet its meaning in practice tended to exclude foreigners, the landless, slaves, and women. In these cases the biological threshold of the human obviously did not overlap with the effective threshold of rights or the law, which the ongoing struggle for human rights aims to make overlap.

Equality beyond the perceived biological threshold of the human is however a matter entirely distinct from equality between humans. Moreover, human rights claims are often articulated by reinforcing this very border, by marking the distinction between humans and animals. Many human rights claimants protest that they are human, not animals; that is to say, that they are on the side of the line where rights should be in force, but still treated as if they were on the other, like dogs, insects, apes, or sheep. Such a threshold also tends to exist in the eyes of perpetrators of violence, for whom actions are often justified by the "animalization" of the stranger, the enemy, the terrorist, the indigenous, or the barbarian. In the nineteenth century, pro-slavery politicians were, according to Cribb, Gilbert, and Tiffin, more inclined to accept the possible humanness of the orangutan, for if the ape was part of humanity, humanity could more justifiably be stratified into a hierarchy of races, with the white man on top, the orangutan at the bottom, and the pigmy, blacks, and other peoples in between. These advocates of slavery also recalled a Javanese belief that the orangutan was able to speak but chose not to do so for fear of being put to work, taken as a slave, or made to pay taxes. Ape-like characteristics have been applied to indigenous peoples throughout history in order to justify slavery as an act of "civilization" and redemption. Abolitionists thus sought to keep the threshold of humanity tighter, and humanity smaller. Yet if human rights claims demand to be remedied by the "humanization" of people who are already human, what can remedy the violation of nonhuman rights?

Orangutan Rights (Notes for the Next Chapter)

Given that apes, like orangutans, were considered to be part of a fuzzy definition of humanity until being "expelled" at the end of the eighteenth century, current attempts at granting apes legal personhood and some form of nonhuman rights do not amount to a simple admission into an expanded humanity, but rather re-admission. Much has changed, however, in the intervening 240 years: the human population has grown sevenfold, undertaken colonialist, imperialist, and genocidal projects, and destroyed the earth's ecosystem to the extent that it has now critically endangered its own survival. In so doing, humans have almost completely wiped out the ape population and concentrated the remaining survivors in tiny islands of forest. If, as some proponents of rights seem to suggest, the orangutan could want, would it want to join our species? Maybe. Maybe it would have no choice. Yet this reunion could take place along different terms than those of the perpetrators. If survival in the era of global warming indeed requires humans to consider themselves as belonging to one biological species amongst others, as Dipesh Chakrabarty suggests, the threshold of the human stands to be crossed in the opposite direction, away from *Homo sapien* in a process of becoming-hominid. We would also, then, have to invert the problem of rights: rather than demand individual human rights for apes, we would rather need to seek something resembling "orangutan rights" for humans.[21]

This text is a kind of epilogue to Hila Peleg and Anselm Franke's "Ape Culture" at HKW, and a prologue to a collaboration between Forensic Architecture and FIBAR: Baltasar Garzon. This text is also greatly indebted to conversations with Paulo Tavares, Thomas Keenan, Eduardo Cadava, Mauricio Corbalan, Bernhard Siegert, the IKKM fellows program in Weimar, and Giorgio Agamben.

1 This has been revealed by new technologies for extracting carbon traces from arctic ice. See Jed O. Kaplan, Kristen M. Krumhardt, and Niklaus Zimmermann, "The prehistoric and preindustrial deforestation of Europe," *Quaternary Science Reviews* 28 (2009): 3016–34.

2 For more on the reading of this image see Giorgio Agamben, *Stasis* (Stanford: Stanford University Press, 2015).

3 Paulo Tavares, *On the Ruins of Amazonia* (London: Verso, forthcoming).

4 Donna Haraway, *Primate Visions* (London: Routledge 1989), 10.

5 Robert Cribb, Helen Gilbert, and Helen Tiffin, *Wild Man from Borneo: A Cultural History of the Orangutan* (Honolulu: University of Hawai'i Press, 2014), 57.

6 Ibid., 32.

7 Giorgio Agamben, *The Open: Man and Animal* (Stanford: Stanford University Press, 2004), 24.

8 Both *Pan* (chimpanzee and bonobo) and *Gorilla* (gorilla) are indigenous to the forests of central Africa. *Pongo* (orangutan) are indigenous to the forests of Sumatra and Borneo. *Homo* has grown indigenous to the rest of the world.

9 Robert M. Yerkes, *Almost Human* (New York: Century Co., 1925); Cribb, Gilbert, and Tiffin, *Wild Man from Borneo*, 46.

10 Hugh Williamson was the first to use the term "change of climate." Williamson also proposed a programmatic change of climate by landscape modifications. Thomas Jefferson wrote: "In order then that we may be able to form an estimate of the heat of any country, we must not only consider the latitude of the place, but also the face and situation of the country, and the winds which generally prevail there, if any of these should alter, the climate must also be changed. The face of the country may be altered by cultivation, and a transient view of the general cause of winds will convince us, that their course may also be changed." Eduardo Cadava, *Emerson and the Climates of History* (Stanford: Stanford University Press, 1997); Hugh Williamson, "An Attempt to Account for a Change in Climate which has been Observed in the Middle Colonies

of North America," read before the Society (American Philosophical Society), August 17, 1770; Thomas Jefferson, *Notes on the State of Virginia* (Philadelphia: Richard and Hall, 1785), 273. Noah Webster provided a rebuttal. Noah Webster, "On the Supposed Change in the Temperature of Winter," The Connecticut Academy of Arts and Science, 1810. For more of the Webster-Jefferson debate see: Joshua Kendall, "America's First Great Global Warming Debate," smithsonian.com, July 14, 2011. Nineteenth-century forest polices were based on "dessicationist" (extreme dryness) beliefs that deforestation caused local, regional, and even continental drought. Note that none of these theories thought of the planet as a whole. J. R. Fleming, *Historical Perspectives on Climate Change* (Oxford: Oxford University Press, 1998); Richard Grove, *Ecology, Climate, and Empire* (Cambridge: White Horse Press, 1997).

11 Thomas Jefferson, *Notes on the State of Virginia.* A discussion of this issue exists in Henry Louis Gates, Jr. and Jennifer Burton, *Call and Response: Key Debates in African American Studies* (New York: W. W. Norton & Company, 2011), 17–24; see also Richard Grove, *Green Imperialism: Colonial Expansion, Tropical Island Edens and the Origins of Environmentalism, 1600–1860* (Cambridge: Cambridge University Press, 1996), 163–68.

12 Today we know that these treetop structures are used differently, that they are not roofs for rain, but rather floors for nests, not luxury but necessity, as a form of protection from predators.

13 Jean-Jacques Rousseau, *Discourse on the Origin of Inequality* [1754], trans. Donald A. Cress (Indianapolis: Hackett Publishing Co., 1992), 44.

14 Gilles Deleuze and Félix Guattari, *A Thousand Plateaus* [1980], trans. Brian Massumi (Minneapolis: University of Minnesota Press, 1987), 232–309.

15 Rousseau, *Discourse on the Origin of Inequality.*

16 Cribb, Gilbert, and Tiffin, *Wild Man from Borneo*, 43.

17 Ibid.

18 One can also look at the same issue differently: the idea of "human exceptionalism" that saw humans uniquely distinct from animals is echoed in the idea of the Anthropocene, with exceptionalism this time articulated as being not heroes but villain-gods, alone in our ability to transform the material composition of the planet. The term "Anthropocene," coined in the early 1980s by Eugene Stoermer, was popularized by Paul Crutzen in 2000. Crutzen proposed the emergence of the steam engine as the historical marker. Since 2008, the Anthropocene Working Group has proposed the scientific adoption and formal ratification of the Anthropocene epoch, the first step of which took place in 2016. See Damian Carrington, "The Anthropocene epoch: scientists declare dawn of human-influenced age," *The Guardian*, August 29, 2016.

19 Bernhardt Seigert, in a spring 2016 seminar at the IKKM in Weimar, speculated that the *Declaration of the Rights of Man and of the Citizen* and the exclusion of the orangutan from humanity might be related in other ways too. Text forthcoming.

20 Thomas Keenan, "Claiming Human Rights," in *Thinking Out Loud Lectures* (Western Sydney University, April 2016). Lynn Hunt, *Inventing Human Rights* (New York: W. W. Norton & Company, 2008).

21 Dipesh Chakrabarty and Eyal Weizman, *Forum,* "Dictionary of Now #2," April 11, 2016, hkw.de/en/app/mediathek/video/50126; Anna Lowenhaupt Tsing, *The Mushroom At The End of the World: On The Possibility of Life in Capitalist Ruins* (Princeton: Princeton University Press, 2015).

Designer and Discarded Genomes

Ruha Benjamin

Field Note Excerpt I
Designer Genomes: By Invitation Only
Harvard Medical School (Boston, Massachusetts, USA),
May 10, 2016

Anticipation was in the air. Old friends, new acquaintances, and profitable collaborations. "History is being made," said one speaker after another. History *and* synthetic genomes.

I did not realize until sitting at the airport on my way to Boston that this was intended to be a "closed session." The organizers asked participants not to contact any media outlets or tweet about the meeting:

"We intentionally did not invite the media, because we want everyone to speak freely and candidly without concerns about being misquoted or misinterpreted as the discussions evolve."[1]

In response, synthetic biologist Drew Endy tweeted: "If you need secrecy to discuss your proposed research you are doing something wrong."[2]

Originally, the meeting was called the "Human Genome Project II" (HGP II), a successor to the first initiative that culminated in the early 2000s with a map of humanity's genetic blueprint. But in response to criticism (source unknown), the HGP II organizers rebranded the current initiative "Human Genome Project-Write." We were moving beyond reading *what is* to composing what *should be*.

Designer DNA. Couture cells. Prada proteins. Must-have mitochondria.

One of the first pilot projects to come out of HGP-Write raised quite a bit of discussion. A team of researchers were working to synthesize a "prototrophic human" that could produce all needed amino acids so there would be no need to eat.

I hear someone sitting next to me whisper to their neighbor, "But what if I *like* to eat?"[3]

The researcher continues, "We've been experimenting with nutrition and food since the Old Testament." *What's the big deal*, he implies.

The entire project is framed in the context of global food scarcity. But several of those in attendance politely object:

"I would venture to guess people suffering from malnutrition are not looking for synthetic genomes."

Another person exclaimed, "I urge everyone to think very hard about the problems you're trying to solve, like 'feeding the world.' There's enough food, it's just not distributed well enough ... Think hard about whether a technological solution is even necessary."

The presentations continue. Technological fixes for social problems, where "fixing" is not only about solving, but also holding some things in place.

A schedule change is announced: the addition of a last-minute lunch panel focused on ethics.

"It's unacceptable that there is only one panel on ethics at the end of the day!" (some influential person must have told the organizers).

I am used to it by now: the ethics panel at the very end of the schedule. It usually runs over onto the last page of the program, standing between exhausted (and hungry) meeting-goers and a fancy reception. But not this time. Now we also have a last-minute lunch panel, and unlike all the other sessions where pins can be heard dropping, the ethics are hard to hear.

Between bags of chips popping open and sandwich wrappers peeling apart, three panelists address the relevance of what one participant referred to as "sexy eugenics questions," for HGP-Write.

Among the many ethical issues on the table, the tension between underreporting research and overpromising breakthroughs to the public was of great concern to those deeply invested in the initiative.

What, after all, is the perfect amount of information to generate support without frightening people? "Surely we shouldn't mention prototrophic humans right off the bat!" someone in the second row chimed in. "Even I'm freaked out by that."

Then there was the ethics panelist who described his company's effort to grow therapeutic human cells in pigs. "Will pigs have human feelings?" an audience member asked to nervous laughter.

"If this meeting was in Europe you'd have protestors at the building entrance," said a man standing in the back.

And finally, the question of who is (and should be) captaining this ship was asked, again and again.

Field Note Excerpt II
Middle Passage Mitochondria
The Voyager (Somewhere between The Door of No Return and the New World), May 10, 1816

"Who's captaining this ship?" whispered the woman crammed next to me. She was the only one I knew, another Mende from a neighboring village.

A voice not far away was singing in a language I didn't understand. She was trying to soothe the shivering boy curled next to her. But mostly there was silence. And the murmurs of those who are trying to make sense of where we are. In several dialects I understand the words "aliens," "catastrophe," "abduction," and "jump." All of us packed so tightly. Lying on my back I cannot bend my knees without bumping the slab of wood holding the person above me.

Finally, it's time to go above deck for the afternoon meal. But most of my companions refuse to eat the daily ration of horse beans. A man with leathery skin and a limp threatens us with his cat—a multi-tailed whip interwoven with wire that smells of dried blood. After a few dozen lashes, a few slowly open their mouths and take the ration. But most of us absorb the sting, squeezing one another's hands, in stubborn refusal.

We have extra time on deck today. The smell from below had finally grown so strong that the captain ordered the crew to fumigate, scrub, and rinse. Pouring vinegar on the floors and smoking the cargo area with tobacco, they eased the stench of excrement and urine, and tried to dissolve the dried filth of vomit, blood, and mucus.[4]

Meanwhile, the one trying to feed us turned from frustrated to furious. He stormed toward the front of the ship and came back with a hideous contraption to force our mouths open. One by one, he poured spoonfuls down our throats. We could hear the captain shouting, "Don't choke the bloody devils! We need them alive."

Finally, it was my turn. As he forced my lips open and struck the back of my throat with the wooden lever, I could feel the nasty beans roll over my tongue. When I started to cough it back up, I could feel his foul breath on my neck as he growled, "It's too bad we can't breed you fuckin' heathens without mouths. Would make my job a whole lot easier."

Just then, I felt the chain around my ankle yank, and caught the eye of the Mende woman on the end of the line. In seconds we all made it overboard, and hovering over the restless sea, I looked back at the alien ship one last time before we flew away.

Field Note Excerpt III
Discarded Genomes: Restricted Access
Foodie Colony M4E5T8 (Island in the South Pacific),
May 10, 2216

As the aerotrain pulled out of the station, the captain reminded everyone to strap in. The trip to the colony was shorter than I expected. The Transportation Authority caution notices always made it seem as if it were another planet and that the foodies were a different species. But when we pulled up along the shore, close enough to see the inhabitants, excited chatter turned to shock as everyone realized that the stories we grew up with—foodies with protruding jaws and bloated bellies whose babies hung from their mother's breasts like monkeys—were flat-out lies.

The figures staring back at us from the island did not seem alien. Most looked just like protees—the vast majority of all the other humans genetically edited to self-sustain.

As the earth entered a period that our ancestors dubbed the "Anthropocene," and the ecosystem began to collapse as a result of human gluttony, food supplies could no longer sustain the growing population. But initial breakthroughs stalled, and dozens of failed clinical trials on four continents failed to produce a viable protee genome. It was three generations before researchers were able to figure out the exact synthesis.

Colony M4E5T8 is one of nine filled with the children and grandchildren of those failed trials.

The public, as it turns out, is hungry to learn more about the foodies, which is where my research comes in. While I wait for my team to arrive in a few days, I'll set up the interview schedule and other logistics with the colony administrators. After the guide walked me from the aerotrain to the guest quarters, I looked over my notes.

To keep things simple, I grouped the respondents: breastfeeders, children, teenagers, and all other adults. I'll decide whether to disaggregate after the first round of pilot interviews. I've already configured the coding software using the themes outlined in my proposal: nursing and attachment in small children, food preparation and gender roles, hospitality and religious customs, diet and self-image, generational exchanges and family traditions. We'll incorporate other forms of foodie sociality as they arise... "grounded theory" and all that.

What's that old saying? *We don't know what we don't know*.

Just as I sat down in the corner of the dining hall to observe the first meal, I was startled by a child with a crown of fluffy brown hair and sticky hands grabbing my fingers, saying, "You're new! Come on, you can sit with me."

Postscript

Beauty. Health. Fitness. Intelligence. These are not static universals, but lively battlegrounds; routinely violent, casually eugenic, and euphemistically wrapped in a moral prophylactic. Human betterment. *But better for whom?* We rarely ask.

Experimenting quite literally with a sociological imagination, this piece employs speculative methods through a series of field notes: the first describes a meeting I personally attended to kickstart the Human Genome Project-Write initiative in Boston, USA; the second depicts a hunger strike on a ship carrying human cargo in the Atlantic two centuries before; the third imagines a colony of excess humans whose passé relationship with food burdens the planet, two centuries later. Each note is necessarily partial, with multiple possible beginnings and endings.[5]

One of the aims of this experiment is to explore the *relationality* of innovation and containment—*who and what is fixed in place*, corralled and coerced, so others are free to fabricate the future?[6] In the process of designing ideal genomes, what versions of humanity are potentially discarded?

Producing speculative field notes as a methodological exercise is a way to fashion possible futures and probable pasts, enabling analysts to critically reflect on the present. In experimenting with the line between fact and fiction, we can begin to question the assumption of inevitability that surrounds technological development.

After all, why is it that we can so readily imagine growing heart cells in a lab, but not growing empathy for other human beings in our everyday lives? For many, the idea that we can defy politics as usual and channel human ingenuity toward more egalitarian forms of social organization is far-fetched. Our collective imaginations tend to shrink when confronted with entrenched inequality and injustice, when what we need is just as much investment and innovation in our social reality as we pour into transforming our material lives.[7]

1 Email communication from Human Genome Project-Write organizers to participants, including the author.

2 See twitter.com/DrewEndy/status/729777013213401088.

3 All quotations in the first field note are paraphrases (unless otherwise noted), revised for grammar, tense, or emphasis.

4 Christopher Hudson, "Cargo of the living dead: The unspeakable horror of life on a slave ship," *Daily Mail*, December 13, 2007.

5 For more on speculative methods, see "Social Fiction: Writing Social Science Research as Fiction," sociologicalimagination.org; "Ethnography, Speculative Fiction, and Design," "Speculative Ethnography," and "Ethnographies from the Future: What can ethnographers learn from science fiction and speculative design?," ethnographymatters.net; and "Design Fiction: A short essay on design, science, fact, and fiction," drbfw5wfjlxon.cloudfront.net/writing/DesignFiction_WebEdition.pdf.

6 For more on the relationship between innovation and containment, see Ruha Benjamin, "Catching Our Breath: Critical Race STS and the Carceral Imagination," *Engaging Science, Technology and Society* 2 (2016): 145–56.

7 For more on political imaginaries that animate biotechnology, see Ruha Benjamin, *People's Science: Bodies and Rights on the Stem Cell Frontier* (Stanford, CA: Stanford University Press, 2013).

Spaces of the Learning Self

Tom Holert

Self-Directed Exit Education

> They called me a "snob," which, obviously, left me overjoyed. I was inventing culture for myself, and at the same time inventing a character and a personality.
> —Didier Eribon[1]

In *Returning to Reims*, a 2009 autosociographic account of class flight and proletarian self-hatred, French philosopher Didier Eribon, author of a well-known biography on Michel Foucault and several books on *la question gay*, emphasizes the role of autodidacticism and self-directed subjectivization as a social and existential exit strategy in the Althusserian scenography of ideological interpellation. These processes stand for a particular mode of organizing one's own intellectual formation in order to emancipate oneself from the confines of class origin. As a high school student from a proletarian background growing up in a French provincial town in the late 1960s, Eribon discovered the mobilizing pleasures of modern literature through a friend from a bourgeois family. Reading as such, but especially reading according to a literary canon constructed in seeming autonomy, proved to be essential for Eribon in escaping the social context that he experienced as constraining and repressive. Around the same time he designed an education, a "culture" for himself, started fashioning a political subjectivity as a member of Trotskyist group, and began acknowledging his sexual desire as a gay man. This education required seceding from the homophobic and anti-intellectual milieu of his family, and was to a large extent autodidactic; cruising, taking a test-drive along various avenues of subjectivization, both intellectual and sexual.

In retrospect, equipped with a sociological sensorium shaped by the study of Pierre Bourdieu, Annie Ernaux, Raymond Williams, Michel Foucault, and others, it appears obvious to Eribon how much his autodidacticism and aspiration to become an academic intellectual owed to the naïveté and ignorance of someone whose "educational choices ... bear the mark of the deprived social circumstances."[2] On the other hand, the choices he made to liberate himself from the strongholds of class and to distance himself from his origins—socially, geographically, and psychologically—were constitutive of the person he aimed to become. Though they caused feelings of guilt at the moment of his father's death, Eribon acknowledged the extent to which his emancipation was based on self-hatred and a shameful denial of class, as well as a gradual insight into the reality of social stratification. He observed how his futile attempt to inhabit the self-conception and attitudes of those claiming to own the privileges of middle class/bourgeois culture separated knowledge from his own social praxis and experience. Yet however suspiciously his younger self is revisited, there is a peculiar pride tangible in Eribon's renditions of such self-directed learning.

Returning to Reims may be considered a typical narrative of self-design, or, as Spinozist philosopher Chantal Jaquet calls it, the quintessential story of "class-passing" and "non-reproduction."[3] These modes of constructing a self may testify to the plasticity of social existence, but are, for Jaquet, too often bound to the "illusion of the self-made man," driven by guilt and shame in a solitary quest for self-invention.[4] And while Eribon does not deny the solidarity and collectivity of the various milieus he dwelled in to become who he did, he nonetheless considers his trajectory in terms of building a singular self.

Architecturality of the Self

One of the crucial political fantasies surrounding '68 was to escape the confines of milieu and to move swiftly across the social spectrum. Vital interest in matters of class was displayed by members of the bourgeoisie, students, and artists. Searching for a political subject outside of themselves, they turned—for the last time—to the working classes, while simultaneously rehearsing a variety of other escapist methodologies, from hallucinogenic drugs and dropout communities to the science fiction of hyper-personalized mobility.

In one of her rare, brilliant interventions in the pages of *Architectural Design* in the late 1960s, architect and artist Ruth Lakofski (Denise Scott Brown's sister) speculated about how "one's life's work becomes one's own physical vision of oneself perfecting it, choosing the perfect skin, hair, body, eyes, soul and spirit to feel magical—narcissus watching him/herself reflected in the water and gradually, gently changing all the time."[5] Lakofski's comments were partly instigated by the catalogue of a 1968 exhibition on "body covering" at the Museum of Contemporary Crafts in New York that featured, among other things, survival gear like an individual inflatable life raft garment made for NASA and a one-piece air-ventilated protective suit. Her column reflected upon "the use of cyborg clocking into homeostatic systems" and addressed the whole gamut of life- and performance-enhancing technologies imaginable in 1968 that were capable of propelling humans into a posthuman process of coming "into our own again as anything at all."

Considering its context, Lakofski naturally invoked Archigram member Mike Webb's mid-1960s "Cushicle" project when writing about homes to be carried "around with us." Webb's customized two-part mobile enclosure synthesized mechanical and biological systems.[6] It was to provide a cybernetic environment designed to anticipate the nutritional, metabolistic, and affective needs of the dwelling person, lending them sustainable autonomy in the face of increasing physical and communicative demands in a near future of (post)humanity. The narcissistic monadism of such self-containment (or, arguably, containment of the self) made Lakofski think of "the addict with his paper bag," an association she elaborates upon almost twenty years later in another essay. With the "Soul Box," Lakofski reflects particularly on "people who have managed to make themselves into containers of their own souls."[7]

> A bag lady (vagrant) carries with her in her endless journeying through the streets, night and day, her myriad paper bags, each containing a fragment of a soul. A poet, painter, writer, musician, or indeed carpenter, boat-builder or person with a hobby, must have a place to work relentlessly to develop and house the developing soul, without which she or he feels and is dead. Studios and workshops, "A room of one's own," are spirit houses, containers of the exploring soul.[8]

Clearly sympathizing with the model of the apparently-chaotic-though-in-fact-meticulously-organized mobile architecture of the "bag lady," Lakofski connects the psychic life of the searching individual—the "developing" and "exploring" soul—with issues of housing and dwelling. Emphasizing the inherent spatiality and three-dimensionality of the dweller's immaterial activities, she points to the intricate relation between self and architecture, if not to a veritable architecturality of the self. To conceive the individual's inner workings in topological or spatial terms has a long tradition; just think of the theaters of memory or the intersection of the dreaming self and the place where it dwells, from psychoanalysis to surrealism and onto various lineages of the horror genre.[9] As Anthony Vidler aptly puts it, architecture "manifests itself in that most ambiguous of all elements—space—within which psychic projection and introjection move freely and without fixed boundaries. It is thereby a site for all the spatial terrors and phobias that have haunted the medicine of the mind since the late nineteenth century."[10]

The identification of architecture and subjectivity operates at the heart of numerous projects that promise the enhancement of the subject's capacities of learning and cognition. Probably one of the most comprehensive investigations into the "spatial terrors and phobias" and their connection to architectures of learning was undertaken by the artist Mike Kelley. His *Educational Complex* (1995–2008) project, "a large architectural model made up of individual models of every school [Kelley] ever attended, plus the house in which [he] grew up," not only explored the repressed memories and traumata of education by reconstructing past, autobiographically charged places of learning, shame, lust, and fear, but also forcibly underscored the inseparability of physical architecture(s) and subjectivization.[11] By the same token, *Educational Complex* renders the rift between the psychic, often entirely imaginary or dreamlike reality of learning environments, and their manifest physical outside. Howard Singerman compares this "non-correspondence between exterior elevation and interior life" to the antagonism between "the clarity and transparency of modern educational architecture, and of the reasoned pedagogy it at once figures and informs" and "a distinctly antimodernist, even gothic, darkness" to be found in the rituals of education and the cultural resistance of those supposed to be educated.[12]

Autonomy of Learning, or the Global Classroom

As if to free the individual not only from the constraints of class but also from the obsolete structures of an outworn educational system, designers and architects of the late 1960s increasingly focused on models of personalized learning environments that were to foster autonomy and mobility. Chris Abel, for instance, an architect and urban planner who advised on the architecture of schools for the Greater London Council, in 1969 proposed designs for "mobile learning stations." Conceived to be largely independent from their surroundings, these stations were to be equipped with different filing systems, display panels, work surfaces, technological aids, and media.[13] The individual student could either learn on their own by immersing themselves in a tailor-made, controlled, and programmed environment, or by connecting with other stations to generate variable learning groups. Contrary to what it might seem, however, Abel and his colleague Chris Dawson's deliberations were less about an Archigram-type space capsule of technologically supported independence, than addressing a "new system" to "emerge from a *change in the organization* of educational and community provision."[14] They envisaged a "coordinated network" and "interdisciplinary resources of a radical nature" of which the "mobile learning stations" were to be only one part.

In a February 1969 article on the "university environment," Berkeley-based ecological designer and architect Sim Van der Ryn, founder of the Farallones Institute, friend of renegade designer-educators Ant Farm, and state architect of governor Jerry Brown's California, developed ideas concerning such a coordinated network, though from a somewhat different angle than the London planners. Criticizing the frenetic postwar production of modernist campus planning and buildings in the United States, Van der Ryn accused planning of operating like a "closed system in which the users do no really participate."[15] Drawing on environmental psychologist Robert Sommer's 1969 classic *Personal Space: The Behavioral Basis of Design*, he emphasized the extent to which architecture shapes the individual's learning and social intercourse as well as how physical forms and administrative arrangements account for significant changes in patterns of human activity. Van der Ryn recommends that instead of being controlled by standardized institutional architecture, people should be encouraged to change their environments, taking benefit from the flexibility that comes, for instance, with new plastic building materials.[16] Rather than constructing everything anew and forcing students and faculty to move into "bright shiny new quarters," negatively modifying their behavior, a "sense of community" should be provided by creating "'waste space' that serves as neutral turf for people to come together." However, according to Van der Ryn, evidence suggests that "open inquiry and independent scholarship, the development of individual student capacities on their own terms, and the production of measurable material benefits for society are increasingly divergent activities. They do not and perhaps cannot co-exist in the same psychic and physical space."

Referring to exceptions such as the Esalen Institute in Big Sur, the Free University in Palo Alto, Fresno, and Mountain View, and SUNY College Old Westbury, Van der Ryn underlines that "there is a limit above which a spatial concentration of educational resources is self-defeating, dehumanizing and wasteful." "Spatial diffusion" is therefore key, given the "extended mobility of most students, and the non-spatial orientation of learning media such as computers and television."[17] The future of university education is, accordingly, media-based, "self-programmed instruction," and "the place for individual learning will be the home, or a personal study station." Van der Ryn was an early, though arguably unintentional, proponent of the Californian Ideology, a believer in the potential benefits of networked learning, and the emancipatory effects of technological progress. His anthropology is based less on organizational theory than on a philosophical outlook on the challenge of radical freedom—freedom both from religious norms and the capitalist economy's demands of productivity. The "future learning environment," as a space of "genuine social innovation, or exploration of self," will be "grounded in each man's [*sic*] belief in his [*sic*] own interior potential, the new 'soul.'" Tellingly, Van der Ryn brought discourse on the design of future learning environments together with musings about the inner life of the learning subject whose "new soul" is the resource to be cultivated and looked after. However, the "soul box" of the learner in a spatially "diffused" educational geography should be considered in terms other than the physical campus building, the mobile study, or even Kelley's educational complex.

In the 2015 UNESCO-sponsored policy paper entitled "The Futures of Learning," notions such as "active learner," "metacognitive development," and "participatory learning" abound. The most important, however, seems to be the "personalization" and "customization" of learning, or even "learner-designed learning." As if copy-pasted from Van der Ryn's 1969 tract, the advice reads as follows: "With personalized learning, individuals approach problems in their own way, grasp ideas at their own pace, and respond differently to multiple forms of feedback."[18] Neuroscience research is cited to the effect that the instead of preparing "lessons" (so old school), the task of a instructor should be "designing project-based forms of learning." This proposition rests on the assumption that learners improve better on "core subject matter" and benefit from emphasis on "depth over breadth" when learning in a personalized environment.[19] "Instructional design" is presumed to become the central agency of such infinitely customized collaborative pedagogy. The key instructional designer, however, is going to be the learner herself, equipped with networked handheld devices: "Future learning processes will inevitably take place in environments in which learners select their own modes of learning and bring personal technologies into education," thereby dissolving not only any difference between formal and informal learning, but also between inner and outer, psychic and physical spatialities of learning.[20]

This exit from the old systems and architectures of both education and class and entry into mobile learning capsules, however they may be defined, has been a political project and designer's dream since at least the 1960s. Yet considering Didier Eribon's self-critical account of class flight into self-organized learning, Ruth Lakofski's appreciation of the bag lady's mode of spatializing her "exploring soul," or Sim Van der Ryn's proposals for an education revolution based on radical individualism, the vista of "pedagogy 2.0" and lifelong personalization (read: commodification) as is promoted today is truly disheartening. That said, the self still waits to be designed. Improved enclosures for enhanced learning experiences will be proposed, with no end in sight. The paradox of programmed autodidactism and the responsibilization of the neoliberal subject to watchfully manage their own lifelong learning curriculum will stimulate the knowledge industry of instructional design schemes. It might thus be convenient to recall what Ivan Illich, author of the influential 1971 *Deschooling Society*, self-critically wrote in retrospect when he called for "the reversal of those trends that make of education a pressing need rather than a gift of gratuitous leisure." Drug-like addiction to education, Illich bemoaned, would make "the world into a universal classroom, a global schoolhouse."[21] Something surely to be avoided, at all cost.

1 Didier Eribon, *Returning to Reims* [2009], trans. Michael Lucey (Los Angeles: Semiotext(e), 2013), 175.
2 Ibid.
3 Chantal Jaquet, *Les Transclasses ou la non-reproduction* (Paris: P.U.F., 2014).
4 "Le self-made man est une illusion: Interview with Chantal Jaquet," by Antoine Louvard, *Marianne*, June 8, 2014.
5 Ruth Lakofski, "Come Back Narcissus – I Love You/Me," *Architectural Design* 39, no. 6 (June 1969): 293.
6 The Cushicle consisted "of a chassis with appliances and personalized apparatuses and an inflatable envelope. The chassis is structured like a spine and would include a heating system. The helmet would contain the radio and mini-TV. Food and water modules could be added to the chassis as attachments. The two skins would be envelopes for the rider, covered with viewing screens. The two could be used independently or simultaneously." See https://architecturewithoutarchitecture.blogspot.de/p/cushicle-and-suitaloon-were-conceptual.html.
7 Ruth Lakofski, "Gedanken über die Seelen-Kiste/Reflexions on the Soul Box," *Daidalos. Architektur – Kunst – Kultur* 28 (June 15, 1988): 92–103.
8 Ibid., 93.
9 Frances A. Yates, *The Art of Memory* (London: Routledge and Kegan, 1966).
10 Anthony Vidler, "Fantasy, the Uncanny and Surrealist Theories of Architecture," *Papers of Surrealism* 1 (Winter 2003): 3.
11 Mike Kelley, "Educational Complex" [1996], *Mike Kelley. Educational Complex Onwards 1995–2008*, eds. Mike Kelley and Anne Pontégnie (Zurich: JRP Ringier, 2009), 21.
12 Howard Singerman, "The Educational Complex: Mike Kelley's *Cultural Studies*," *October* 126 (Fall 2008): 48.
13 Chris Abel, "Mobile Learning Stations," *Architectural Design* 33, no. 3 (March 1969): 151.
14 Ibid.
15 Sim Van der Ryn, "The University Environment," *The Daily Californian*, February 18, 1969. Reprinted in *Architectural Design* 33, no. 11 (November 1969): 618–20.
16 Ibid., 619.
17 Ibid., 620.
18 Cynthia Luna Scott, "The Futures of Learning 3: What Kind of Pedagogies for the 21st Century?" *UNESCO Education Research and Foresight: Working Papers* 15 (December 2015): 4.
19 Ibid.
20 Ibid., 9.
21 Ivan Illich, "Foreword" [1995], *Everywhere All the Time: A New Deschooling Reader*, ed. Matt Hern (Oakland, CA: AK, 2008), iv. See also Rosa Bruno-Jofré and Jon Igelmo Zaldívar, "Ivan Illich's Late Critique of Deschooling Society," *Educational Theory* 62, no. 5 (2012): 573–92.

History for an Empty Future

Sylvia Lavin

The first and sometimes last thing an architect designs is himself. Andrea Palladio was born Andrea Di Petro della Gondola in 1508, but became Palladio only in 1538. The new name, concocted out of Pallas Athene, the goddess of wisdom, and the name of a character in a play by Palladio's patron, Gian Giorgio Trissino, designated Andrea as a master of languages, of both humanism and architecture. John Swan is the forgotten son of a mason, but also the moderately known architect John Soan, as well as the very well-known John Soane and the prodigiously known Sir John Soane. He is not Baron John Soane because despite the architect's evident aristocratic ambitions, becoming a baron would have required John to leave his estate to his detested son, George. McKim, Mead & White might well have designed their firm name alphabetically, as did Skidmore, Owings & Merrill in reverse order. This corporate nomenclature was as mechanically generated and organizationally driven as the steel frames such offices worked in and on. Le Corbusier designed two names for himself, using one for his work as an architect and the other for his work as a painter, which is to say, he designed his names to affirm an essential distinction between mediums. Charles Moore was a serial renamer, going by Charles Moore at various times and at others by MLTW, Centerbrook Architect, Charles W. Moore Incorporated, Moore Ruble Yudell, and Urban Innovations Group, to name just a few of his names, hidden identities, and personae. And of course, the infinite array of acronyms, monikers, and brand names designed by contemporary architects is just the most obvious symptom of the virtually universal desire to become a "signature architect," a goal that requires a near total immersion of the self in the design of hyperbolic singularity and distinction.

The history of most things, or at least modern things, could be redesigned through an archaeology of proper and improper names, pseudonyms, alibis, forgeries, and makers' marks. This history would reveal misalignments between consciousnesses, individuals, persons, people, and subjects, and in turn reflect a history of definitions of the human. The language games implicit in the design of "Palladio" belonged to a then emerging association between the human and the capacity not just to *use* language but to design it, just as the humanists did when they refashioned Latin and reordered architecture. Soane's modifications to his name were a central component to his continual effort to make the representation of his self and the self align, to produce a perfectly transparent *cogito* in accordance with the classical episteme that allowed no other possibility than the identification of "the human" with knowledge. Yet the rationalization of corporate name design in the late industrial age reflects the growing conflation of human and machine. Le Corbusier's schizophrenic essentialism, for instance, grounded the human not in bedrock but in plastic—a twentieth-century material infinitely powerful (and totally vulnerable) in its capacity to be endlessly remade. Plasticity became the ontological principal of the nuclear age, where matter became not a substance of essences and unities but the explosive potential to rive the human species to death. Only modern design could hold matter together until, perhaps exhausted by the effort, a new sort of human shifted his focus towards the design of death itself. Charles Moore performed his own death again and again, precisely in the period during which it was possible for people like Andy Warhol and Ronald Reagan not only to live life as a perpetual performance but to be shot, to die, and to come back to life.[1]

A history of architects' names would be less a collection of biographies than an anthology of traces left by existences, traces that became more articulated in their design as those existences were shaped by an increasing number of increasingly denaturing systems of production, structures of power, and abstract epistemologies.[2] Palladio may have been widely known by a specially designed name, but architects did not commonly sign things until well into the eighteenth century. By then, a name alone was insufficient for the complex task of authentication required by a culture organized around the circulation, collection, and exchange of images. Palladio's name printed in a book was enough to spread Palladianism, but Piranesi needed both a name and an identifying signature to function as avatar and keep him attached to his drawings as they dispersed, image by image, across Europe.[3] As industrial modernization further alienated the architect-as-person from his productions, compensatory architectural signatures proliferated until even buildings themselves were signed. From the mid-nineteenth century on, the quotidian architectural counterparts of often insignificant existences, like the innumerable apartment blocks that built the modern European city, sported signature plaques near their front doors. These signs of self-importance, bits of advertising for an often anonymous architect, were small tokens of self-design offered in compensation for the increasing absorption of human presence in the metropolis as a layer of design. Auguste Perret scratched his name into a wet ceramic tile on his apartment building at 12 bis Rue Franklin in Paris, leaving behind a signature more like a child's scrawl on a sandy beach than an exemplar of art nouveau design.

A name signed in wet sand that cannot be erased is evidence of the effects on architectural design of nineteenth-century concepts of geological time and history outside human experience. If, in the wake of the invention of the Darwinian past, history was no longer to be recorded on paper, motivated by the acts of individuals, and authenticated by signatures, but rather buried within layers of rock, where, how, and for whom were traces of individual existence to be deposited? For architects of the latter half of the nineteenth century, in other words, how to design history and the place of the human within it became a central preoccupation, one that can be read through the redesign of names, signatures, and their division into two increasingly irreconcilable forms, each with a distinct mode of address. Growing separations between museums and archives, drawings and documents, and monuments and habitations produced cleavages between histories addressed to individual human experience and those addressed more abstractly to the human species. Charles Garnier, for example, became a designer both of architectural monuments and of human beings. On the one hand, the Paris Opera came to be so identified with the architect that it was known as the Palais Garnier. To reinforce the building's function as a signature, Garnier had a monument to himself—an autograph, in effect—erected in front of the entrance bearing his bust, his name, his drawing of the Opera, and the dates of his birth and death. As vertical and visible as the building's grand facade seen at the end of the long perspective, the monument addressed itself to man, he who walked erect through the city on its new boulevards and who understood his place in the present empirically, as a reality derived from the conditions of his human experience. On the other hand, Garnier also styled himself as an ethnographer, constructing at the 1889 Exposition Universelle a display of human habitation from the prehistoric to what he called the "contemporary primitive": forty-four buildings concerned not with individual existences but with the "march of humanity through the ages."[4] This panorama of prehistory required the suppression of Garnier's signature to produce its reality effects, and therefore more design than ever: to be perceived as prehistoric, each house had to be fully furnished, inhabited by living human specimens in costume, and visitors had to be distracted from their temporal incongruity with the present. In the book published as a scientific record of the spectacle, the extraction of the species from the present continued. Each house is presented as if drawn on a separate sheet of paper and the papers piled up on each other and strewn haphazardly across the page, deposited like so many strata in a geology of paperwork. The individual drawings aspire to the status of anonymous documents, lest evidence of their design lessen their capacity to appear as architectural fossils at the limit of human history. *L'Habitation Humaine* required nothing more than the printed identification of Garnier as coproducer.[5]

If the human and its place in history were both designed during the second half of the nineteenth century, the second half of the twentieth century redesigned the human without a place in history. By the 1960s, cultural attention was shifting to the end of the species rather than its origins—a potential death that was making its way into thought, redesigning neural pathways and the epistemic substrate of life. The advent of a geological era designed by humans, today commonly known as the Anthropocene, was therefore raising the question of what kind of signatures, what signs of life, would be useful for a time *after* the human—for a historical age without human posterity. Those becoming architects as these questions were taking shape are the architects associated with postmodernity and its anxieties about history. These architects constitute the last generation for whom the use of their own name as avatar, linked to their biographies and personal experience, appeared to be a natural selection rather than an act of design. This generation was scrupulously attentive to how they would enter the historical record, constructing elaborate and explicitly designed genealogies of architecture into which they inserted their names. Above all they self-archived, almost continuously, and while their obsessively constant choices about what to keep and what to expunge from the design of their future memory produced an almost comprehensive record of their existences, their efforts nevertheless contain gaps—evidence of moments when they appear to have been distracted from posterity by the exigencies of immediate events. And in these unintended lacunae, self-designs not only without designers, but more importantly without designated or even imagined recipients, begin to appear.

Peter Eisenman and Robert Venturi are two architects who were particularly consumed by self-archiving in the 1960s, although they followed apparently opposed design methods in this enterprise. Eisenman allowed relatively little material to find its way into the archive of House 1, for example, which is evidence of the great deal of material he elected to repress.[6] He included only drawings, largely by his own hand, and no paperwork, thereby eliminating any trace of constraints on him and exposing his desire to appear absolutely autonomous, which is to say self-regulated and self-designed. His protocol recalls that of an art collector or museum curator, carefully picking and choosing things according to criteria designed to appear subjective and hence able to produce a record of a human existence identified as such by its pure and autonomous subjectivity. Many of these drawings are signed. Venturi, on the other hand, kept and included everything: every scrap of paper, specification set, and phone memo.[7] His protocol was clinical and scholarly, designed to appear objective, and his archive contains far more signatures on typed letters, contracts, and other mechanically produced documents than on drawings. Where Eisenman's archive is holographic, like a handwritten last will and testament, with his name appearing as an intrinsically authenticating autograph, Venturi's archive is an accumulation of copies, typesets, and transcripts—the sort of documents that require notaries to authenticate their signatures. The former imagines its salience in terms of its capacity to record the unfolding of a personal history—what the field calls a "design process"—addressed to other persons with histories, while the latter imagines its salience in terms of its capacity to record the traces of functions deposited in an impersonal mountain of paperwork addressed to other operatives.

Despite the significant differences in the design of the selves they contain and the human types they address, both archives are above all containers for the afterlife of these various self-designs. They design both the past and the future, but it is in the projection of the future that the archives capture traces not only of design intention but of designs without designers that anticipate the potentiality that these future addressees may not be human in any recognizable sense. Mixed in among the autographs on drawings that appear with a systematic deliberateness on the lower-right-hand corner and the signatures of documents that consistently follow bureaucratic regulation on the proverbial dotted line (which is to say mixed in with designs of selves and their place in the human world), there appear a loose scattering of letters: a free floating "P," an "E" in axonometric projection, and an "RV" here and there. These initials neither reinforce nor undercut the self-archiving impulse but instead appear simply to disregard the self as an a priori category and, without a self to recognize them as signs, they mutate into elements of a code that is already obsolete, bits of data prepared for algorithmic operations that unfold without design. If Palladio used digits to regulate the orders, he did so to make them more communicable to other humans, not less. Eisenman and Venturi's digits operate with no guarantee that a human will be their ultimate recipient.

The political context of this design of history without humans is made evident in one of the first collaborations between Robert Venturi and Denise Scott Brown, a design submitted to the Fairmount Park Fountain Competition of 1964, shortly after the Cuban Missile Crisis. As befits the ontology of the nuclear age, the architects describe their proposed fountain, the central point of an artificial interior grotto, mossy and filled with a misty yellow haze, as a plastic shape, even though it was to be made of sand-blasted aluminum and designed to amplify the mechanical roar of its sixty-foot-high jet of water. The shape, in fact, is that of the tip of a missile ready to rocket into space—a potential escape pod and weapon. Lettering at the base was designed for humans walking upright in the park: for them, the legend read "Here Begins Fairmount Park." These Homo sapiens, however, were only part of the missile's intended target. To those humans redesigned by mechanization, who traveled in cars at high speeds and moved low to the ground, the message compressed into an instruction: "Park Here." While working on this design, using the standard lined yellow paper

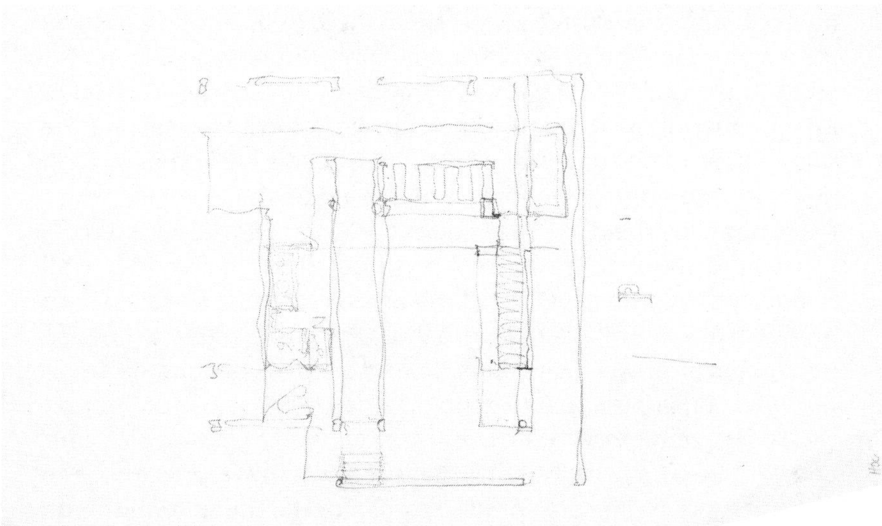

Top: Peter Eisenman, Barenholtz Pavilion (House 1), Sketch, 1967–68.
Bottom: Monumental Fountain on the Benjamin Franklin Parkway, Competition. Fairmount Park Art Association.

on which he signed his name and tagged his initials, Venturi also seems to have considered sending a message to a future reader who had mutated beyond the recognizably human altogether. For no apparent reason, in between sketches, initials, and arbitrary marks on paper, he wrote, "Ask not what your country can do for you"—the first line of the famous couplet from John F. Kennedy's inauguration speech. Venturi, however, did not write the second line that concerned the importance of human action: "Ask what you can do for your country." Instead, he simply marked the paper with ditto marks, as if to repeat the negation of human action, ad infinitum.[8]

If the premodern architect was a demiurge, a designer of all things, and a being at the very limit of the human, and if a modern architect like Garnier could write that "there is no need to choose among the arts: one must either be God or an Architect," the architect who considers the Anthropocene has the task of confronting the design of history for neither man nor god but instead for an empty future. Yet even that thought relies on a theory of design, the oldest theory of design—*creatio ex nihilo*—because for humans there is no thought outside design, not even the thought of nothing.

1 This is the subject of a forthcoming book by Peggy Phelan, *Death Rehearsals: The Performances of Andy Warhol and Ronald Reagan.*

2 On the relation between signatures and the notion of an anthology of existences, see Michel Foucault, "Lives of Infamous Men," in *The Essential Foucault: 1954–1984*, ed. Paul Rabinow (New York: The New Press, 1994), 157–75.

3 On the history of the artist's signature, see Nicole Hegener, *Künstlersignaturen von der Antike bis zur Gegenwart: Artists' signatures from Antiquity to the present* (Petersberg: Imhof, 2013).

4 For an historical account of the exhibit, see G. Fraipont, *Histoire de l'habitation humaine: Constructions édifiées par Charles Garnie*r (Paris, 1989).

5 See Charles Garnier and Auguste Ammann, *L'Habitation humaine* (Paris: La Librarie modern, 1892).

6 Peter Eisenman's official archive is held at the Canadian Center for Architecture.

7 Robert Venturi's professional archive forms part of the Venturi Scott Brown Collection, held in the Architectural Archives, University of Pennsylvania.

8 This particular sheet is misfiled and located among the papers concerned with the Guild House. On the completion, see Robert Venturi, "3 Projects," *Perspecta* 11 (1967): 103–11.

Masters and Slaves

Lydia Kallipoliti

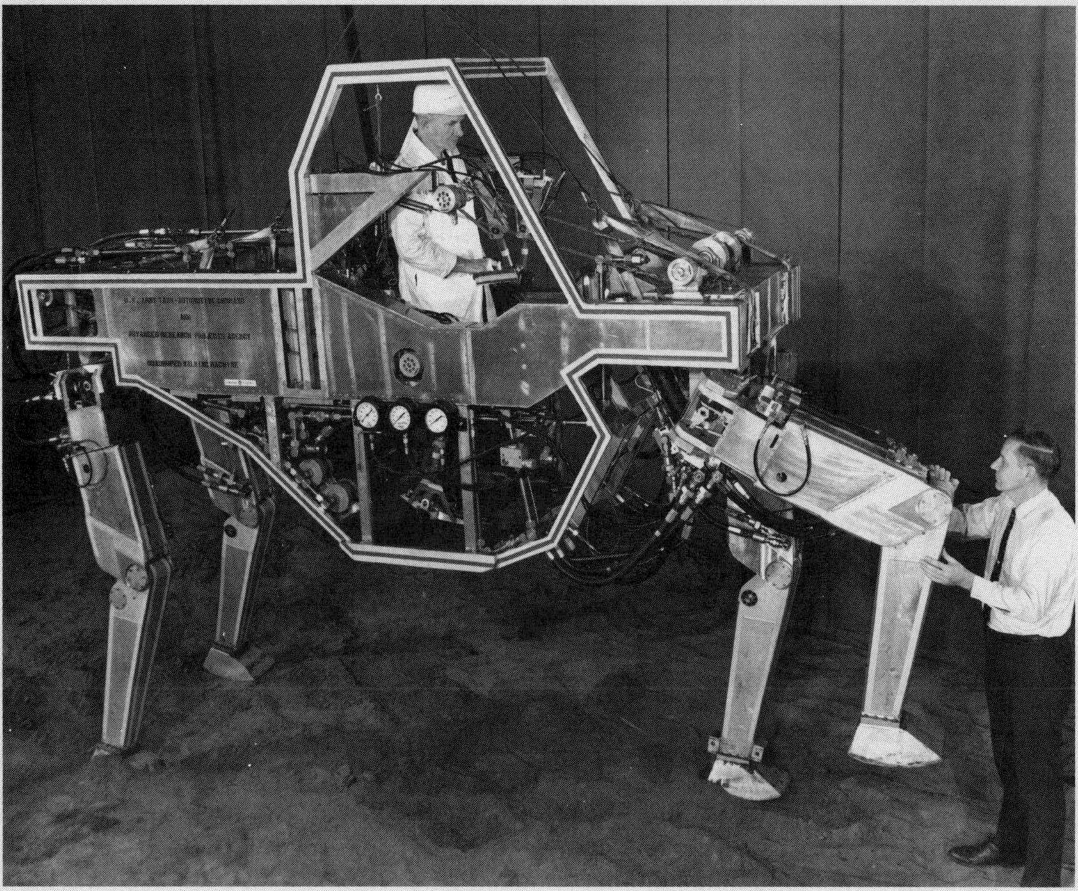

General Electric Prototype for a Versatile Walking Truck developed by Ralph Mosher and R. A. Liston in 1969.

When Aristophanes was summoned in Plato's symposium to speak of *eros* (έρως), he reverted to the root of human nature, the natural bodily reality of three sexes: male, female, and the vanished *male-female* (αρσενικοθήλυκο).[1] The latter was the strongest and fastest of all, combining both male and female attributes. Its appearance was whole and round with four hands and legs, two faces, and a back on all sides. The creature was not erect and would never stand vertical to the earth. It did not walk, but tumbled after taking a spherical shape. Its power of completeness became a threat to the gods, so Zeus invented a machine, destined not to eliminate the third sex, but to fade its supremacy; he sent a lightning bolt to split the sex.[2] As soon as the creature was fractured, each half would run with passion to the other because its desire for reunification was greater than hunger or survival. So according to Aristophanes, *eros* is inherent to human nature as the tormented journey for the reunion of original descent.[3] *Eros* attempts to make the two more than one and thus remedy the original shortcoming of each as a split symbol.

Aristophanes's duality was displaced later in the *Symposium* by Diotima's version of *eros* (narrated by Socrates) as a multidimensional *diaspora* (διασπορά) of the body in floating fragments—a fractured ego looking not simply for the other, but for pieces of one's body. Following this, it becomes evident that *eros* is as much directed to the "other" as it is to the "self" of one's body, as it narrates erotic desire stemming not merely from a longing for completion, but also from an intense desire to replicate the "self," one's body and identity—to enlarge and prolong it to eternity.

The story of designing, editing, and replicating ourselves is as much a story of love as one of slavery. Jumping from circa 380 BC to 1974, the desire for a replicate body that would complement and exponentially augment its carrier returns as an advanced engineering experiment filed by NASA in United States Patent #4046262.[4] Under the rubric of experiments for man-machine integration, the contentious term "master/slave" has consistently been used since the late 1950s for anthropomorphic manipulator systems, and later on for computer networking. In the patent, the "slave" is a mechanical replica of the body and armature of the "master," designed to carry unimaginable loads and endure all possible injury, all virtually without consequence to the user. The term-pair was later used to define a centralized communication protocol: one device or process, the master, would control all others, the slaves. In 2003, with the rise of distributed computing, "master/slave" was banned by the County of Los Angeles, and subsequently by the Global Language Monitor, as one of the most egregious and offensive terms of the year. Nevertheless, if we allow ourselves to look beyond the politics of domination restated as computer theory, one can find a story of melancholy and deep anxiety as much as one of mechanized authority. As we travel in time from an unsubstantiated myth to a carefully designed patent, the replication of our bodies quite clearly demonstrates the persistence of our schizoid existence and delusion for wholeness.

At present, the pervasive use of social media (Facebook, LinkedIn, Twitter, Instagram, et al.) requires us to carefully construct and steadily edit digital identities, projecting the "self" into a carefully designed entity assembled of data fragments. Although this practice is unlike the mechanical anthropomorphic body that literally replicates the physique of the body, the reproduction of the self online still enforces a type of master/slave relationship and a yearning for a mirror image either materialized or narrated. Our digital selves are possibly even more accurate versions of us than our raw physical bodies walking in flesh. In every post, we review, control, and refine with utmost care how to project our own design. As Sherry Turkle argues, posting allows us to present the self we want to be—not too little, not too much, but just right.[5] Who is the slave, though, in this newer nuanced version of self-replication? Is the ethereal online identity we build analogous to NASA's patent? Or is it the other way around—are we in fact voluntary slaves of what we have earnestly designed with love?

Augmented Man+ / Atrophic Man-

In the Cold War period, the design of the body was reflected in both the astronaut and aquanaut who promised to conquer uninhabitable regions with armored suits carrying earth-like environments inside. An augmented and engineered type of man became of larger cultural interest, portraying a new universal human subject. Unlike the Vitruvian Man or Le Corbusier's Modulor that idealized a cosmic subject representative of humanity as a whole, these mechanized figures were put forth as guinea pigs: delegations of human agency in precise input/output measurements.

The 1974 master/slave patent filed by NASA has a long line of precedents. Spearheaded by major subcontractors such as General Electric with joint support by the US Navy and Army, the 1950s and 1960s witnessed several programs that sought to augment human capabilities with mechanized slave limbs. The augmented man, with replicate bionic components and mechanized parts, was not merely preparing for a future of space exploration, but was an active attempt to design exoskeletal armor for war.

General Electric engineer Ralph Mosher pioneered an extensive investigation on Cybernetic Anthropomorphous Machines (CAM), developing several robotic prototypes with extra limbs that would be directly tied to the human nervous system rather than operate autonomously. Mosher envisioned this type of union—our neurons translating desire into kinesis—as a wedding of sorts. In his own words, "Man and machine can be combined into an intimate, symbiotic unit that will perform essentially as one wedded system. The cybernetic anthropomorphous machine (CAM) will respond to irregular force and position patterns with the alacrity of man's information and control system coupled with the machine's power and ruggedness."[6] The wedding was further consummated by the key feature of force feedback that Mosher applied to all CAMs. In his machines, a mediated level of force was fed back to the human operator to give him a sense of the environmental interaction of the limbs under control.[7]

Mosher's master/slave manipulator projects included the "Yes Man," which was featured in *Life* magazine in 1956 as a robot assisting a lady into her coat; "Handyman" in 1958, a set of robotic arms controlled from a distance by an operator; a walking machine from 1962 called "The Pediculator"; a four-legged "Walking Truck" in 1969; and finally, "HardiMan," developed between 1965 and 1971, which was an acronym for "Human Augmentation Research and Development Investigation," plus "Man" from "MANipulator." "HardiMan" was the first experiment with a powered exoskeleton framework and the controller inside the suit. Whereas Handyman was remotely controlled, the user would sit inside HardiMan's skeleton, directly amplifying the wearer's lifting ability and strength.

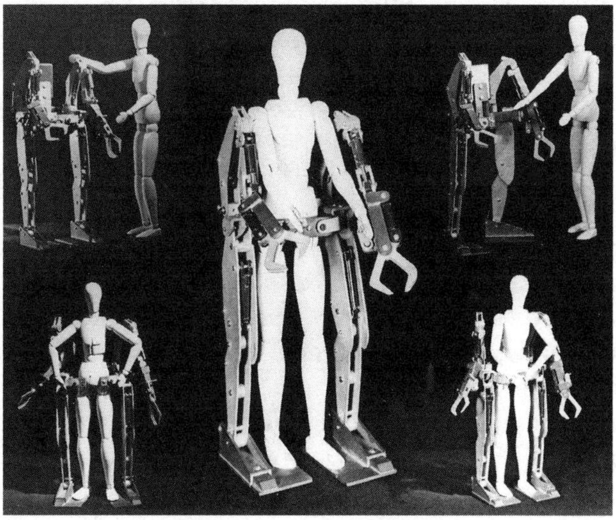

Model of HardiMan, 1965–1971, developed by Ralph Mosher for General Electric.

Other agencies quickly got involved with General Electric and Mosher's man-machine control interfaces, including ARPA (Advanced Research Projects Agency), the Department of Defense, and the US Navy.[8] HardiMan's exoskeletal harness system was further developed by Cornell's Aeronautical Laboratory, which appeared on John McHale's *Design Quarterly* magazine cover from 1968 and ended up becoming one of his most lasting fixations. In his seminal book *The Future of the Future,* McHale invented the term "Man+" to speak not only of elaborate mechanical bodywork encasing humans, but also of solid feedback loops between man and machines in which motor impulses from nerves and muscles were picked up and fed to artificial muscles.[9] As Mark Wigley argues, McHale's fascination with artificial limbs and arthropod-like joints did not merely reflect a prosthetic desire for accessorizing and augmenting the human body, but also a desire to reconstruct the body as a type of controlled artificial ecology.[10]

In many respects, the extension of the human nervous system is analogous to connecting the body to a computer. In a computer interface, the human and the logistical operating system are interconnected on multiple levels; both sides are influenced by each other. The computer relays information that enhances the knowledge of the human and depicts its motives. In some cases, the computer/machine can overpower the human to the point where it is no longer needed. Such was the case with "Posture Chair," a prototype designed by Greek architect and cybernetician Takes Zenetos in 1967.[11] The chair was intended to accommodate all human activities as a duplicate body receptor—including sleeping, working, exercising, having sexual intercourse, and enhancing one's leisure with digital projections and immaterial microenvironments—all managed by a keyboard fastened to its arm. Equipped with a group of electromechanical devices for the control of temperature, sound, and visual effects, the chair was a replicate body intended to resensitize the muscular and nervous system and to "decrease the disadvantages of daily routine life of the men involved in tertiary production."[12] Through a control processing system, the user could customize temporal microclimates, soundscapes, and electronic digital displays. Zenetos describes the project as "a mobile spinal agent equipped with a remote control for tele-activities and a control center for optical-acoustic contacts, which will aid in the execution of tele-activities."[13]

Even though Posture Chair extended the body's capabilities, it introduced a different type of subject than the one featured inside McHale's exoskeleton and Mosher's HardiMan. If Man+ was stronger by virtue of anatomical replication, this was "Man-." Posture Chair's subject was tightly fastened, but not erect—soft and hairless, mushy, and passive. It was designed as premature, portraying a new soma, stripped both of plethoric physical functions—such as too much movement—as well as physical object-like extensions—such as clothing and other prosthetic accessories. Man- was in a state of regressive corporeality. Posture Chair was designed to eventually immobilize the body, even lead it to atrophy while nourishing the mind and the senses.

In some sense, Man- silently hoped that brainpower would become the ultimate computing device and directly control the environment. The brain was conceptualized as an information processor and transmitter able to project—with the aid of hypersensitive receivers of electro-mental waves—instructions for spatial reform, broadcasted directly by the brain with no circuitry. Mechanical limbs, wires, and infrastructure were dematerialized into wave spectrums, magnetic fields, and energy flows.

Augmented Agency

In hindsight, the legacy of human augmentation thrives up until this day in an enormous amount of research going into military and commercial applications of body prosthetics and remotely controlled robots. Boston Dynamics's BigDog is the most advanced, seamlessly roaming through rough terrain with four legs articulated like an animal's, able to absorb shock and recycle energy from one step to the next.[14] Recently, the MARCbot (Multi-Function Agile Remote-Controlled Robot) created by Exponent Inc., was lethally deployed as a bomb disposal machine for the first time by US police.[15]

Considering today's ubiquity of different genres of machines and machine learning with big data and responsive systems, master/slave devices exhibit little (if no) computational intelligence—that is, intelligence exhibited by machines with a learning capacity.[16] Although referenced as reconnaisant robots, Amazon's flying drones expected to pervade our skies by 2020, BigDog, and MARCbot are controlled by a master user in a linear chain of command. Each master/slave machine might be limited in its operational intelligence, yet nevertheless, as Benjamin H. Bratton suggests, it is the vastness of their pervasion, spinning out on their own, that might have already formed the body of an accidental megastructure.[17] Despite their differences, Man+ and Man- form a comprehensive understanding of the modern human condition, allowing us to witness how we safely reconstruct ourselves, believing in vain that the design is our own.

Master/slave designs can partly be seen as the aspirational projection of the world based on potentiality and connectivity that was presumed to accompany the emergent reality of digital information. They exhibit the impasses of our capitalist society—delusions of efficiency, flexibility, ubiquitous access to information, and totality. The replicate body of the master/slave envisions a world entirely based on mediation, both between individuals and with space. Our constantly connected existence allows individuals to affirm themselves by augmenting their containment as something simultaneously interiorizing and exteriorizing. Yet the passage from introspection to projection requires the design of a replicate body and self, and this is where our dreams for a new communal existence and public space occur. Even though the master/slave model reflects, and even materializes, an absurdity of self-love, it is perhaps the truest version we have of human nature and its absence.

1 Plato, *Symposium and Critias,* vol. 15 (Library of Ancient Authors), translated in Greek by B. Dedousis and G. Kordatos (Athens: Zacharopoulos Publishers, 1999), p.141–43.
2 In ancient Greek, "machine" means invention or craft.
3 The original descent refers to the vanished male-female, which preceded the two sexes—male and female—according to Aristophanes's myth in Plato's *Symposium.*
4 Hubert C. Vykukal, Reginald F. King, and Wilbur C. Vallotton. 1974. Anthropomorphic master/slave manipulator system. US Patent 4046262 A, filed January 24, 1974, and issued September 6, 1977.
5 Sherry Turkle "Connected, but Alone?," TED Talk, February 2012.
6 Ralph S. Mosher, "Handyman to Hardiman," SAE Technical Paper 670088, 1967, doi: 10.4271/670088. Research and Development Center, General Electric Co.
7 Jon Turi, "GE's bringing good things, and massive robots, to life," *Engadget*, January 26, 2014.
8 Ibid.
9 See John McHale, *The Future of the Future* (New York: George Braziller Inc, 1969). See also John McHale, "Toward the Future," *Design Quarterly* 72 (Walker Art Center: January 1968); and John McHale, "The Future of the Future," in "2000+," ed. John McHale, special issue, *Architectural Design*, February 1967.
10 Mark Wigley, "Recycling Recycling," in *Eco-Tec: Architecture of the In-Between* (New York: Princeton Architectural Press, 1999), 38–49.
11 Zenetos designed and manufactured Posture Chair in the framework of his major research project Electronic Urbanism, which ran from the 1950s to the 1970s. The design for the Posture Chair won an honorable mention in the "InterDesign 2000" international design competition, in October 1967.
12 Takes Zenetos, "City and House of the Future," Οικονομικός Ταχυδρόμος – *Economy Postman* 924 (January 6, 1972): 10–12.
13 Ibid.
14 Boston Dynamic, "BigDog," bostondynamics.com/robot_bigdog.html.
15 Mark Prigg, "First use of a lethal robot by US police: Details emerge of bomb disposal machine Dallas cops used to kill shooter Micah Xavier Johnson," *Daily Mail*, July 8, 2016.
16 Evangelos Kotsioris and Molly Wright Steenson, "Computational Intelligence," panel announcement for the forthcoming 105th ACSA Annual Meeting "Brooklyn says 'Move to Detroit,'" Detroit 2017.
17 Benjamin H. Bratton, "The Black Stack," *e-flux journal* 53 (March 2014).

On Snow Dancing

Ina Blom

Philippe Parreno, *Snow Dancing*, 1995. Installation detail.

Some twenty years ago, the effects of an expanding regime of design were starting to be felt in the field of contemporary art. Increasingly, designers seemed to use art contexts as platforms for non-pragmatic reflection and expression. Increasingly, design was also becoming a catalyst in so-called social art practices, artistic efforts to engineer or test-drive new social and/or economic relations. In the work of collectives like Superflex or Atelier van Lieshout, for instance, design was an all-important feature of their manufacture of innovative objects or technical solutions, as well as the branding of the groups themselves. Concerned discussions about the aestheticization of anything and everything abounded: design should, apparently, know its place. But this new design ubiquity might have actually been grounded less in a political appeal to the senses over reason than in rapidly expanding processes of informatization and a growing preoccupation with their social and economic effects. A wider concept of design thus established itself: Defined as "the conception and planning of the artificial," it reflected the fact that, with computation, design was no longer the final outcome of a process, but an interdisciplinary activity embedded in all aspects of production. This was "design thinking," a systematic approach to a plastic environment that more than ever seemed subject to human construction and control.[1]

Yet this was perhaps not all there was to design thinking. Some twenty years ago, a more subterranean art-and-design discourse also emerged, one that was perhaps harder to appreciate due to the curiously indirect way in which it seemed to associate design with the operations of new media. In 1995 Philippe Parreno had just completed a project called *Snow Dancing*—supposedly a film, although without cameras, editing, or projection in any ordinary sense. To most of the people who knew about it at the time, *Snow Dancing* was mainly a social event, an open party at Le Consortium in Dijon, immediately followed by an exhibition of the rooms in which the party had taken place and a number of objects or spatial arrangements that had played some part in the staging of the evening.

If the question of design could be said to have been at the center of this project, it was only in the sense of something at once ubiquitous and discreet. This was not a project invested in producing the design for this or that; nor could the situations and behaviors it contained be said to have been "designed" in the strong sense of the word. Design issues were above all present in a text that served as the point of departure for the cinematographic logic that informed the work. Recounted by Parreno to Jack Wendler and Liam Gillick, who wrote it down, it is a loosely scripted scenario providing the outline of a situation or a sequence of events to be produced: notably, the party and subsequent exhibition at Le Consortium.[2] As scenarios go, it is a peculiar exemplar. Neglecting the scene-by-scene action that defines the genre, the text conjures up something more atmospheric and static, in between environment and situation—essentially an extended stage direction. It describes in great detail a world where the design of the social environment and related questions of self-styling play a major role. But these details are not simply descriptive: they could also be seen to indicate a particular type of activity or action. To insist that this never-filmed, never-projected, design-obsessed text, social event, and exhibition is still a "film" is to associate design itself with a certain machinic or mediatic logic. It is to imply that design is interchangeable with the production, manipulation, and distribution of time materials characteristic of a postindustrial media age and its intensified exploitation of the temporalities at work in cognitive and affective processes. If design is at once ubiquitous and "cinematographic" in this scenario, it is because it consistently highlights complex temporalities of shape-shifting—the breaks and shifts of genetic processes that are not rooted in any clearly established point of origin, agency, or plan.

• • •

At the outset, the scenario mainly seems to focus on the question of setting and location, the *type* of place in which the film action may unfold. A fictional yet familiar type of building or building complex is conjured up, one that seems to embody, in a dreamily condensed form, the key traits of urban gentrification. It is a place whose original function obscured, but which retains a vague aura of past significance. It may have been a school, it may have been a hospital. It may also have been a site of industrial production, but exactly what type of industry is unclear. The important thing is that the place bears the visible traces of a long series of recent appropriations, mainly for the purposes of alternative cultures and the more or less ephemeral programs of beneficial rehabilitation to which spaces like these are typically subjected. The text is quite specific about the score. Concerts and other cultural events routinely take place here. It is also the officially sanctioned place of demonstrations, union meetings, and other forms of political activity. And when not otherwise occupied, the place is subjected to more random forms of appropriation: parking, skating, etc. What is important in this context is the fact that such alternative cultures are implicitly centered on issues of style and design, not only as to demarcate a distance from "official" culture, but also to give visible expression to a shared belief in different, if not always too specific, futures. Design, here, is about projection and imagination rather than problem solving—a constant activation of time materials, splicing together future, present, and past. The scenario places great emphasis on the way in which the paraphernalia of such imagined futures, many of them incomprehensible in their current state of neglect or disarray, litter the floors and walls of the large rooms. Having survived repeated cycles of use and reuse, they end up as mutant objects, like colorful Christmas ball ornaments repurposed as door knobs.

In reading the scenario, it gradually becomes clear that the setting it describes is not just a framework for action, but represents a form of action in its own right: media action; cinematographic (or televisual) processes in the widest sense of the term. Only media references, it seems, can fully do justice to this particular type of space. The rooms are described as having been painted in a now-dirtied off-white and illuminated in a way that recalls the even, shadowless distribution of light in sitcom productions, where everydayness reigns and equal attention is given to a host of characters. The changing weather patterns—the snow and rain that can be seen and heard through the open doors—are very explicitly "special effects" and experienced as such. And the traces of spatial appropriations—all equally visible in the bright and even light—are compared to the vast range of sketchy image elements that make up a cartoon; isolated, frozen fragments on their own, they become a shape-shifting life-form the moment they are filmed in the correct succession.

In short, the building seems to have the dynamic and responsive fluidity that characterizes today's information-driven architectures.[3] And the people who will inhabit it for the purpose of a party—according to the scenario, a promotional event for some unnamed purpose or product—are a piece of this general design velocity. They are described in terms of stylistic mobilities and mutations rather than character, action, and dialogue. They are said to carry enormous slogan T-shirts, as if an extension of the graffiti on the walls and the torn posters on the floors, or padded jackets whose filling material has been exposed so as make their bodies appear like amorphous blurs. They favor the "mullet" hairstyle that signals a consciousness of working-class identities, but visit shops that offer rapid makeovers in the name of a variety of commercial sponsors. They talk about the special-effect weather, smoke for show, and are generally obsessed with self-styling and style judgments. They are wildly different, yet very much alike, a heterogeneous crowd-subject. Under their influence, the building also takes on an increasingly person-like complexity and subjectivity. New rooms mysteriously appear in the middle of existing spaces with a matryoshka doll–like effect. Hence the building is also described in psychological terms as suffering from multiple personality disorder. Aligned with a media apparatus vested in the production and manipulation of time and events, "design" now apparently signifies

Philippe Parreno, *Snow Dancing*, 1995. Installation details.

the emergence of any possible situation or function, from the environmental to the psychological.

To what extent is this particular fantasy of design ubiquity compatible with the idea that design in the digital age produces an increasingly human-centric universe? Perhaps the most remarkable feature of *Snow Dancing*'s scenario is the way in which its mutating, shape-shifting, living architecture appears to be an effect of noncoordinated collective actions rather than any one, conscious, central agent. The setting it outlines is at once the medium and the effect of the passing passions of a great number of different bodies, projects, and organizations. In this sense, the scenario not only extrapolates the pragmatics of any cinematographic or televisual project ("auteurial" or not) about design and architecture, since any such project is the more or less fortuitous effect of a vast number of disparate competences, technologies, and desires (sometimes held together by no more than the paragraphs of a contract that assigns body-part stand-ins to certain sequences and final cut to a producer). It also underscores the way in which this living, shape-shifting space undercuts a number of commonly held ideas about design, most notably that it is the outward result of purposeful creative effort and control.

To some extent, such control fantasies have only grown stronger with digital technologies, which make it possible to compute and hence to build any possible form. In *Contagious Architecture,* Luciana Parisi describes how informatization has produced a mode of design that fully relies on computation to produce new architectural forms and surfaces: by drawing on biological notions of morphogenesis and the capacity of forms to change over time, algorithms are the generative components in a new architectural form-finding and pattern-making. This is, apparently, design at its most ambitious and pervasive. Yet, there are limits to this concept of generative control. As Parisi shows, a closer look at algorithmic procedures indicates that incompleteness in axiomatics is actually at the core of computation. Due to the entropic tendency of data to increase in size and thus become random, infinite amounts of information may not only interfere with but also actually reprogram algorithmic procedures. The rationality of digital quantification is thus not simply challenged by random inputs from the outside (as described in traditional cybernetic feedback models), but produces its own internal contingencies. Digital design generates its own forms of thought and sensation, clearly distinct from human concepts of logic and aesthetics.[4]

Such ideas not only seem to give credence to the shape-shifting media/design dynamics intuited twenty years ago in *Snow Dancing*, but also seem to resonate with two themes constantly brought out in Parreno's oeuvre: the question of self-organization, and alien presences. At the most obvious, narrative level, the building described in the scenario houses typical instances of political and cultural self-organization. But self-organization—the unpredictable effects of multiple noncoordinated agents—also informs its mediatic status as an emergent location, an event-location housing "social events." Yet the question of the relationship between self-organization and design (in the broad sense of the word) is hardly new. It was, for instance, the subject of intense discussion in the early Enlightenment, where the new emphasis on rational individual agency was challenged by an interest in self-organizing systems, in which unrestricted agency could be combined with deterministic outcomes. Against a "designed world" indicating an anthropomorphic order (governed by a divine architect), notions of design and providence were even then combined with chance and inherent variation. Design theory had, as Jonathan Sheehan and Dror Wahrman have put it, become complex and creative.[5] A couple of hundred years later, in the context of the more restricted twentieth-century design discourses that underpin almost every single word of the scenario for *Snow Dancing,* "design ubiquity" had also become precisely that which undermined computation-based notions of an increasingly human-controlled world. In this work, self-organization is less a political ideal to be realized than the projection of a social reality animated by an unruly composite of sentient beings. In Le Consortium, the half-empty rooms and disparate object arrangements exhibited to the public on the day after the party (some walls covered in blue denim, an empty hair-dressing station, a giant T-shirt limply present) were not the dismal relics of a past event or series of events, but elements in that same projection: part of the inherently messy shaping of things to come.

1 David Berry, "The Post-Archival Constellation: The Archive under the Technical Conditions of Computational Media," in *Memory in Motion: Archives, Technology and the Social,* eds. Ina Blom, Trond Lundemo, and Eivind Røssaak (Amsterdam: Amsterdam University Press, 2017), 112–13.

2 Philippe Parreno, "Snow Dancing," in *Speech Bubbles* (Paris: Les presses du réel, 2001), 40–63. I am indebted to Jörn Schaffaf's thorough description of all aspects of the entire *Snow Dancing* project in *Philippe Parreno: Angewandtes Kino* (Cologne: Walter König, 2010).

3 Lisa Blackman and Janet Harbord, "Technologies of Mediation and the Affective: A Case-study of the Mediated Environment of MediacityUK," in *Cognitive Architecture: From Biopolitics to Noopolitics*, eds. Deborah Hauptmann and Warren Neidich (Rotterdam: 010 Publishers, 2010), 303–21.

4 Luciana Parisi, *Contagious Architecture: Computation, Aesthetics, and Space* (Cambridge, MA: MIT Press, 2013), ix–xviii, 1–71.

5 Jonathan Sheehan and Dror Wahrman, *Invisible Hands: Self-Organization and the Eighteenth Century* (Chicago: University of Chicago Press, 2015), 33.

In the Skin of a Lion, a Leopard ... a Man

Lesley Lokko

> Man is alone, desperately scraping out the music of his own skeleton, without father, mother, family, love, god or society. And no living being to accompany him. And the skeleton is not of bone, but of skin, like a skin that walks.
> —Antonin Artaud, *The Peyote Dance* [1]

> "Black" and "white" signify their own arbitrariness, and are a deliberate way of maintaining and affirming a kind of colour-blindness. When I name myself or another as "black," I mean "one whom others regard as "black." I could not use the words "red" or "brown" or "yellow" in the same way unless they too had a political profile, and summarised and signified the value and effect of colour, rather than the colour itself. Black and white are therefore markers of "chromacity," so to speak, designators of attitudes towards colours, rather than the colours themselves. In using the last phase, I do not mean to imply a distinction between the conventional associations of colours and the physical facts of colours themselves, for what I mean by seeing colours as colours is precisely seeing the cultural meanings they carry. The distinction I imply between chromacity and colours is not a distinction between culture and nature.
> —Steven Connor, *The Book of Skin* [2]

How *does* the world design me? Well, it depends who the "you" in question is, of course. Nine years ago, the *New York Times* ran an article which read, "Barack Hussein Obama was elected the forty-fourth president of the United States, sweeping away the last racial barrier in American politics with ease."[3] Yet another article from the same newspaper published last year paints a rather different picture: "The heavily armed sniper who gunned down police officers in downtown Dallas, leaving five of them dead, specifically set out to kill as many white officers as he could, officials said Friday."[4] Suddenly, James Joyce's assertion that "modern man has an epidermis rather than a soul" is disturbingly apt.[5]

Of the three main criteria that constitute our understanding of "race"—skin color, hair texture, and facial features—it is skin color that most readily asserts "difference." This association is not arbitrary: skin *is* color, and vice versa. Bleaching and tanning aside, it is not possible to separate skin from its hue. It is not unreasonable, therefore, to assume that the significance of skin color in human history exists precisely because color and what it signifies are generally regarded as one and the same thing. But what it *means* varies enormously across time and place. Eighteenth-century Europe marks the beginning of skin color as the overwhelming factor in theories of racial difference with which this essay is partly concerned. I say "partly" because of equal interest to "difference" is an interest in "origin." And for the purposes of this essay at least, that's where the thread of what it means to be human begins.

Here's Where It Starts

In Setswana, one of the indigenous languages of southern Africa, the word "Maropeng" means "returning to the place of origin." Maropeng is also the name of a paleo-anthropological site of 180 square miles, located about forty miles north of Johannesburg. Known in English as the "Cradle of Humankind," Maropeng was declared a UNESCO World Heritage Site in 1999. Buried deep within its geological strata are clues to the origins of mankind. It is a site of outstanding natural beauty—a rocky "highveld" grassland of rolling hills and frequent wildfires—and a complex of limestone caves which have yielded up more than a third of all known early *hominim* fossils since the 1930s, some dating as far back as 3.5 million years.[6] In October 2013, two recreational cavers, Rick Hunter and Steven Tucker, discovered fossil skeletons in the Dinaledi Chamber ("chamber of stars"). A month later, the National Geographic Society and the University of the Witwatersrand funded the Rising Star Expedition, which sent six women scientists—chosen for their combination of paleo-anthropological caving skills and small size—into the caves. Their "find" of 1,500 fossils led to the formal announcement in 2015 of the discovery of an extinct species of early *hominim,* which scientists have assigned to the genus *Homo*. Although the description has attracted controversy, with a number of scientists arguing that the classification of *Homo naledi* requires more testing, one of the key arguments from the forty-seven-member international team is that *Homo naledi* buried its dead, an act of "deliberate cultural deposition," which we might also consider to be an act of design.[7]

There are two competing views about the origins of *Homo sapiens*: the Recent African Origin (ROA) and the Multi-Region Origin (MRO). MRO holds that humans first arose around two million years ago, and that all subsequent human evolution has been within a single, continuous species. The ROA, also known as the "Out of Africa" theory, suggests that modern humans evolved somewhere between two hundred thousand and one hundred thousand years ago, with members of one branch leaving Africa some sixty thousand years ago and populating the rest of the world. ROA is based on fossil evidence (much of which was found at Maropeng over the past seventy-five years) and is the general consensus among the scientific community. DNA, the "mother" of all design applications, is surprisingly clear on this point: there is more genetic

A view of the highveld at the Cradle of Humankind, South Africa. Photo: Eric Wright.

variance on the African continent than the entire rest of the world put together. This fact is, to a paleontologist, proof enough that we all originated somewhere on the African continent. So at one level, yes, we're all (or were) black, and at another, we're all African. But that does little to explain history—or, perhaps more specifically, the history of skin and our troubled understanding of its hues.

The Skin That Walks

Both the Greeks and the Romans had a variety of words used to describe skin. *Chros*, in Greek, is a common name and often expressed the idea of proximity—*enchroi* means "close to the skin." *Homochroma* refers to the "evenness of color" or "complexion" of the skin. *Derma*, meaning "hide," was also used, akin perhaps to the English word "rind." The two major words in Latin for skin were *cutis*, signifying living skin, and *pellis*, signifying dead, flayed skin, used for animals and to convey dread or horror. Aristotle's belief that the "skin cannot feel"[8] contributed greatly to a general understanding of the skin as a "thin," rather than "thick" surface, whose importance lay in its breach. Like Aristotle, the Syrian philosopher Job al-Albrash believed that skin was an aftereffect, the result of the actions of drying and hardening, like scum upon boiled substances. "The skin came into existence in an outside position because, when the humidity of the outside portion met the air, the latter destroyed the thinness which it possessed and it thickened."[9] But by the third century BC, a classical taboo of cutting or breaking open the surface of the skin had relaxed sufficiently for the first dissections of dead bodies to take place at the medical school in Alexandria. In Galen's *De anatomicis administrationibus*, the order in which aspiring medical students should learn about the body was laid down: bones, muscles, veins, arteries, nerves, intestines, fat, and glands. The skin, the surface to be punctured in order to gain entrance to the workings of the body below, appears not to merit mention. Sixteenth-century anatomical illustrations such as those by da Carpi and Vesalius tend to depict the skin as a dainty, drawn-back apron, hanging from the extremities of wrists, elbows, and ankles.

Through Thick and Thin

This difference between skin as a "thick" or "thin" surface is of particular interest because of the importance many African cultures place on the body and its skin as both the primary medium for creativity and artistic talent as well as the primary resource and repository of identity and self-expression. From oral history to body art, the body is simply another surface into which culture is carved, sculpted, cut, patterned, and tattooed. In this context, skin acquires depth, becoming a "thick space" in which memory, history, tradition, and testimony are literally inscribed. In contrast to the Western tradition outlined above of seeing skin primarily as the last, protective barrier that keeps the "outside in," African traditions of the skin encourage its "inside"—blood, tissue, secretions—to interact with its surface, such as in the case of raised keloid scars that swell the skin's surface and give it profound, almost elastic depth. The tendency amongst peoples of African descent to keloid scarring has produced a highly distinctive art form in the practices of scarification and cicatrice.

Traditionally, sub-Saharan African body art practices fall into three varying levels of penetration: *scarification*, where the surface of the skin is cut, irrigated with materials such as charcoal, certain insects with medicinal or healing properties, or herbs to encourage the formation of keloids; *tattooing*, where a colored substance is pricked or inserted into the outermost layer of the dermis, producing a dull stain; and *painting*, where patterns, combined in a dizzying array of permutations, are applied to the surface of the skin to depict beauty, tell a story, or indicate age, rank, and status. Children are often given their first incisions immediately after birth. Further incisions are then added at regular intervals, like at the onset of puberty, after the birth of a first child, or after breastfeeding has ceased. These decorations—often involving considerable pain—are seen as a way of improving physical appearance and are often erotic in connotation. Together with ceremonial patterns, these markings do not simply proclaim cultural values and histories: they pass them on, reinforcing them in a tightly knit mesh of ceremony, ritual, and aesthetics. Design, in this sense, is less something done *to* the external world—the external envelope of the body (clothing) or society (buildings), for example—as it is something to bring the world *in* to the body.

Color, too, often plays an important and symbolic role in many African societies, although it is not possible to attribute a general or unvarying significance across cultures. For some, the color of blood is the color of life, joy, and good health, while for others it signifies death, grief, and transience. In some Central African cultures, for example, traditional healers paint the sick with ochre to stimulate life force, while for the Ghanaian Ashanti, red is the color of mourning. The diversity of languages within Africa also makes it difficult to judge color accurately. Some take into account texture, the nature of surface, or shadings or patterns, which result in concepts of color arising that have no equivalent in European languages and can only be described through paraphrase. Amongst the Ga of Greater Accra, for example, there are distinct words for "red-with-a-rough-texture" and "black-which-is-shiny-or-dull." Colors also make temporal references: for example, white often symbolizes links with the ancestors or underworld, but usually only in a ritual or ceremonial context. Color therefore takes on different meanings according to the measure in which it is used.

DIY Self-Design and/or Design of the Self

Our contemporary obsession with our skin complexions is everywhere: from its exposure in cinema and advertising to our efforts to modify and control its appearance with cosmetics and plastic surgery, our skin has suddenly assumed center stage. Both the *idea* of skin and its literal *surface* have gained a prominence in modern thinking.[10] Since the 1930s, the language of critical and cultural theory has been full of the presence of skin: Roland Barthes worked on the erotics of texture and tissue;[11] Emmanuel Levinas asserted that the exposed skin of the face signifies the sign of ethical nudity;[12] and Jacques Derrida's concepts of "double penetration" (of the body, the hymen, and the pen and the paper it punctuates) brings the idea of skin into a wholly new dimension between form, surface, and performance.[13]

For the most part, Africa is absent from this discourse, yet skin and particularly the *color* of skin is associated with Africa and people of African descent in ways that are unlike any other supposed "cultural" association between people and place. For the most part, to be African is to be black, and vice versa. A century ago in the United States, Americans of African descent were referred to as "Colored." In the 1920s and 30s, W. E. B. Du Bois ushered in the term "Negro," which was supplanted in the 1960s by "Black." At a press conference in Chicago in 1988, Reverend Jesse Jackson declared that the preferred term was "African-American," and this name has more or less stuck. But the interchangeable nature of the terms "Black," "African," and "Afro" points to a deeper complexity than Western thinkers have historically allowed for.

The intertwined relationship between self, cultural identity, and skin color is both overwhelmingly superficial (in the Aristotelian sense of a very thin covering), and profound. If we think about the skin's surface less as a *screen* onto which our fears and fantasies about power, class, and even sexuality are projected, and more as a literal *space*, something with depth, mass, and volume, it allows us to think more deeply and creatively about the elements that make up our identities, from history and shared experiences to ritual and mythology. Claude Levi-Strauss described the body as "a surface waiting for the imprintation of culture."[14] The appreciation of skin as a deep and pliable medium is embedded in many African artistic practices and holds provocative potential for contemporary design, particularly architecture, which has historically been viewed as the envelope of the body, separate from it, housing rather than embodying. In his "Notes for a Research Program," Stefano Boeri describes the spatial and territorial uncertainty of a new Europe, stating that our "now-useless vocabulary continues to make the distinction between 'center' and 'periphery,' between 'public space' and 'private space.'"[15] Boeri makes a compelling case for the development of new vocabularies—what he terms "eclectic atlases"—that better correspond to new spatial realities. Boeri's lexicon offers an unexpected insight into the way in which different understandings of space, form, and place might be combined and read. Using "real" spaces scattered across the "new" European territory, he speaks of "inundation," "osmosis," "transplant," and "pulsation." The corresponding lexicon of African "space" might draw on similar uncertainties: skins that are "thick," "thin," "branded," "carved." We might begin to speak of "ruptures" and "folds," of surfaces that are "stretched," of "supple and pliant spaces" and not the petrified monuments that underpin so much of Western architectural history and praxis. "Uncertainty," as Boeri writes, "transforms into innovation."

1 Antonin Artaud, *The Peyote Dance*, trans. Helen Weaver (New York: Farrar, Straus and Giroux, 1976), 37–8.
2 Steven Connor, *The Book of Skin* (Ithaca, NY: Cornell University Press, 2003), 148.
3 Adam Nagourney, "Obama Wins Election," *New York Times*, November 4, 2008.
4 Manny Fernandez, Richard Pérez-Peña, and Jonah Engel Bromwich, "Five Dallas Officers Were Killed as Payback, Police Chief Says," *New York Times*, July 8, 2016.
5 James Joyce, *James Joyce in Padua*, trans. and ed. Louise Berrone (New York: Random House, 1977), 21.
6 The highveld is the portion of the South African inland plateau that has an altitude between 1500 meters and 2100 meters.
7 P. Dirks, L. Burger, E. Roberts, H. Kramers, P. Randolph-Quinney, M. Elliott, C. Musiba, S. Churchill, D. de Ruiter, P. Schmid, L. Backwell, G. Belyanin, P. Boshoff, K. Hunter, E. Feuerriegel, A. Gurtov, J. Harrison, R. Hunter, A. Kruger, H. Morris, T. Makhubela, B. Peixotto, and S. Tucker, "Geological and Taphonomic Context for the New Hominin Species *Homo naledi* from the Dinaledi Chamber, South Africa," elifesciences.org/content/4/e09561, September 10, 2015.
8 Aristotle, *Historia Animalium*, trans. D'Arcy Wentworth Thompson, in *The Works of Aristotle*, eds. Smith and Ross, vol. IV, III.11.518a.
9 Job of Edessa, *Encyclopaedia of Philosophical and Natural Sciences, As Taught in Baghdad About AD 817, or Book of Treasures*, trans. A. Mingana (Cambridge: W. Heffer & Sons, 1935), 88.
10 Connor, *The Book of Skin*, 10.
11 Harari, "The Maximum Narrative: An Introduction to Barthes' Recent Criticism," *Style* 8, no. 1 (1974): 56–77.
12 Emmanuel Levinas, *Collected Philosophical Papers*, trans. Alphonso Lingis (Boston: Duquesne University Press, 1987), 116.
13 Jacques Derrida, *Spurs: Nietzsche's Styles*, trans. Barbara Harlow (Chicago: University of Chicago Press 1979), 37.
14 Claude Levi-Strauss, *Structural Anthropology* (New York: Basic Books, 1963), 144.
15 Stefano Boeri, "Notes for a Research Program," in *Mutations*, eds. Rem Koolhaas et al. (Barcelona: Actar, 2001), 356–77.

As if by Design

Raqs Media Collective

In 1936, the equation wasn't yet common knowledge and it was still decades before you could look things up on a search engine.[1] If you forgot something or had a gap in your understanding, sometimes you still needed to "phone a friend." The best and most efficient design for information retrieval still required you to know people who knew things. Isamu Noguchi wired his friend Buckminster Fuller, an admirer of Einstein, to ask if he knew it.[2]

Fuller's reply to Noguchi—a five-sentence, 264-word Western Union telegram—is a model of how to be wildly rambling and tightly precise at the same time.[3] The designer-engineer and not-yet-visionary messes with the physicist's equation to answer the artist's question. In his own way, Fuller redesigns, clarifies, compresses, and complicates Einstein in response to Noguchi.

We take the bare bones of this episode to be a kind of methodological exemplar for the problem of how to answer questions like *are we human?* or *how to be human?* and variations thereof. What else can you do when you have to respond to a question with an answer that was till just now at the tip of your tongue?

Fuller's response is the kind of answer that we suspect the Vikram would have had to offer twenty-five times to his mentor and tormentor, the goblin Betaal (whose name means "out of time," pun intended): one for each time Betaal posed a riddle, the solution for which would free Vikram from the task of having to carry the out-side-of-time being as he sojourned in the world's charnel house.[4]

Perhaps Betaal asks Vikram, "When life and death run a race, who wins?" Perhaps Vikram answers, "Life is the counterclockwise motion of clock-hands on a clock-face that runs clockwise towards death. Both life and death must read the numbers, one to run away from, and the other to run towards the direction of time. Death doesn't yet win, life still doesn't lose, but the referee's finger is always pulling the trigger on the starter gun, and the alarm never stops ringing." Perhaps Betaal says, "Bravo wise King, well played, but let's see if you can get to the heart of my next and best riddle." And so on, and on.

We could say that Vikram's answers, or the tensegrity ("tensile integrity," to user a Fullerism) of Fuller's telegram, is symptomatic of a kind of controlled communicative chaos. It features a startling but coherent conclusion that we are still trying hard to understand:

> ... SPECIFIC QUALITY OF ANIMATES IS CONTROL WILLFUL OR OTHERWISE OF RATE AND DIRECTION ENERGY RELEASE AND APPLICATION NOT ONLY OF SELF MECHANISM BUT OF FROM SELF MACHINE DIVIDED MECHANISMS AND RELATIVITY OF ALL ANIMATES AND INANIMATES IS POTENTIAL OF ESTABLISHMENT THROUGH EINSTEIN FORMULA

Isamu Noguchi seated with three Akari Light Sculptures, c. 1950s.

In other words, the mechanism of life (the property of animates) features the ability to achieve willful or involuntary control over the rate and direction of the release of energy along with the capacity to divide, and to create relationships with other animates and inanimates that are a result of that division, or that are present anyway. Life is that which coheres, divides, multiplies, relates, and by doing so, flourishes. Human life is that which knows that it does so, and presumably, still enjoys doing so.

Seen this way, every human, and every living being, is a temporary defeat of the second law of thermodynamics, which would ordinarily have the universe, and all matter in it, fritter itself away perennially towards chaos as time passes. But the accident, or blueprint, of Life, while it lasts, features biology outsmarting physics, one infinitesimal life at a time. We are as ephemeral and as strong as a thread in a spider's web. Gone in a breath, enduring a storm. Everything else is ordinary.

To embody a peak of concentrated living intensity even while caught in the undertow of thermodynamic dispersal is to be both in and out of time. To live, leaping from one such peak to the next, is to experience the intensity of the flux, flow, crossovers, inversions, collisions, loops, folds, and confusions of all kind of durational influences and processes. Time is a shape-shifting entity made up of layers, arranged in folds, latticed by cracks. Time waxes, wanes, wavers, winds up, and winds down. Time is a trickster, wears disguises, plays hide and seek, plays for time.

The forces of time impacting upon us, burning us, oxidizing us, answer to different kinds of acceleration—of the planet and off the planet, to their entanglements. We have only a dim awareness of the disruptive power of these forces on our metabolic processes. And yet at a fundamentally cellular level, we tend to want to stay organized till we must die. Eventually, thermodynamics reigns supreme but every life is a conscious insurgency of the will of each cell against the way of all atoms. To stay human we have to stick to this plot and to this hunger. This is the only design. There is no plan B.

While we live, we betray a tendency towards the maintenance or increase of relatively high levels of information, despite a simultaneous, constant, and counterweighted tendency towards entropy and meaninglessness. Eternity would freeze design and melt disorder, but we aren't there yet. We will never be, even though we act like creatures that run counterclockwise in a clockwise universe.

Now, Vikram asks Betaal, "Are you done?"

The goblin cackles in reply.

He is never done; always, already, undone.

The daily plebiscite against time that unites every cell in the body's unruly democracy requires a lot of energy, which we mine from a cold, cold universe. From the sun, our nearest fireplace, our farthest gold mine. If the universe is a cold, ghostly, deity, a Shiva-sovereign drunk with *datura* and other poison, then the suns and the stars and the planets and comets are his host of spirits, burning, dancing, spinning merrily around him as he goes to fulfill his tryst with time.

What does it take for us to join this cosmic raucous wedding party, this blazing, drunken cosmic orgy between cold space and hot time?[5]

We run till we drop. Our sun burns because it has no choice. Although it is in some fundamental way the source of all life on earth (and as far as we know, in the universe), it is not itself a living thing and so cannot, not even momentarily, reverse its tendency towards disorder. In ceaselessly dying, the sun generously endows life with its energy. This is the power that we use to stay up and running. The good saint Bataille taught us that the sun shits out a dying light, which we eat to stay alive. We, humans, are knowing solar scavengers, the sapient vultures, hyenas, and pigs of solar time.

Basically, we harness light. We harvest other animates (other forms of life) that either turn light into life-force (by photosynthesis—such as all plants) or we prey on other life-forms that in turn prey on plant life. We live by eating the life that eats light to live. In the current scheme of things, this guarantees abundance for all, because the sun is too distant a source of sustenance to play at favorites by parceling out the consequences of its combustion into greater and smaller portions.

We in our turn are eaten by darkness. And this is our design flaw. We look into the mirror and see mortality looking back. It tells us that we will run out of light in the end. Perhaps uniquely amongst creatures (with the possible exception of elephants and their close cousins, the cetaceans—some whales and dolphins), we know death, our own, that of our species, even that of our sun. One day, eons from now, we know that our sun will grow cold, and that we will either have to prepare to outlive that freezing point by finding places to nest and scavenge in the light of other stars, or accept that our days of eating light will have come to an end.

At more modest scales, the metaphor of the frozen sun may find other applications. We are aware that it's possible to get social hypothermia from capitalism's subzero dive into a zone of total alienation, where our social relations become too brittle, too frozen to be supportive of any desire for life. Sometimes when markets crash, we see this happen. Capital then comes into its own as the death drive, the *alp* or goblin of dead labor that sits on the chest of living labor. Like Betaal, it is no longer a friendly imp, but an icy, sclerotic, anacoustic interrogator whose questions are sharp icicles.

When the weight of dead labor gets too heavy, then the only way that capital knows to lighten its load on the earth is by shedding some ballast. In our times, this takes the form of wholesale destruction of constituted infrastructure, life, and nature. The descent and ascent of societies into and through war is a measure of a generation's willingness to commit mass ritual suicide rather than to consider an exit. There can be no greater design flaw. The problem is, how is one to live, knowing as one does the possibility of personal tragedy, social death, and natural disaster?

Sometime in 1972, Fuller came to the conclusion that he "seemed to be a verb."[6] To describe oneself as a verb rather than a noun is to insist that one is *doing* rather than *being*. To be, to just be, one can claim the ontological privilege of an accident. But to do, one has to have working parts, one has to have a design. Life, as in the fact that there should be any animate beings at all, may well be an accident. But once "life" gets going, then each life must adhere to the dynamism of the design for what it needs to do in order to be what it is.

From Hayden Herrera, Noguchi's biographer, we learn that while working on this frieze-mural in 1936 he wrote an article in *Art Front*, the magazine of the New York Artists Union. The text calls for the abandonment of traditional forms, materials, techniques, and styles and advocates investigation and experimentation with new media, with new forms and materials. Even with new tools, such as spray guns, drills, and pneumatic hammers. "Why not paper or rubber sculptures?" he asked. Noguchi championed the cause of art in public contexts, and advocated for its embedding in life. He says, "Capitalism everywhere struggles with inevitable death—all the machinery of war, coercion and bigotry, are as smoke from that fire."

We need not share Fuller's faith in a "divine designer," or even Noguchi's sense of historical destiny in order to cleave to a sense of one's design as a continuing argument with the weight of accumulated dead labor. Design, in this case, is polemic of verbs against nouns, of "doing" as opposed to "being." It is also the question of how to harness the light to keep the desire for life—for an aesthetic and ethic of dividing, multiplying, relating, flourishing alive despite the retrospective and anticipated burden of the dead. It is a property of the phylogenetic emergence of a life-form in conditions of entropy, or, the decision by Vikram to keep walking with the burden of Betaal on his shoulders while continuing to search for an answer to the riddles of time, life, death, truth, justice, beauty, and love.

Design, unlike nature, does not abhor a void. Sometimes, while waiting for a really good answer, it can make do with whatever is at hand, until the just and/or elegant answer finally comes calling.

It is said that while Noguchi waited for Fuller's telegraphic response to his question to arrive he happened upon another answer. One of the Mexican workers working with him smiled and gave him another way to understand Einstein's famous equation.[7]

He said, "$E = mc^2$ means *'Estado = Muchas Cabrones'* or 'The State equals many sons of bitches.'"

This is as valid an answer as the one that says:

QUOTE ENERGY EQUALS MASS TIMES THE SPEED OF LIGHT UNQUOTE SPEED OF LIGHT IDENTICAL SPEED ALL RADIATION COSMIC GAMMA X ULTRA VIOLET INFRA RED RAYS ETCETERA ONE HUNDRED EIGHTY SIX THOUSAND MILES PER SECOND WHICH SQUARED IS TOP OR PERFECT SPEED GIVING SCIENCE A FINITE VALUE FOR BASIC FACTOR IN MOTION UNIVERSE STOP.

1 "The equation" here is Einstein's equation expressing special relativity, $E = mc^2$.

2 Isamu Noguchi, the Japanese-American sculptor, had forgotten the $E = mc^2$ equation for special relativity while working on a frieze mural in brick and cement marking the forces of his time at the Abelardo Rodriguez Municipal Market in Mexico City in 1936. He needed to put the equation into his design. He had in mind a quiet corner by a window, with a young boy contemplating the equation, surrounded by the turbulence of history. For details of this episode, see "Mexico," in Hayden Herrera, *Listening to Stone: The Art and Life of Isamu Noguchi* (New York: Farrar, Straus & Giroux, 2015).

3 For a full transcript of Fuller's telegram to Noguchi, see "ENERGY EQUALS MASS TIMES THE SPEED OF LIGHT SQUARED STOP," lettersofnote.com, August 19, 2011.

4 The goblin Betaal's questions posed to King Vikramaditya (Vikram) feature in a famous set of "riddle stories" known as the *Vetālapañcaviśati*, or *Betaal Pachisi* (Twenty-Five Tales of the Betaal). The Wikipedia entry on the story cycle has the following succinct plot summary: "The legendary king Vikramāditya (Vikram) promises a sorcerer that he will capture a vetala (or Betaal), a spirit analogous to a vampire who hangs from a tree and inhabits and animates dead bodies. Vikram faces many difficulties in bringing the vetala to the sorcerer. Each time Vikram tries to capture the vetala, it tells a story that ends with a riddle. If Vikrama cannot answer the question correctly, the vampire consents to remain in captivity. If the king knows the answer but still keeps quiet, then his head shall burst into thousand pieces. And if King Vikrama answers the question correctly, the vampire would escape and return to his tree. He knows the answer to every question; therefore the cycle of catching and releasing the vampire continues twenty-four times. Finally, the twenty-fifth question stumps the king, and so the goblin consents to be made captive." For a note on Raqs Media Collective's work refracted through the prism of the Vikram-Betaal motif, see Aarti Sethi, "In Rarer Air: Ten Entries in an Untimely Calendar," *Take on Art Magazine* 16 (2015).

5 For a description of Shiva's "wedding party," see "The Hideous Groom," in Devdutt Pattanaik, *Myth=Mithya: A Handbook of Hindu Mythology* (New York: Penguin Books, 2006).

6 Buckminster Fuller, *I Seem to Be a Verb* (New York: Bantam Books, 1970).

7 See "Mexico," in Hayden Herrera, *Listening to Stone: The Art and Life of Isamu Noguchi* (New York: Farrar, Straus & Giroux, 2015).

An Apology to Survivors

MAP Office

> If I am not drowned or killed trying to escape in the next few days, I hope to write two books. I shall entitle them *Apology for Survivors* and *Tribute to Malthus*.
> —Adolfo Bioy Casares[1]

Addressing politics in the Anthropocene, Jodi Dean identifies three possible roles for humans: observers, victims, and survivors.[2] Her analysis of these differing human trajectories exists within a clear Darwinian perspective of the world. The division of humans into passive victims, active survivors, and those who watch is embedded within a "survival of the fittest" ethos and an acceptance of a world where the act of survival is defined as an individualistic performance, suspiciously responding to "the struggle for existence."[3] Her definition also echoes that of Elias Canetti in *Crowds and Power*, for whom the survivor—along with the ruler—stands alone, as a hero. In this same line of thinking, philosophers and writers such as Hannah Arendt and Primo Levi approach survival as a form of culpability, inexorably linked to the traumatic experience of the Holocaust. In addition to, and perhaps beyond, these heroic figures of modernity, we propose another reading of the act of survival as a collective performance and the survivor as a collective being. This understanding shifts the frame of the Anthropocene from a spatial struggle to a temporal practice—not a point of departure toward new colonies, but rather a dimension of the present to be handled now for the time that is to come.[4]

Supersimple

The figure of the castaway, and Daniel Defoe's emblematic *Robinson Crusoe* in particular, is a helpful guide to understanding the condition of the survivor. Crusoe's survival on the island is only possible thanks to the supplies that were cast away with him, namely, the building materials and tools salvaged from the shipwreck. In this sense, the various saws, jackscrew, hammer, nails, spikes, grindstone, spare ropes, canvases, cables, and hangers were instrumental in Crusoe's survival of his misfortune. With the Bible in one hand and his tools in the other, Crusoe confronted the adversity of his situation and his lack of society. In fact, this very adversity—combined with years of patient labor—led to a mastery of many occupations: agriculture with a wooden spade, carpentry, earthenware, wicker weaving, and many others, all of which allowed him to satisfy his basic needs and beyond.

Similar to Robinson Crusoe, the story of Tuscan farmer Zeno Fiaschi, narrated by Superstudio in 1978 for the Venice Biennale, questions the autonomy, needs, and behavior of a single individual.

Emphasizing an objective of autonomy, *Project Zeno* calibrates the concept of "home" to what can be produced and is necessary for the sustenance of a single individual, and presents all the tools and supports required to do so. The *supersimple* life of Zeno parallels the economy Defoe developed with Crusoe, where the consumer is also the direct producer of what is consumed. Within this simple framework, both Zeno and Crusoe have created an economy that is antagonistic to accumulation and other forms of capitalism.

The example of Zeno serves as a way to establish a critique of design under the conditions of capitalism. Superstudio returned to fundamentals—historical knowledge, creativity, and survival—to propose and sustain a new relationship between man and object, and further, between man and nature. By applying the survivor's economy to design, Zeno and Crusoe are nonetheless exposed to major risks. Like any other heroic figure, the survivor cannot afford to be sick or to experience an extended period of unproductivity without putting their own life at stake. If production for complete self-sustenance is the basic condition of the survivor, the risk encountered in ensuring its continuance requires the same amount of energy, if not more.

Supercommunity

> The people who were dancing up on the hillside, the vicious leaves, the roots that tasted of the earth, the hard, the fibrous bulbs—all these were enough to convince me that I should enter the museum and look for some bread and other real food.
> —Adolfo Bioy Casares[5]

The question of risk is at the core of many economic theories. As it is impossible to eliminate risk, distributing it is the best way to reduce it. Despite the fact that this distribution is not always even, this simple idea is at the origin of any community or society. For Crusoe, this process started with the rescue of Friday, an escaped native prisoner who shares his condition of survival and becomes both his "society" and companion.[6] Furthermore, this is the starting point of a desire that increases in the second and lesser-known volume of the story, where Crusoe comes back to the island after having left for the comforts of home.[7] During this return visit, Crusoe discovers that a new society had developed, composed of Spaniards, British, and other natives, first having warred with each other, but eventually settling and prospering.

Here the concept of "community" offers an alternative to the logic of competition proposed in evolutionist theory and in the figure of the individual survivor. Surviving by collaboration, as first suggested by Russian anarchist Peter Kropotkin, differs radically from Darwin's theory.[8] Kropotkin proposes cooperation as a mode of constructing societies. In his early studies for the Russian Geographical Society, he observed birds' ability to collectively migrate across continents and over oceans in search of food. In contrast to a typical predator or flora, the avifauna he observed collaborate for their continued collective existence. Learning from those observations, Kropotkin proposed survival as a communal form of existence—sharing the risks of production and consumption.

This proposition was further developed by the Soviet agrarian economist Alexander V. Chayanov, who advocated for new forms of agrarian cooperatives.[9] His proposition for a collective rural economy reused some facets of Crusoe's economic model—producers becoming their own direct consumers—but he reduced risk by increasing the size of both the household and the collective. Considered too distant from the social organization that existed for peasants at that time, Chayanovism failed under Lenin's social model.[10] Nevertheless, from the perspective of Soviet economic models, Chayanov highlighted the principle of balance between consumption and labor, as well as the dominant role of use value in rural communities. He also demonstrated that in order to survive, communities need to incorporate nonproductive members by capitalizing on productive ones, which could, by way of social hierarchy, lead to a form of capitalism. Even if the Chayanovist model never really shaped the Soviet economic model apart from highlighting the interaction between agriculture and capitalism, its influence remains by advocating for community as a way to escape individualistic modes of survival and production.

In this collective form of existence, Kropotkin defines migration and processes of deterritorialization as principal characteristics of the survivor as one who can adapt and cope with change. Like a nomad, the survivor reinvents the territory as they move on. We would like to identify a parallel between the figure of the survivor and that of the refugee. The refugee can be seen as the ultimate figure of survival by their migratory avoidance of conflict or climate change. The negative connotations of victimization that often characterize both the migrant and the refugee are therefore not only misleading but also contrary to the base logic of survival Kropotkin proposed.

Superself

... when one is alone it is impossible to be dead.
—Adolfo Bioy Casares[11]

Recognized as one of the main inspirations for *Robinson Crusoe*, Ibn Tufail's *ayy ibn Yaqān*, the first Arabic novel, narrates the story of the autodidactic child from whose name the book gets its title. Raised by a gazelle on an isolated island in the middle of the Indian Ocean, the sudden death of his mum (the gazelle) drove the young ayy into a process of self-learning based on experimentation and empiricism. His first encounter with civilization only happens later in life thanks to Absal, a castaway who introduced him to religion and the culture of materialism. Rejecting both as distractions from spiritual life and the search for truth, isolation is framed as a way to develop fundamental human values. Ḥayy became a voluntary castaway, promoting self-awareness, critical consciousness, intellectual autonomy, and altruism as virtues.

Endurance appears to be a desirable quality for responding to the harsh life of isolation. This additional virtue offers a possible escape from the thesis and antithesis proposed by Darwin and Kropotkin, and can be identified in the concept of *survivance* (survival + endurance) first proposed by writer and ethnographer Gerald Vizenor.[12] In his studies of Native American populations, Vizenor defined survivance as a renunciation of dominance, tragedy, and "victimry." Endurance shifts the question of survival from a spatial struggle, like territorial domination by an individual, a group, or a state, to a temporal practice and the possibility of sharing a single territory among multiple communities. Duration—recording the time—becomes the symbiotic rhythm to reconceive an environment based on behavior, reconnected to the stars, mobility, and production based on atmospheric conditions.[13] The concept of survivance is also developed by French philosopher Jacques Derrida as an existence between life and death, a spectral form of living death.[14] For both Derrida and Vizenor, survivance is marked by the production of an archive, of a memory, and can be seen in Crusoe's logbook as well as Zeno's inventory of tools. The systematic inventory and accumulation of knowledge allow the survivor to not only survive the space they find themselves in, which is often a hostile environment, but also time, in the duration and transmission of knowledge and a general awareness of self-existence. Archives weave making and repairing, reusing and recycling, together to propose new relationships between individuals, communities, and the environment. The millions of castaways/refugees already on the move and those more to come are both displaced from their original environments and distant from the ones to come. Divided, they are unable to form an act of collective production, but are rather forced to develop specific forms of self-endurance and cultural preservation. They propose alternative processes of self-management that stand to be explored outside normative urban cultures.

The question of self-organized, self-regulated processes and networks presents a logical extension of Ḥayy's quest for self-awareness. In the age of the superself, a conscious position towards the host environment includes the possibility to transmitting this conscience to "the other." This consciousness takes the form of a production and consumption that adapts to where it takes place. The superself, here defined as a collective individual, fragmented and dispersed in various localities, holds the possibility of expanding knowledge beyond the Capitalocene and an accumulative form of production.[15] In surviving the Anthropocene, the superself resides beyond tools and technologies, beyond exclusive communities, and beyond self-centered heroes. It becomes diffused within the territories of the simple, communal self—the one still able to dream of and form a project for a better future.

1 Adolfo Bioy Casares, *The Invention of Morel* (Buenos Aires: Editorial Losada, 1940).
2 Jodi Dean, "The Anamorphic Politics of Climate Change," *e-flux journal* no. 69 (January 2016).
3 Charles Darwin, *The Origin of Species* (London: John Murray, 1859).
4 Andy Weir, *The Martian* (2011).
5 Casares, *The Invention of Morel*.
6 Friday was named after the day Crusoe rescued him from being eaten by his captors. It is gratitude for this act that led him to become Crusoe's servant.
7 Daniel Defoe, *The Farther Adventures of Robinson Crusoe* (London: W. Taylor, 1719).
8 Peter Kropotkin, *Mutual Aid: A Factor of Evolution* (London: William Heinemann, 1902).
9 Alexander V. Chayanov, *The Theory of Peasant Economy* (Madison: University of Wisconsin Press, 1986).
10 Lenin uses the classic Marxist theory by proposing a three-tiered structure: rich, middle, and poor peasants.
11 Casares, *The Invention of Morel*.
12 Gerald Vizenor, *Manifest Manners: Postindian Warriors of Survivance* (Middletown: Wesleyan University Press, 1994).
13 Farmers often refer to atmospheric, rather than chronological, time.
14 Jacques Derrida, *The Beast and the Sovereign*, vol. 2, trans. Geoffrey Bennington (Chicago: University of Chicago Press, 2011).
15 *Anthropocene or Capitalocene?: Nature, History, and the Crisis of Capitalism*, ed. (Oakland: PM Press, 2016).

Couple Format:
The Identity between
Love and Work

Shumon Basar

As of September 2016, "Brangelina" was no more.

That most super-famous of celebrity portmanteaus "Brad + Angelina" which began in 2005, during the pre-social media age, ended eleven years later, in a feverish hysteria of cruel/funny Twitter/Facebook memes.[1] This supercouple, who had surrendered their individual identities to become a clickbait-friendly brand (worth an alleged $400 million), were breaking apart. And there was nothing any of us could do about it. Some of us schadenfreuded. Others lost faith in eternal love. The rest couldn't care less.

Truth is, couples do matter.

They're vessels of human hope.

Whether doomed and romantic or cynical and wrong, couples are design projects with narrativity, predestination, and failure built into their wiring. A couple is, mathematically speaking, the smallest unit of collaboration and perhaps therefore the most potent (or poisonous).

Inspired by a comment made by Jean-Luc Godard—"The identity between love and work"—can we think of a working life together, in tandem, as something possessing shape, or format? Whether beds are shared or not, couples who make their love their work remain as compelling for us as they seem to be for each other. Is this the "Couple Format"?

A powerful, pervasive idealism often drives people in their late teens or early twenties. Passion! Immortality! This heady cocktail delivers a delusion that the person you love is the one you *must* work with. Thus, the Couple Format becomes the ultimate public/private *Gesamtkunstwerk,* a total theater of reciprocities and supposed syntheses.

In the design world, the 1920s and '30s produced female pioneers such as Charlotte Perriand and Lilly Reich. They remained forever in the shadows of their male architect counterparts, respectively Le Corbusier and Mies van der Rohe, with the not-so-subtle subtext being that buildings are made by men while interiors—from furniture to soft furnishings—are the necessary province of women. Power lay with the former, prettiness with the latter.

Disentangling the major and the minor in a couple-unit is like trying to measure the color of love itself. The continued ways in which couples are erroneously remembered and credited proves that lazy, male hero worship still wins the messy custody battles of legacy and myth. It usually occludes the true nature of creative authorship, making the close study of Couple Formats forensically relevant.

In summer 2016, I organized a series of conversations at the Architectural Association in London, where guests were invited to share one Couple Format that had made some kind of mark on them.[2] I asked each guest "from the worlds of art, architecture, curating, literature, and philosophy" to present the ways in which their chosen couples' roles were delineated; the ways in which the things the couples produced shaped the relationship; or the ways in which the relationship itself may have been a kind of work or product. It was inevitable that we would also consider how couples come together and what mystical force sustains their bond—a force that might end up being the very same force that ultimately tears them apart. Of which the best possible outcome, in the twenty-first century, is surely Gwyneth Paltrow's "Conscious Uncoupling," where mutual consent negates the more typical toxic meltdown.[3] Arguably, the worst kind of breakup, which was unfolding as these conversations were taking place, is that of the United Kingdom's referendum to leave the European Union. It too produced a quippy portmanteau, such that the end of "Brangelina" marked the beginning of "Brexit." Or perhaps more conspiratorially, did the sudden advent of "Brexit" mean the ensuing end of "Brangelina"?

Below are selected excerpts from the seven Couple Formats that were presented. Throughout, we ask, "What was the identity between love and work; or, what was the love found in working together?"

Charles and Ray Eames by Catherine Ince

Ray Eames's position in their career has often been marginalized. Charles Eames was a strong character, somebody who put himself to the fore. Ray was from the generation where she was perhaps happy to step back at certain periods, and let Charles be more the "office of Charles Eames" than the "office of Charles and Ray Eames." A lot of work has been done, in particular by Professor Pat Kirkham, to correct this view, or, to look again at the role of women in professional and personal creative partnerships. Kirkham produced the definitive biography [of the Eameses] in the early 1990s, the consequence of ten years of looking at their work. Some of the things she talks about are still aspects that you have to explore and defend today, i.e., what was Ray's role in the office? How do you delineate a personal and professional relationship in an office? And is it even interesting to think about what "X" did or what "Y" did? And how do you "uncouple" the work? Charles was definitely the photographer and the filmmaker. Ray was the master of form and color. What unites them is an interest in structure, architecturally, sculpturally, and conceptually. There has been a lot of critique from people who used to work at the Eames office, that Ray was marginal, that she hid herself away. But you can read the archive legacy in quite a different way. [In the exhibition I curated at the Barbican] I was interested in bringing her out of being "just" the textile designer and the painter. She has the equivalent eye to Charles, it just happens to get expressed in a different way. Ray is the ultimate art director. Their work often happened in very private moments, at home ... notoriously, for six-and-a-half days a week, often eighteen hours a day ... They tended to document themselves, a kind of self-branding ... There is this togetherness in the early years that starts to disappear as their office gets very, very big ... They had a uniform. They cultivated a particular look for lots of different reasons to project a persona in the business, art, and corporate worlds of the 1950s ... They liked entertaining other couples at their house, and they clearly enjoyed the Couple Format. It was socially manageable for them. Throughout their working lives, Charles would speak for them, and Ray would not speak publically. Only once Charles passed away, in 1978, did Ray finally came to the fore.

Robert Venturi and Denise Scott-Brown by Sam Jacob

Denise Scott-Brown takes Robert Venturi to Las Vegas. They make incredible pictures of each other.

Denise takes a picture of Bob, next to a broken-down shack. You can see The Strip in the distance. Him with his back turned to us, the viewer, like a Magritte painting.

And then there's Denise. Standing in the landscape like the most electrified person you could possibly imagine. I've never seen someone look so absolutely excited by the idea of the urban environment. The photographs are part of a studio they're running at Yale University in 1968. They're taking their students to Las Vegas. What they're doing there is looking for weirdness. Bob's love of Rome and Denise's love of the West Coast produce perhaps the most important book about twenty-first century architecture: *Learning from Las Vegas*. It describes architecture's relationship to modernity. But at the same time, it's the most touching, beautiful love letter to a moment in time, to a place. That comes partly from a moment in their relationship where the world looked absolutely and endlessly fascinating ... When you see some of the photographs—and Denise took endless photographs—you realize that the books is full of beautiful images. The one I love the most is an intimate moment between Bob and Denise driving down The Strip, Bob with his arm on the back of Denise's seat. At this moment you can see an absolute love of architecture and a love between them, a romance of all these things simultaneously. And it produces a new way of looking at architecture, of seeing the world. It is a period of psychedelic joy in the possibilities of the world.

Gilles Deleuze and Félix Guattari by Aaron Schuster

What is friendship? What is a couple? What is love? There is a strange figure of the "two" that runs through Gilles Deleuze's collaborative work with Félix Guattari as well. Deleuze is known as a philosopher of multitudes, speed, and becoming. More profoundly, though, Deleuze was a thinker of solitudes. He hated travel. The most exciting encounter, he'd say, is to stay at home and read a book. Solitude remains an essential category of his thought ... For friendship to be true, there needs to be something that remains mysterious. You don't know when the friendship *happened*, but, it occurred. Deleuze and Guattari also developed this idea together. If you're really friends with somebody it's because you're able to grasp something in them that somehow takes them out of themselves. Deleuze would call this their "grain of madness." This is the real charm of a person. The two of them met in June 1969 and then they worked together for more than twenty years. Guattari was one of the directors of a clinic called La Borde, where he was thinking about groups, in terms of institutions. How do institutions function and malfunction? For Guattari, the therapeutic relation was not a couple, not a patient and an analyst; instead, he asked, how can the group itself become a therapeutic environment? This is Guattari's early work on "transversality." He already felt a kinship with Deleuze's ideas before he met Deleuze. And Deleuze himself was interested in clinical problems, and particularly in psychosis. But he had no direct access to psychotics or schizophrenics. So, when Deleuze meets Guattari, sparks fly, and the first discussions end up in their book *Anti-Oedipus*. However, their work together was not without trouble. Deleuze described their roles thus: "Guattari was the diamond miner, and I was the polisher." A few years later, in 1973, Deleuze wrote to Guattari, "You respected my solitude, and I your groups, without interfering." How is it that these two positions would come together? How does that allow us to think what a couple is? Is the real figure of the couple perhaps not two people, but more abstractly, more metaphysically, a combination of solitude and a group? One finds this precisely articulated in their 1980 book, *A Thousand Plateaus*, where they speak about a "populous solitude." Multiplicity? Yes. And also elements that remain unconnected to each other ... Deleuze and Guattari were both deeply engaged with psychoanalysis. Yet, in all his writings, Freud never gives a definition of love. But, he suggests, it's through the distortions of love, the way love fails, that we can grasp what love is. Which is: *a set of mutually compatible symptoms* ... Instead of a dialogue, love is a matter of intersecting monologues.

Gertrude Stein and Alice B. Toklas by Guy Mannes-Abbott

They met in Paris in September 1907. Gertrude asked Alice to go on a date the following day, after which they remained together until Gertrude's death in 1946. Gertrude was living with her older brother Leo, in an apartment on Rue de Fleurus that was covered with the modernist art she had collected since settling there in 1903: Matisse, Cézanne, and Picasso. For a while this was the only place that Picasso could show his work to anyone interested in it, and Gertrude and Alice's Saturday salon became a famous institution amongst artists and émigrés, and a legend beyond that. Quickly Alice took on the key role of typing up Gertrude's nightly productions, a role she performed for decades. They were living together within a year, sidelining Leo, who got a studio elsewhere and was shunted out finally in 1914. Brother and sister never spoke again. Let's focus on their passion: the love and work. The following is from Diana Souhami's glorious book *Gertrude and Alice*:

> "Our pleasure is to do every day the work of that day," wrote Gertrude, "to cut our hair and not want blue eyes and to be reasonable and obedient ... Every day we get up and say we are awake today ..." Alice's work of the day was to serve Gertrude, who liked to read, write, wander around, drive cars and talk. Alice was secretary, cook, publisher, housekeeper and ministering angel. She did the knitting, sewing, housekeeping, dusting, typing, ordered books from Mudie's lending library in London, supplied etymologies of words, references for poets, pronunciations of Spanish, corrected Gertrude's French, kept the house filled with acacia, honeysuckle, roses and tulips, answered the telephone, did the filing, carried Gertrude's bag and served all meals promptly. When they went on holiday Alice did the packing. "She is very necessary to me ... My sweetie. She is all to me," wrote Gertrude, who was freed from all domestic chores and could concentrate on her work. "It's hard work being a genius. You have to sit around so much doing nothing," she said.

So we circle back to *The Autobiography of Alice B. Toklas*, which wasn't of course an autobiography. What was it? ... It was a biography: not one authored from outside, but from inside, albeit in another's voice ... I linger with this because while this is one of the most conventional prose-like works of Gertrude's, it is also *properly* strange. That is, Gertrude adopted Alice's recognizable voice, exorcising as many Gertrudisms as she could identify, though not all, to write a memoir of her own life and times.

Marina Abramović and Ulay by James Westcott

Marina Abramović and Ulay lived, loved, and worked together for thirteen years in an incredibly intimate, intense, and explosive all-consuming relationship. Their performances together were basically a series of contracts. And those contracts dictated how they lived. They tried to give those contracts sacred status by devoting unimaginable amounts of work, unimaginable amounts of effort, and unimaginable amounts of pain to them. In retrospect, there's a sense that Marina and Ulay were both pushing themselves, individually, over a cliff just before they met each other. There was no further they could go by themselves ... They didn't have a marriage contract but they did buy a Citroën HY van together and write a manifesto. They called it *Art Vital* and it was a list of rules for their life on the road together. Their relationship would consist of a set of ideals and pure ambition, to see what their bodies could do together. This contract between them became so stringent that it gathered the force of a covenant. And each individual performance was like entering into an individual covenant—there was no question of breaking it. If great relationships need to be about a third thing, theirs was about a performative mode of living on the road. Marina would take on the traditionally feminine roles in the relationship: cooking, cleaning, knitting, and entertaining and charming the art world. Abramović lapped up the adulation; Ulay hid from it. Ulay would handle paperwork and finances. They were starting to become symbiotic. They called each other "glue" ... The closest they got to a ceremony was when they each got a tattoo of the number "3" on each of their ring fingers in lieu of wedding rings. I think the "3" symbolized the third thing their relationship was about: the work. The tattoos would fade after a few years ... A paradox begins to seep into their work: the more raw and authentic it is, the more it feels like the performance of a series of *metaphors* for relationships, for desire. The more "real" it is, the more abstract it gets. But they were tied to a contract, a promise they'd made to each other. They'd stated that they would perform *Nightsea Crossing* ninety times. That means ninety days. Only then would it be done. Even though their contract with each other was already being broken, they were still willing to fulfill its other terms—it almost had the force of a covenant. In a kind of recurring nightmare around the world, they'd reperform *Nightsea Crossing*, in galleries, basements, even in a plaza and once, in Japan, in a pit. The work compelled them to carry on. They'd been planning a walk across the Great Wall of China for several years. They would each start from opposite ends. It would culminate in them meeting in the middle and getting married. Instead, it was an arduous divorce ceremony, called *The Lovers*. That was the end of their collaboration.

Broadway and Fifth Avenue by Natasha Sandmeier

Hundreds of years ago, the Wickquasgeck Trail was carved into the landscape of Manhattan, winding its way through swamps and around rocks. It now calls itself Broadway and is the only street that cuts across Manhattan's otherwise resolute grid. Broadway runs the entire twenty-one kilometers of Manhattan and then carries on for a further thirty-two kilometers through the Bronx and Westchester County. It runs from the very bottom of Manhattan at Battery Park, up through Lower Manhattan. Once it hits 10th Street it gets derailed from the grid and begins its diagonal cut through the city until it hits West 79th, at which point it straightens out and shoots through the rest of the island until it exits via the Bronx into Yonkers and beyond. It keeps going for another twenty-nine kilometers. Fifth Avenue, on the other hand, was commissioned in 1811 and for many years remained a predominantly residential street until 1893, when the Astoria Hotel was built. Fifth Avenue was already the home of the elite by the mid-to-late 1800s, and today of course it has become one of the most expensive shopping streets in the world. For more than a third of its length it runs along the east side of Central Park. The meeting of the grid and the diagonal triggers a confetti of triangular or otherwise angled plots. The collision creates weird residual spaces that are too difficult to develop. Some are empty. But the most famous of these residual spaces is The Flatiron Building. Designed by Daniel Burnham in 1902, its iconic shape marked an area that became known as the Flatiron District—after the building which took its name, predictably, from the shape of an old iron. Regardless of the building's own identity, it is absolutely the prodigal son of Fifth Avenue and Broadway. Two streets each with their own identity, whose trajectories literally shape their offspring.

The Empire State Building and the Chrysler Building by Madelon Vriesendorp

It was the early 1970s. Rem [Koolhaas] was very interested in the future, and I was interested in the past, what the past was like. That divided our collections very much: his postcards of New York and my souvenirs of Americana. I had already made one painting of Lady Liberty [i.e., the Statue of Liberty] falling backwards onto New York while we lived in Ithaca, in Upstate New York. In Manhattan, I started the paintings of the buildings in bed together. In the 1930s, the Empire State Building and the Chrysler Building were being built and were sort of competing: Which was going to be the tallest? Both were important in Rem's story of the beginning of the skyscraper. It struck me that the Empire State was masculine, and the Chrysler Building was sort of dressed up with lots of jewelry and little details that were very feminine. There is a phenomenon called "Object Affection," where people fall in love with inanimate objects. For example, a woman fell in love with the Berlin Wall. If this was possible, then inanimate objects should be able to fall in love with each other too. I did lots of little sketches with the Empire State and the Chrysler in bed with one another, then Rem said, "Modernity has to come in." So he forced me to put the Rockefeller Center into the scene, catching the other two in the act. It's about relationships.

1 Jenny Awford and Chris Spargo, "'And that, my friends, is what they call closure': Brangelina break-up immediately inspires hilarious memes—and they've all got one thing in common ...," *Daily Mail*, September 20, 2016.

2 "Couple Format," *Format*, format.aaschool.ac.uk.

3 Habib Sadeghi and Sherry Sami, "Conscious Uncoupling," goop.com/conscious-uncoupling-2.

Lesser Worlds

Felicity D. Scott

Speaking at the Conference on Space Manufacturing Facilities (Space Colonies) at Princeton University in May 1975, German-American aerospace engineer and science-fiction writer Jesco von Puttkamer reported on NASA's long-range plans for manned space flight missions, inflecting his remarks to account for "such far-future undertakings as space colonization, space industrialization, and manned planetary exploration."[1] The conference was dedicated to demonstrating the technical and economic viability of Princeton physics professor Gerard K. O'Neill's rather hallucinatory visions for "Earthlike" space colonies, also seeking to enhance the profile of, and hence mechanisms of financial support for, his endeavor. To these ends, discussions were to focus on "construction methods, productivity, and payoff to the Earth of permanent industrial habitats near the L5 Earth-Moon Lagrange libration point," a point of stable gravitational equilibrium between the sun, the earth, and its moon.[2] The first colony would be located at L5, or so it was imagined, remaining in line with the moon as it orbited earth but not needing to expend fuel to maintain this position indefinitely. From this base, ever-more-gigantic colonies and industrial installations would be built in line with O'Neill's bootstrap narrative.[3] Always optimistic and in tune with the import of rapid return on investments, O'Neill estimated that one could "put the earliest technically possible date for the first space community at somewhere between 1988 and the year 2000."[4]

Achieving this goal would take more than enormous monetary funds. Additionally, creating entirely new *worlds*—what von Puttkamer termed "man-made worlds," to distinguish them from transport vehicles or lunar mining settlements—would require advancing scientific and technical knowledge towards the design of such unprecedented artificial territory as well as expanding knowledge about the humans and human communities that would be sent to populate and work within or upon it. Space colonies, that is, required an integrated environmental design strategy appropriate for such a complex biopolitical apparatus—a design strategy operating at once in the material, informatic, social, political, physiological, and subjective or psychological domains. Yet the simultaneous design of the human and their physical environment was not exactly unique to space colonies, and by 1975, earth itself was already extensively a "man-made world," which an engineer like von Puttkamer must have been known. But in being called upon to imagine how NASA's existing and future space technologies might be directed not just towards manned space exploration (ostensibly in the name of science) but further instrumentalized for the design of space colonies and their inhabitants, he introduced—among an array of more pragmatic diagrams, flowcharts, tables, etc.—a symptomatic and fantastically ambiguous image of post-Vitruvian Man.[5]

Appropriating Leonardo da Vinci's famous late-fifteenth-century drawing, von Puttkamer's diagram, "Evolution of the Earth Orbit Space Community," seems, in retrospect, to be haunted by disturbances in the anthropocentric, anthropometric, and anthropogeographic logics informing traditional Western conceptions of architecture and design. Prompted by his encounter with space-colony visions, von Puttkamer's image also allegorizes the constructive tension between aesthetics and instrumentality that renders design practices so provocative and problematic. In harboring such an extreme or literal notion of how design practices are always and already designs of the human, it is my hope that space colonies and the cultural imaginaries to which they give rise can serve as a productive vehicle for reflecting upon the ontological and epistemological stakes at play in design.

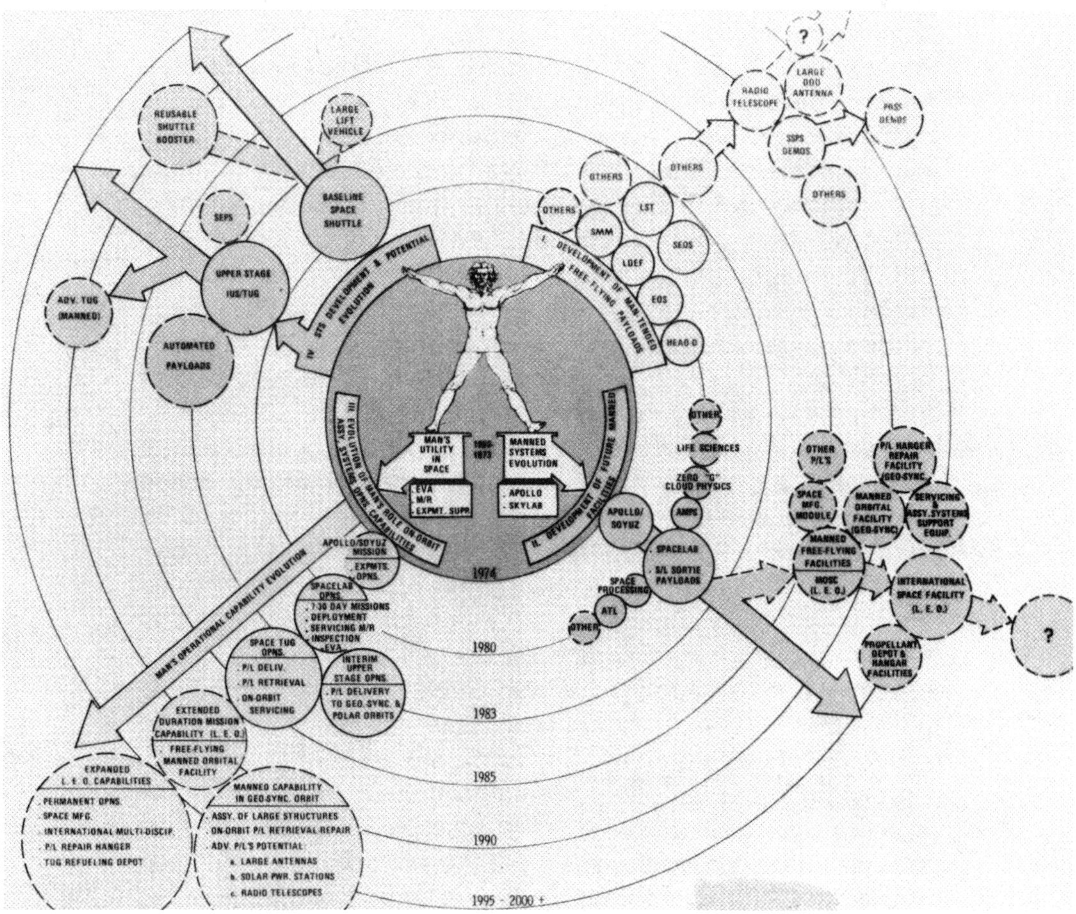

Post-Vitruvian man: "Evolution of Earth Orbit Space Community," from Jesco von Puttkamer, "Developing Space Occupancy: Perspectives on NASA Future Space Program Planning" in *Space Manufacturing Facilities* (Space Colonies), 1977.

Occupational Prerequisites

In 1962, von Puttkamer joined the aeroballistics division of NASA's Marshall Space Flight Center in Huntsville, Alabama, at the invitation of German-American rocket scientist, space architect, and fellow science-fiction writer Wernher von Braun, who had been instrumental in developing the V-2 rocket for Nazi Germany. Von Braun's team in Hunstville developed the Saturn V rocket used in the 1969 Apollo Lunar Landing—a euphoric moment in US history, galvanizing national pride at the height of the Cold War space race—and von Puttkamer worked, in turn, on the ill-fated Skylab space station and solar telescope after von Braun's departure. Launched into orbit in 1973, Skylab was abandoned in 1974 as funding priorities shifted, and in 1979 its debris was scattered in Western Australia. In 1974, the year before the Princeton conference, von Puttkamer was transferred to NASA headquarters in Washington, DC and put in charge of long-term planning as the agency transitioned from a research phase to "a new era of applications-oriented space operations based on the space shuttle."[6] NASA's space shuttles bore the pressure of commercial applications and were cast as elements of an international space transportation system (STS), more than mere examples of US technical supremacy.

Among NASA's main goals at this time, von Puttkamer indicated, was "to continue to provide the capability for man to operate effectively in the space environment." Extending knowledge of human physiology and psychology was central to this techno-scientific enterprise, as was imagining what the "good life" might be in outer space. The capability of which he spoke was therefore not just that of enabling humans to physically and psychologically survive within extreme environmental conditions, but to "operate effectively" as productive subjects when suspended within a space colonial apparatus. To ensure the desired operationality of the human in such a unique and untested, although still distinctly biopolitical (and in this sense all-too earth-like), environment entailed not only scientific study and measurement of the human but also its redesign. What von Puttkamer called the "increasing penetration of space by man" remained the shared ambition of this international phase of space research. Yet the collaborative design of artificial environments for extraterrestrial forms of human life involved an increasingly complex articulation of techno-scientific know-how with territorial ambitions and economic logic. This application of science and engineering expertise to space colonies, moreover, implicitly called into question ideals of anthropogeography, of the human notion of being in our proper or natural place.

Von Puttkamer remained evidently more skeptical than most conference participants about imminent prospects for actually realizing human colonies in outer space, repeatedly situating totally designed worlds in the years 2000+. Yet the conference had implications bearing on future NASA funding, so he offered a series of four overlapping evolutionary scenarios for the potential phasing of "space occupancy," suggesting that the knowledge to be gained was relevant whether the end result was a space colony or not. His narrative began with "permanent occupancy of near-earth space," such as a space station or orbital launch facility, followed by "permanent occupancy of Earth-Moon space," in the form of a manned geosynchronous space station or orbiting lunar station, then "full self-sufficiency of man in Earth-Moon space," in which he situated the L5 community along with lunar colonies and space cities like Krafft Arnold Ehricke's dream of "astropolis," and ended with "permanent occupancy of heliocentric space," such as asteroid colonies or radiation-protected Mars settlements. In addition to artists' renderings depicting spacecraft, bases, and other settlements replete with control rooms and geodesic domes in a familiar pop-realist science-fiction aesthetic, von Puttkamer supplemented his narrative with extensive diagrams, charts, and tables illustrating, in a scientific and pragmatic tone, how environments proper to his four scenarios related to "technological prerequisites without which those utopias will always remain pipe-dreams."[7] He organized these prerequisites into six categories (transportation, habitation, engineering technologies, life sciences, operations technology, and advanced management concepts), analyzed components of each, and detailed multiple connections and nodes between them within the larger system. But as suggested above, the by-then customary artistic renderings, scientific diagrams, and data tabulation were less remarkable than his appropriation of Leonardo's Vitruvian Man, which von Puttkamer situated at the center of a depiction of four possible evolutionary trajectories pertaining to the lowest category, near-earth space. Nowhere in his text does he mention or account for this gesture.

Leonardo's anthropometric drawing superimposes two figures of man, each cast as a geometric proportional measure: one is depicted with legs held vertically and arms held horizontally, his proportions inscribed neatly within a square; the other has legs splayed and arms raised at a higher angle to be inscribed similarly within an overlapping, albeit not squared, circle. The drawing is typically read to privilege man's dual position at the center, and as a proportional measure, of both earthly and cosmic (or secular and divine) domains, respectively. It returns us to the problem of conceptualizing the mutual reciprocity of humans and their environments, in this case at both microcosmic and macroscopic scales, for Leonardo read the body in relation to both its interior workings and to the earth and cosmos, referring to man as "a lesser world."

Von Puttkamer's rendering eliminated the square/earthly module and dislodged the latter, spread-eagled cosmic figure, recontextualizing it within contemporary techno-scientific agendas and implicitly dismantling Leonardo's metaphysical ideals.

It is perhaps not surprising that von Puttkamer would remove the earthly side of the equation, for space colonies are by definition extraterrestrial, having departed quite literally from the terra or earth. But the valence of what we might call "once-cosmic" man is perhaps even more violently shifted in this gesture. The figure is grafted, somewhat awkwardly, to stand on two platforms occupying the lower quadrants of the circle—on the left, "man's utility in space," leading to the evolution of a human's "operational capability," and on the right, "manned systems evolution," leading towards the development of "future manned facilities." The former privileged the role of humans within this techno-scientific apparatus, the latter machines. On the upper part of the diagram we find the figure's hands pulled beyond the circle, not in the form of a measuring device but to tie him to two further trajectories—"sts [space transportation system] development and potential evolution" and "development of man-tended free flying payloads." Components of the bubble diagrams attending to each of the four trajectories become increasingly tentative or hesitant as the figure's scientific and technical extensions pull him outwards towards the year 2000+. The overall image hesitates to even imagine future scenarios beyond the international space facility upon which von Puttkamer worked.

In von Puttkamer's diagram, Vitruvian Man no longer serves as a bodily analogy or proportional measure able to shift back and forth between earth and the heavens. Yet remnants of Leonardo's artistic figure continued to haunt the engineer's conception of a man-made world in outer space. The archaic figure representing the cosmic pole was in fact suspended just as ambiguously in his new context as he was in Leonardo's diagram, if now embedded within a speculative field of space operations. We can read it either as the ghost of humanism stretched to its limit (crucified?) by this new epistemology and the apparatus it sought to create, or by contrast, as another kind of center or privileged node within an expanded system of science and technology, a point that might somehow hold together possible futures, deploying them as yet-further extensions of man. The latter reading raises the specter of engineering hubris, as humans like O'Neill sought to replace God's power in creating future worlds. The former reading brings me back to the less god-like status of humans within the larger picture.

Within space research, the human remained a *key* component, the site of extensive measurement and calculation, the very medium through which to collect data about physiological, biochemical, mechanical, psychological, and social systems. It was not of course ideal measures or proportions that were sought, but data establishing normative standards and degrees and frequencies of deviation from them—data that could be statistically fed into a new set of depictions. These notably include ergonomic figures (symptomatically absent from von Puttkamer's illustrations), the dimensions of which were quite literally inscribed within space vehicles.[8] The translation of such applied research from the space transit system that remained the focus of von Puttkamer's work to the expansionist agenda of O'Neill and his followers' vision of space colonization, with its search for new *lebensraum*, implicitly recast any such instrumentality of the human, raising the question of just who the figure at the center might be. Under the category of "life sciences," von Puttkamer listed environmental control and life support systems, radiation shielding, physiological adaptation, spacesuits, "training/simulation/indoctrination requirements," psychological factors of long-duration flights, and sociological factors of extended missions as critical points of study. All such measures, including indoctrination, were of course necessary "to continue to provide the capability for man to operate effectively in the space environment"; they were biopolitical elements crucial to optimizing this system's productive capacities.

Decentered

In "The Living and its Milieu," Georges Canguilhem offered a distinct reading of mutual reciprocity between humans and their environment, one seeking to complicate or counter politically ambivalent claims that a determining influence "authorizes man's unlimited action upon himself through the medium of the milieu," the implications of which seem relevant here.[9] Tracing within modern science intertwined archaeologies of mechanistic and biological conceptions of relationships between organisms and their milieu, he insisted that inherent to such relations was a persistent indeterminism and multiplicity, and hence structural mechanisms of diversification, negotiation, and change. Canguilhem underscored that a human milieu was not natural but artificially constructed: "It is a fundamental characteristic of the living thing, that it makes its own milieu: it builds one for itself," he wrote, adding, "the milieu on which the organism depends is structured and organized by the organism itself."[10] When Canguilhem inverted the primacy typically afforded to environmental influences on the human, arguing that "to the extent that he exists in history, man became a creator of the geographical configuration; he is a geographical factor," he was not imaging entirely new man-made worlds in outer space. Moreover, Canguilhem reminds us that a living being—as a

A cutaway view of the 1975 Stanford Torus space station design. The rotation of the torus provides Earth-normal gravity on the inside. Illustration by Rick Guidice for NASA.

center, medium, or milieu—does not "dissolve into its environment. A living thing does not reduce itself to an intersection of influences." Living beings, we might say, are not simply scripted by environmental apparatuses, even complex and highly scientific ones, just as human bodies never fit quite so neatly within humanist systems of geometrical proportion wherein man appears as a lesser world.

When Canguilhem sought to denaturalize the conception of environment, and when he insisted on the irreducibility of the human to it, he was not seeking to shore up humanist assumptions of primacy and centrality or notions of agency and subjectivity. Rather, he was seeking to undermine metaphysical foundations and scientific blindness that read the world as given or absolute and as lacking potential for decisions (including political ones) and for change. This is rendered more explicit when he recalled the need to make political choices between "existential security and the demands of scientific knowledge" when confronted by the scientific revolution's shattering of the cosmos, after which man was "no longer at the center of the world." Following this event, he suggested, "it became necessary to choose between two theories of milieu, that is, in the final analysis, theories of space: a centered space, defined as being where the mi-*lieu* is a center; a decentered space, defined as being where the *mi*-lieu is an intermediary field."[11]

Von Puttkamer's diagram suggests an even more radical decentering than that produced when Copernicus, Kepler, and Galileo dislodged earth's, and with it man's, position from the center of the universe. His graft of the Vitruvian Man onto an indeterminate field of techno-scientific potentials of outer space, I propose, hovers ambiguously between a centered and decentered paradigm, no longer bound by linear geometries or Western metaphysics of space. Indeed, faced with the translation of man into biopolitical data, the Copernican revolution might well have started to seem modest in its manner of deposing a humanist subject from the center of his universe. This is precisely where Canguilhem's reading of the indeterminacy and multiplicity inherent to such decentering becomes critical, as does a politics of taking a position and making decisions. Faced with the structural ambiguity attending the mutual reciprocity of a subject and his or her milieu, one is called upon to recognize the importance of ongoing negotiation and choice. That is, whether we are talking about an evidently artificial environment like a space colony, or its allegorical double in an earthly environment, functioning similarly as a biopolitical apparatus of subject formation, there remains the possibility for spaces of more progressive subjective and political revalencing, just as there remains space for a politics of design.

1 Jesco von Puttkamer, "Developing Space Occupancy: Perspectives on NASA Future Space Program Planning," in *Space Manufacturing Facilities (Space Colonies): Proceedings of the Princeton/AIAA/NASA Conference, May 7–9, 1975*, ed. Jerry Grey (New York: American Institute of Aeronautics and Astronautics, Inc., 1977), 209.

2 "Abstract," in ibid., v.

3 As O'Neill explained of this orbit, in the "L5 Lagrange libration point, 60° behind the Moon in the orbit of the Moon around the Earth ... an object located at L5 would stay there forever." Gerard K. O'Neill, "The Colonization of Space," in ibid., A-5.

4 Gerard K. O'Neill, "The Space Manufacturing Facility Concept," in ibid., 8.

5 There are actually two similar drawings reproduced alongside von Puttkamer's presentation. I will focus on the second, in which Leonardo's drawing is not simply retraced but mechanically reproduced.

6 Von Puttkamer, "Developing Space Occupancy," in *Space Manufacturing Facilities*, 209.

7 Ibid., 217.

8 On ergonomics, see John Harwood, "*Skylab,* or the Outpost," *AA Files* 61 (2010): 93–99; and Harwood, "The Interface: Ergonomics and the Aesthetics of Survival," in *Governing by Design: Architecture, Economy, and Politics in the Twentieth Century*, ed. Aggregate Architectural Collective (Pittsburgh: University of Pittsburgh Press, 2012): 70–92.

9 Georges Canguilhem, "The Living and Its Milieu," trans. John Savage, *Grey Room* 03 (Spring 2001): 23.

10 Ibid., Canguilhem, 19, 26.

11 Ibid., Canguilhem, 24–25.

Spatial Thought

Daniel Birnbaum and
Sven-Olov Wallenstein

> I was thinking of a book, but I didn't like that idea.
> —Marcel Duchamp[1]

> Posthumous books are published, why not a posthumous show?
> —Philippe Parreno[2]

Can an exhibition be a productive medium for thinking *through*, and not just a kind of pedagogical illustration *of*, extant ideas? Certainly there have been works of literature, art, and music with such magnificent ambitions, and intellectuals who have attempted to articulate the philosophy of, say, the novel, modern music, or cinema. Consider the case of Jean-François Lyotard. At the very peak of his fame in the mid-1980s, Lyotard, one of Europe's most prominent thinkers, staged an art-world intervention. He did so with essentially a short piece of writing and one major exhibition. The essay, "The Sublime and the Avant-Garde," appeared in the April 1984 issue of *Artforum,* just as he was also preparing *"Les Immatériaux"* ("The Immaterials"), a sprawling, pan-historical installation that opened the following year at the Centre Georges Pompidou in Paris. His intention with the exhibition, Lyotard explained, was to produce "unease" in the viewer.

Lyotard's massive project swept in during an exciting moment in continental philosophy, when the ways in which one might "do" philosophy were being radically rethought. A decade earlier, Jacques Derrida had proclaimed the end of the book, and in *Différence et Répétition*, Gilles Deleuze stated that the "search for new means of philosophical expression ... must be pursued today in relation to the renewal of certain other arts, such as the theater or the cinema." Lyotard shared Deleuze and Derrida's overtures to other media, but there is something quite original in his own wild texts from this period. These were not really books, but experimental and open-ended projects. Lyotard stressed the need to render philosophy visual—not only in the sense of illustrating concepts with striking and sensuous images but also through spatialization, in a way reminiscent of Mallarmé's famous throw of the dice. Perhaps the recent English translation of Lyotard's first major book, *Discours, Figure*, is evidence of a new interest in his attempt to reinvent philosophy through confrontations with art.[3] He was not happy with this book. What it ought to have been, he suggests, is a dislocated body, where fragmented speech could be joined together in various ways. "A good book," he stated, is "a book the reader could dip into anywhere, in any order." A good book, Lyotard seems to say here, is not a book at all, but an exhibition.

More like an environment than a traditional exhibition, *"Les Immatériaux"* was a scenography, an informational space or interface where objects, sounds, projections, music, and texts conveyed an image bordering on an "overexposition," as Lyotard says, drawing on Paul Virilio's concept of the "overexposed city."[4] Unlike the nineteenth-century world exhibitions, the aim of such an overexposure was not to project a sense of newness and amazement—not to simply affirm the seductive power of the new—but rather to trigger a "reflexive unease" in our relation to things that we already dimly sense.

In a conversation with Hans Ulrich Obrist, Phillipe Parreno recalls visiting Lyotard's exhibition:

> *Les Immatériaux* was an exhibition producing ideas through a display of objects in space. It was very different from writing a book or developing a philosophical concept. And that's precisely what I loved in that exhibition, that it wasn't a conceptual exhibition. I learned later that Lyotard wanted to do another exhibition, *Resistance*. "Resistance" isn't a good title. You immediately think of a series of moral issues. But when I met him, I understood that he meant in fact resistance in another way. In school when you study physics you are told that frictional forces are not important—the forces of two surfaces in contact let certain axioms become uncertain. I think that's what *Resistance* was to be about.[5]

Wittgenstein never made an exhibition, and neither did Adorno, nor Heidegger—thank god. Lyotard was the first major modern philosopher to make this leap, though others would follow. *"Les Immatériaux"* was an ambitious experiment concerning the impact of information technology on human life and the ways in which the exhibition format itself might become a spatial practice of philosophy. The exhibition, which contained scientific instruments, technical devices, and works of art, has often been seen as a celebration of information technology and a new postmodern world based on the immateriality of flows of information. But anyone willing to look a bit closer will discover that the underlying conception was far more ambivalent, not in the sense of some psychological hesitation on the threshold of the new, but rather as something inherent in the things themselves, most importantly because the very sense of thing and "thinghood" was at stake here.

A sequel entitled *"Résistances"* was indeed planned, and would have dealt with the underside of communication, noise, distortion, and the dimension of experience that resists both consciousness and language. This part was never completed, and what remains are only the accounts of participants in Lyotard's seminars.[6] It can however be understood as aligned with the direction in which Lyotard's own research was moving at the time, away from the postmodern as a universe of messages and codes, and once more approaching the idea of touching, of the event, and what he called "passibility" (neither an activity nor the simple passivity of receiving, but rather—in continuity with the central theme of *Discours, Figure*—a "donation" as something fundamental and originary). The 1985 exhibition must then be seen in conjunction with this second project that never took place, which of course is a tenuous proposal; we have no way of knowing what it would have looked like, and any claims about it must remain conjectural. Nevertheless, if one wants to continue the line of thought sketched out in 1985, it is important to note the element of indeterminacy that is inherent just as much in immateriality and ideality as in matter and its various cognates. From this perspective, the celebration of various forms of dematerialization in the first exhibition was always paired with an attentiveness to forms of resistance, and perhaps the sequel was, at least to a certain extent, already present from the outset as a kind of undercurrent or possible counterpoint reading against the grain.

In many ways the proposals of *"Les Immatériaux"* retrieve the promise of *indeterminacy* of the early avant-garde of the twentieth century. While we seem to be faced with an infinity—and the experience of infinity as an abyss is a fundamental feature of *"Les Immatériaux,"* as well as of Lyotard's writings on the sublime—of possible modes of experience, this just as much produces anxieties and fantasies, precisely the kind of "unease" that the exhibition wanted to provoke: a loss of self, identity, and stability, a disconnection from the space-time of perception, from matter, materials, and materiality, from the *ground* in all senses of the term. The question is how to make such an unease productive, how to make it into the *matter* of thought, in all senses of the term; how to allow for the "foundation crisis" not to be resolved too quickly by appeals to either the synthetic constructions of techno-science or a naive, sensory given, but to make the "unease" that it produces become a condition for an experimental thinking and making.

The philosophical task proposed by Lyotard—if we see *"Les Immatériaux"* and the conjectural *"Résistance"* together with the many essays and writings that surround the first project and may be understood as pointing to the second—is to determine how to approach artworks that, while actively resisting (at least from conceptual art onward) traditional modes of aesthetic enjoyment, nevertheless do not just amount to a withdrawal of sense or sensibility. Rather, they open up to a restructuring of the sensorium that allows representation and its underside to enter into a new constellation that is in tune with the mutations of our present space-time. For this, the term "postmodern," as suggested by Lyotard, was perhaps a deceptive one, since it tends to enclose us in the schemas of cause-effect and before-after that his thought on the temporal knots of presence precisely took as its task to undo. Something similar must of course be said of all claims to locate the mutations of our present. For who would claim to know what the present is, what its limits and possibilities are? Just like any other temporal category, the present is only given in anamnesis, through a rewriting and working-through; "*Les Immatériaux*" was such an attempt, unfinished, incomplete, and even contradictory, which is why it still demands to be not only thought, but also continued.

In its experimental layout, "*Les Immatériaux*" intensified the reflection on the exhibition as a form of communication, as an interface that need not limit itself to the presentation of objects, but can expand into a kind of immersive space.[7] Immersion should however not be understood as the intoxicating and overpowering space of the *Gesamtkunstwerk*, but rather as an exploration of differences and discontinuities that have already begun to inhabit our sensorium; it directs the subject back to a space for reflection and questioning, not only of what is there to be seen, but also of what it means to see, and of who is its subject. Thus, the prying apart of the subject and its faculties not only occurs on the level of thematic content, but just as much on the level of the exhibition layout as such, which on several levels works to achieve a kind of parallelism of multiple sensory and cognitive events.

A show curated by a ghost: from the point of view of communication, Lyotard's second exhibition would probably have focused on its obverse side: noise, loss, scrambling, and disorder—all of those facets of experience that offer a resistance to transmission. Beginning in the physical sense of resistance (as in the resistance produced in electric circuits), the theme may obviously be expanded to cover all facets of experience, and it belongs to the indeterminacy that is inherent just as much in immateriality and ideality as in matter and its various cognates. Thus, even if the first exhibition can at first sight be taken as championing various forms of dematerialization, the attentiveness to forms of resistance was in fact present throughout, although in an oblique manner—which is why one might assume that the planned sequel, at least to a certain extent, was already present in "*Les Immatériaux.*" What such an exhibition would have looked like in the mid-to-late 1980s must of course remain purely conjectural. More important is the question to which Philippe Parreno wants an answer: What would it look like today?

In hindsight, one cannot avoid noting that most of the technological inventions that appeared new and exciting in the 1980s have either become part of everyday life, and in this sense lost their capacity for producing both unease and thought, or, more alarmingly, turned into an increasingly hegemonic system of information and surveillance. All of this could be taken as simply an intensified version of what Adorno called the "administered world," and one in which the techniques of administration have grown infinitely more subtle, insidious, and difficult to resist. In the world of global capital, where the ubiquity of information ensures that all thought is transformed into bits of exchangeable digitized units, identity and difference go together, and the unifying and leveling power of what was once called the "culture industry" have been replaced by a smooth production of differences, in taste, desires, lifestyles, and affective dispositions. Variation, specification, and infinitesimal penetration into the local are the forms through which capital works, and how it sustains its ordering and regimenting function on a higher level.

It is against this development that one could pit the insistence on zones of resistance to information: opacity, inertia, friction, physicality, all seem to offer other possible avenues, as does the thinking of the sensible that Lyotard engages in his last writings. The sequel to "*Les Immatériaux*" could in this sense have amounted to a counterstatement, or to an obverse side that was already present in the first exhibition, perhaps even as the possibility of completing its trajectory in the opposite direction, from language to body, from the immateriality of information to a kind of resistant materiality that is inherent in information as such.

The first problem with such a countermove is that it inevitably—as we saw in many instances in Lyotard's own writings—runs the risk of reactivating regressive ideas of art and drawing on what are in fact highly traditional ideas of painting in particular, which since the advent of modernism in the mid-nineteenth century has, for a host of historical reasons, been accredited with the potential for providing an alternative to technological mediation. While obviously not simply exhausted as such, ideas of touch, gesture, and the presence of color, together with many other similar moves that emphasize the irreplaceable *here and now* like in body art and performance, often function as integral parts of the system they supposedly dislodge, and in this they are akin to the movement of differentiation that is the other side of systemic control and may exert a compensatory function.

Such returns to the sensible can sometimes be uninterestingly conservative, in simply claiming that we need to regress to some earlier point in time. Others have a more complex agenda though, for instance as in theories of "obsolescence," where the strategic return to technologies and mediums that are no longer considered up to date allow for a different take on historical genealogies without making any claim that we could return to the past without further ado. Both of these returns however share a focus on the medium, no doubt as an echo of a formalist legacy that can be retrieved in any number of ways, and yet remain caught in a theory of art and an aesthetic that begins by shunning the present. The convergence of material "carriers," or at least their almost infinite variability—which was one of the basic claims of "*Les Immatériaux*"—poses problems that are unlikely to be addressed in a relevant fashion by reclaiming obsolete technologies. This is obviously not to deny the force, critical value, or interest of any particular form of artistic practice, but rather to note the complexity of the problem of resistance, which, as already the classical formulations of information theory show, is a necessary part of transmission (and not something that would form a radical outside). It would seem that Lyotard poses the problem of countermovement, but then, as he moves away from the seemingly celebratory stance of "*Les Immatériaux,*" somehow ends up being trapped in his own examples, which limit the force and scope of his philosophical claims.

Secondly, if we begin with a theory of resistance—which must also be thought as a resistance *in* or *to* theory itself, if we follow Lyotard's mediations on passibility, the event, and other related concepts—that takes its cues from the physical features of circuits and information systems, how can we move upwards to the dimension of subjectivity and social practice? If a concept like resistance is to be at the center, the political dimension that seemed more or less absent from "*Les Immatériaux*" must somehow be addressed, in a way that articulates the physical with the social. In terms of exhibitions as physical sites, an ulterior issue would be the possibility of pursuing the inverted trajectory in the form of an exhibition that takes account of the transformations of space itself that have occurred since "*Les Immatériaux.*" Could the move back from language to body—or on the level of an exhibition, from information to space—be undertaken at all in the sense that it would project an abstract level into a circumscribed location? If so, such a move must produce its own space as a different kind of interstice or interface in a way that takes into account the shifting relations between the abstract and the concrete, the material and the immaterial. The sites of the work and the exhibition have long since become, if not wholly obsolete, then at least far removed from the phenomenological coordinates that once upheld the first discussions on site specificity, and have since gone through many stages, from the various attempts to inhabit institutions in a reflexive and critical fashion to the complex overlays of places, times, and representation that characterize much of contemporary art. Thus, spiraling downwards, we pass from what appears as spheres of pure ideality—a weightless realm of information circulating frictionlessly—to inertia, body, visceral grounding, and incarnation. But to *which body, which ground*?

Every route through the exhibition represented not only the transition from a modern past to a postmodern future, but more emphatically, a journey from body *to* language*—from the density of physical and corporal experience to the seemingly frictionless realm of information. Each trajectory through the exhibition explored dichotomies like body-code and substance-logos, and many statements seem to present this as a one-way process. "The individual paths all lead from the body to language,"*[8] *Lyotard claimed, as is indicted by the two decisive sites that frame the exhibition, "Theatre of the non-body" and the "Labyrinth of language." It is this unidirectional movement, while part of the curatorial statement, that must be interrogated—for if language is a labyrinth, should it not just as much be able to take us back to the body, not as it was at the outset of the journey, but in a transformed fashion? This is at least the hypothesis that we are forging, and which in what is to follow will guide our reading. Even if the exhibition on one level seemed to champion various form of dematerialization, the attentiveness to forms of resistance, or at least ambivalences, were present throughout, and perhaps the planned sequel was, to a certain extent, already there. Would walking through the exhibition in the opposite direction, i.e., entering through the exit and exiting through the entrance, represent a version of "Resistance"? The reply, to be spelled out elsewhere, is, we believe, no.*[9]

1 Marcel Duchamp to J. J. Sweeney, quoted in Jean-Francois Lyotard, *Duchamp's TRANS/formers* (Venice: The Lapis Press, 1990).

2 Philippe Parreno and Hans Ulrich Obrist, *The Conversation Series 14* (Cologne: Walter König, 2008), 17.

3 Jean-François Lyotard, *Discourse, Figure*, trans. Antony Hudek and Mary Lydon (Minneapolis: University of Minnesota Press, 2011).

4 Paul Virilio, "The Overexposed City," *Zone* 1–2, trans. Astrid Hustvedt (New York: Urzone, 1986).

5 Parreno and Obrist, *The Conversation Series 14*.

6 Ibid.

7 For a thorough analysis of the exhibition layout, see Antonia Wunderlich, *Der Philosoph im Museum: Die Ausstellung "Les Immatériaux" von Jean-François Lyotard* (Bielefeld: Transcript, 2008), part III; and Francesca Gallo, *Les Immatériaux: Un percorso di Jean-François Lyotard nell'arte contemporanea* (Rome: Aracne, 2008).

8 Jean-François Lyotard, "Qui a peur des 'Immateriux'?" *Le Monde*, May 3, 1985.

9 See *Spacing Philosophy: Jean-François Lyotard and the Idea of the Exhibition* (Berlin: Sternberg, 2017).

Down with the World

Tony Chakar

I

> You burn me
> —Sappho, addressing passion

A song from my childhood, by Fairuz, Lebanon's most famous singer, goes like this:

> I wish
> You and I were in a house
> A house the furthest house
> Erased behind the frontiers of darkness and wind
> And snow falling, wounding the surface of all things,
> Making you lose your way, so that you would never leave,
> And you would remain,
> Next to me you would remain,
> While a thousand seasons of jasmine would blossom,
>   and wither
> And you would remain,
> Next to me you would remain,
> Next to me you would remain,
> And not one drop of oil would be left in the lantern
> I wish
> I wish

The song is considered romantic, like most of her songs (except the patriotic ones); the musical arrangements are vanilla-sweet, and the tonality of her voice is pure, with a touch of melancholy. These are all the ingredients needed to make a cheesy pop song about love, which the YouTube videos uploaded by fans have internalized, adding images of isolated cottages, flowers, and hearts to the formula.

But is this song about love, really? One could argue that it isn't, that the lyrics—which were actually written by a man—are more about possessing the Other rather than loving him, which leaves no place for love or desire to unfold, to blossom. This is perhaps true; the lyrics' juvenile character, their immaturity, their remoteness from how love is experienced in today's world, make them very unconvincing.

But in spite of all that, there is something very strange about these lyrics: they are knit together to create a universe of total darkness, "behind the frontiers." The singer wishes to redesign the entire world in order to keep the man she loves next to her, which she does not by inventing a new world but simply by rearranging the elements that make up this one. In this universe there are no paths, because they are covered by the violent snow falling on the world, making it impossible for the man to leave the house even if he so wishes. This situation presupposes that the woman is already contained in the house and it is the man who arrives, after which the elements of Nature, redesigned by the woman, keep him from leaving. In this universe, there is no time: the moment of intimacy lasts for a thousand years, while flowers come into being and collapse into oblivion. In this universe there is no light; it is a universe of total darkness, where the absence of light is necessary to abolish the act of seeing, further locking the man in a universe with no points of reference that would help him orient himself.

II

> The earth was formless and void, and darkness was over the surface of the deep, and the Spirit of God was moving over the surface of the waters.
> Then God said, "Let there be light"; and there was light.
> God saw that the light was good; and God separated the light from the darkness.
> —Genesis 1:24

In God's design, light is crucial. It gave form to the earth and filled the void; because of the separation between light and darkness, the rest of the plan of creation became possible. Who, then, is this woman singing that song about that house, that dwelling "erased behind the frontiers of darkness"? Who is she who wishes to reverse all of God's design? Is she even human? And what does she replace it with? What is her design for the world?

The funny thing about devils and demons—at least the way they are understood in popular culture—is that they never really try to undo God's design of the world. They instead try to control it by manipulating humankind, but that's not exactly the same thing. Why didn't Satan try to gain control of all plant life, for instance, and use it to attack humans and subjugate them? In the popular imagination, it seems that the devil, however he's called, accepts God's order of things; he lures and seduces and leads humanity astray, but that's about it. He competes in order to take over, but does not propose a different plan, a different design.

There is one exception though: the "other" woman, the first woman, Lilith. In the Bible, when God created Adam, it was not only Adam he created: "So God created man in His own image; in the image of God He created him; male and female He created them."[1] The shift in pronouns, from "him" to "them," suggests that there was a female as well, and that she was equal to the male because she was created from the same substance as the male and at the same time. Her name was Lilith, and she is associated with the night. Her name in fact shares the same root with the word "night" in Arabic (L/Y/L, ليل), and she still lives on in popular culture as the Succubus, or in Arabian mythology as "Qarinah" (قرينة), an old silent woman connected to every man who appears in dreams. Lilith refused to be subservient to Adam, so she grew wings and flew out of Eden. She coupled with the demon Samael and begot hordes of demons until God castrated Samael and made Lilith eat her children. Lilith's domain is the night, where and when she roams, to have sexual encounters with sleeping men and to prey on pregnant women, attempting to steal their unborn babies.

Lilith's domain is exactly what God tried to suppress and banish from His design: formlessness, void, darkness. One might think that it was probably a good thing, what God did, but if we think of this void not as pure emptiness but rather as something containing millions of possible universes, then a million "what ifs?" spring to mind. This is precisely what Lilith has to work with: millions of possibilities, millions of other universes that do not necessarily begin with "Let there be light," where humankind is not necessarily at the center of all creation (and, knowing why Lilith flew away from Eden, universes where Man, or the male element, is not necessarily "on top"), where life is not necessarily intermingled with death, love with hate, war with peace; a gentle universe where it does not hail violently on defenseless parsley leaves. This universe is one where the foolishness of creation, God's design, the design that we've been told for thousands of years is perfection, is replaced by something else, let's call it "tenderness," or "*Hanaan*" (حنان) in Arabic; a universe where things long for each other, where everything waits for the other, listens to the other, and lets the other grow, separate, then return in an endless dance, the dance of life.

Lilith's design is not one of control. She wanted to be free, to liberate herself from the control of the one who was supposedly created as her equal. In order to do so, she first had to blaspheme; by pronouncing the Tetragrammaton, she was able to grow wings and escape to the other side of the world that God designed where millions of other possibilities lay dormant. But in order for these possibilities to come to light, so to speak, the existing order, the order of domination of the equal by his equal, had to be undone; and this is, I presume, the real purpose of the nightly wanderings, the hauntings, the silence. This is the real meaning of the "furthest house erased behind the frontiers of darkness," where light and time are erased, or where everything is undone in order to start anew.

Tony Chakar, *The Eighth Day: God Created the World in Seven Days. This Is the Eighth Day*, 2009.

III

> O you who fly in (the) darkened room(s),
> Be off with you this instant, this instant, Lilith.
> Thief, breaker of bones.
> —Incantation against Lilith, seventh or eighth century BCE, Syria

Undoing the world—God's Design—and opening up all the latent possibilities that were banished into darkness—everything that can be imagined, everything that can be possible—does not go unopposed. In the story of Lilith, it is said that God punished her by making her eat all her children at the rate of one hundred every day. Consequently, the story says that her actions are driven by rage and revenge. Needless to say, this account was written from the side of the established order, from the side of the forces who were victorious, and who are still shaping our world today, dictating what and how we see, listen, smell, taste, and touch; how we establish relationships with everything that is outside of us: people, things, nature, the cosmos.

It's not easy to think of other possibilities, but there are always moments of lucidity. On October 14, 2011, in a small village in Syria called Kafranbel, a banner was held up by the inhabitants during a demonstration. The banner read:

> Down with the regime and the opposition...
> Down with the Arab and Islamic Nations...
> Down with the UN Security Council...
> Down with the world...
> Down with everything
> Occupied Kafranbel 14 10 2011

In the photo documenting the event, we can see the villagers holding the banner and making an upside-down V-for-victory sign with their fingers. After that date, "Down with the World" graffiti was spotted in different cities around the world: Cairo, London, Baghdad, and so on.

The banner sounds nihilistic, bitter, politically naive even. At first glance, one would think that it was written by people who have reached the bottom, the last level of desperation. But the moment of an absolute absence of hope can usually lead to a moment of absolute clarity. The Syrian revolution started as peaceful protests against a dictator. The response of his followers was "Bashar [Assad] or we will burn Syria." And they did. While the world was negotiating with Mr. President, Destroyer of Cities, talking about a "peaceful solution," worrying about ISIS before ISIS even existed, organizing "peace conferences" with self-proclaimed oppositions, sending weapons to different factions, refugees were being treated as if they were garbage, politely referred to as a "problem" to be dealt with. Someone who has lost everything, who takes a perilous journey across seas, forests, borders, cities, and security forces to finally arrive at his or her coveted destination only to discover that he or she is merely a "problem" ... The world order that allows for such a thing to happen should be destroyed and trampled under foot. This order of things should be undone—and this is what the banner is saying. It is not nihilistic; it is an absolutely viable political program. The precise moment that allowed the residents of Kafranbel to see the truth of the world is the moment that allows the rest of us to think of other possibilities, of other worlds where such things are simply not possible.

IV

> I speak to you over cities
> I speak to you over plains
> My mouth is against your ear
> The two sides of the walls face
> my voice which acknowledges you.
> —Paul Éluard

Undoing the world means unlearning everything that we were taught, from the way we see to the way we hear and smell and touch. Everything. Could design, as a specific practice, play a role in that plan? It is possible, but it needs to stop believing in the world-as-it-is in order for that to happen. Design needs to let go of the primacy of the individual, something that is so deeply embedded in the idea of design itself, or else it'll remain stuck in creating objects of comfort (what is comfort? whose comfort?) that would "make life better." I am not advocating for social design or the social responsibility of design; if we are to undo the world, then the first thing to unlearn is all that what we have been taught about the individual, his completeness, his well-being, his emotions, his states, his sociality. Instead of the hermetic individual who finds it increasingly difficult to inscribe themselves in the world, we should opt for another mode of inscription, that of an ongoing, incomplete, enriching conversation that would blow up the borders between us and the things of the world. Or as Friedrich Hölderlin once put it, "*Cette conversation que nous sommes.*" "This conversation that we are."

1 Genesis 1:27

The One-Foot Shop

Rupali Gupte and
Prasad Shetty

A one-foot pan shop at Null Bazaar, Mumbai.

One morning, while a man busied himself opening his shop, Design and Accident entered into a conversation.

Design proclaimed: "I have created humans; humans differ from others because of me; I shape their minds and lives. Their families, friends, gods, religions, organizations, communities, and nations are me; their homes, schools, factories, temples, cities, and graveyards are nothing but me; there is no human universe without me; I am what they eat, wear, and think; I create sense in them; their souls and bodies are shaped by me; they imagine their past and future through me; I create order; I create ethics; I create beauty; I create emotions; there is no life without me; I am life."

Accident enquired: "Are you the one?"

"Yes, I am that one ... But I am not just 'one.' I am different for different humans. I take different forms and therefore am formless; I create unending pasts, presents, and futures and hence am endless; I can create joy for some and grief for others at the same time and hence am characterless; I am many."

"If you have created humans, who created you?"

"I have created myself."

"How?"

"Do you see that shopkeeper who is opening that small shop on the wall? Some years ago, his uncle had made a shop like that after renting a part of a wall. The uncle had embedded the shop a foot inside the wall and also extended it a foot outside on the street. He sold his homemade soaps from this shop. There were many such one-foot shops in the city. The uncle had seen these shops and had decided to build one for himself. The nephew has recently made this one-foot shop after seeing his uncle's shop. He sells assorted perfumes in this shop. I manifested myself in the uncle's shop after the uncle learnt from other shops and then again in the nephew's. The nephew had learnt to make the shop from his uncle. I continuously create myself through humans."

"But who is the first one to make the one-foot shop? The first one who made you?"

"The uncle's shop is right next to the nephew's shop. Do you see it? Isn't the nephew's shop very different from the uncle's? Do you see the doors of the uncle's shop? They open in a peculiar way; the two shutters do not open sideways, but flap upwards and downwards. The shutter that flaps upwards creates shade and the one that flaps downwards creates a seat for the uncle. The uncle has extended his shop one more foot onto the street through his shutters. Now look at the doors of the nephew's shop. The shutters are thick and open sideways. Within their thickness they hide another set of shutters that open in all directions, making the shop look very large and capable of swallowing the world. These shutters have multiplied space for the shop. Within the secret warmth of these tiny spaces created by the shutters, exquisite perfumes are kept. Every human who has made a one-foot shop, learning from other shops, has made her own small change. His shop will become a reference for someone else, who will make yet another small change. After some time, there may be no reminiscence of the one-foot shop and something else would emerge in its place. So there is no one human who is the first one to make me. There is no first human who thought of a one-foot shop or a museum, or a hospital, or a school. These have been created slowly over time and constantly change. I remain in a constant state of becoming. Humans are instruments, who manifest me. But who are you?"

"I am born when two of your manifestations collide. Do you see that man carrying a large box? That box opens into a perfume shop too. This man is a street vendor and creates his shop wherever he stands and opens the box. Look, he is walking on the street where the uncle and nephew have their shops. He is looking for a place to set up. If he sets up close to the nephew's perfume shop, then I will be born. The box vendor's design will collide with the design of the one-foot shop. Many things can happen then. The box vendor may attract the customers from the one-foot shop and annoy the one-foot shopkeeper. The shopkeeper may then call the police or the municipality to drive away the box vendor. Or, the box vendor may attract casual walkers and get them interested in perfumes, and they may then visit the one-foot shop for more options. The box vendor and the one-foot shopkeeper would then become friends and may collaborate. The shopkeeper might then offer the box vendor storage space for the perfume box in one of the shutters. Or the box vendor and the one-foot shopkeeper may not affect each other at all and may remain oblivious of each other's presence. Then again, the box vendor may attract other perfume vendors and the street could turn into a perfume street. Anything can happen here. I am the moment of encounter between two Designs. I am not deliberate and deterministic like you. I am unpredictable. In many ways, I am your other. I also produce life."

"How can you produce life? You are just a consequence of me."

"Do you see that woman's blue house? It was built over many years. Five years ago, the municipality had demolished the house with many others in the neighborhood as they were unauthorized. The day after the demolition, this woman and some of her relatives salvaged some corrugated tin sheets and wood and erected a tiny shed with tin walls and tin roofs. The woman works as a maid in a few houses. She managed to get money from some of her employers. She got a local mason and replaced the four tin walls with brick walls. Later that year, when she got some more money from her chit-fund savings, she built a floor above. But this had to be done very quickly and only on the second or the fourth weekend of the month, as those are holidays for municipal workers and no one comes to monitor construction. So the top floor was built out of tin sheets, as it was very quick to assemble. Some bribe was nevertheless paid to the local police.

Three years ago, another demolition took place nearby. Many shops were broken down. But this demolition was by a developer who had bought the shops and was demolishing them to build a new building. A lot of old furniture was removed from the site. Numerous trash dealers were called to pick up the furniture. When the woman came to hear about this, she rushed to the spot and negotiated a deal with the contractor to get three old showcases from a jeweler's shop. The showcases were brought to her house, and she got a carpenter to modify them to fit them in her house and to make some storage space. The three disparate showcases now melded together beautifully like patchwork on a quilt. The carpenter made many shelves and small storage units within them. From the remaining wood, he made a beautiful tiny table with a glass top. Last year, the woman's brother decided to discard his steel cupboard. She immediately brought the cupboard home, but realized that there was no space to keep it. So she got the carpenter to remove some old shelves from one of the walls and make space for the cupboard. The incremental process through which the house was put together followed a bizarre logic, made up of strange negotiations and unpredictable accesses to resources. This logic, my logic, is different from your logic, which is deliberate and deterministic. You don't produce or shape life here; I do. You actually don't produce or shape life anywhere. I set the tone for you to happen everywhere."

"That is not true; I set the tone for myself. You are just a residue that will wither away. I am the one who creates life. Life happens through my perpetual manifestations. I create desires. Without me, humans would not even know that they are alive."

"You cannot exist without me. I create you by constantly challenging humans. Life happens through me. You are superficial and don't make much difference to humanity. Without me, there is no evolution, no necessity, no need, no desire, and no you."

For eight days, Design and Accident continued their dispute over each other's primacy. Their arguments became intense and aggressive, reaching a point where nothing could be heard anymore. Their conversation had turned into deafening noise. They had both started speaking over each other. By the ninth day, they both said the same thing and sounded like each other's echoes. Soon their voices became one, resonating like the beats of a drum. They kept repeating: "I create life ... I create life ... I create life ..."

Meanwhile, the box vendor had consolidated his shop on the street in front of the one-foot shop. He seemed to be attracting a lot of customers and doing quite well. Though the box vendor had no substantial effect on the one-foot shop, it's keeper did not particularly appreciate the situation; he was not happy with another perfume seller establishing himself so quickly.

Suddenly, while Design and Accident were continuing their arguments, a fight broke out on the street. The woman from the blue house started shouting at the box vendor. She had bought a bottle of perfume from the box vendor just a few days ago, but the scent from the perfume had already disappeared. The woman accused the box vendor of cheating her by selling only water in place of perfume. She asked the box vendor to return her money. The box vendor, on the other hand, counter-accused the woman of finishing off the perfume in the bottle and filling it up with water. The quarrel became noisy and several people gathered around. Design and Accident also became inquisitive about the matter. The one foot shopkeeper saw an opportunity in the situation and soon dived into the quarrel. He took the woman's side and started yelling. He made allegations that the box vendor sold only water in place of perfume. More people from the street joined the shopkeeper and soon the situation became precarious. A few rogues started pushing the box vendor and throwing his bottles around. He was about to be beaten up when a group of four men led by a large old man intervened. These men pushed the rogues away and took the box vendor to safety. The one-foot shopkeeper and the old woman continued to yell, and felt a sense of achievement. They knew that they had been successful in evicting the box vendor from the street.

Accident: "This is puzzling. Why did the people gather?"

Design: "It is because of the spectacle of a street brawl and an inquisitiveness to see how it unfolds."

"How does it matter to them? Were they really interested in the scentless perfumes, or did they desire to see the box vendor beaten up? Where did the inquisitiveness and desire come from?"

"I had nurtured their inquisitiveness and desire."

"Why did some men roughen up the box vendor and others save him?"

"They were both expressing their masculinity. I had nurtured that too."

"But I produced the moment of quarrel for the inquisitiveness and the desires."

"So life gets produced through both of us; one nurtures and the other produces the moments to manifest."

"Yes, but why was the old woman happy with the eviction of the box vendor. She has herself suffered evictions. How did you nurture this desire for someone else's eviction? Where did that come from? Where did that desire come from in the one-foot shopkeeper? He wasn't particularly affected by the box vendor."

"I am not sure anymore. And what about the street? You produced the moment of discord, but the street seemed to take over as if it had a life of its own, that breathed for that moment. You did not produce it and I certainly did not."

"I am not sure anymore either."

The ninth day passed and on the tenth day, Design and Accident start humming together: "We create life, but we are not sure anymore ... We create life, but not sure anymore ..."

They then started looking for the box vendor to see what had happened to him. They found him on another street selling perfume. He had added many legs to his little box which could now perch daintily on the pavement, yet folded away when he left the place. He had painted the insides of his box pink and had made friends with the young girl who sat on the pavement next to him selling flowers. People who came to buy flowers stopped to look at the perfumes in the box and vice versa. As Design and Accident watched the box vendor and hummed their song, Friendship interrupted them, "It's me, it's me—I am the one who created human life—I created community, society, and the public. Without me nothing is possible." Annoyed with this, Design and Accident yelled back at Friendship and all three entered into an argument.

Designer Sex

Rubén Gallo

Marcel Proust's bedroom, including his cork-paneled walls, as recreated at the Musée Carnavalet in Paris, 2009.

There is something elusive about the term "design." English dictionaries tell us the word comes from French, French dictionaries point to an Italian origin (*disegno*, drawing), but modern Italian uses the English word "design." French and German have also adopted the English term, while Spanish prefers *diseño*. Most cultures, it seems, project the idea of design into the sphere of international English and the cool modernity it represents.

In these languages, "design" has several meanings that include: plan, trick, and deceit (as in "to have designs"). In French, for instance, the word *dessein* refers to this kind of cunning: in one of Edgar Allen Poe's stories, this is the term that C. Auguste Dupin inscribes on the purloined letter that inspired Jacques Lacan to write one of his most famous seminars. As Derrida pointed out, Lacan misread *dessein* as *destin*, transforming "design" into "destiny" and producing one of the most famous misreadings in the history of literary theory. Design, Derrida argues, was not destined for this epistemological turn.

Design is a slippery term: it cannot be pinned down to a specific origin, to a specific tradition, and when invoked it often leads to Freudian slips. As we will see in the following cases and their missed encounters with design, "design" becomes an especially unstable territory when it overlaps with sex ...

Proust

Dessein is a term Marcel Proust used often when relating tales of seduction. In *Time Regained*, the last volume of *À la Recherche du temps perdu* (*In Search of Lost Time*), one of the characters uses it to describe Baron de Charlus's seemingly boundless appetite for young men (who seem to get progressively younger as the novel progresses). Near the end, a decrepit Charlus—having suffered several strokes that leave him blind and bound to a wheelchair—is cared for by his lover Jupien, who explains to the narrator that ill-health has not hindered Charlus's "cunning designs":

> One day ... I was returning from one of these supposedly urgent errands, all the faster because I guessed it to have been arranged on purpose [*arrang*ée à dessein], when as I approached the Baron's room I head a voice saying: "What?" and the Baron reply: "You don't mean that this has never happened to you before?" I went into the room without knocking, and imagine my terror! The Baron, misled by a voice which was in fact deeper than is usual at that age (remember that at this period he was completely blind and in the old days, as you know, he had always been partial to men who were not

> quite young), was with a little boy who could not have been ten years old.[1]

Charlus's elaborate designs have a singular purpose: to ensure his erotic satisfaction. And it is the perversity of these designs—today they would be associated with child abuse and in most cultures this passage would provoke the ire of the censors—that interests the narrator. Here, *design* refers to the creative mechanisms—and cunning stratagems—deployed to achieve libidinal satisfaction.

Was Charlus's design successful? It would seem so, since it allowed him to find a sexual partner and to carry the act to completion. But Jupien seems to imply that the adventure concluded with a comic failure, since the Baron made the wrong object choice, in part because of his blindness (there is a blind spot in his design). This point is ambiguous, however: the object-choice seems inappropriate to Jupien—and to most readers—but Charlus seems perfectly satisfied—even if a bit surprised by the outcome of his adventure. His *design* had, in any case, a happy ending.

Proust was not what we could call today a *design queen*. He lived in a dusty apartment filled with the dark, heavy furniture he inherited from his parents. Though he wrote his novel during the heyday of art nouveau—called "modern style" at the time—he had no interest in updating his furnishings or modernizing his living space; visitors recall a dusty and claustrophobic space where the curtains were always drawn and the rooms were airless. Nor was he a *label queen*: in his youth he spent countless evenings *dans le monde*, attending dinners and parties and cocktails, but most of his friends recall him as a poorly dressed man, halfway between a clochard and a ghost. In his diary, Jean Cocteau recalls that one day Proust called and asked him to accompany him to the Louvre so he could see Andrea Mantegna's *Saint Sebastian*: it was midsummer but the novelist, pale as a ghost, showed up wearing a fur coat, gloves, and a scarf. "No one in the galleries looked at the paintings," Cocteau writes. "They were too busy looking at Proust."

Proust is often linked to dandyism, and it is true that many of his friends—like Robert de Montesquiou—and some of his characters—like Charlus and Robert de Saint-Loup—are sharp dressers, but in real life (and especially in his later years) he seems to have been completely uninterested in either his appearance or the design of his clothes. His unfashionable overcoat has recently been the subject of a book by Lorenza Foschini, *Proust's Overcoat*. Could it be that all of Proust's design energies went into literature and sex? One of the most detailed descriptions of interior design in Proust's novel appears in the section devoted to Jupien's male brothel. The living quarters of the Duchesse de Guermantes or Charles Swann are never described in much detail, but the interior of this Temple of Sodom gives rise to pages and pages of information: we learn about the layout of the rooms, the number of stories in the building, and even the design of peepholes to satisfy shy voyeurs. The model for this heterotopic erotic space was a hotel on the rue de l'Arcade owned by a Breton by the name of Albert LeCuziat. During the belle époque there were so many establishments of this kind in Paris—including the Chabanais, arguably the most famous brothel in the world—that historians could write a history of brothel interior design, which was not only decorative but also functional; one designer had to go as far as to conceive a special piece of furniture to allow the Prince of Wales to enjoy, simultaneously, the erotic pleasures afforded by the bodies of two female companions.

Freud

Though Sigmund Freud and Proust never met, their lives and interest overlapped. Freud, in Vienna, published his *Three Essays in the Theory of Sexuality* in 1905, while Proust, in Paris, was busy writing his novel. Both were fascinated by the same topics: sexuality, the workings of memory, and the discontents brought about by the demands imposed on us by civilization.

Freud, like Proust, had little interest in either interior or fashion design. Though he overlapped with Adolf Loos, who revolutionized the concept of living space, the analyst continued to live in a stuffy nineteenth-century apartment on Berggasse, furnished with Persian rugs, heavy Biedemaier objects, and thousands of Greco-Roman and Egyptian statuettes. His dress was equally unmodern: in a time marked by dandies and experimental dressers, Freud opted for the most sober and neutral of outfits (in one of his papers on technique, he even recommended that analysts avoid variations in dress from session to session). He was less disheveled than Proust, but equally unfashionable, and could not have been more different than Lacan, who wore designer shirts and dressed the part of the dandy.

Unlike Proust, Freud seems to have been completely uninterested in interior design. Nowhere in his published work does he describe an interior: neither patients' apartments nor brothels. But he did make one telling comment about design. In the *Three Essays* he writes:

> The progressive concealment of the body which goes along with civilization keeps sexual curiosity awake. This curiosity seeks to complete the sexual object by revealing its hidden parts. It can, however, be diverted ("sublimated") in the direction of art, if its interest can be shifted away from the genitals on to the shape of the body as a whole.[2]

This passage is followed by a most intriguing footnote:

> There is to my mind no doubt that the concept of "beautiful" has its roots in sexual excitation and that its original meaning was "sexually stimulating" ... This is related to the fact that we never regard the genitals themselves, which produce the strongest sexual excitation, as really "beautiful."[3]

Freud would have interpreted the aesthetic pleasure generated by well-designed objects as having a sexual origin and being the result of the sublimations introduced by civilization. More surprisingly, however, is the fact that Freud dismissed the genitals as unaesthetic. This comment, which has been analyzed at length by Leo Bersani, reveals that the analyst considered the genitals as poorly designed (they performed a function, but had a disagreeable form), and that in his view all good design (characterized by an agreeable form) originated with a turning away from the genitals: design as an anti-genital turn. Proust too might have shared Freud's vision of the genitals as ill-designed; his novel include painstaking accounts of seductions but not a single description of the genitals, male or female.

Grindr and the Posthuman

Technology has introduced the specter of designer sex, a decidedly un-Freudian proposition. Apps like Grindr sell its users the fantasy of designing every aspect of their sexual encounters, from the partner—entered in the form of height, weight, hair color, and favorite position—to the site and the duration (nsa or boyfriend material). Freud might have wondered whether the rise of Grindr introduced new sexual perversions—technological fetishism? smartphone onanism?—while Proust, germaphobic and bed-ridden, would have welcomed this app with open arms, just like he listened to the opera using the theatrophone, an invention that allowed users to dial into the opera house and listen during performances.

Grindr allows users to upload photos to their profiles: proof that the stats—6'1", bl/bl, top—correspond to what a potential partner might find upon opening the door. Recently a new website, Lurid Digs, ventured to explore the collateral damage—design accidents—generated by users of this app. While the punctum of profile photos is usually the genital area that Freud deemed unaesthetic, it is possible to examine these images for information on current trends in interior design: users pose, most often in various states of undress, in their living rooms, basements, kitchens, and gardens. The queer eye deployed by the editors at Lurid Digs flows in the exact opposite direction than the process Freud described as sublimation: instead of moving from the unaesthetic genitals to the beautiful artwork, the lurid gaze progresses from attractive body to squalid interior:

> In one caption—"Oh come on dude! At least tidy up a little bit first!"—the viewer does not have access to the model's genitals, but he can appreciate the mess—strewn clothes, dirty laundry, computer cables—crowding the apartment.
>
> Lurid Digs presents its project in the following terms: Interior design began with the first cave dwellers. Most likely it was a gay caveman who decided to paint pictures of running bison and other frolicking animals on the rough walls and low ceilings of his abode. Not only were these flourishes artistic and decorative, they also served as a way to feel more comfortable while living in a hole in the earth.
>
> But, my how times have changed. Gone is the stereotypical association of gay men with good interior design. The Internet has shattered the gay style myth forever with its slew of nude amateur self-portraits that clog bandwidth from New York to Sydney and back again. These Feng Shui-challenged souls have proven over and over again that male homosexuals can be just as color uncoordinated, sloppy and nasty as their straight brethren. Yes, the gap between what defines gay and straight is slowly beginning to zipper shut.[4]

Interestingly, Grindr's terms of service (TOS) do not allow users to post images featuring full frontal nudity. Could it be because they agree with Freud that the genitals are unaesthetic? In any case, the app was design precisely to carry out the kinds of erotic designs that Charlus had in mind when he sent out Jupien on a fake errand. In the new world order of app design, users are postsexual beings. Body contact—such a twentieth-century notion—has been replaced by one-click, slide, and screen taps. Freud once wrote of mechanical excitations: Could these touchscreen excitations characterize the design of a new, twenty-first century sexuality? In any case, Proust's dusty, dark, and stuffy interior—the room of a germaphobic asthmatic—would fit right into the gallery of interior design follies highlighted in Lurid Digs.

1 Marcel Proust, *In Search of Lost Time, Volume VI: Time Regained* (New York: Random House, 2000), 251–52.

2 Sigmund Freud, "Three Essays in the Theory of Sexuality," *The Standard Edition of the Complete Psychological Works of Sigmund Freud*, vol. 6 (London: Hogarth Press, 1953), 155.

3 Ibid., 156.

4 See luriddigs.com.

Storage Space

Giuliana Bruno

"Are we human?"[1] A possible way to answer this question is to ask someone who is not human. So let me ask a "replicant." This, you may recall, was the name given to the nonhuman figures in the Ridley Scott film *Blade Runner* (1982), adapted from Philip K. Dick's novel *Do Androids Dream of Electric Sheep?*[2] The replicant was a robot that understood humans well. A sophisticated type of android, it fulfilled a series of literary dreams and cinematic fantasies: the desire to "replicate" the human.

The question "Are we human?" emerges as a fundamental issue in the effort to design a nonhuman entity in the history of cinema as well as in literature. On the eve of the invention of cinema, Auguste Villiers de l'Isle-Adam's novel *L'Ève future* imagined an android created by Thomas Edison, the inventor of light and film, and marveled at its human-like capacities.[3] Many Frankensteins followed, originating in the literary mind of Mary Shelley and subsequently visualized in the history of film.[4] But the replicant of *Blade Runner* is more equipped to answer our question, for technology has by now grown in its capacity to replicate the human. Anticipating reality, in cinema a human being can now design a nonhuman copy of itself that is no longer approximate, grotesque, or monstrous. The replicant is superior even to the android of Fritz Lang's *Metropolis* (1927), whose body double still suggested mechanical behavior. No longer machinic, this new replicant is perfectly designed. It is a "skin-job," and it appears utterly human.

But is it human? Yes, it has the looks. But to look human is not enough to be human. What is the difference, then, if a flawlessly engineered body shows no such difference? Well, the main thing is: the replicant does not have a memory. With no sense of the past, it not only lacks a history but the capacity to recall and to store personal and collective events in its mind. A replicant is unable to express the affect that a memory brings to human features.

To be human, then, means to have a cultural memory. The replicants knew this, and did everything they could to fabricate visual memory. They were obsessed with collecting photographs that could make up for the memories they lacked. If they could only have a past in this way, they could possibly have a future, and live like humans. In the end, then, all the replicants needed in order to be considered human was an archive. Perhaps they simply needed the internet.

Art of the Archive

The story of the replicant asks us to care for our memories, to cultivate their relational qualities and carefully reflect upon forms of cultural amnesia and obsessive recording. It impels us to consider the design of memory and the configuration of our cultural archives, for, in turn, this is what designs the human condition. At stake here is an important aspect of the design of the self.

This tale also suggests that, in some way, we have all become replicants. We are in constant search of ways to create, store, and recall our collective memories. The internet has become a quotidian source and repository of shared information, turning into a vast, virtual storage space. Shelving away our lives has turned into a daily habit, even an obsession, and takes up considerable amounts of our time. We constantly manage the files of our professional and personal lives, and deposit loads of visual and written documents of our collective existence in our computers and various digital devices. As soon as we record the development of our life, we store it away. But are we all archivists? Does the capacity to store information constitute an archive? Is the database machinic and the archive human? If we wish to understand how the design of cultural memory designs human culture, we should go to the root of the issue. What is this fundamental desire to memorialize, and to archive? "Archive fever," as Jacques Derrida reminds us, is a phenomenon that has roots in the word *arkhē*, which "names at once the *commencement* and the *commandment*."[5] The term contains, and correlates, two principles at once. The first configuration of the archival is "where things *commence*—[the] physical, historical, or ontological principle"; the second is "the principle according to the law ... *there* where authority, social order are exercised, *in this place* from which *order* is given."[6] The archive thus stores within itself the origin of the foundational principles that give it its name; it holds its very memory. But it also tends to forget this history, especially when resistance to inherent order is expressed.

Think of the way the archive has emerged as inspiration as well as model in the visual arts. Here, the idea of the archive has often arisen precisely to counteract machinic behavior and to resist commencement, order, and completion. A poignant example is Gerhard Richter's artistic archive, *Atlas* (1962–2013), a collection of the pictures, both historical and personal, that the artist has accumulated across five decades.[7] It is an archive of images of landscapes, urban plans, views, travel sites, peopled places, bodyscapes, objects, and interiors, often marked by slashes of paint. The fragments are set in an orderly fashion but with no systematizing goal or taxonomic obsession to control the contents. In this mnemonic archive, the photographic material is not forced into fixed schemes of memorization; nor is it driven to exhaustion, according to a logic of enclosure. The work is boundless, and yet bound. This cartographic archive is not designed to give categoric form to the knowledge it presents; rather, it conveys a material work of mourning.

Richter's *Atlas* thus presents an archive that works against its own principles. He is not alone in the effort to design such an archive of human memory, which is, in a way, like a fictitious museum. Yet the art of the archive goes beyond the use of pictures and found objects, the remaking of cabinets of curiosities, or the reenactment of the narratives of former cultural archives. In some way, the contemporary artistic archive has had to come to terms with the old laws of the *arkhē,* which have reemerged in the digital age in the form of the systems and logic of the database. This phenomenon provokes in art a discussion of the difference between an archive and a database, and the possible tension between human and nonhuman factors. For his part, Hal Foster argues that "the archives at issue here are not databases ... ; they are recalcitrantly material, fragmentary rather than fungible, and as such they call out for human interpretation, not machinic reprocessing."[8]

The issue of materiality is complex and full of nuances that challenge binary oppositions between archive and database, or human and machinic design. Historically, informational databases were themselves recalcitrantly material, and they are currently subject to a process of rematerialization by contemporary artists in immaterial ways. Take the Archivio Storico del Banco di Napoli in Italy, three hundred and thirty rooms filled with records of every monetary transaction that ever took place in this ancient bank. In the largest assembly of this kind in the world, the information—mechanically taken down by a human—is bound in dusty leather volumes and even hangs from the ceilings, collected in suspended columns of paper. At the end of a corridor, in a dark room, one now encounters a moving projection of still images onto the storage space. In the installation by photographer Antonio Biasiucci, titled *Moltitudini* (2016), a multitude of inscriptions and a population of faces are projected as if emerging out of the informational material, in this way drawing out historical narratives.[9] After all, when the transactional records dryly inform us that the Prince of San Severo bought alchemical tools and cadavers on such-and-such dates and for these exact sums of money, the alchemy of a city can come to life.

Antonio Biasiucci, *Moltitudini*, 2016. Installation view, Archivio Storico del Banco di Napoli.

Material Archives

We are witnessing renewed attention to informational modes and models in various ways, which are in turn informing the design of the archive. In speaking of contemporary visual culture, David Joselit has pointed to a "shift from object-based aesthetics in both architecture and art to a network aesthetics premised on the emergence of form from populations of images," which constitute "formats," that is, "dynamic mechanisms for aggregating content."[10] This shift demands further reflection on the status of things such as images, their forms of collection, strategies of aggregation, patterns of memorization, and dynamics of circulation—in other words, on the archival design.

It is interesting to note that an intense interest in material culture and a deep fascination with the materiality of the archive has emerged in the digital age, characterized by networks and their seeming immateriality. New disciplines, methods, and forms of scholarship have originated from this tension between material and immaterial culture, and they express this very tension in their development. Think of the rise of "media archaeology," which, in some ways, is an (in)discipline of all things archival.[11] In this new field of media studies, one can see a deep interest in the material history of things combined with a fascination for systems and networks. In some aspects of this archaeological excavation of mediums and their cultural memory, emphasis is put on machinic conditions, organizational principles, and systems of cataloguing.[12] At times one senses an impulse to search for methods to control the ever changing flux of stored information. But rather than reverting back to the *arkhē* of archiving, one could more productively resist this impulse and instead work through the dynamics and tensions expressed by the aggregates of disparate mnemonic materials.

Materiality is, in fact, a gray zone, and a place of complex mnemonic relations. It is not a question of materials themselves or a matter of "thingness" per se; rather, it concerns the substance of material relations and connections and how they are configured on the surface of different media.[13] We live in an active zone of encounter and admixture, a site of mediation and projection, memory and transformation. The surface of objects and the structure of entities, including screens and their networks, haptically convey energies, for we entrust to our screens memories that are layers of experience and residual existence. (Im)material things such as screens—architectural, cinematic, digital—activate connections between persons and with objects and have acted as the surface of material relations throughout modern culture. Concern with such gray materiality, then, does not put an end to the agency of human subjectivity, for this is fundamentally a relational matter.

So, ultimately, the question "Are we human?" concerns the issue of how to implement our relational capacities. One must resist the oppositions between human and nonhuman and the rooted conviction that things are the opposite of persons, and finally recognize the full extent of the dynamic connections and interactive designs that have shaped the history of cultural productions, as well as their forms of memorialization. To this end, as the political theorist Jane Bennett would also suggest, it becomes ever more necessary to draw out the vibrant entanglements and vital force of things, and to rethink the agency of assemblages.[14]

This means putting the body, and the body of things, back into the work of cultural design. In fact, as the philosopher Roberto Esposito proposes, a possible way to untangle the "metaphysical knot between thing and person is to approach it from the point of view of the body. Because the human body does not coincide with the person or the thing, it opens up a perspective that is external to the fracture that one projects on the other."[15] Indeed, the body is not a singular entity but rather functions as a social, relational matter, and as a vehicle of mediation. It is not the sole property of humans, for there is also a body of things, even immaterial ones, which themselves have a vibrant material consistency and form a corpus of aggregations and systems of connections that are also mnemonic. In this archival sense, a corpus constitutes a "medium," that is, a form of relational in-betweenness. It is a shared depository and interactive material. Thinking in this hybrid, material way, one can activate relations that are not reducible to a binary logic of opposition between humans and nonhumans and instead implement the flow of intersections, interactions, and transformations that produce the cultural design of the self. After all, thanks also to biotechnologies and techniques of replication, these distinctions are now definitively blurred. The human body itself has become an aggregate of different corpora and data, with mixed organic and inorganic elements. In the end, we are all replicants, equipped with digital memories.

1 This question formed the theme of the 3rd Istanbul Design Biennial 2016, curated by Beatriz Colomina and Mark Wigley.
2 Philip K. Dick, *Do Androids Dream of Electric Sheep?* (New York: Doubleday, 1968).
3 Auguste Villiers de l'Isle-Adam, *Tomorrow's Eve* (1886), trans. Robert Martin Adams (Urbana: University of Illinois Press, 2001).
4 Mary Wollstonecraft Shelley, *Frankenstein: or, The Modern Prometheus* (1818) (Oxford: Oxford University Press, 2008).
5 Jacques Derrida, "Archive Fever: A Freudian Impression," *Diacritics* 25, no. 2 (Summer 1995): 9.
6 Ibid.
7 See *Gerhard Richter: Atlas of the Photographs, Collages and Sketches*, eds. Helmut Friedel and Ulrich Wilmes (New York: D.A.P., in association with London: Anthony d'Offay, and New York: Marian Goodman Gallery, 1997), exhibition catalogue, which features a catalogue raisonné of the oeuvre. For a critical reading, see, among others,

Benjamin Buchloh, "Gerhard Richter's *Atlas*: The Anomic Archive," *October* no. 88 (Spring 1999): 117–45; and Giuliana Bruno, *Atlas of Emotion: Journeys in Art, Architecture and Film* (London: Verso, 2002), ch. 10.

8 Hal Foster, "An Archival Impulse," *October* no. 110 (Fall 2004): 5.

9 Artist Antonio Biasiucci has also produced a large photographic installation, titled *Codex* (2016), that revisits the same archive. See Antonio Biasiucci, *Codex: L'Archivio Storico del Banco di Napoli*, ed. Gianluca Riccio (Rome; Contrasto, 2016).

10 David Joselit, *After Art* (Princeton, NJ: Princeton University Press, 2013), 43, 55.

11 For a survey of this field of scholarship, see Erkki Huhtamo and Jussi Parikka, "Introduction: An Archaeology of Media Archaeology," in *Media Archaeology: Approaches, Applications, and Implications*, ed. Huhtamo and Parikka (Berkeley: University of California Press, 2011), 1–21.

12 See, for example, Wolfgang Ernst, *Digital Memory and the Archive* (Minneapolis: University of Minnesota Press, 2013).

13 For further treatment of this subject, see Giuliana Bruno, *Surface: Matters of Aesthetics, Materiality, and Media* (Chicago: University of Chicago Press, 2014).

14 See Jane Bennett, *Vibrant Matter: A Political Ecology of Things* (Durham, NC,: Duke University Press, 2010).

15 Roberto Esposito, *Persons and Things*, trans. Zakiya Hanafi (Cambridge: Polity Press, 2015), 10.

Real Estate Porn; or, How to Liberate Us from Being Slaves of Our Own Houses

Ingo Niermann

The New Old Gentry

Housing is meant to make our lives more comfortable from the outside. Besides walls that protect us from hostile circumstances, we have equipped the interior with an accumulation of tools and devices. To be spoiled by all those belongings has only been followed by even more things. Digitalization marked a shift in the minimalism of interior design; while it was first about shrinking, smoothing, and hiding those tools and devices, 3-D printing and the cloud enable us to live with almost nothing aside from what we need at this very moment.

The only thing that cannot be expanded out of nowhere is our exclusive living area. Earth's surface is fixed and the population continues to grow while further building is restricted. The result is a cult of vast, empty, naturally lit space, in densely populated areas, if possible. After thousands of years of civilization and mass murder, we are talking square meters. The medium-rich are selling shares or their companies to buy architectural jewels, devote years of their lives to polishing them, live in them like in a shrine, and make a living by occasionally renting it out for special occasions.

Walled space has become the ultimate luxury. Even more—as everyone needs a minimum of shelter—to have a place to put a bed and your clothes is just as important as having an address to gain the status and benefits of a full citizen. Still, while lots of states guarantee their inhabitants food, clothes, and health care, they don't guarantee shelter. At most they pay your rent up to a certain amount.

Virtually everywhere on earth, the prices to rent or buy residential space have been rising faster than the average income, the result of which is a mass speculation for a further rise in prices. If you don't buy a house or apartment now, you probably won't be able to afford a similar one for the rest of your life. You are under the gun to start climbing the real estate ladder as fast as possible, and to already include space for your eventual kids so that you won't be forced to move to a worse part of town when you actually start a family. Couples stay together only because of the decent piece of real estate they once got together. Maybe the piece of real estate is so exquisite that it becomes the true love interest, effectively turning the marriage into a ménage à trois. *Ghost*, *8½ Weeks*, *Sleepless in Seattle* ... since the 1980s, many famous erotic thrillers and romantic comedies have shown an uninhibited level of real estate porn.

Nothing has created more millionaires than the worldwide boom in real estate. Yet at the same time it enslaves a majority of people to a life-long mortgage and flawless career. With prices for real estate skyrocketing, it gets harder and riskier for every new generation to secure decent housing with their income. Even if you could sell something you were able to buy and make a profit worth a couple of annual salaries, it wouldn't be worth moving into a cheaper area as its underperforming job market and poor infrastructure would cost you even more.

A decent inheritance is the last chance. People who don't have to pay their rent or take out a mortgage are the new old gentry: highly privileged but often hardly solvent. Maybe it's the creative class, but I know an increasing number of people who own huge flats and have hardly enough to eat. The rising cost of utilities are eating them up, and renting out the flat can be against house rules. Or, renting can make property lose value. In Germany, this can be up to fifty percent, as it's quite difficult to kick out tenants, and rent can only be increased slowly without renewing the contract. As a result, many private owners prefer to keep their property empty or only offer it on Airbnb.

Airbnb officially started as the possibility to rent out your flat when you are not home, or to rent out an extra room when you don't need it. But in fact, Airbnb reduces permanent living space, and by increasing the possible income from owning flats or houses, prices are being pushed up even further.

The Landlord's Guilt

Six years ago I had saved and inherited enough money to buy a decent flat in a mildly gentrified part of Berlin. Compared to other European capitals and many other German cities, prices in Berlin were still amazingly low, just like the rents and wages. The population hadn't been growing since reunification, even though Berlin was Germany's new capital and the country's economy was finally booming again. Berlin's economy was still doing bad and there weren't enough international bohemians moving to the city to compensate for a new suburban flight. During the Cold War, the Western, capitalist part of the city had been encircled by a wall, and the Eastern, socialist part had left people without personal fortune, so the possibility of building your own house outside the city was still new.

But the global 2008 economic crisis in general, and the 2009 Euro crisis in particular, was about to have a drastic impact on Berlin's real estate market. The crisis had been triggered by mortgages being belligerently issued to Americans with precarious income. From a self-fulfilling prophecy, the housing boom had turned into a worldwide pyramid scheme. To stop the crisis, national banks flooded the market with cheap money. Yet as interest rates plummeted, where could money be safely invested? Again, the main idea was private housing.

Whether at art events in Berlin or private parties in Nairobi, everywhere I went I heard people talking about Berlin's spectacularly cheap real estate. People hardly knew the city but their pronunciation of up-and-coming quarters like Moabit, Schöneberg, or Neukölln was remarkably good.

I had been based in Berlin for more than twenty years and finally I could profit from my deep knowledge of the city. Different from the outsiders, I would focus my search on Wedding, a part of the city where I had been living for a couple of years. Wedding neighbors Mitte, the historical center of the city, and despite its exquisite location, gentrification was still sparse.

The longer I searched, the more it became clear that it would be hard to find a flat that I would like as much as the one where I lived. My flat was small but extremely quiet, had a lot of light and a spacious balcony. Situated on a pedestrian road with no shops, gentrification could not manifest in an accumulation of neat cafes and shops. And still, Mitte and Prenzlauer Berg were only a stone's throw away.

But of course, my rent would rise and the house could eventually be sold to a rigorous investor or even torn down. Besides, at some point in my life I might stop traveling a lot and be fed up with living on my own in only one room. So I continued to search for a two- or three-room apartment in Wedding. As I wouldn't need this apartment right away, my search wasn't limited to ones that were already vacant. I wouldn't want to be a mean investor, and I would be fine as long as the current tenants paid enough rent to cover running costs and taxes.

When I visited the first flats I realized that either I detested the tenants so much that I would never be able to deal with them, or I liked them too much to make them fear that one day I could kick them out to move in myself. Just the idea of standing again in someone's apartment as its potential owner became unbearable. Renting out an apartment was far too personal to be acceptable as a business relationship. I couldn't do it, just as I could never go to war.

The Housing Lottery

The fear of losing your familiar shelter might be banal compared to the fear of dying from sudden cancer or being killed. In the worst case you have to commute longer, have less space and less sunlight. But unlike finding a job or staying healthy, we get no practical support in securing our living space (neither from scientists nor from politicians), making it one of the things that causes us to feel most responsible for ourselves. A large part of our courage and energy is absorbed by finding and paying off a proper living space. Real estate is the enemy of love, fun, and generosity; it makes our lives fearful and boring. We don't own our houses, but our houses own us.

"What have you been doing all your life?"

"Oh, I secured a really nice piece of property. It's unaffordable now."

Only for the really rich is it not enough to reside in an architectural jewel. They instead feel compelled to activate their villas, gardens, and islands for very special moments and encounters, or to transform them into residencies for artists or shelters for refugees.

What would a society that provided generous hospitality to everyone look like? A "basic habitat"—similar to a basic income—is not easy to offer. People have different needs and desires, and existing houses cannot be cut into similar slices as in land reform. But perhaps every year, or every other year, there could be a compulsory lottery to redistribute housing among an entire population.[1] As personal material belongings are no longer so relevant, moving from one living space to another is simple. And if you were to draw a small living space in the lottery, you could put most of your belongings in storage. You could also put them on display from time to time in a public showroom. Conversely, if you draw a huge space, you can earn extra money through aquaponics, an illegal swap, or the production of actual real estate porn.

The redistribution lottery is a transitory phase until genetic engineering (à la CRISPR) enables a future us to comfortably live outdoors in any climate. When that time comes, there'll be endless virtual possibilities to find seclusion, when desired. People who continue to insist on a vast physical space just for themselves will appear as unacceptable burdens on the environment.

1 This concept goes back to Thomas More's *Utopia* (1516): "At every ten years' end they shift their houses by lots."

Our Heads Are Round, Our Hands Irregular

Hu Fang

1.

I saw the white light through the monitor of my mobile phone—a burst of white light that spread from the upper-left corner of the frame the moment the surveillance camera at Istanbul's Atatürk airport captured the detonation of the suicide bomb—and this fleeting white light meant that some people's lives had been cruelly taken from them without any warning.

This was neither the first nor the last time a suicide bomber would strike innocent people in a modern public space, and it is precisely due to the innocence of their victims that these violent incidents create such great terror: no one will be spared until the objective of the violence can be achieved.

This was neither the first nor the last time that I would be struck by such news through the tiny screen of my Apple iPhone. Gripped in my hand, the iPhone almost becomes an extension of my senses, and it is exactly through such technological sensibility that we inevitably become a part of the contemporary order. This order was built up by technological acceleration, the innumerable plans to "improve" the social system and raise the quality of life that were brought about by the Industrial Revolution. In the course of the construction of this new order, human life was increasingly subjected to the active intervention of knowledge/power—the ongoing phenomenon described by Michel Foucault as "biopolitics." If technology (which of course includes politics) is an extension of human sensoria, and design a means for the integration of technology into daily life, then today, all thresholds that technology and design attempt to reach and encompass are already extending into the body itself—to the control and management of life's resources.

The suicide attack throws the corporeal body—the core of biopolitics—back into sacrifice. Suicide bombers typically employ simple techniques to make homemade bombs that are assembled from cheap, everyday materials. Escaping the control of the global military-industrial complex (which also means that of the lucrative military-industrial economy), such devices are expedient for allowing nonspecialists to join the ranks at any time. What the combination of the "homemade bomb" and the suicidal body has brought about is perhaps the most severe challenge to the history of humanity: after large-scale modern warfare, the battlefield has shifted to everyday space. In fact, while the world's consumers are caught up in buying their iPhone 6s and iPhone 6 Plus's, these homemade bombs are being made out of fertilizer.

2.

> The great turning point in the modern history of corn ... can be dated with some precision to the day in 1947 when the huge munitions plant at Muscle Shoals, Alabama, switched over to making chemical fertilizer.
> —Michael Pollan[1]

At the end of World War II, the US government found that it was stuck with a tremendous surplus of military-grade ammonium nitrate, the principal ingredient in explosives. In response, experts in the Department of Agriculture came up with an excellent idea: the ammonium nitrate could be turned into a source of nitrogen for plants and sprayed onto fields as fertilizer. And thus fertilizer was born, through the peacetime reappropriation of the war apparatus. But who could know whether this would truly dispel the ghosts of modern warfare?

More than a half-century after the invention of fertilizer, bombs combining ammonium nitrate and fuel oil—so-called "fertilizer bombs"—are now widely used by today's international terrorists. As one of the main ingredients of nitrogen fertilizers, ammonium nitrate, along with fuel oil, can be easily purchased at low cost, therefore lending them the name "poor bombs."

The "poor bomb" is derived from the material of industrial society and produced according to homemade methods that even evoke the idea of "poor design," or any social project applied in a DIY sense to resolving the ills of poverty. With its means of production and its declared objective intricately linked, the poor bomb can easily become a radical statement of critique with no compunction about the price of other people's lives, making the terror it spreads reach far and be pervasive. When a high-school student in Texas, Ahmed Mohamed, put together his own homemade clock, it was mistaken for an explosive device and the student was detained by the police. Although Mohamed was released two days later, just what is it that has made the distinctions between homemade explosives and homemade clocks—between the capacity to destroy lives and the capacity to investigate the world—so tenuous?

3.

As a basic means of investigating the world, "self-design" endows us all with the potential to explore our relations to it. But the value of life has become so skewed, and the boundary between preserving and destroying life so fragile, that when we talk about "self-design" today we must confront this situation and ask: How can we regain our curiosity about the diversity of life? How can we relearn to turn the limited resources for survival into the conditions for living together? It's like an exercise in reestablishing everyday routines in the midst of a crisis.

Where are the technologies for protecting, preserving, and providing for life? Through what media must the secrets of human existence and culture ultimately pass in order to be propagated? This is how "craft" once again enters the picture. In contrast to the somewhat romantic "Arts and Crafts movement" of the start of the last century, the significance of "contemporary craft" lies not only in craft practices that continue the "traditional categories" of the "past," but also extend to all kinds of creative labor that turn our bodies into media; through people's intelligence, vision, and technology, the material elements of survival are transformed and molded into the shareable material of human life experiences. As such, sound technicians, film editors, instrument makers, storytellers, cooks, landscapers, practitioners of Chinese medicine, brewers, and beekeepers all could be thought of as the "craftsmen" of today.[2] In encountering these laboring individuals, in touching and in listening to materials that are intimately connected to the experience of human existence, we can perceive life forces and the meridians of cultural practices of survival, such that it even becomes possible to recover the original power of daily practice possessed by "craft" itself and build connections between self and community, between "my existence" and "the other's existence." What accumulates through day after day of tempering is not hate but an appreciation and reverence for life.

"Our heads are round so our thoughts can change direction." These words of Francis Picabia are perhaps the best encapsulation of "human design," and, in the end, "as lacking as humans are in wisdom, so that of nature is all the more profound."[3] Life is an extremely arduous journey, and our deteriorating senses and bodies, already accustomed to air conditioning, often appear powerless when confronting such an expansive and profound world as ours. But even so, this is neither the first nor last time that humanity has sought in the synthesis of mind and hands, body and material, the ability to reconcile ourselves with the world. Nor is there any need to overemphasize the morality of "craft," as "the truly moral age is a time when morals are no longer even thought about, rather than a time when they are constantly glorified. Could not the same be said for craft?"[4] Among the achievements of human labor that can be shared by "craft," people may constantly wonder at the richness of humanity and the vastness of the world, but the power of death always hovers behind that of life.

Franz Kafka's *In the Penal Colony* comes to mind here, in which the proud apparatus that once represented absolute justice has gradually deteriorated amid the world's vicissitudes. Over time this precisely designed "peculiar" apparatus (one of the components of which is indeed called the "Designer") has become a completely irrational killing machine. Except for people like the Officer who "dedicates" his body to the apparatus in willing "sacrifice," later generations will no longer believe in, and instead struggle to get away from, this machine that requires human lives as its lubricant.

Translated from the Chinese by Andrew Maerkle.

1 Michael Pollan, *The Omnivore's Dilemma: A Natural History of Four Meals* (New York: Penguin, 2006), 41.

2 In "The Storyteller: Reflections on the Works of Nikolai Leskov," Walter Benjamin writes, "The storytelling that thrives for a long time in the milieu of work—the rural, the maritime, and the urban—is itself an artisan form of communication, as it were." He continues, "In fact, one can go on and ask oneself whether the relationship of the storyteller to his material, human life, is not itself a craftsman's relationship." From *Illuminations: Essays and Reflections*, trans. Harry Zohn (Random House, 1968).

3 Yanagi Soetsu, "Kitaru beki kougei" (The Crafts of the Future), in *Kougei no michi* (*The Way of Crafts*) (Tokyo: Guroriasosaete, 1929); published in Chinese by Guangxi Normal University Press, 2011. [Passages cited here and below are translated from the original Japanese by the English translator.]

4 Ibid.

The Birth of Design

Spyros Papapetros

Frederick Kiesler, Table on “Abstraction” and “Design,” preliminary illustration for *Magic Architecture* (ca. mid-1940s).

Per Frederick Kiesler, design is born from a crocodile—a reptile caged inside the architect's genealogical table alongside a solitary piece of metal.[1] Were it not for the vertical line dividing the two figures, one could picture the crocodile snapping the hard rock with its open jaws and swallowing, slowly but steadily, the large mineral specimen. Design, Kiesler implies, is born by the omnivorous appetite of animal beings seeking to assimilate the most indigestible things, including inorganic substances by a transgressive territorial act of cross-species incorporation.

The second row of this evolutionary chart displays the first offspring of the crocodile, another crocodile, but unlike the one of "nature," a larger, smoother, and "abstract" animal-machine. Just like the metal slab is a different *animal* from the crude rock above, so is this "abstract" *superanimal* a different *thing* from its natural progenitor: its atrophied feet having turned into pliers, its tail into an airplane's metal end, and the winding texture of the reptile's scaly skin minimized into an undulating line of welding seams connecting patches of metal cladding. The croc has devoured the rock and is now ready to snatch the metal slab as well—the rectangular formation of its belly anticipating the homophagic inception. Design for Kiesler is birthed by such a sequence of unlikely cannibalisms between animate and inanimate objects. The inorganic animal of the "abstract" crocodile is the original "product design" of both the rock and the reptile, suggesting that the lines of descent in this table are more diagonal than vertical. Based on such diagonal correspondences, the evolution of design proceeds along a zigzagging pathway, as marked by the lines of the crocodile's crusty texture.

Another preliminary draft from Kiesler's book manuscript on "Magic Architecture" explains this design process: "Design is abstracted from nature (animals, plants, rocks), as metals are abstracted from nature (ore)."[2] Design, then, is the combined product of mental abstraction and material extraction—a physical pulling from the surfaces of animal skin and geological ground, which in the architect's diagram bear more than a morphological affinity with one another. A series of enumerated steps unravels the knots of such extraction. From the "natural animal" of the crocodile (1), a patch of its skin is extracted and framed by a rectangle via the act of "painting" (2). This chaotic bundle of lines then turns into the regular *cosmos* of a geometric "ornament," which is the first work of design, *proper* (3).

Returning to the third transformation from the first chart, we see that the body of the crocodile is replaced by an ornamental swatch bearing a pattern that emulates the zigzag line previously crisscrossing the crocodile's metallic skin. Early-twentieth-century ethnologists note that African ornamentation is marked by a pronounced presence of snakes and lizards—the terrestrial animals

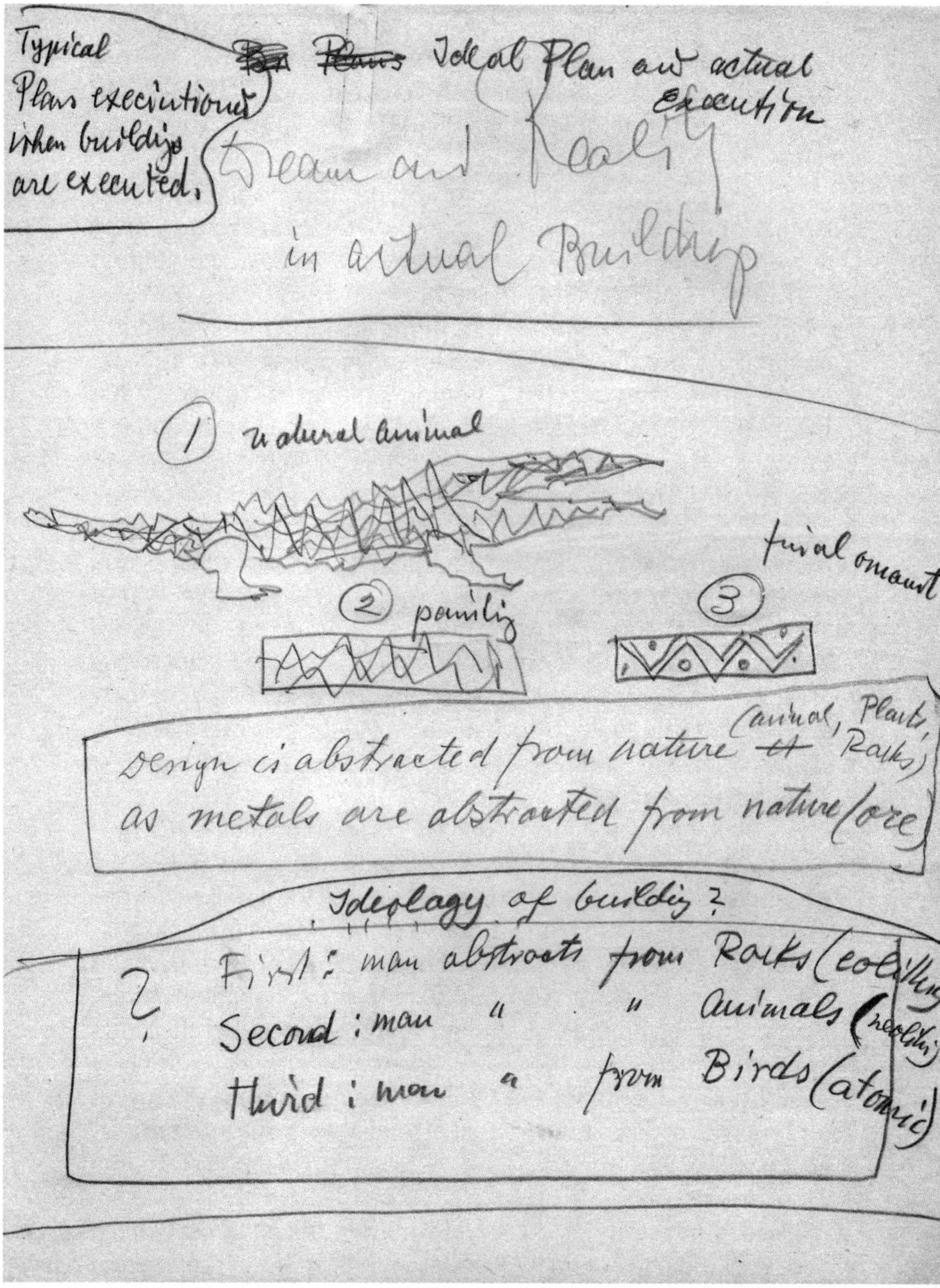

Frederick Kiesler, Notes and sketches on "Abstraction" and "Ideology of Building?," preliminary draft for *Magic Architecture* (ca. mid-1940s).

that move closest to the ground. There, the earthly ground often transforms into a painted background for the ornamental arrangement of the lizards' diminutive appendages drawn in orthogonal schematizations.[3] The ornament extracted from Kiesler's "big lizard," on the other hand, knows no distinction between figure and ground; it is all ground punctuated by a series of dots resembling the circular eyes of the "abstract" crocodile. Just when we thought the crocodile had vanished, it now looks at us from all around; anywhere we stand we could be stepping on its tail.

To the right of this swatch, the metal slab has given birth to a spiral ornament made of wire. Thus, the geometric abstraction of the painted ornament is supplemented by a three-dimensional (albeit flat) artifact that signals the emergence of "applied" arts, a system of detachable nonnatural layers. Design is fully born when these ornamental surfaces become attached to the human body, which is what happens in the fourth and final stage of Kiesler's diagram through textile art and metallurgy, as represented by a fabric skirt and metal earring worn by an African female. These bodily layers elevate both the subject and the artifact to the plateau of what Kiesler in his idiomatic English calls "over-nature"—essentially a *supernature*, amalgamating *superhumanity* with *superanimality* through the transformative power of design.

And so it is that the human body, or rather, the human type—as morphed by the anthropological principles of ethnologists such as Leo Frobenius (whose works Kiesler had in his library and cites in his writings)[4]—stands as the end result of this birthing process. Here, we move from the abstraction of nature to applied "art" and the *supernature* of the ornamentally enhanced human—not in a vertical progression, as the orthogonal structure of the table would have us believe, but in a spiral rotation, reminiscent of the wire earring. The spiral artifact posing in the middle of the chart is not simply another product of design, but an ideogram for its evolutionary process, following which, the culminating point of the human is at once a return to its animal or mineral origin and a deviation from it by an increasing margin. The fact that this spiral is made of metal "wire" gives us another perspective onto the affinities of this primeval adornment with man's technological extension via modern infrastructural networks, bridging the gap between the "eons" of prehistory and the "Atomic" era inhabited by Kiesler.

The reciprocal displacements and material transformations in Kiesler's table suggest that design consists of a periodic sequence of subtractions and additions. In the chart's first two levels, abstraction equals a physical tearing from the raw material and the animal skin. In the lower two, the design of bodily ornament restores the attachment of the natural specimen (either animal or mineral) to the earthly ground by affixing the sample of an artificial ground onto the surface of the human body, whose own geological consistency is entirely restructured by the inorganic character of the ornamental envelope. In that, the architect's evolutionary chart depicts not simply the birth of design but also the birth of the human *by* design.

The chart itself is the ultimate design. The principle of "sympathetic magic" (a term from James Frazer's *The Golden Bough* that exists in Kiesler's library in a two-volume edition), where "like produces like" (and, here even *eats* like) simultaneously consolidates and unravels the chart's vertical composure.[5] The same telepathic force allows the objects of the right column to communicate with those of the left while maintaining their distance. We could imagine an expanded history or even a historiography of design based not on a vertical genealogy of manmade artifacts but a series of reciprocal exchanges between nature and "over-nature" that are not limited to the domain of the human, but are willing to include the animal territory of the crocodile and its elective affinities with metal.

Ornaments and Implements

The "birth of design," writes Kiesler, describes the moment when "man discovers his capacity to convert his own body into a dream image through painting or makeup."[6] This conversion proceeds from the thick surface of painting to the three-dimensionality of physical bodies and manmade artifacts, yet also maintains the ethereality of a "dream image," projected most prominently on the screen of the human skin, the first canvas of human design. While other design (pre)histories present the hand axe—a stone implement detachable from the body—as the first product of human artifice, Kiesler prioritizes a form of design that is applied onto the body itself. The body performs both as an instrument and a surface for design upon which the instrument *draws*.

Design proceeds by a leap to the animal. The facial makeup Kiesler cites is patterned to imitate animal skin—such as the striped fur of a tiger—in the attempt to endow the wearer with a semblance of the superhuman strength of the animal. Paint here represents a tectonic psychological support that is embedded on the surface of the body. The first human design is the image of an animal worn on top of the human skin, allowing the human to shift places in the evolutionary continuum instead of consolidating its superior position. The painted skin in this case is an implement (both for attack and defense), as well as an article of bodily adornment. For Kiesler, there is essentially no ontological distinction between ornament and implement—two object categories that are rigorously differentiated

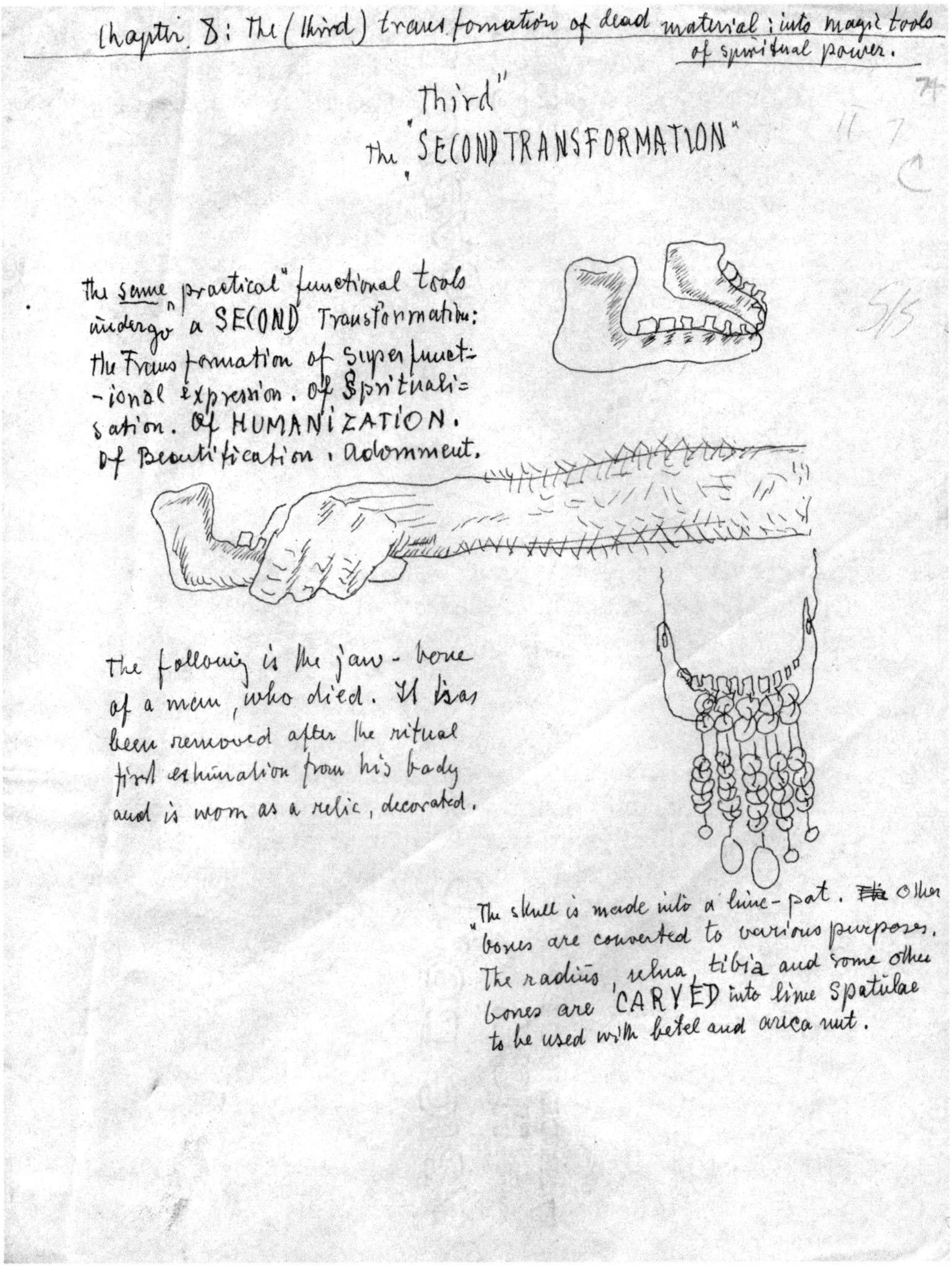

Frederick Kiesler, Drawing and notes on "The SECOND TRANSFORMATION (transformation of dead materials into magic tools of spiritual growth)," illustration and diagram for *Magic Architecture* (ca. mid-1940s).

in modern histories of design (the distinction even becoming constitutional in certain histories of modern architecture).

In another diagram of "transformation" illustrating the process of "humanization" in tandem with techniques of human "adornment" and "beautification," Kiesler draws a human hand (with intense hair growth) holding a jawbone. The bone is initially employed as a weapon or functional implement, but is then turned into a "decorated relic" by hanging strings made of plant or animal fibers with small natural objects attached to them from the jaw's remaining teeth.[7] The previously inert instrument is now a vibrant decorative relic oscillating by the swaying movement of its pendants. Here, design coincides with the origin of adornment, since when it was used as weapon or spatula, the jaw bone was essentially unaltered. Echoing this original "transformation," adornment constantly reclaims objects of design and tries to redesign them for its own (side-)purposes.

Atomic Birds

The final design stemming from Kiesler's crocodile is neither an implement nor an ornament. It is, in fact, not a material object at all, but another grand theoretical and historical schema comparable to the table we saw earlier. Returning to the second sketch discussed earlier, with the crocodile on top illustrating the process of design abstraction, we see at the bottom of the same page another chart in the form of a rectangle with a trapezoid simulating the roof of a building. This theoretical crown contains the title of the diagram: "Ideology of building?" The question mark is repeated inside the rectangle containing a theoretical outline divided into three chronological eras: "[E]olithic," "[N]eolithic," and finally in a transhistoric leap, "[A]tomic." These three phases correspond to sources of design "abstracted" from "rocks," "animals," and "birds," respectively. We have already familiarized ourselves with design abstraction from minerals and animals in Kiesler's previous charts, but "birds" are a new addition in this totemically classificatory scheme. How and from where do birds fly into the architect's theoretical "building"? And if the "ideology" of that building represents a genealogy of design, why do "birds" correspond to the architect's own "Atomic" era—the period in which he is jotting most of these notes and diagrams?

Perhaps appropriately, the answer to this hovers outside this draft and the tripartite scheme of its theoretical enclosure. In 1944, Kiesler sketched a few preliminary proposals for an exhibition on "Ecology" from a "geological" perspective to be installed at the Natural History Museum in New York, which was never realized.

One of his drawings depicts the placement of all organic species in relation to the ground, which represents the geological origin of life: from starfish and seaweed at the bottom of the ocean to worms and multi-leg lizards which move closest to the earthly ground, to quadrupeds and the (few) biped species whose "forefeet" are "up [from] the ground," and finally, aerial creatures that fly in the "air."[8]

Strikingly, the human species figures not in the biped category, which is occupied by a kangaroo, but rather finds itself airborne. Superimposing Leonardo's sketch for a flying "man-machine" and the design of a modern airplane, Kiesler's human appears along with a bat to fly high, "up free" and "detached" from the earthly "ground." The aerial domain, and by extension, the spatial spheres far beyond the envelope of the earth, constitute the human being's projected milieu—the endpoint of man's endlessly expansive design orientation. It soon becomes clear, however, that this birdman is no free creature flying carelessly in an idyllic heaven but is instead the harbinger and eventual agent of mass destruction from the sky.

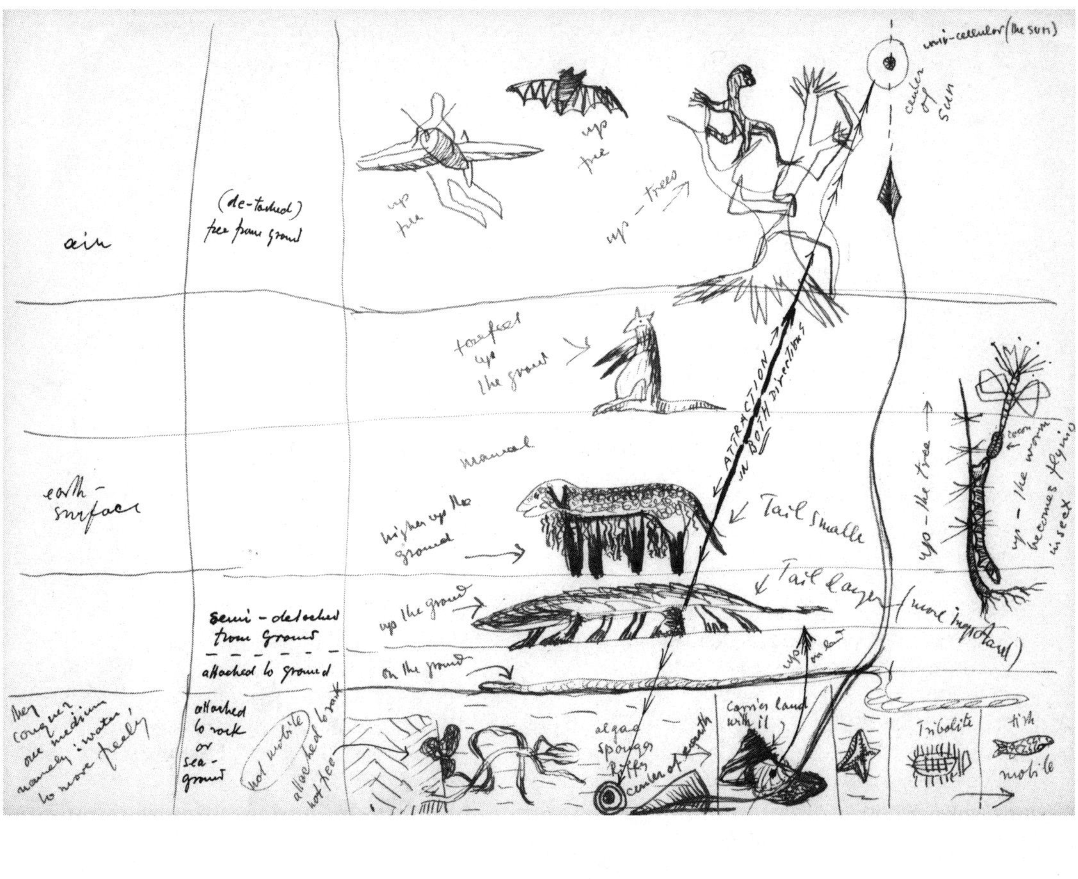

Frederick Kiesler, Diagram for the "Ecology" exhibition, study for a project in the Museum of Natural History, 1944.

"And the greater his civilization the farther away will he take his stand for the kill ... His ultimate dream of safety is to be able to shoot from interstellar space—unseen, unheard, with nothing of his scent coming down wind," writes Kiesler in a chapter of his *Magic Architecture* titled "Fear of the Unseen."[9] The "birdman" of the Atomic age is the human inside the airplane, a metal-insulated body reminiscent of the geometric figure of the "abstract" crocodile and its metallic tail. The birdman condenses all three developmental phases of Kiesler's "Ideology of Building" diagram and their corresponding natural models—rock, animal, and bird—into one composite figure. In effect, all earlier states survive in the latest one: there are still fossils of the "Eolithic" rock and organic rudiments of the "Neolithic" crocodile inside the chassis body of the "Atomic" bird.

Following Kiesler, one can argue that there are basically two types of design instruments present throughout human history: "tools for attack" and "tools for defense." While other forms of design, such as ballistic devices and aerial military technologies, produce "tools for attack," houses function primarily as "defense mechanisms." During the Atomic era, air and ground switch positions in the stratospheric classification of human design. Instead of being the space of transcontinental exchange and universal communication (the infrastructural extensions of the metal "wiring" technologies originating in the spiral earring pictured in the architect's first diagram), the air becomes the stratum of imminent death—a sky persistently darkened by the possibility of aerial attack—while the underground or the mineral enclosure of a "cave" becomes the protective environment shielding the preservation of life. Both the departure and endpoint of human design signal a return to the "rock"—the inorganic condition represented by the "metal" at the top of Kiesler's original diagram next to the crocodile of "nature." The reptile's open jaws transform into an abstract arrow, pointing towards a redirection of the "birth of design" from life's mineral and animal origins to its (super)human extinction.

1 Frederick J. Kiesler, *Magic Architecture. Origin and Future. The Story of Human Housing*, unpublished book manuscript (ca. 1945). Archive of the Austrian Frederick and Lilian Kiesler Private Foundation Vienna. Hereafter cited as MA, TXT_6806_0_N2.
2 MA, TXT_6806_0_N1.
3 Karl Weule, "Die Eidechse als Ornament in Afrika," in *Festschrift für Adolf Bastian zu seinem 70. Geburtstage* (1896), 169–94.
4 In particular, Leo Frobenius, *Kulturgeschichte Afrikas* (1933).
5 James Frazer, *The Golden Bough: A Study in Magic and Religion*, abridged ed. of 1922 (1996), 15.
6 MA, TXT_6689_0_N1.
7 MA,11_SFP_6662_0_N6.
8 Frederick Kiesler, *Ecology Exhibition*, study for a project in the American Museum of Natural History, New York, 1944. The Kiesler Foundation, Vienna, SFP 6614.
9 MA, TXT_5877_0_N015-16.

Beyond the Gene

Alexander Tarakhovsky

> There are no depths. Appearance is the summary of phenomena.
> —Joseph Brodsky

Life on earth is a narrative written by the deoxyribonucleic acid (DNA). The chemical design of DNA is uniform among every form of life, but its sequence is different between species and individuals. DNA sequences are comprised of millions of differentially combined chemical letters (A, T, C, and G) and yield most of the current diversity of species, as well as offering an endless blueprint for the future design of life-forms. Once established, life-forms tend to stay within the borders of their species, one generation after the other. However, no two individual organisms, even twins, manage to follow precisely the same script. The reason for this is the so-called "epigenetic" impact that expands the boundaries of the DNA language and generates another level of diversity by incorporating life experience in its different forms.

What is epigenetics? In the mid-1960s, Conrad Waddington, one of the founders of epigenetics, wrote:

> Some years ago [in 1947] I introduced the word "epigenetics," derived from the Aristotelian word "epigenesis," which had more or less passed into disuse, as a suitable name for the branch of biology which studies the causal interactions between genes and their products which bring the phenotype into being.

"Epi" means "upon" or "over," and "genetics" implies that genes are involved, so the term reflected the need to study events "over" or beyond the gene.

What is beyond, or over, the gene? The DNA of a single human cell is 1.2 meters long and is tightly packed within the micron-size cell nucleus. The packed ball of DNA string has a levitating 3-D structure where the different strings overlap and loop around each other like folded fishing line. Each loop contains genes that encode proteins as well as numerous regulatory elements that define the gene activity. Epigenetics addresses the mechanisms that define gene activity without interfering with the gene structure. Thus epigenetics is more a censorship of the DNA "reading" than an editing of the text.

DNA "reading" involves thousands of different proteins that move with extreme precision and sensitivity over the DNA structure, like a blind reader's fingers over brail. DNA reading molecules are sensitive to environmental impacts, and the longer and stronger these are, the more likely it is that cells will tune the pattern of DNA reading to environmental pressure. The meaning of the environmental impact differs between distinct cells and the organisms. For example, in the brain neurons, persistent fear of aggression affects the activity of hundreds of genes responsible for the immediate reaction to aggression, as well as a long-lasting adaptation to life in fear, meaning that many of the genes that operate in the brains of "free" individuals are either silent or abnormally active in the brains of those who live under conditions of oppression or fear. The scope of gene activity and patterns of genes within each given cell generate an individual cell dialect. As cells operate together they form a library of dialects that will eventually drive the emergence of novel and stable features that could not have been predicted by the DNA sequence alone.

The emergence of a common cell language is similar to the emergence of linguistic dialects that liberate individuality from the rigid constraints of scholastic grammar. As genes interact with each other and with the "readers," life within the cell nucleus appears strikingly similar to life in the ancient Greek seaport of Piraeus, inhabited by Greeks looping into Athens from all around the Mediterranean. The mixture of dialects and the contact between multiple varieties of the same language brought about a new language, "koiné." Koiné languages do not change any existing dialect, but instead emerge as a spoken dialect in addition to the original ones. As with koiné, our cells do not attempt to change the original DNA language, yet *koiné ad libitum* in response to environmental influences.

The supposed virginity of our genome becomes challenged as soon as we tap into the "dirt" of the world. Bacteria and viruses invade our bodies already in the womb, and even more after we are born. The total mass of bacteria living in a single human can be measured in kilograms. Bacteria have no preconceived knowledge of the future host, and likewise, we are not aware of the invaders. To reach a symbiotic relation, both our body and the collective body of invaders need to adapt to each other to avoid the excessive stress of futile intolerance. In essence, the birth of a human is not merely the origin of a new individual, but the onset of a new community. Exposed, the cells of our body tune their genetic language to help achieve the life-long symbiosis between us and "them." Since partners in symbiotic relationships frequently belong to different kingdoms, yet may be so intimate with each other that one may reside in the other's tissues and/or cells, their shared "language" tends to be a basic—and ancient—form of communication. Such communication blurs the boundaries between different living entities, giving rise to a single biomolecular network: a "holobiont" with a "hologenome."[1] At the bottom of all of this are our genes, carrying the burden of the environment throughout our life.

Similar to bacterial invasions that challenge our immunity, the brain of a newborn becomes exposed to the limitless number of new signals that will continue to arrive for as long as we live. Similar to how genes in the gut and skin adapt to bacterial presence, the genes in our brain cells become part of a virtual "hologenome," where not bacteria or viruses but information imprints its presence on the genes and alters their function. A baby screaming in a cradle in the feverish embrace of the world reflect a struggle where our genetic script, which really has not changed that much over thousands of years, experiences the burden of novelty in a cruel and unanticipated form.

Can the burden of novelty be reduced by passing a memory of ancestral experience to the next generation? Can information about ancestral environments be transmitted to offspring via sperm cells? Early in the twentieth century, Dr. August Weismann removed the tails of sixty-eight white mice repeatedly over five generations, and found that while "901 young were produced by five generations of artificially mutilated parents ... there was not a single example of a rudimentary tail or of any other abnormality in this organ." Intuitively, Weismann chose mutilation as the most likely experience that could lead to heritable changes. Naively, however, Weismann mistook a sign of mutilation for its consequences. While tail-shortening is obviously not heritable, the trauma of mutilation left a lasting hereditary impact. It turned out that fear can be passed to new generations. Mice were found to pass on the memory of a smell if it was coupled to a strongly painful experience. In the experiment, a particular odorant was paired with foot shock. Offspring of the males treated in this way showed increased sensitivity to that specific odorant, while no change in sensitivity was registered with another. This study suggests the somewhat shocking possibility that parents can inform offspring in an extraordinarily complex chemical milieu via sperm.

While these experiments were done in mice, there is no reason to think that humans are different. Instead of being individually discrete, our flesh and mind may be hostage to our ancestral experiences. While the ancestral influence may have a positive impact, it may also narrate defeat and leave us inept in the face of danger. Maybe revolution and its ensuing calamity is merely an evolutionary tool to erase the memory of the past, to start from a clean slate.

1 Lynn Margulis, *Symbiosis in Cell Evolution* (New York: W. H. Freeman, 1981).

Aestheticization and Democratic Culture

Juliane Rebentisch

Newsreel cameras, teleprompters, and other equipment set up in the Oval Office for President Truman's address to the nation on international arms reduction, 1951. Photo: Abbie Rowe.

The 1990s were dominated by debates about postmodernism, one strand of which was concerned with the so called "aestheticization of the life-world." Wolfgang Welsch, for example, wrote in *Grenzgänge der Ästhetik*: "The facades get prettier, the shops more animated, the noses more perfect. But such aestheticization reaches deeper, it affects fundamental structures of reality as such."[1] For aestheticization means "basically that the non-aesthetic is made aesthetic or is grasped as being aesthetic."[2] However, what counts as aestheticization and which concept of the aesthetic is presupposed can vary, as he goes on to explain:

> In the context of an urban environment, aestheticization refers to the expansion of the beautiful, the pretty, and the stylish; in advertisement as well as in self-understandings it means the growing importance of performance and lifestyle; in view of the technological determination of the objective world and the social effects of the media, "aesthetic" primarily designates virtualization. Finally, aestheticization of consciousness means: we no longer see first or last foundations, instead reality takes on a condition we formerly only knew with respect to art—a condition of being produced, changeable, noncommittal, levitating etc.[3]

Whereas Welsch, from the perspective of a somewhat generalized constructivism, affirmed these developments as a move towards the freedom of designing ever more spheres of life,[4] others were more skeptical. Not only did they doubt that postmodern urban space should indeed be characterized by an "expansion of the beautiful and the pretty," they also saw in the postmodern emphasis on the surface a symptom of an ugly social truth: that of a profound alienation. In their view, the postmodern cult of the surface was a symptom of a novel domination of simulacra that erodes the substance both of our ethical self-understandings and our political culture. "Reality," Rüdiger Bubner wrote, "gives up its ontological dignity in favor of an applauded semblance."[5] Both sides of the debate, however, assumed that aestheticization is not just a question of design, but that this question itself should be seen in a broader social context. "Aestheticization of the life-world" is thus a formulation with which both sides tried to find a tangible concept for the state of contemporary Western societies.

However, the agitated argument over the *status* of a supposedly obvious societal development that dominated the 1990s was soon to be deflated by sociology, for the philosophical debate remained unfounded as long as it was possible to question the actual scope of this development.[6] As a result, attempts to empirically substantiate the thesis of the aestheticization of the life-world quickly came in for criticism, such as Gerhard Schulze's thesis of an "experience society" brought about by affluence.[7] Schulze was in turn accused of falsely generalizing a phenomenon located in the more privileged part of society.[8] Today, the parameters of this debate seem to have shifted: a much more prominent role is played by studies which show that aesthetic motifs such as creativity, spontaneity, and originality are no longer signs of a sphere of freedom lying beyond the necessities of social reproduction, but have themselves become an important productive force in the capitalist economic system. According to this research, these motifs have turned into crucial social demands, representing an increase of constraints rather than freedom.[9] In any case, sociology seems to have become the central location for serious debate on how to appropriately describe, explain, and evaluate the crucial position of aesthetically connoted criteria both for individuals and for the organization of society in Western democracies.

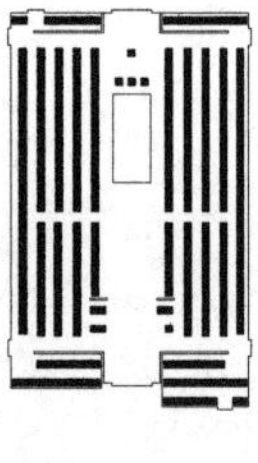

Opposing Benches
House of Commons, United Kingdom

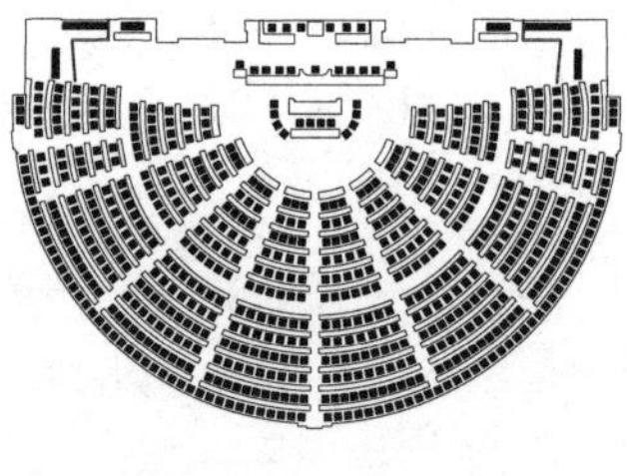

Semicircle
l'Assemblée Nationale, France

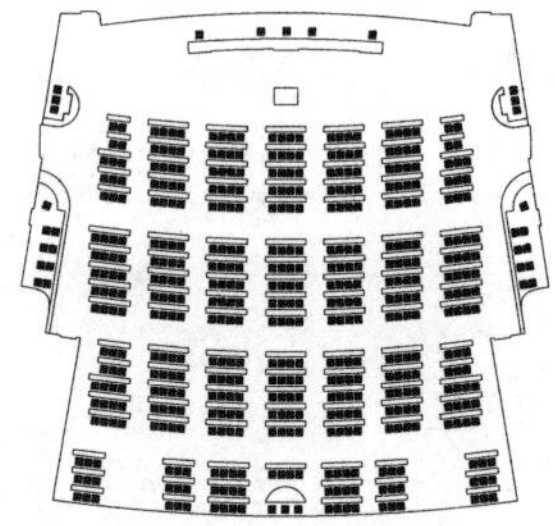

Classroom
Duma, Russia

Three examples of parliament floorplans arranged by typology: opposing benches, semicircle, and classroom. Drawing: XML.

But as relevant as these debates are, I believe that philosophy has been wrong to retreat from them. After all, the diagnosis of aestheticization implies an assumption about the undistorted essence of both ethics and politics, which is not merely an empirical, but systematic question. The specific approach of philosophy in the context of contemporary diagnoses, however, can only become fully visible once we turn away from the business of diagnosing the present and turn to the history of philosophy. Contrary to the impression raised by recent debates, aestheticization in no way represents simply a contemporary problem; and traditionally, the concept is much more philosophical than is suggested by the largely sociological character of the current discourse. In fact, philosophical discussion of the challenges posed by certain aesthetic motifs for understanding ethics and politics even goes back to antiquity. The history of practical philosophy can even be seen as a history of crisis-diagnoses that have sought to combat the invasion of the aesthetic and its disintegrating effects into the spheres of ethics and politics. Without a reflection on the long history of this discourse, the claim that the "aestheticization of the life-world" represents a new phenomenon and a new epoch will remain questionable. Without a detailed discussion of the problems that practical philosophy has historically ascribed to "the aesthetic," our judgment of current developments will be in danger of either merely carrying over old prejudices into the present, e.g., by criticizing a supposedly novel domination of simulacra, or we will end up becoming a part of an old problem rather than a part of the solution, e.g., by becoming proponents of a supposedly new, constructivist relation to ourselves and the world. In order to clarify the philosophical assumptions that at least indirectly influence these debates, we require a historical and systematic discussion of the history of the philosophical critique of aestheticization.

As I have already indicated, this history begins in antiquity, or more precisely, with Plato's critique of democratic culture in *The Republic*. Plato mistrusts the "colorful" plurality of life-forms in a democracy, as well as the "dazzling" democrats that have learned from (theater) poets that it is possible to adopt several roles in life. He even sees a major problem in the pretty appearance of democratic culture and its privileged life-form. For according to Plato's diagnosis, the logic of appearances constitutes the essence of democracy itself: the ethical commitment to the good gets replaced by an aesthetic stylization of existence, while good government (i.e., government that is committed to the good) gets replaced by an uncontrolled spectacle that seduces the people. For Plato, this logic is a small, dangerously subtle step on the path from democracy to tyranny. What is astounding about this diagnosis from antiquity is how familiar its central motifs are even today. Indeed, these motifs were picked up again in the philosophical discourse at the beginning of modernity (around 1800) and have continued to play an important role into the twentieth century and beyond. But why does Plato, of all thinkers, prove to be such a decisive source when it comes to naming the problems of modern democracy, or rather the problems associated with its aestheticized culture? After all, the model of democracy in antiquity cannot be applied to modern democracies; just as little can the arts of antiquity, which Plato criticized for their subversive influence on morals, be equated with modern art forms. Nevertheless, it is no accident that modern philosophical thought on the matter draws on the work of Plato.

Plato invented a type of critique that has become so crucial for modernity that, despite the obvious differences between antiquity and modernity, a good deal of conceptual effort has been undertaken to revive it. Plato connects his analysis of various forms of government with his investigation of—to put it in modern terms—forms of subjectivization. The connection between government and self-government takes on greater significance in modernity, despite the fact that the organization of the state is no longer regarded as mirroring that of the soul, as is suggested at several points in *The Republic*. However, if we take a closer look at Plato's account of this connection, we find the more complex argument that government and self-government are not merely similar to each other, but rather that they form an analogous unity via their respective relation to a value that is central to both, which in the case of democratic culture, is freedom. This thesis on the relationship between ethics and politics is what has remained crucial to the modern critique of aestheticization, and the key to the modern debate on aestheticization is likewise the problem of freedom. If the diagnosis of aestheticization sometimes more, sometimes less explicitly refers to democratic culture, then the freedom that defines this culture is the systematic problem with which it is both ethically and politically concerned.

More precisely, what is at stake is a concept of freedom associated with aesthetic motifs, namely a form of freedom that contradicts social practices, their normative orders, and the corresponding identities or roles. It does so by giving private motives (moods, pleasure, taste) such a clear priority over conformity to a given social order that they come to dominate the way that individuals determine their own lives. Critics of aestheticization fear that such a private model of freedom, if successful in establishing itself in society, will have a disintegrating effect on the political community. At best, social bonds will be replaced by "aesthetic" relations; and where there are no longer any social bonds, the staging of community becomes a politically decisive force. Yet the staging of community, as critics of aestheticization go on to argue, does not create community. On the contrary, not only does it barely conceal the fact that it is only necessary because the collective has been undermined from within by the aesthetic self-understandings of its (non) members, but it is only capable of producing a community to the degree that it simultaneously establishes a divide between those that produce the community and those who—again in the form of moods, pleasure, and taste—receive it. The political community thus disintegrates into a spectacle and an audience.

Because of its disintegrating effects, the aesthetic form of freedom has been denounced as a "degenerate freedom" by Plato or as "caprice" or "arbitrariness" (*Willkürfreiheit*) by Hegel. In the history of the philosophical critique of aestheticization, very different conceptual presuppositions have been employed in order to deliver proof, and it is here that the gap between modernity and antiquity becomes particularly visible. However, since Hegel's objection to the romantic ironist, this critique has taken the shape of a reference to the constitutive role of social practices for the unfolding of individual freedom. Without question, this reference is still justified today. It captures extreme constructivist positions that reduce the possibility for shaping one's own life to a question of individual ethics,[10] as well as all those who argue that Foucault's demand "not to be governed like that" refers to the entirety of life—as if a life beyond all social determination were desirable or even possible.[11] Not only is everybody always involved in social practices, but any understanding of the self requires social recognition in order to be realized.[12]

But by exclusively associating "aesthetic" freedom with freedom *from* the social *in toto*, the critique of aestheticization conceals another, more productive interpretation: distance from the social does not necessarily entail a distance from all social determinacy—a distance that would be as abstract as indeed imaginary. We could also grasp this distance in a different way: not as a *model* for the life of the subject, but as a productive *element* of it. Referring to aesthetic existence, to "dazzling" life-forms, does not mean demonstrating and defending abstract freedom from the social, but rather the mutability of the social itself. The aestheticization of freedom would then no longer stand for the misunderstanding of a kind of freedom *from* the social, in a kind of nondialectical opposition, to freedom *in* the social. Rather, it would express the tension at the heart of the life of every individual. Changes of the self are not brought about by a pseudo-superior subject standing above all social identity. Instead, such changes are rooted in experiences of self-difference, which compel the subject to reconceive of itself, its self-understanding, and the meaning of its subjectivity from a distance. I do not distance myself from an overly disciplined self-understanding, for example, by placing myself over this understanding—as if I were the sovereign of my own sovereignty—but, on the contrary, by experiencing desires that counter them in such a way that I (by laughing about myself) become free for new, probably more appropriate self-images. Whoever lives within the misunderstanding of solipsistic self-production is thus just as unfree as those who have never had the experience of distance from themselves, their social roles, and its corresponding expectations. It is only possible to mediate between both sides of this tense relationship if we grasp them as elements in a process in which we can change both ourselves and the social practices of which we are a part.[13] Indeed we would misunderstand the changes in ourselves if we took them to be merely private changes. Through these changes we change the practices of which we too are a part. Occasionally this can occur without our noticing, while in other cases it can lead to collisions between ourselves and existing practices, a collision that can only be removed by making explicit changes to either ourselves or the world. That I now choose to understand myself differently can also mean that in order to be able to live out my new self-understanding I must enter into a struggle for recognition.

To defend the possibility of such change, however, means to defend the possibility of changing given determinations of the good as a good in itself. The form of government that has integrated the possibility of questioning given determinations of the good into the concept of the good itself is—as Plato already clearly recognized—democracy. It is the only form of government in which it is allowed to publicly criticize everything, to publicly call everything into question—including the shape of democracy itself. Because it remains open, despite all the risk involved, to re-determinations of the good, and thus to the possibility of a more just order, democracy remains—to cite the now famous formulation employed by Jacques Derrida—"to come."[14] Yet this is not meant, as Derrida is often misunderstood, as an eternal suspension until the arrival of a coming messiah of democracy. On the contrary, our determinations of the good are all that we have for realizing our freedom in the here and now. Democratic openness to future events neither means openness for the sake of openness, nor is this a fundamental criticism of normative determinations in general. Rather, it emphasizes the possibility of historical revision. For precisely this reason, democracy, to cite Claude Lefort, is the "historical society par excellence."[15]

Yet due to its insight into the historicity of the good, democracy indeed has an internal connection to what has been criticized as the "aestheticization of the political." We can make plausible that participants in social practices are always potential nonparticipants, and thus also that members of society are potential nonmembers, such that the meaning of social practices can be called into question at any time. If this is the case, then the immediate result will be a critique of prepolitical conceptions of the order and unity of the political collective. Neither the order nor the unity of the community can simply be presupposed; rather, its character is revealed to be a political determination. Furthermore, this means that the unity of the community, along with the order within which it is grasped, must be politically created, produced, staged. Because democracy knows neither order nor unity beyond political representation, it not only stands in clear opposition to Plato's antidemocratic conception of the natural political order, but also concerns the idea of collective self-government, an idea that is central to the modern understanding of democracy. This latter point has far-reaching consequences, for if it is true that the self of collective self-government cannot be assumed to be a unified will and that it must first be brought forth by political representation, then this means that the *demos* of democracy can never exist beyond the separation thereby established between representatives and the represented, producers and receivers, the rulers and the ruled, performers and the audience. The *demos* can therefore never exist outside of relations of power and domination; it never exists as such. In fact, sovereign power and authority are presumed the moment someone steps forward and claims to speak for everyone, yet the people being spoken for are helpless against this presumption of power only to the extent that they are blinded by measures designed to conceal the elements of sovereignty and rhetoric entailed by this act. The democratic answer to the problem of sovereign power does not consist in concealing the latter, but in exhibiting it and thus exposing it to an examination of its legitimacy. For it is precisely through this democratically understood "aestheticization of the political" that democracy preserves its openness to the future. On the democratic political stage, the representatives of the *demos* must justify themselves before those whose will they represent; they must face a heterogeneous audience whose members always potentially have or develop alternative conceptions of the democratic general will, which can ultimately be asserted publicly as a (counter)power in opposition to the currently prevailing conception.[16]

Such a defense of an aesthetic, even theatrical dimension of democracy, of the necessity of representation (and the sovereignty that comes with it) does not mark the end of a critique of representation but its beginning. Contrary to the generalized critique of all forms of political stagings or "the media," we now need a critique in the original sense of the term, i.e., as differentiation. First of all, we must distinguish the aesthetic of totalitarian stagings of unity and of post-democratic disintegration from the political stagings in which democratic power justifies itself before the *demos* that it claims to represent. Within the framework of totalitarian mass spectacles, for example, everything serves the ideological expression of *unity*. However, the realization of such a totality, which excludes any kind of division, can only be had at an extraordinarily high price. To the degree that power succumbs to the "madness," as Claude Lefort and Marcel Gauchet write, of embodying the position of universality and articulating the true general will, power necessarily passes over into the particular: "Instead of the universality to which it lays claim, we only perceive the arbitrariness of rules and decisions, the narrow bias of judgment and the constant resort to brute force."[17] The contradiction of totalitarianism consists of the fact that "the sought-for elimination of all divisions within society requires a power that separates itself from this society and thereby divides itself between the claim of its transcendence and its factual social immanence."[18] The fact that totalitarian rule is "doomed" in spite of "all the compulsory measures at its disposal" does not eliminate the possibility that the totalitarian vision can succeed in reality—even if only for a certain time, which history has shown to be necessarily too long.[19]

In its own way, post-democracy, too, is determined, like totalitarianism, by the ideological conception of a complete accordance of power and society.[20] Only this time the idea of accordance is accompanied by a visual culture that is not shaped by an aesthetic of unity, but by an aesthetic of disintegration; it is precisely the endless openness of this culture which proves to be especially inclusive. Post-democratic power denies itself up to a point at which it negates its own sovereignty to define the common good and instead merely claims to manage economic necessities and constraints.[21] To the degree that power legitimates its actions by invoking its own powerlessness, the responsibility for the state of society and the situation of each individual is pushed onto the governed (and no longer onto the government), thereby equating itself with the image of a (neoliberal) classless society that embraces even the poorest of the poor by according them the potential for creative self-realization. Each individual should see himself "as his own militant," as a bundle of energy that can be molded to fit into continuously new contexts with new contracts, all the while viewing themselves as being in pursuit of their own pleasures.[22] You just have to want it. In terms of a politics of representation this corresponds to a "regime of the all-visible" which eliminates the distinction between image and reality; all citizens are granted the opportunity to present themselves and their individual particularity, but they are no longer met with the expectation of a demand for political representation. By granting each person the possibility of individual visibility, post-democracy claims that it has given each person his or her just due. In both aesthetic and political terms, this recalls the nightmare of a society that has taken on the form of an afternoon talk show.

Both extremes demonstrate the urgency to not only defend a democratic setting in which power appears and must legitimize itself as such, but also the many stages on which arguments about the appropriate representation of the *demos*, about the respective version of the general will, can be carried out. These are the different, partially interlocking dimensions of democratic life on which the self-difference of the *demos* can occur: it not only appears in the relation between the government and the non-parliamentary opposition, but also in the relation between the government and the parliamentary opposition; between politics and the media; between the media and the citizens; and finally, between citizen and man, the limit of democratic community. Those cases in which one or more of these differences are absorbed or ignored should appear to be a problem, such as whenever human rights are equated with the civil rights granted by nation-states, or when the relationship between the government and the opposition is eliminated in favor of a one-party state; when free speech and the right to protest are restricted, or when the influence of economic and/or political power blurs the line between politics and the media. Within this perspective, discussions about different formats and strategies of political communications, or the role of new technologies and media for the formation of publics and counterpublics, gain critical relevance.

Defending the levels of democratic life that bear witness to a conflict over various views of what is publicly relevant, of what constitutes the common will, means abandoning the conception of democracy as the final, good form of rule in which the problem of sovereignty has been overcome, because "the people" itself takes up the position of the sovereign, for this conception presupposes the problematic fiction of an identity of the *demos* with itself. Given the unforeseeable heterogeneity of its (non)members, this notion of democracy is a structurally totalitarian one. The insight that the *demos* never exists outside its representation implies, as we have seen, the recognition of an element of sovereignty at the very foundation of democratic societies. However, this is not the unfortunate death, but the beginning of democratic politics. For this is the kind of politics whose dynamic derives from the experience of the self-difference of the *demos*, in which democracy is realized only by means of a constant struggle over the nature of its very concept.

The text documents a lecture in which the author summarized for discussion some of the theses from her book The Art of Freedom: On the Dialectics of Democratic Existence *(Cambridge: Polity Press, 2016).*

1 Wolfgang Welsch, "Ästhetisierungsprozesse – Phänomene, Unterscheidungen, Perspektiven," in *Grenzgänge der Ästhetik*, 1996: 20.
2 Ibid, 20f.
3 Ibid, 21.
4 Ibid, 55.
5 For this position see Rüdiger Bubner, "Ästhetisierung der Lebenswelt," in Ästhetische Erfahrung (Frankfurt am Main: Suhrkamp, 1989), 150.
6 This is Axel Honneth's justified objection to this past discussion. See Axel Honneth, "Ästhetisierung der Lebenswelt," in *Desintegration: Bruchstücke einer soziologischen Zeitdiagnose* (Frankfurt am Main: Fischer, 1994), 29f.
7 See Gerhard Schulze, *The Experience Society* (London: Sage, 1995).
8 For a critique on Schulze, see Honneth, "Ästhetisierung der Lebenswelt," 37f.
9 For the more recent tendency, see Luc Boltanski and Ève Chiapello, *The New Spirit of Capitalism* (London: Verso, 2007).
10 On the justified critique of a reduction of life to the "disposable material of an individual who is proud of his autonomy," see the discussion in *Kritik der Lebenskunst*, eds. Wolfgang Kersting and Claus Langbehn (Frankfurt am Main: Suhrkamp, 2007), 8.
11 See Michel Foucault, "What is Critique," in *The Politics of Truth*, ed. Sylvère Lotringer (Los Angeles: Semiotext(e), 2007), 44.
12 See Axel Honneth, "Diagnose der Postmoderne," in *Desintegration*, 18f.
13 Because there is a tension between the individual and the social good, which are nevertheless interwoven, both sides cannot be reconciled with each other by relegating them to two separate spheres, as Richard Rorty suggests when he locates self-creation in the private sphere and solidarity in the public sphere. See Richard Rorty, *Contingency, Irony and Solidarity* (Cambridge: Cambridge University Press, 1989), 13f., 142.
14 See the compact determination of "*démocratie à venir*" in Jacques Derrida, *Rogues: Two Essays on Reason* (Stanford: Stanford University Press, 2005), 86.
15 Claude Lefort, *The Political Forms of Modern Society: Bureaucracy, Democracy, Totalitarianism* (Cambridge, MA: MIT Press, 1986), 305.
16 See also Jacques Rancière, *Dissensus: On Politics and Aesthetics* (London: Continuum, 2010), 34.
17 Claude Lefort and Marcel Gauchet, "Über die Demokratie: Das Politische und die Instituierung des Gesellschaftlichen," in *Autonome Gesellschaft und libertäre Demokratie*, ed. Ulrich Rödel (Frankfurt am Main: Suhrkamp, 1990), 102.
18 Ibid, 104.
19 Ibid.
20 Jacques Rancière, *Disagreement: Politics and Philosophy* (Minneapolis: University of Minnesota Press, 1999), 102.
21 Ibid, 113. The self-emasculation of power thus goes along with the naturalization of a specific economic order, a specific form of capitalism.
22 Ibid, 114.

Beyond the Self

Jack Self

If you spot a "throbber," you've probably got an issue with your hardware. These small digital animations, more commonly known as buffer icons, only appear when your internet connection or browser speed is too slow to manage the volume of incoming data. In the 1990s almost every web page used to buffer before it loaded; the old Netscape throbber (depicting a meteor shower over a hilltop) was practically the unofficial logo of the World Wide Web for many years. These days you will only see a throbber when handling large media files like video, or when a so-called "infinite scroll" page loads a new segment.

A throbber frequently resembles a rolling wheel, spinning bar, bouncing ellipsis, or (more uncommonly) a set of grinding gears. These forms are designed to suggest that, while no immediate change is evident, the computer is nonetheless hard at work behind the scenes. In the absence of a percentage bar, we simply have to wait and trust that the throbber's motion does indeed represent some form of progress.

The throbber is a sign of temporal rupture. It is the last barrier to a perfectly smooth and seamless virtual experience. It draws attention to an asynchronous maladjustment, or misalignment, between the space of our bodies and the infinite atopian fluidity of the digital world. As such, the throbber stands for wasted time, with all the implications of subversive indolence and anti-industriousness this evokes. The elimination of the throbber is therefore integral to the fantasy of "real-time," a paradigm of total coherence in which events are instantly known to all agents in a network. For several decades the neoliberals that posited such an exchange assumed real-time would improve the quality of collective decision-making and resource distribution. It is only now, as technology catches up to the vision, that real-time systems are revealed to be as ineffective as any other model. They perpetuate the hegemonic inequalities of previous systems, and in fact accelerate the polarization of wealth and power. They make the same logical errors as before, only much faster—and they often create disproportionate feedback loops in the process. Any improved efficiency of real-time exchange (which is, in the long run, minimal, as demonstrated by the Grossman-Stiglitz paradox) stems purely from its speed. The pursuit of real-time increasingly means either abandoning human engagement in the network altogether (as with fully electronic trading platforms like the NASDAQ), or operating at the very limits of human conscious thought, in the half-waking peripheral glaze of the mind (as with models that require large data volumes for marginal consumer returns, like Instagram). The throbber, as a trigger for critical reflection, threatens to disturb this soporific state.

Advocates of real-time imagine humanity as progressing towards a utopia of self-regulating supplies and demands. To achieve this presupposes several conditions. First, all individuals have to be incorporated into a single global network. Second, the network must be universally robust, with all parts accelerated to a uniform speed. Lastly, any remaining inconsistencies or internal delays within the network have to be reduced or mitigated as far as possible. In truth, this process is almost complete: there are seven billion people in the world with 6.8 billion active mobile phones between them (of which more than a billion are smartphones). By the end of this year, 85 percent of the world's population will have access to a 3G network; by the end of next, 50 percent will be on 4G.

Nonetheless, some internal barriers cannot be eliminated. Even at the speed of light, large geographical distances produce latency. We will always need the throbber because we will always have to mitigate the effects of network inequality. The throbber's role is therefore to mollify a user sufficiently to keep them within the general flow of information by reframing nonaction as a normalized process of data exchange. There is a critical threshold to this period of inactivity, a suggested duration of about two seconds. Beyond this time the throbber is unable to hold the subject's attention and the entire illusion of smoothness breaks down. The function of this element is therefore to massage irreconcilably unequal agents into an elastic, but unbreakable, continuum. The throbber is thus integral to maintaining the illusion of inescapability, dissimulating the possibility of exiting the network—one that has become both spatially and temporally coextensive with the world. This is the truth of the real-time we now inhabit: a surreal simulation so perfectly smooth it is indistinguishable from, and indeed preferable to, reality.

The all-encompassing space of synchronization reframes the individual as a hapless Mechanical Turk engaged in endless self-exploitation—the victim of a profoundly dehumanizing informatic process in which they voluntarily render every aspect of their being into commoditized data. It is an exchange dominated by the obligation to create, where individuality and personality are useful only inasmuch as they provide information diversity. In essence, real-time is a model that treats all humans as merely homogenous and interchangeable data input nodes. We are no longer freethinking beings; we are bundles of particulars and pre-prepared preferences. We are poor collages of discrete data blocks, constantly compiled for cross-comparison and analysis.

This unraveling of the individual appears only as the latest phase in a history of Western personal subjectivity that began with the rise of democracy in the late eighteenth and nineteenth centuries. At that time, for a citizen to vote successfully, they had to be able to understand the soundness and consistency of public rhetoric. This legibility relied on a general comprehension of cultural logic, which was defined by the philosophical and scientific canons.

This was the basis of John Stuart Mill's argument that university graduates should get two votes—because education equated to better clarity of reason. Leisure, or nonwork, was recognized as a necessary ingredient for the formation of the voter, as it provided the time needed for contemplation and reflection, or wisdom. Nonwork, particularly of the passive kind, is central to the synthesis and critical evaluation of different structures, patterns, arguments, facts, and the relative weighting of opinions. In this sense, pointless leisure produces considered opinions. Idleness is quite literally the time needed for subjective formation as a civic individual.

Since the throbber has appropriated nonaction, it has made leisure—and thus the individual—impossible.

The idea of the individual and its inviolable existence is unquestionable today; however, it is important to remember that for the ancient Greeks and Romans, there was no such concept. The individual was effectively invented during the Enlightenment, alongside the scientific method, a realization of humanity's non-privileged position in the universe, and the consequent shift to an anthropocentric cosmology. As described above, the individual was also a precondition for modern democracy, and indeed was a development that came from religious ideas. In order to govern feudal societies effectively (and to generate a financial model), medieval theology reframed salvation as a personal project that related to the "soul." The democratic individual is largely the product of a reconfiguration of the "soul" into a secular, intellectual, and politically indivisible voting unit. Today, the individual has been transformed into a purely economic agent: rational, dumb, and self-interested. The fallacy embedded within the concept of the individual consumer (who "votes" with their dollar) is simply the impossibility of self-determination in the marketplace; while each individual's specific interests may indeed belong to the self, the self is not where they originate. Interests can easily be manufactured through numerous strategies, most prominently seductive advertising. The so-called individual's "self-interest" is frequently nothing more than an emergent product of inculcation by market forces. Under these conditions, individualism becomes merely the illusion of diversity, where the identity politics of infinite and marginal differences dissimulate the mechanisms of network flow that are transforming us all into a homogenized, standardized, globalized population of data providers.

Any attempt at self-expression (whether political or aesthetic) involves the donning of a persona, or even just a costume. There is no meaning to subcultural styles or fads, because they are all united by the same payment methods and social platforms. There is no meaning to protest, which at least since the Iraq War has assumed a symbolic status as the public theater of mock-resistance. The concept of the individual once seemed to offer the possibility of liberty, self-realization, and manifestation of personal and collective will, yet it is now the mechanism of our subjugation and control. Maybe it always was? Regardless, all the things we associate with individual subjectivity are illusions. There are no meaningfully distinct identities. There are only economic metrics of the self. Every category you use to define the limits of your ego is an invention.

This is not to say that the singular body does not still exist. I recognize myself by my distinct voice, the hands I first see when I wake, the itch of stubble piercing my skin, and I know I am a unique organism. This condition of incomparability is not in any way related to the concept of individuality. As long as we insist on exclusively pursuing our self-interests, we continue to assert the myth of individualism and we contribute to (or perhaps even accelerate) our own exploitation. By insisting on the self, we limit the possibility of change in the world. Self-concern has become the single largest barrier to any meaningful assertion of our collective rights.

In spite of this apparently dire situation, humanity's long-term prospects do remain positive. As the twenty-first century progresses we will no doubt face a number of truly existential threats, most notably from the effects of global warming. Fortunately, we have the technical means in the real-time network to act cooperatively at scales unmatched by any other species on the planet, and that is remarkable. Even in a worst-case mass extinction scenario, the latent wealth polarization in global society will probably allow at least a small population to survive.

Humanity today is genetically indistinguishable from its ancestors that walked the earth two hundred thousand years ago. As a species, we survived all those eons by adapting our behavior, and not our genes. One of the most successful behavioral evolutions was a willingness and capability for collaborative action. This trait first assisted group hunting and the construction of shelter, but later made possible language, the rapid dissemination of shared knowledge, complex social structures, and finally digital technologies. Humanity not only domesticated animals, it also domesticated itself to operate as a pack. Within this narrative, the rise of the real-time makes complete sense. A highly individualistic species would be the total opposite of our genetic lineage thus far. In fact, the extent to which the network dissolves the individual is wholly commensurate with its power for unprecedented collectivism. The conclusion is clear: atomization of the individual is the only source of unity.

Images throughout: Lazy loading patterns designed by Alan Woo for the e-flux.com website and based on the pattern recommendations issued by the US Federal Geographic Data Committee. Lazy loading patterns appear as placeholders for images while they are loading on a website.

The Duck Is the Übermensch

Chus Martínez

It's just been scientifically proven that ducks have abstract thinking.[1] The discovery neither alters nor surprises ducks, since they've known this fact, since they are ducks. The discovery just reveals that we, non-ducks, are deeply fascinated by sharing with ducks traits that are relevant to our idea of rationality. If taken really seriously, the discovery is a revolution, marking, in a very nice, duckish way, the impossibility of taking the premises of humanism and humanists seriously. And following this argument, only those who still believe in humanism—and the controlling, man-taming humanists with their corresponding animalistic and technological representations of the world—are going to see this as a minor discovery. Those who are unable to let go of the false contest between culture—simplified to literacy—and the beast—the ignorant—will be unable to embrace these ducks as the true coming of the Übermensch. But don't dare consider ducks' abstract thinking as less important than our own! On the contrary, this revelation only shows that animals, to use Nietzsche's perspective, may be able to perform a maximization of all that is very human. Think about animals—and plants—as beings who bring to light the dangers of the humanistic horizons of sitting and reading and breeding and taming and training. The duck is the Übermensch, who takes into consideration the intimate constraints of our humanistic hopes and opens up a spacious new arena that, in light of the previous long millennia, offers us a (sufficiently) radical suggestion: the encouragement to reflect anew on the need, more than ever, for philosophy. True, this turning-into-others, into animals, this continuous expansion of gender, this impossibility of returning to the concept of man as a rational animal, at first unleashes a feeling of decline in awareness as presented by hermeneutical criticality. The fear produces the claim that statements like "the duck is the Übermensch" may just be a new twist on a premeditated anthropotechnology in disguise. But if one wants to speak anthropologically, one could say that humans of the historical period were animals, while the animals of today suggest possibilities for future humans.

You might think it's a trend to embrace them, but it's a true evolution, one that, once and for all, proposes to challenge the way we see all existing and functioning organs—not just the brain—as producers of a radical mutation of our culturally acquired ideas of experience. There's undeniably an element of kitsch here, since the jump from one form of life to another is so big that even in literature it's a difficult illusion, one only achieved by Greek myths or ambitious minds like Kafka's. How wise it was of Anderson to propose a Little Mermaid; we all imagine her being half-fish, half-girl, but we should see her fish tail in place of legs and female sexual organs first instead of her little girl's head. All kinds of ideas related to her not being sexual might appear in that image of her as a virgin-fish, with all the beauty of youth, all the appeal of the female gender, and all the freedom of an animal living in a realm beyond the laws and institutional restraints of the humans' earth. At least in theory, look more closely at the tail, that fish tail. Having had a normal sexuality and digestion all its life, the mermaid body is now under the pressure of a head that aspires to air and language imposing itself upon the fish tail and its animal sexuality. Why on earth do we think about these two bodies in contradiction? They're just not. These two creatures together are in fact one, and it is this possibility of merging lives of different kinds that has been announced since ancient times as the very form of future intelligence. We keep reading this story metaphorically, but reading it literally would be a true act of revolution. A revolution that will involve a radical metabolic change with incredible epistemological consequences.

I. Hylomorphism

Apparently, the architect Louis Kahn once posed this question to a brick: "What form do you want to take?" He used to tell his students:

> If you are ever stuck for inspiration, ask your materials for advice. You say to a brick, "What do you want, brick?" And the brick says to you, "I like an arch." And you say to the brick, "Look, I want one, too, but arches are expensive and I can use a concrete lintel." And then you say: "What do you think of that, brick?" The brick says, "I like an arch."[2]

One might think that Kahn, for the sake of pedagogy, turned his materials into eloquent substances, and that he performed some sort of animistic, ventriloquist theater with a brick in order to stress the importance of change and transformation. But Kahn's introduction of the brick's desire into the dialogue between the maker, the architect, and the material also constitutes a critique of the paradigmatic theory of Aristotelian hylomorphism, the theory that describes each body and object as a combination of form and matter. We could enter into numerous digressions about what exactly Aristotle meant by this, but to cut the story very short, hylomorphism is the base of our most accepted understanding of unity, and the simple division contains our inherited model of individuation. The philosophical problem of how to account for unity and individuation is a rather obscure and complicated one. One might wonder why it's even worth considering. Yet Deleuze was captivated by the medieval problem of what makes an individual an individual, and how an individual can be distinguished from other individuals. The aim of the French philosopher was to produce a concept of difference that would no longer be bound to the primacy of identity or representation. For Aristotle, matter was a substance in search of a form, and form was not "whatever" form but an intrinsic feature that can be inscribed or even reinscribed in matter. But Deleuze was committed to the thesis that identity is just a product, and representation just an effect. In *Difference and Repetition* he argues that in post-Darwinist biology, the individual precedes the species, and species are just populations.[3] Here, Deleuze stresses the notion that we need a dynamic conception of individuation. In other words, we need a concept of individuation that relies on a continuous process and not on an intrinsic feature of an individual.

II. The Cloud

Federico Manuel Peralta Ramos (1939–92) was an Argentinian artist of the 1960s who captured my attention with the large egg—titled *Nosotros afuera* (We, the Outsiders)—he produced in 1965 for an exhibition at the Torcuato Di Tella Institute in Buenos Aires. Peralta Ramos was awarded a Guggenheim Fellowship in 1968, and he became famous for having used the scholarship funds to organize a splendid dinner with friends at the Alvear Palace Hotel—still an emblem of luxury in Buenos Aires—and to acquire artworks by the most successful artists of his time (to please his family, he claimed, who could relate to the new artistic languages emerging at Di Tella). I recall this anecdote here because one might think of it as a performance, or as Peralta Ramos's very personal take, as he stated, on merging art and life, but in fact this recollection marks an interesting division. On the one hand, it embodies the awareness of Peralta Ramos and his art far beyond his local context: the Guggenheim Fellowship marks the coming-into-the-present of the artist not only in his country, but his "synchronization" with the art of today; his identity as an Argentinian artist became equal to "an artist." However, that dinner at Alvear—that incredibly bold gesture of generosity and disregard for money as potential matter that may serve him well in the process of becoming even more of "an artist" and produce more artworks—put into reverse Peralta Ramos's very synchronicity with the art world, sending him back to the "past." His expectations did not match those of the American institution, and so he was to "remain" an Argentinian artist.

It is interesting to think about the desire for recognition and visibility as similar to a process of transubstantiation between a local time and place—the here and now—and another time and place that is "bigger" or "larger" or just more universal, to borrow modern terms. Peralta Ramos, however, found a way to escape. In 1969, the artist started to sing and perform on TV shows, and, in 1970, he recorded what he called "nonfigurative" songs: "Soy un pedazo de atmósfera" ("I am a little piece of atmosphere") and "Tengo algo adentro que se llama el coso" ("I have something in my innermost called the thingamajig"). He once said he wanted to become a cloud, and added "a little piece of atmosphere." Becoming atmosphere is even better than becoming a recognized artist; it is far more complex, literally far more universal, and far more defiant of any theory of difference and individuation. One might say that the cloud, or atmosphere, has long been both an image to express an organ of sentiment and, at the same time, part of the painterly effort to address space, mass, and mood. Indeed, Peralta Ramos was trained as a painter, but wanting to become a cloud is wanting to abandon any idea of a solid body, of sharp visibility, of clear distinction. Becoming atmosphere—and not even the whole but a "piece"—challenges us with a mysterious volume without surface and embraces indeterminacy as the one and only identity.

III. Indeterminacy

For decades artists have understood that the only way to regain an understanding of form demands losing it completely. The renewed interest in becoming a cloud or a rock or a plant or a turtle is an interest in separating identity from identification. I still remember my surprise when, ten years ago, I met two artists in two different latitudes proposing to get into somebody else's body: Eduardo Navarro, in Buenos Aires, and Roberto Cuoghi, in Milan. During one of my first conversations with Eduardo years ago in 2005, he told me about how he once dressed up as a "fat" young person on a group tour to spot UFOs in the north of Argentina. I remember meeting him in his studio, where he explained his decision to join the already established group that met regularly and organized trips to experience extrasensorial life, to wait for UFOs. In a quiet voice, Eduardo explained how he couldn't go on the trip as "himself," so he decided to create a costume, an inflatable dress, which made him look very overweight. It was a radically naive attempt to become another person, but what I liked about it was its total absence of ambition to make it look "realistic." But why become "fat"? One simple answer: fat is a way to win more space between an artist and others. Eduardo not only told me about the long sessions of invoking spirits and looking for signals, but also how they found him too weird, too awkward, despite the fact that they were all open to the extrasensorial. The group thought he didn't belong, and yet the artist was far from an impostor or a spy. If infiltration was his goal, he could have done it better. Instead, pretending to mutate into somebody else turned empathy into a radicalized performance, testing the many ways we need to exercise the human capability of training our senses differently.

Not long before this meeting with Eduardo I met Italian artist Roberto Cuoghi in Milan, who told me about a similar pursuit. In 1998, at the age of twenty-five, Cuoghi attempted to take on the appearance of his father, who was becoming seriously ill. Within just weeks, Cuoghi transformed himself into an old man. In an attempt to accelerate biological time, he gained forty kilograms, dyed his hair white, grew a long beard, and began to dress and behave like his father. Neither enacting a performance nor wearing a disguise yet existing somewhere between fiction and reality, Cuoghi maintained this new persona for years. And although he created no artworks about it, news of Cuoghi's attempt to "life-share," to duplicate and consequently prolong his father's existence, spread by word of mouth until it passed into art-world lore. Cuoghi's imitation survived the original, but his body paid a high inheritance tax: when his father passed away, the artist began to reverse the premature aging, but the stress he had subjected himself to over the years rendered the process extremely slow and painful, even necessitating surgical operations.

IV. Quī Fuit Rāna, Nunc Est Rēx

As in gender and biology, all these projects reveal an art that moves away from essentialist ideas of what we and things are, which can only be contested by a radical expansion of what we can feel or sense, since it is in the senses that thinking breathes. But they also represent a powerful attempt to contest and overcome solitude, a funny word, which I associate with form. Even more so, I pair solitude with modernity; it is a projection of course, but in my imagination the modern condition implies isolation, autonomy, absorption, solitude. The modern spirit says that the "good" thing is a separate thing, a particular, a body, a fortress, a nation-state. It is this logic that we need to contest, the logic of an undisturbed solitude. Our solitude cannot but be disturbed and start a radical process of *mixtio*, allowing forms and bodies and formats and languages and genders and nations to blend. Solitude needs to learn how the "entering" of one another is possible. We fear that in this process of fading individuality there will be no becoming, no future. Indeed, we will (yet already) need a totally new concept of the social in order to understand a notion of *life* in which we recognize that what we share with others is not our individualities, but our singularities. In other words, we need a concept in which the social does not rest on a contract, but on an experiment with what precedes both the individual and collective forms of life.

To play with the idea that a duck or an octopus or any nonhuman form of intelligence is what Nietzsche meant by the Übermensch is to reject anthropodicy and to negate the humanist paradigm aimed at establishing a distance between the human and all that is dehumanized. Art is our chance to imagine this form of a decentered perception system; it enables us to sense the world in ways beyond language. Art is the thinking duck. It transforms of our way of conceiving the social, its institutions, and the hope we all have for perceptual inventiveness and a more complex notion of experience. Traditionally, we are the ones who perceive art, and art is the provider of that particular experience that surpasses all other experiences without resembling any of them. Yet we can still think and judge when perceiving art. Separation and difference is key to a centralized way of sensing that still allows for distinction and the valuation of everything that touches our skin.

The history of aesthetic experience is the history of solidification, of a materialistic idea of the production and possession of a certain determinate feeling that we can both isolate thought and communicate socially. Aesthetic experience is like a rock and its enemy is liquid, fluidity. It is said that all began in water, and indeed, it took us centuries to control our relationship with fluids. The history of hygiene is not only the history of epidemiology, but also the history of a strong—and necessary—boundary-making between the body and fluids. The history of these norms that prohibited us to "be fluid" is the history of governance. It is illegal to urinate or defecate in public, or to throw unclear water on the streets; condoms are used to prevent semen from entering the body of another. These are ways to draw boundaries, to understand our body as a container that is separated from what is outside of it, from others. But this does not only include the toilet or the condom or the hygienic pad or systems of sanitation; aesthetic experiences are also part of this economy of cleanliness and separation, of objects and bodies that evoke a more pristine, unpolluted kind of experience. I used to love the writing of Zygmunt Bauman, until he also started to elaborate on liquid as a problem. Baumann illustrates liquid as a trait of our postcapitalist condition, but not as the necessary opening of boundaries of identity and the body. Instead, he explains it as a new return to a Sisyphean condition, only now instead of a solid rock, we spend unending hours digitally tasking with smartphones and computers. Baumann's hero is condemned to texting and internet dating. In his words, the liquid modern is forever at work, forever replacing the quality of relationships with quantity.

It's a pity that Baumann sees the problem in the streams of water and fluid and the indistinctiveness between us and machines. His perspective is similar to complaining about new generations being "absorbed" by screens or not being able to read linearly. But things are only this way because we invest so much in a technology that allows us to break the straight line. To navigate today is to move and flow in a complex stream of text, to engage with a collage of words, phrases, and images that make some people believe we are losing our focus. Philosopher Vilém Flusser is one of the few who thinks positively about this abandonment of the line, of definitive forms. In 1988 Flusser visited the Ars Electronica festival in Osnabrück, Germany, where he gave an interesting interview in which he tells how words simply cannot describe the world anymore. He explains how we are at the end of a single code: the alphabet. The alphabet was not only a radical invention that—more than 3,500 years ago—provided a unique code to form words and describe reality, but it was also at the core of the genesis of our notion of "historical time." The end of the alphabet's hegemony implies the possibility of finally embracing a "broader" stream. Here, knowledge gets its form not from a single argumentative and critical logic, but from a dance of a million entanglements and ideas and materials that compose a convoluted new ocean of knowledge. We are not ready to take this as it is now; we first need a different notion of the sensual and the senses, as well as different hypotheses to link biological organs with material and technological ones.

There is nothing metaphysical or magical or esoteric or even irrational in a potential return to a defense of liquidity. It merely designates the happy difficulty we have with amorphous life and our fear of being gobbled up by it. Culture has expressed this fear many times, and it was probably the seventeenth-century French humanist François Rabelais who articulated it best. In his literature, Rabelais stressed two key notions for the time to come: extravagance and the importance of unintelligibility. It does not work to take Eduardo Navarro's artistic attempts too seriously. There is a brutal lightness in the way Eduardo proposes to be a turtle, and even more so in becoming an octopus (a later work with eighty dancers), because it is something bigger, it makes him need other humans to volunteer to become one with him; it is Pantagruelian and beautifully extravagant. His imagination and the ability for others to participate in it are motivated by an out-of-proportion kind of humor; otherwise, he would be just another power-seeker leading a group into a conversion that will transform nothing but life into its eventual destruction. It is very radical to invite someone to become an octopus, and even if it's thought of as a fiction, a temporary metamorphosis, its effects and the power of the transformation will never be known until you actually do it.

Eduardo's octopus is not the same as that incredible animal living under the sea, but imagine the thoughts of each and every individual attaching to each other. Imagine being hungry and not being able to stop and eat or even claim hunger because—once attached to that enormous body that exercises synchronicity—it is unempathetic to drawing attention to just one small stomach. There are at least eighty stomachs in this octopus, one hundred and sixty ears that hear differently, eighty noses that smell differently, another one hundred and sixty eyes that see the body, the structure, space, light, forms, textures differently. Think about how many square meters of skin and millions of nervous terminations this "dry" octopus has. The complex intermingling in becoming-mollusk is some sort of simultaneous self-discovery and discovery of the animal. I quote Michel de Montaigne on the "life" of the male sexual member in order to explicate and defend this thesis:

> How often do the involuntary movements of our features reveal what we are secretly thinking and betray us to those about us! The same cause that governs this member, without our knowing it governs the heart, the lungs, and the pulse, the sight of a charming object imperceptibly spreading within us the flame of a feverish emotion. Are these the only muscles and veins that swell and subside without the consent, not only of our will, but even of our thoughts? ... How much more justifiably can we brand [our will] with rebellion and sedition, on account of its constant irregularities and disobedience! Does it not often desire, to our obvious disadvantage, what we forbid it to? Does it let itself be guided, either, by the conclusions of our reason? In short, I ask you on behalf of my noble client kindly to reflect that, although his case in this matter is inseparably and indistinguishably joined with that of an accomplice, nevertheless he alone is attacked, and with such arguments and accusations as, seeing the condition of the parties, cannot possibly appertain to or concern the said accomplice. Wherefore the malice and manifest injustice of his accusers is apparent.[4]

"Metamorphosis" implies fluidity, liminality, and processes of change. As a scientific term, it characterizes the abrupt biological development of a species after hatching or birth. This idea of an in-between space or state of growth, transition, and transformation has captured the imagination of philosophers, poets, and writers throughout history. In rejecting essentialist fixed identity categories, feminist scholars too have sought to understand how gender intersects with other identities, paying attention to how these are performed in and through gendered bodies.

1 Alex Kacelnik and Antone Martinho III, "Ducklings imprint on the relational concept of 'same or different,'" *Science* 353, 6296 (July 15, 2016): 286–88.
2 Louis Kahn, quoted in *My Architect: A Son's Journey*, dir. Nathaniel Kahn (Louis Kahn Project Inc., 2003).
3 Gilles Deleuze, *Difference and Repetition* [1968], trans. Paul Patton (New York: Columbia University Press, 1995), chapter 5.
4 Michel de Montaigne, *Essays* (1580), 42–44.

Amplified Humanity and the Architectural Criminal

Lucia Allais

Prosecutor Fatou Bensouda and the accused, Mohammad Al Mahdi, during Al Mahdi's International Criminal Court trial in the Hague.

Over the past twelve months, two international initiatives have been closely watched because they appear to set the terms for a new, globally punishable architectural criminality.[1] The Italian-Jordanian initiative *Protecting Cultural Heritage: An Imperative for Humanity* mobilized the UN, Interpol, and UNESCO to stem the looting and smuggling of antiquities out of war-torn Syria by demonstrating that their traffic "finances terrorism" and is "linked to international crime."[2] At the same time, the International Criminal Court of the Hague tried and indicted Ahmad Al Faqi Al Mahdi, a Malian citizen who orchestrated the destruction of ten mausoleums and mosques in Timbuktu on behalf of Ansar Dine (an affiliate of Al Qaeda in the Islamic Maghreb, AQIM), in the broadest-ever judicial ruling that architectural destruction is punishable as a war crime.[3]

These two projects promise to bridge two notions, "heritage" and "humanity," that have been separated in international law for at least a hundred years.[4] Legally, the bifurcation can be traced to the aftermath of World War II. Since the 1954 Hague Convention, heritage laws have protected architecture as a kind of collective property, whereas texts such as the 1948 Human Rights Declaration codified humanity as an attribute of individual personhood. Any reference to cultural heritage was deliberately excluded from the 1948 Genocide Convention, signed that same year.

But historically, the split predates these laws. World War I was the first conflict where modern nation-states competed and collaborated to protect their art and architecture. In fact, these protective measures were so well-publicized that after 1918 Europe's cultural elite became consumed with debates about whether armies had been more concerned with their art than with their citizens. Fearing that humans and things might have to *compete* for protection in future wars, international lawyers found themselves split for much of the twentieth century in an apparent opposition: advocate either for culture or for human rights.[5]

Fast-forward to September 2016. The ICC's judgment against Al Mahdi explicitly seeks to move past this split legacy. "Crimes against property are generally of less gravity than crimes against persons," states the ICC Chamber, but this particular attack was "heightened by the fact that it was relayed in the media"—that is, it was amplified by its consequences for the international community.[6]

So if protecting heritage has become an "imperative for humanity," it is by undermining the early-modern and Enlightenment definition of the human as distinct both from things that are less than human (such as barbarians, animals, or inanimate objects) and also those that are more than human (such as gods).[7] At the ICC trial, the religious aspects of destruction took a notable back seat, while its technical and material logistics, and the nature of Timbuktu's mosques and mausoleums as "living" heritage, were emphasized.

To be sure, tensions lie just beneath the surface of the apparent consensus that the Al Mahdi case is groundbreaking. Critics point out that Al Mahdi's confession and cooperation with the court mean that the case sets no new evidentiary standards.[8] Human rights advocates worry that a victory in punishing violence against buildings might obscure crimes against persons, including the widespread sexual violence committed by the very same group, during the very same period, and in the same urban spaces of Timbuktu. The Malian association for Human Rights and Amnesty International have both called for "an expansion of the charges" against Al Mahdi.[9] The stakes of punishing architectural destruction are therefore clear: is it a proxy for exposing more pervasive but more invisible human rights abuses, ones whose victims are chosen for their collective identity but targeted as individuals, living in a city under siege.

If the relationship between heritage and humanity has been reconfigured from one of opposition to one of *proximity*, what are the architectural terms of this proximity? What are the operations through which the "expansion" or "widening" of crime and punishment alike are imagined? In this essay I probe these questions in two parts. First, the accused's discourse, in court and in abundant video evidence, provides an entry point into the logic of sincerity that motivated the design of the destruction of Timbuktu. Second, an analysis of the practices that authenticate Timbuktu as an international treasure—both in court and in ongoing preservation—reveals the techniques of amplification that are embedded into the built environment to hold together an agreement, on both sides of the law, that the target of this new criminality is humanity itself.

Life on the Architectural Surface

Heritage and humanity are becoming proximate notions under the sign of a dialogue, or negative mirroring, between the ideologies of Western humanitarianism and global jihad. In his remarkable book *The Terrorist in Search of Humanity*, historian Faisal Devji shows the confounding parallels between the structure and functioning of these two movements: both operate through widely distributed networks whose endgame is nongovernmental, who claim to occupy a privileged place of morality, and who recruit young and idealistic individuals "in search of humanity."[10]

Devji's work is informed by Hannah Arendt's 1957 definition of humanity as produced through "negative solidarity, based on the fear or global destruction."[11] Arendt proclaimed that humanity had "become an urgent reality," but one realized only in the face of the possibility for total extinction. Devji argues that something resembling this negative solidarity animates the suicide bombers of Al Qaeda for whom the "globe" (*al-alam*) can be unified only at the moment when it is left behind. To be sure, there is a difference in the two sides of Devji's comparison: the search for empathy leads humanitarian workers to seek out sites of bare life, whereas the jihadist's path culminates in sacrificial suicide. But two of Devji's lessons are clear: first, assuming that Western humanitarianism is modern and secular while the Islamic militant project is fundamentalist and anti-modern only obscures the analysis of both, and second, destruction plays a crucial role in humanity's coalescence.

Because Devji relies on Arendt, he already offers us a way of thinking of humanity and heritage laws as *historically* proximate. If a new humanity coalesced in the face of mid-century mass murder, so too was the notion of international heritage worked out in response to massive scenarios of destruction during the tumultuous decades before its codification in the 1972 World Heritage Convention.[12]

Furthermore, Devji has updated his analysis to encompass the rise of the Islamic State, describing how, against the commonly assumed rift between modern superficiality and traditionalist depth, IS recruits are asked to live what he calls "a life on the surface."[13] "Efforts to explain terrorism tend to be structured as efforts to plumb the movement's depth," he writes, but in fact most recruits obey "banal forms of reasoning" that explicitly mirror the actions of the West, to expose its insincerity. Thus, "it is not the content of the West's actions that is put in question" by militant rhetoric, "but simply its hypocrisy."

Devji invites us to see in destruction the "logic of equivalence that marks militancy." For Al Qaeda, he cites Vyjayanthi Rao's reading of the Mumbai bombing as an infrastructural counterpart to the smart bombs of the West.[14] For ISIS, he diagnoses a "hatred of all historical, sociological and ideological depth" as motivating the architectural destruction "of pre-Islamic monuments, [and] also of all 'traditional,' 'heretical' or 'infidel' sites."[15]

Returning to the case of Timbuktu, then, we find destruction that *both* echoes Al Qaeda's concerns for global belonging, *and* constitutes an early example—an experiment, really—of the attacks on funerary structures that the Islamic State would later make systematic, beginning with the invasion of Mosul.[16] In Timbuktu, Al Mahdi leveraged both the infrastructural, networked nature of the city, and its nature as a historical root. Additionally, I would like to argue, the attack on the mausoleums and mosques was motivated by an almost superficial reflectivity, a ghostly mirror of the profundity that is assumed to be granted by the West to these locally revered objects.[17]

Consider, first, the carefully timed game of retaliation that motivated the destruction. Ansar Dine monitored the activities of local inhabitants at ten mosques and mausolea for several months, but only ordered their destruction after they were inscribed on UNESCO's list of heritage under threat in June 2012.[18] In October, the group restarted destruction on the eve of an international meeting in Bamako, and in December, it was in response to a UN security resolution to send an occupying force to northern Mali that further "hidden mausoleums in the city" were found and attacked.[19] In interviews with the Western press, Ansar Dine spokesperson Sanda Ould Boumama performed this mirroring, asking, "We are Muslims; what is UNESCO?" and continuing, as if to question the moral authority of the West's cult of monuments, "For us, their indignation is an atonement."[20]

Next, consider Al Mahdi himself. A religiously educated member of a Tuareg family, he was a teacher of literary Arabic and a schoolmaster by the time he was recruited into Ansar Dine in April 2012, when he took the name Abu Turab and began travelling as an acolyte of Abu Zadine. When the group returned to Timbuktu to occupy the city, Al Mahdi was enlisted to act as local mediator and, given a choice of positions, became the chief of the "morality police," al-Hesbah. Video footage from this period (captured by a rare embedded journalist) shows him to be living exactly the kind of life on the surface described by Devji: going from his day job teaching Arabic to a child, to donning a special "vice police" jacket on top of his clothes before he sets off on vice patrol.[21] This squad is in charge not of beliefs but of mores; not of the content of the Koran but of its respect; not of the rules but of the sincerity with which they are followed.

Following Al Mahdi on his routine as a morality policeman, the camera catches him alternately conducting online research on Koranic law in a session of the local Islamic court, patrolling the streets with Kalashnikov and megaphone in hand, inflicting the first three of a hundred lashes to an adulterous couple in the public square, assisting in the assassination of one of Ansar Dine's own, and leading a group of men in the destruction, by pickax, of a number of buildings.

The architectural destruction fits seamlessly into the joint policing of local morality and global sincerity. "We have destroyed these cemeteries as a preventative measure," Al Mahdi explains at one point, "in order to make sure the people don't use them as idols."[22] In fact, Al Mahdi is not originally convinced that the mausolea need destroying. But when he is finally pressured to write a radio sermon calling for their destruction, he finds a Koranic verse forbidding any construction higher than an inch on top of a tomb.[23]

What ensues is a two-week performance of regulating architectural volumes and surfaces through destruction. At stake is the superficiality of the Western notion of heritage "protection," to which Ansar Dine counterproposes that it is the globe and its surface that should be the true object of protection, and not have objects built upon it. Thus tombs are sinful protuberations and their razing "brings protection of Sharia of the unicity of God."[24] Destroying buildings creates a place "upon which the law of Allah can now be applied."[25] Al Mahdi vows to "remove everything that doesn't belong on the landscape," as if to prime the surface of the earth for a guest.[26] Thinness and superstition are also conflated when the mob arrives at one of Timbuktu's revered monuments—a sacred door. "There was a legend that if you opened this door it would be the end of the world. We are charged with fighting superstition. This is why we decided to fix the construction of the door."[27] Exposing superficiality, Al Mahdi helps rip out the door by hand to expose a bricked-up, solid wall.[28]

One of the more remarkable allocutions of Al Mahdi's destructive rationale comes retroactively, in court, when the presiding judge inquires about the sincerity of his remorse and asks whether he has had to renounce his religious belief to plead guilty. Instead, Al Mahdi notes that this is not his first, but his second change of heart, thereby assuring the court that he had simply learned to live with "the contradiction that the mausoleums represented."[29] To be sure, this represents a betrayal of Al Qaeda's sacrificial quest, but it also retroactively confirms that this sacrifice was originally demanded in the name not of a historically grounded tradition but rather to publicize (and destroy) modern hypocrisy.

In court, Al Mahdi himself takes on qualities of an architectural mediator. He is tried not only as the "author" of destruction but as a "media spokesperson," for his design of a sequence for the destruction. He is charged with "heightening the suffering" of Timbuktu's population by allowing "armed groups to reach and thus to victimize a broader audience."[30] His choice of destruction techniques (instead of a bulldozer he purchases pickaxes, which distribute the destructive tasks) also confers mediatic properties to his mob: they transmit ideology through their actions.[31]

But if AQIM relies on Al Mahdi as a local connector for implanting itself in Timbuktu, the ICC equally requires him to use his own personhood to depict an expanded field of applicability for international law. The same qualities that Al Mahdi offered to the terrorist network are fully exploited by the ICC: he is a person who can "expand" his identity and belonging concentrically. This is particularly evident in the way Al Mahdi structures his guilty plea, in a statement that repeats atonement in a scalar progression from local brotherhood, to national citizenship, to global humanity:

I am sorry. I am really remorseful and I regret all the damage that my actions have caused to my family. And to my brothers in Timbuktu. And to my home country, the nation of Mali, in general.

And to the whole of humanity around the world.[32] (*al bashariyyati jamaa fi anha' al alam*)

When Al Mahdi uses the word "humanity," he evokes a ribbon of persons across the globe. But the French and English translations (both in court and in official transcripts) replace this with "international community," taking advantage of the discursive structure that is shared between humanitarian activism and Islamic jihad.[33] Indeed, even if Al Mahdi's language is far more colorful than its translations, it conveys a struggle with superficiality. He speaks of being "swept up" in an "intense whirlwind," but argues that despite this destructive force the "deep historical roots (*al jothoor al amiqa*) of the city of Timbuktu and its inhabitants" cannot be erased. The court translators substitute "root" with "heritage," and "whirlwind" with "evil wave ... of deviant people." But these substitutions are altogether seamless, because Al Mahdi is one of the few people who can make these linguistic substitutions possible. From an anonymous official, he becomes throughout the trial a crucial operand, who can perform the scalar shift from personal brotherhood to global humanity that is consistent both with the imagined territory of humanitarian law and with the global surface of jihad.

What, then, about heritage practices that were called upon to remediate Al Mahdi's cultural vandalism? Devji's concept of "life on the surface" helps to locate the criminalization of architectural destruction within humanitarianism as a privileged vector of moral sincerity in the West, as well as within terrorism and its publicity goals. What is the relationship between this dynamic and the international preservation community, with its well-known preoccupation with integrity and authenticity? Here too the answer lies less in the symbolic weight of Timbuktu's architecture than in the technologies of protection that have been used to manage its decay, its destruction, and now its reconstruction.

When Old Ontologies Were New

Two conceptions of heritage were brought to trial in the Hague. The first associates architectural objects with depth and fundament. It offers a vision of heritage as local, situated, and connects the architecture of the buildings to the earth itself. The prosecutor in Al Mahdi's case, Fatou Bensouda, adopted this view in her opening statement. She invoked the "deep connection between the mausoleums and the inhabitants," called the destroyed buildings "roots of an entire people" and "important foundational blocks" for the city's life and recalled their "inherent" or "intrinsic value" which, "once destroyed, restoration can never bring back."[34] For her, Timbuktu was targeted as an emblem of cultural diversity, a union of human and material tolerance that was dissolved as soon as "authentic materials [were] destroyed."[35] She further functionalized this architectural ontology in her legal argument, by resorting to the doctrine of military objective (which objectifies the built environment by classifying all buildings as *either* civilian *or* military).[36]

This argument is entirely in keeping with prevalent international preservation theories that hold that the gap between heritage and humanity can only ever be bridged by a deep essentialism of place. "In order to maintain its authenticity and truthfulness," Jukka Jokilehto writes, "space must be alive." Any local community "produces" space through dwelling, and therefore all spatial history ("inheritances," in this language) is necessarily local, while any contact with a "globalizing world society" provokes an uprooting.[37] What is lost in destruction, therefore, is architecture's inherent sincerity.[38]

But the material continuities that apparently authenticate these historical lineages are hard to trace. Thus a second view of heritage extends a testimonial power to buildings and affords more room for historical and material ruptures. Here, Bensouda appealed to the continued "memory" of these buildings in several generations, as "living testimony to Timbuktu's glorious past ... a unique testament to the city's urban settlements."[39] One step removed from ontological dwelling, this chain of communication proceeds through history witness by witness.

In fact, Bensouda also speaks of the mausoleums as media of amplification, and of herself as a transmitter. "It is the voice of the mausoleums, of monuments, which ring out like a bell through my voice ... a voice that brings with it echoes for its audience, of hatred or violence or anger." Bensouda—who has been applauded for her willingness to leverage the "symbolic power" of the ICC—repeats this amplification in her concluding statement giving weight to the judge's ruling in a scalar concentricity. "Your judgment is awaited from the ancient streets of Timbuktu and throughout Mali to all four corners of the world."[40]

It is this media-enabled, amplified humanity (and not a fundamentalist architectural essence) that the judge ultimately designates as the victim of Al Mahdi's crime. In the final judgment, the court refuses to accept either the "religious nature" or the "high-profile quality" of the attack as an "aggravating circumstance." Instead, the "far-reaching nature" of the crime is essential to the fact that it is aimed at "multiple victims."[41] The gravity of the crime is measured spatially but indirectly, with the idea that international humanity is a mediated, amplified multiple of the local inhabitants.

How did the heritage experts who helped rebuild Timbuktu beginning in 2013 take up this challenge of reconciling essentialism and mediality? It was not in fact difficult. Their task was facilitated by preexisting efforts to bring techno-scientific building practices to bear on a primarily artisanal building tradition. Consider a *Manual for the Conservation of Timbuktu*, published in 2014 to herald the cultural rebirth of the city, but based on research conducted by Italian architects and archaeologists between 2002 and 2006 to protect the city from climate change. The manual depicts the city as a natural product of the "constructive culture of earth."[42] Yet the conservation techniques prescribed in this manual are almost exclusively drainage practices that control the external surfaces of the city's vernacular construction. One section shows a typical city street with a Tuareg scale figure surrounded by meticulously layered paving and walls. Another shows how to protect the joint between earth and building from water infiltration. Another embeds toilet plumbing inside banco walls. From the care given to these technical images, a casual reader of this manual would be forgiven for thinking that the world-heritage status of Timbuktu pertains only to the thinnest of its outer layers.

"Facade Ouest" and "Facade Est" for the Cheikh Sidi Ahmed Ben Amar Arragadi, in Pietro M. Apollonj Ghetti, *Etude sur les Mausolées de Tombouctou* (Unesco, 2014).

But international expertise is concentrated on these surface details for good reason: because the more tectonic aspects of building are delegated to a local community of masons who have for generations, we are told, conserved the city through embodied building know-how.[43] They use earth to make either rounded or rectangular earth bricks; they also replaster outer walls periodically by hand using sand and water. The material link between these masons and the "earth" out of which they build their architecture is a human, transgenerational apprenticeship, *itself* designated as intangible heritage under threat.

Implicitly, then, the reasons for this ecological intervention in Timbuktu's architecture are aesthetic: together, climate change and declining know-how have conspired to undermine the objecthood and legibility of Timbuktu. Increased rains mean that water stagnates in the cityscape, and earthen walls are not able to dry through natural evaporation, especially as sand piles surrounding outer walls give water a place to collect and walls rot from within. Masons have responded to the increasing frailty of their architecture by using hybrid building techniques, such as using adding cement to adobe, CMUs, and banco bricks, or shoring up failing walls with banco buttresses that jut out into streets. These new practices create an increasingly pile-ridden, formless, ill-defined urban streetscape.[44] In other words, the guardians of World Heritage find themselves policing Timbuktu's masons by constraining their work so that it may only result in sharply outlined, monolithic objects.

All of these aspects of the thick-thin theory of Timbuktese earthen architecture have made their reappearance in the UNESCO-sponsored reconstruction of Timbuktu's mausoleums, but the contradiction between depth and surface has now been reconfigured. While ecological disaster seemed to call forth nostalgia for a disappearing tradition, the threat of terrorist destruction makes architecture a medium for the transmitting of a newly construed humanity. In the ICC trial the masons appear as "living human treasures" and, by publishing this manual in 2014, UNESCO makes clear that the goal of reconstruction is in part to give them something to build.[45] Through its reconstruction, Timbuktu is now defined as the medial support for the transmission of know-how, not the other way around.

After all, Al Mahdi had intervened in the city's medial landscape with his megaphone and his laptop as much as with his pickax and his Kalashnikov.[46] The contest for defining the global "human" continues now, as international institutions continue to publicize their involvement in Timbuktu, keeping its architecture alive by circulating it on networks of communication.[47]

After the destruction and reconstruction of its mausoleums, Timbuktu's architectural history becomes a media archaeology, one which may help get past the pitfalls of colonialist histories. After all, the inaugural definition of Timbuktu as a place of protuberations was colonial. Robert Caillié's famous engraving of the "city of 333 saints," still reproduced in heritage manuals today, saw religious diversification literally materialized in a proliferation of buildings.[48] Now, instead, the original context in which Timbuktu will take its architectural significance is that of a network of pilgrimage, commerce, and tourism both real and virtual. In the words of the court, Timbuktu is the "protective heart" of Mali's heritage because it has been a focal point of cultural mobility since the Middle Ages.[49] And with protection now understood to be the original function of Timbuktu's destroyed mausoleums, their reconstruction can be seamlessly integrated into their history.[50]

Timbuktu's architectural history as a protective shield has not been interrupted by the destructions of 2012; rather, it has been increasingly materialized. The city was already mediatized when technologies of communication were embedded in its urban architecture and its landmarks.[51] In the 1990s, the Djingareiber Mosque was wired and loudspeakers were lodged among its dome's distinctive wooden stakes. Between 2002 and 2006, Timbuktu's urban fabric was surveyed through plans that encircled buildings with markers signifying the positions of photographers. After their destruction, the rebuilt mausoleums have been inventoried not through simple photography but with data-rich photogrammetric scans, with a ghostly scale figure digitally added in. UNESCO hopes that reconstruction will reclaim the warscape the city had become under Ansar Dine, through new acts of medial-architectural presencing.[52] For example, when masons climb atop mosque towers during their yearly "ritual maintenance event" and pose for a publicity shot, the architectural festival itself is not new, but it is has now become a performance of retracing, reproduction, that takes place on the very surface of what colonial visitors called "a noble pile."[53] Photographic surveying and participatory masonry have created a new standard for authenticity, where geometric exactitude recedes and live approximation triumphs.[54]

The Lure of Evidence

From a place for the multiplication of saints, Timbuktu has become the site for an amplification of humanity. It is undoubtedly this power of amplification that prosecutors and activists are hoping to avail themselves of today to activate the proximity of heritage and humanity. When heritage advocates argue, after Raphael Lemkin, that cultural destruction tends to precede human violence; that vandalism must be prosecuted to "signal" that no other violence will be tolerated—it is because violence against heritage and humanity circulate by the same means.[55] But even when it occurs *in the same place*, the broadening of heritage into humanity is mediated. This is why architectural forensics is an urgent issue, and its practitioners are keenly attuned to the evolution of new media.[56]

Yet when architectural evidence is brought to the Hague, the argument that heritage and humanity are united by collective identity, by dignity cemented through dwelling, is not sufficient. The architects' cameras that penetrated Timbuktu's interiors in the 2000s to survey its urban fabric could not produce evidence of the sexual crimes that those same walls may have witnessed in 2012. On today's international stage, any ontology will be tested against an evolving definition of humanity as fueled by "negative solidarity." The architectural criminal mirrors the morality claims of the humanitarian, including those of her evidentiary regimes. After all, when the court attempted to penetrate Al Mahdi's internal life, he performed an outward extension of personhood instead.

1 This piece was originally written in December 2016.

2 *Protecting Cultural Heritage: An Imperative for Humanity*, United Nations Brochure, September 22, 2016, 10. Produced on the occasion of a "high-level meeting" at the United Nations.

3 Vandalism on the world stage is nothing new, nor is its prosecution as a violation of international norms. A crucial precedent was set by the International Tribunal established in the aftermath of the Balkan wars, which tried and convicted criminals for "intentional cultural destruction." But the Dayton Accords, which this Tribunal enforced, pertained only to one conflict, circumscribed in space and time. On this, see Andrew Herscher, *Violence Taking Place* (Stanford: Stanford University Press, 2010). In contrast, the International Criminal Court prosecuted Al Mahdi for his violation of a prohibition against "intentionally targeting cultural sites" that makes up Article 8 of the Rome Statute, an agreement that originates in a 1998 compact to establish a permanent international judiciary.

4 Among those pushing for this bridging are journalists such as Robert Bevan, "Attacks on Culture to be Crimes against Humanity," *The Art Newspaper*, September 27, 2016; and scholars such as Stener Ekern, William Logan, Birgitte Sauge, and Amund Sinding-Larsen, "Human Rights and World Heritage: Preserving Our Common Dignity through Rights-Based Approaches to Site Management," *International Journal of Heritage Studies* 18, no. 3 (2012), 214–354. In Africa, the phrase "crime against world heritage" has been circulated; see Slimane Zeghidour, "Crime contre le patrimoine de l'humanité," tv5monde.com, March 11, 2015. In Western elite preservation circles, the two terms have also been cross-pollinated, as when Renzo Piano's addition to a building by Le Corbusier was called a "crime against humanity"; see Michael Z. Wise, "Confrontation at Art Museums," *ArtNews*, October 29, 2014. The film version of Bevan's book *The Destruction of Memory* (dir. Tim Slade, 2014) features a number of international figures arguing for now "conjoining" heritage and

humanitarian law. Most prominently, UNESCO Secretary General Irina Bokova declares, "You don't choose between lives and monuments because it's about identity." On the differentiation between humanism and humanitarianism in the construction of international architectural heritage value, see Lucia Allais, "This Criterion Should Preferably Be Used in Conjunction with Other Criteria," *Grey Room* 61 (Fall 2015): 92–101.

5 Rafael Lemkin, the author of the Genocide Convention, originally included "vandalism" in his definition of genocide but dropped this aspect when it threatened the passage of the convention. See A. Dirk Moses, "Raphael Lemkin, Culture, and the Concept of Genocide," in *Oxford Handbook of Genocide Studies* (Oxford: University Press, 2012).

6 International Criminal Court, *Summary of the Judgment and Sentence in the case of The Prosecutor v. Ahmad Al Faqi Al Mahdi*, September 26, 2016, 10.

7 This is a distinction reiterated in 1938 by Erwin Panofsky, "The History of Art as a Humanistic Discipline," reprinted in Erwin Panofsky, *Meaning in the Visual Arts* (New York: Doubleday, 1955), 1–2.

8 The prevalence of video evidence was a factor in the court's decision to take on the Al Mahdi case for cultural property crime alone, producing what *Foreign Policy* calls "an evidentiary slam-dunk." See Marie Forestier, "ICC to War Criminals: Destroying Shrines Is Worse Than Rape," foreignpolicy.com, August 22, 2016. But it was his confession that established the "gravity" of the crime and its punishment.

9 See Association Malienne des Droits Humains, "Mali: La comparution d'Abou Tourab au CPI est une victoire, mais les charges à son encontre doivent être élargies," amdhmali.org, September 30, 2015. To argue for "widening" the charges, they wield a combined language of heritage and humanity. Erica Bussey of Amnesty International argued along similar lines to *The Guardian*; see Ruth Maclean, "'I am sorry': Islamist apologises for destroying Timbuktu mausoleums," *The Guardian*, August 22, 2016.

10 Faisal Devji, *The Terrorist in Search of Humanity: Militant Islam and Global Politics* (New York: Columbia University Press, 2008).

11 Hannah Arendt, "Karl Jaspers: Citizen of the World?" [1957], in *Men in Dark Times* (New York: Harcourt, Brace & World, 1968).

12 Far from a tabula rasa, the landscapes of destruction that increasingly patched the globe after the First World War were shaped around architectural objects that had been designated for survival, singled out for reconstruction, or both. This history of monument survival is the subject of my forthcoming book, *Designs of Destruction: Monument Survival and Internationalism in the 20th Century*.

13 Faisal Devji, "A Life on the Surface," hurstpublishers.com, September 21, 2015.

14 Vyjayanthi Rao, "How to Read a Bomb: Scenes from Bombay's Black Friday," *Public Culture* 19, no. 3 (2007): 567–92. Cited in Devji, *The Terrorist in Search of Humanity*, 51.

15 Devji, "A Life on the Surface."

16 Like many other groups in the Sahel, Ansar Dine has shifting alliances within global terror networks. At the time of the destruction it was allied with Al Qaeda, but also hosted recruiters and preachers coming through Timbuktu from a constellation of other groups. ISIS's cultural targeting became systematic in Mosul in June 2014, when the Islamic State of Iraq and al-Shām issued a "Charter of the City" announcing that "all shrines and mausoleums" would be razed. Cited in Aaron Zelin, "The Islamic State of Iraq and Syria Has a Consumer Protection Office," *The Atlantic*, June 13, 2014.

17 In "Between Cult and Culture: Bamiyan, Islamic Iconoclasm, and the Museum Author(s)," *The Art Bulletin* 84, no. 4 (December 2002): 641–59, Finbar Barry Flood already critiqued the essentialist view of Muslim iconoclasm as a cultural pathology by inscribing the destruction of the Bamiyan Buddhas within tropes of global modernity, especially as a response to the "hypocrisy of Western institutions." I wish to thank Byron Hamman for reminding me of this seminal article and for thoughtful comments on a draft of my own text as well.

18 Ansar Dine's monitoring and patrolling of the sites was one reason for the UN's decision to place them on the list of endangered cultural property. United Nations Press release, "Mali site added to List of World Heritage in Danger – UNESCO," un.org, July 13, 2012. The ICC also noted that the destruction was a response to the initiatives of the Malian Ministry of Culture begun in 2013.

19 "Les Islamistes détruisent les derniers mausolées de Tombouctou," *L'Express* with AFP, December 23, 2012.

20 "Les Islamistes poursuivent la destruction des monuments de Tombouctou," *L'Express* with AFP, July 1, 2012. These remarks were made to Agence France-Presse over the phone, reported widely (see for instance "A Tombouctou, les islamistes détruisent les mausolées musulmans," *Le Monde* with AFP, June 30, 2012). This citation is from the ICC's own "unofficial internal

translation" for the video MLI-OTP-0034-0395: "Our reference is not to international law, nor the United Nations, nor UNESCO ... These international bodies ... don't concern us, and for us their indignation is an atonement ... What is the value of these walls?" See also an interview of Sanda Ould Boumama by Marie-Pierre Olphand of RFI, "Mali: la destruction des mausolées de Tombouctou par Ansar Dine sème la consternation," November 10, 2013, which became evidence MLI-OTP-0007-0228, and MLI-OTP-0020-0584.

21 These videos, which serve as the core evidence in the ICC's case against Al Mahdi, were shown in an elaborate multimedia presentation during trial. Originally they were recorded by a Mauriantian videographer, Ethnam Ag Mohamed Ethman, who was embedded with Ansar Dine for months. Ethman periodically broadcast them on the news website saharamedias.net. Eventually they were acquired by producers and reporters from France 2, and broadcast during the special segment "Envoyé Spécial" on January 31, 2013, as part of the report "Mali: La vie sous le régime islamiste." See youtube.com/watch?v=H-7QMGd2fWI.

22 *The Prosecutor v. Ahmad Al Faqi Al Mahdi*, Transcript, Trial Chamber VIII, August 24, 2016: ICC-01/12-01/15/T-6-ENG, 11. Transcript from ICC trial indictment (January 12, 2015).

23 The ICC documents describe this as a rule against building anything measuring over "an inch" while press reports say "building anything that is taller than the span of a hand."

24 "Envoyé Spécial," 15:07–15:30. "Settling the graves" is *taswiyat al qoboor*. Translation from original Arabic by Leen Katrib.

25 "If a tomb is higher than the others, it must be leveled ... We are going to rid the landscape of anything that is out of place." Cited in *The Prosecutor v. Ahmad Al Faqi Al Mahdi*, Public Judgment and Sentence, September 27, 2016 (ICC-01/12-01/15), 20–21. "Un homme remercie Dieu après avoir détruit un tombeau plus protubérant que les autres; un autre qui loue Allah de leur avoir accordé toutes ses victoires et de leur avoir permis d'appliquer Sa Loi sur terre." "Sahara média accompagne Ançar Edine en train de démolir les mausolées de Tombouctou," saharamedias.net, June 30, 2012.

26 "Les Islamistes détruisent," *L'Express* with AFP.

27 "Envoyé Spécial," 14:00–14:30. Translation from original Arabic by Leen Katrib.

28 "The door was condemned and bricked up. Over time, a myth took hold, claiming that the Day of Resurrection would begin if the door were opened. We fear that these myths will invade the beliefs of people and the ignorant who, because of their ignorance and their distance from religion, will think that this is the truth. So we decided to open it." Cited in Trial Chamber VII, *Prosecutor v. Ahmad Al Faqi Al Mahdi*, Public Judgement and Sentence (ICC-01/12-01/15-171), 22.

29 In response to the question, "Have you changed your religious conviction?" Al Mahdi replies: "If you review my former statements, you will see that I was not convinced originally with the appropriateness to undertake such actions from the beginning because the decisions I had made were made on the basis of a legal decision. I said that what I did was based on a theory according to which one cannot build anything on tombs, and a tomb, according to the religious beliefs, should not be over 1 inch above the ground, and those mausoleums are far higher than that ... But from a legal and political viewpoint one should not undertake actions that will cause damage that is higher or more severe than the usefulness of the action. Such mausoleums I believe are not as harmful as the contradiction they represent as they are built on tombs, but the people who controlled the country at the time considered that such ... Thus, I believe that by doing that I do not change my beliefs, I should not undertake action that will cause damage to others. This is a former belief and a present belief of mine, sir." Trial Chamber VIII, *Prosecutor v. Ahmad Al Faqi Al Mahdi*, Transcript, August 23, 2016 (ICC-01/12-01/15-T-4-Red-ENG), 13.

30 "We are not here to decide on the fate of the author of single act of vandalism, but to render justice to memory and affirm the importance of symbol in the existence of a people." *Prosecutor v. Ahmad Al Faqi Al Mahdi*, Transcript, August 24, 2016. "His role as media spokesperson in justifying the attack" is from *Prosecutor v. Ahmad Al Faqi Al Mahdi*, Public Judgement and Sentence, September 27, 2016, 39–42.

31 This choice of tools was also noted by the press. See "Sahara média accompagne Ançar Edine," saharamedias.net.

32 The English translation and transcription is *Prosecution v. Ahmad Al Faqi Al Mahdi*, Transcript, August 23, 2016 (ICC-01/12-01/15-T-4-Red-ENG), 8–9. The French is ICC-01/12-01/15-T-4-Red-FRA. This and following quotations of Al Mahdi's statement are retranslated by Leen Katrib from the Arabic video, not transcribed but made available by the court as "In the Courtroom Programme," icc-cpi.int/al-mahdi-videos.

33 Also critical to Al Mahdi's performance as an international witness was the somewhat belabored procedure of his choosing a language for

the trial. Being asked which language he preferred, Al Mahdi chose Arabic, indicating that his exographic affinity was with global Islam rather than the State of Mali, whose official language is French. When he indicated this choice through his lawyer, however, the presiding judge replied that he should have spoken this choice himself. Once Al Mahdi obliged, the judge then ensured an Arabic simultaneous translator, and asked all parties not speaking Arabic to pause periodically to allow this interpreter to keep up with proceedings.

34 "This is how deep the connection is between the mausoleums and the people of Timbuktu ... to erase an element of collective identity." *Prosecutor v. Ahmad Al Faqi Al Mahdi*, Transcript, August 22, 2016, 21.

35 Ibid.

36 "He acted with the requisite degree of knowledge. He knew that the buildings targeted were dedicated to religion and had a historic character and did not constitute military objective." Trial Chamber VIII, *Prosecutor v. Ahmad Al Faqi Al Mahdi*, Confirmation of Charges Hearing, March 24, 2015, (CR2016_02424), 25.

37 Jukka Jokilehto, "Human rights and cultural heritage," *International Journal of Heritage Studies* 18, no. 3 (May 2012): 226–30.

38 Accordingly, Bensouda cited an elderly man captured on camera, declaiming the loss of the city's "soul." *Prosecutor v. Ahmad Al Faqi Al Mahdi*, Transcript, August 22, 2016 (CR2016_05767), 19.

39 "These monuments, your Honours, were living testimony to Timbuktu's glorious past ... a unique testament to the city's urban settlements. But above all they were the embodiment of Malian history, captured in tangible form from an era long gone yet still very much vivid in the memory and pride of the people who so dearly cherished them." *Prosecutor v. Ahmad Al Faqi Al Mahdi*, Transcript, August 22, 2016 (CR2016_05767), 17.

40 *Prosecutor v. Ahmad Al Faqi Al Mahdi*, Transcript, August 22, 2016 (CR2-16_05757), 24.

41 The prosecution argued that the "multiple victims" aggravated the crime, while the chamber countered that it had "already taken into account the far-reaching nature of the crime." "World Heritage" status means that the crime "not only affects the direct victims of the crimes (namely, the faithful and inhabitants of Timbuktu) but also people throughout Mali and the international community." *Prosecutor v. Ahmad Al Faqi Al Mahdi*, Transcript, August 24, 2016 (CR2-16_05730).

42 Mauro Bertagnin and Ali Ould Sidi, *Manuel pour la Conservation de Tombouctou* (Paris: Unesco, 2014).

43 See "Analyse et constat: Dégradation des bâtiments" and "Les matériaux de la tradition et le rôle des maçons," in ibid., 61–70. See also Ali Ould Sidi, "Monuments and Traditional Know-How: The Example of Mosques in Timbuktu," *Museum International* 58, no. 1–2 (May 2006): 229–30; Ali Ould Sidi, "Timbuktu: Mosques Face Climate Challenges," *World Heritage Review* 42 (2006): 12–17; and Ali Ould Sidi, "Partnership to Preserve Timbuktu," *World Heritage Review* 29 (2009): 16–17.

44 *Manuel pour la Conservation*, 61.

45 For Bensouda, rebuilding and regular architectural maintenance, in an allegory for peacemaking itself, "contributing to the workshop of peaceful coexistence." *Prosecutor v. Ahmad Al Faqi Al Mahdi*, Transcript, August 22, 2016, 24.

46 I take inspiration here from Brian Larkin's description of the mediality of the loudspeaker in Jos, Nigeria, a city where both daily life and conflict are, as in Timbuktu, mediated through techniques and technologies for attention and inattention. Brian Larkin, "Techniques of Inattention: The Mediality of Loudspeakers in Nigeria," *Anthropological Quarterly* 87, no. 4 (Fall 2014): 989–1016.

47 Pietro M. Apollonj Ghetti, *Étude sur les mausolées de Tombouctou* (Paris: Unesco, 2013).

48 Robert Caillié, *Voyage à Tombouctou* [1830], Facsimile (Paris: La Découverte, 1996).

49 Francesco Bandarin's testimony at the ICC notably weaves together three themes of Timbuktu's architecture to argue for its multivalent historical value: a site of material know-how, of religious aura, *and* an urban network that is a "focus point for religious life, the region ... and focus for pilgrimage." *Prosecutor v. Ahmad Al Faqi Al Mahdi*, Transcript, August 23, 2016, 44.

50 Even Timbuktu's famous manuscripts, which had been meticulously digitized before 2010, have been rereleased into networks of global mobility. Originally housed in new museums on site, they were smuggled to Bamako before Al Mahdi's group was able to get to them, thanks to a network of globally trained curators, funded in part by a Ford Foundation grant. These funds had originally been granted in a "multidimensional and integrated United Nations initiative for stabilization" (MIUNIS) to Abdel Kader Haidara, a collector and librarian in Timbuktu, to conserve these manuscripts on site. They were officially diverted to help with the secret removal of these objects to Bamako by boat and car. "Trois Bibliothèques de manuscripts anciens

réhabilitées à Tombouctou," UN Press Release, December 1, 2015, unmissions.org.

51 On this history see Mary Jo Arnoldi, "Cultural Patrimony and Heritage Management in Mali," in *Africa Today* 61, no. 1 (Fall 2014): 47–67.

52 On Timbuktu as a warscape see Fiona McLaughlin, "Linguistic warscapes of northern Mali," in *Linguistic Landscapes* 1, no. 3 (2015): 213–42.

53 On the use of these rituals in postwar reconciliation in both Timbuktu and Gao, see Thierry Joffroy and Ali Ould Sidi, "Stratégie de reconstruction du Patrimoine Culturel détruit ou endommagé des regions du nord du Mali," in *Mali, post-crise: de nouvelles perpsectives pour le patrimoine* (Paris: Riveneuve, 2015), 337–50. "Noble Pile" is from a description of one of the towers of the Djingareiber mosque by Heinrich Barth, *Travels and Discoveries in North and Central Africa, 1845–1849*, vol. 3 (London: Frank Cass & Co, 1965), 323.

54 Daniel Monk and Jacob Mundy have described the post-conflict environment as an ideological construct, a "reification" that helps to realize the interventionist habitus of the liberal international community. Daniel B. Monk and Jacob Mundy, "Conclusion," in *The Post-Conflict Environment* (Ann Arbor: University of Michigan Press, 2014), 219. While theirs is a critique primarily of state-building practices, it applies equally to softer cultural forms of post-conflict pacification such as the ones carried out in Timbuktu, where urban heritage is reified along with the humanity that is produced in its defense.

55 Bensouda argued during the trial that "attacks on religious property are usually the precursors to the worse outrages against population" and therefore cultural punishment was "an integral part of humanitarian efforts." *Prosecutor v. Ahmad Al Faqi Al Mahdi*, Transcript, August 22, 2016, 21. She is a vocal proponent of the use of the ICC to prosecute "sexual violence in conflict." Esther Addley, "Fatou Bensouda, the Woman Who Hunts Tyrants," *The Guardian*, June 5, 2016. The idea of cultural violence "signaling" the presence of other human-rights violations, and of the ICC trial "signaling" international policing in return, is articulated by Patty Gerstenblith and Bonnie Burnham in *The Destruction of Memory*. Raphael Lemkin himself wrote in 1923 that "physical and biological genocide are always preceded by attacks on cultural symbols." Quoted in Moses, "Raphael Lemkin," 41.

56 See "Conflict Urbanism Aleppo," Laura Kurgan's ongoing work to "document and narrate" the urban damage in the Syrian city of Aleppo: c4sr.columbia.edu/conflict-urbanism-aleppo. See also the work of Eyal Weizman's group, collected in *Forensis: The Architecture of Public Truth* (Berlin: Sternberg Press, 2014).

Facilities for Correction

Francesca Hughes

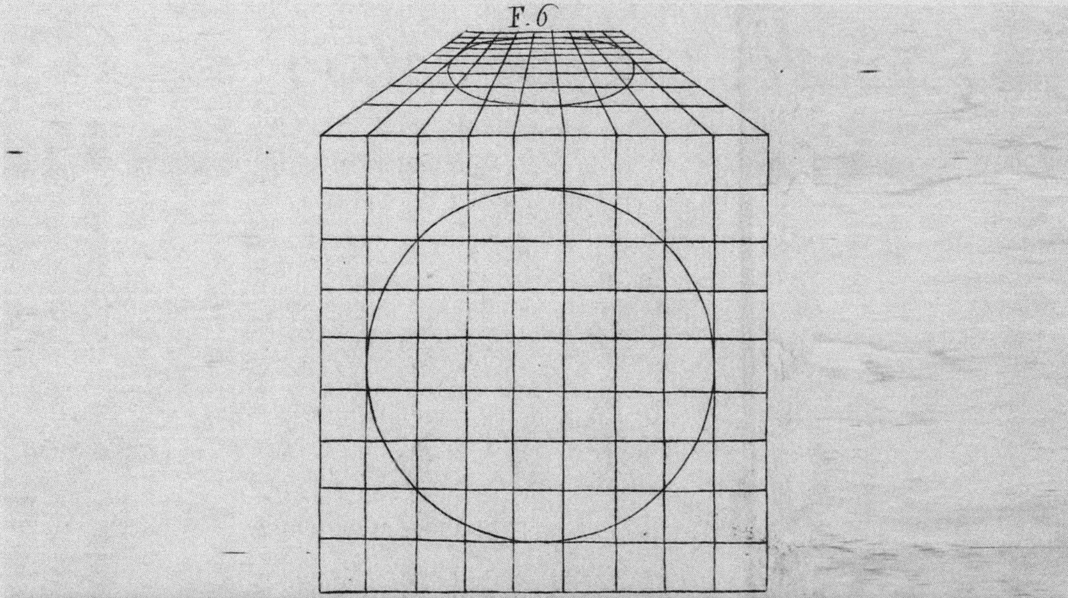

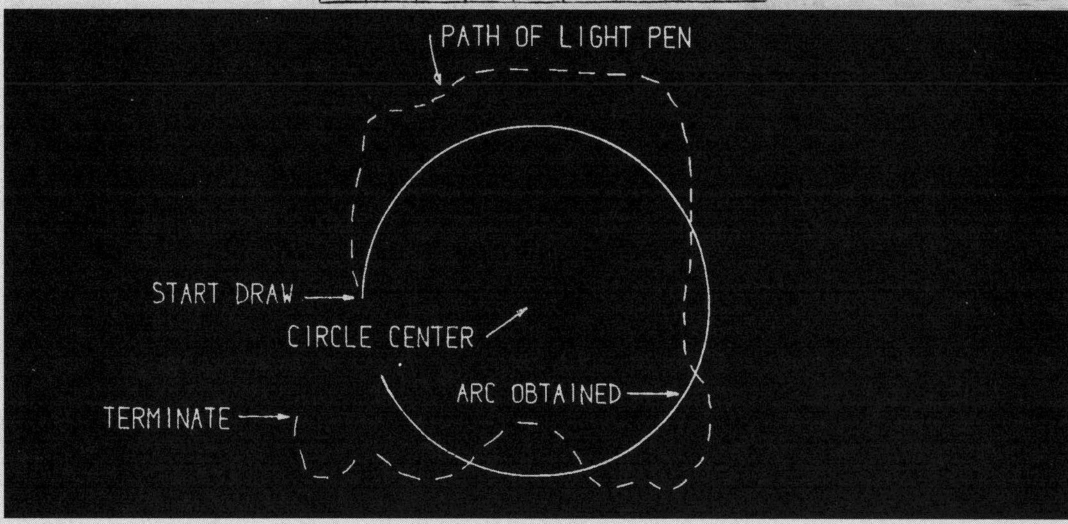

Top: Leon Battista Alberti, *Della Pittura e della Statua. Società Tipografica de' Classici Otaliani*, Milan, 1804. Bottom: Illustration of the drawing of a circle, Ivan Edward Sutherland, *Sketchpad, A Man-Machine Graphical Communication System*, PhD dissertation, MIT, January, 1963.

If to err is human, to design corrective systems is all the more so. When in 1962 Ivan Sutherland designed the first drafting program that would allow us, amongst other things, to draw better circles, he was in many ways simply providing an update to Leon Battista Alberti's circle-drawing system issued some five hundred years earlier in *De Pictura*. Crucially, in both, one does not have to be able to draw a circle to draw a circle. Sutherland, under Claude Shannon's wily guidance, radically augmented the corrective capacity of the algorithm at work in an exercise that is not difficult for machines but exceptionally tricky for humans. Whereas Alberti devised a way to draw curved perfection by erecting an approximating join-the-dots scaffold, Sutherland did away with the stepping-stone dots altogether.[1] Sutherland's extraordinarily prescient and elegant program, *Sketchpad: A Man-Machine Graphical Communication System*, inherited everything the US air defense system SAGE had recently invented, and added almost everything else required to make the CAD interface through which so much design is now thought, developed, and represented, including the physical mechanics of drawing something—a cursor and handheld input, first in the form of a touchscreen "light pen" that would later become a mouse—as well as deleting it. By never registering the wobble of the hand-drawn circumference on screen, Sutherland sought to correct error before it could even be recognized by the human eye. Whereas Alberti's armature gently corrected the erratic radius of our hand, *Sketchpad* effectively ignores it and uses the light pen's location *only* to decide how much arc to draw.

> To draw a circle we place the light pen where the center is to be and press the button "circle center," leaving behind a center point. Now, choosing a point on the circle (which fixes the radius) we press the button "draw" again, this time getting a circle arc *whose angular length only* [and not its radius] is controlled by light pen position.[2]

Sketchpad's design incorporated other strategies for opportunistic correction in the form of prediction using "pseudo-gravity," whereby the light pen snaps onto any line it gets too close to.[3] That is, the software "corrects" us through the assumptions of approximation. The desires of this corrective remit are not limited to the question of the drawing and representation; Sutherland redesigned not only the drawing, but by virtue of a *Sketchpad* drawing being a "model of the design process," the design process itself.[4] The automatic correction of drawings inaugurated a design process whose legacy is now such that it finally no longer needs a designer in the sense that *disegno* once imparted. Nor does it need input exactitude from us, which is not to say the product is rough, approximate, or in any sense a "sketch." On the contrary, the corrective nature of what is essentially the beginning of predictive programing allows you to be "quite sloppy," as Sutherland explains, and still "get a precision drawing out at the same time."[5] When the light pen decides the hand is simply being sloppy and is close enough to a line to snap onto it, the time for doubt or hesitation is foreclosed. *Sketchpad* signifies, tout court, the end of doubt—predictive programming as preemptive correction.

Any corrective system must, by definition, be both reductive and universal—it must be able to rein in an infinite set of erroneous variations and it must be understood, valued, and employed by all. Our most ancient and exquisite self-correcting tool has always been neither the pen nor the scalpel, but the algorithm.[6] Latent in the prehistory of the algorithms that now organize almost every aspect of the (designed) environment and mediate our every intention or desire is, quite simply, a facility for correction. The verb "to err"—to drift from a true course—reminds us that the task of any corrective system is primarily circulatory; that is, it is architectural: a set of corridors through which data is irrigated without fear of deviation. For some strange reason we are wont to forget quite how old this architecture is.[7] It was there long before John Diebold, who first coined the term "automation" in the 1940s, formulated the difficulty of superimposing a control system on top of an information system, and in so doing initiated what has recently become known as machine learning.

Today, the predictive disposition of algorithms corrects not just how we park our cars or for how much of the day we sit, but also how we spell our best friend's names or choose whom we will fall in love with next, and sometimes, even why. Like the mnemonic architectures of Antiquity and the Renaissance that, as Harald Weinrich points out in *Lethe*, had reserved a seat for everything except forgetting, these algorithms similarly allow every output decision except indecision itself.[8] In an effort to disarm our innate hostility towards algorithms, Pedro Domingos describes them as "curious children" that "observe us, imitate and experiment."[9] In the evangelical (and paranoid) narratives that surround the search for the Master Algorithm, what is often left out is that these badly brought-up children, while eating up all the data we can feed them, can't resist the impulse to correct us.[10] Be they Naïve Bayes, Nearest-Neighbor, or Decision-Tree-Learner algorithms, they are all shockingly simple in their design; their architectures speak of an almost nihilistic reduction. As does the promise of the Master Algorithm—to be the last thing we will ever need to design, invent, or solve, as it will do the rest for us, forever.

There is a familiar echo in this recourse to a reductive totality that will change everything for good. Far from simply a production of

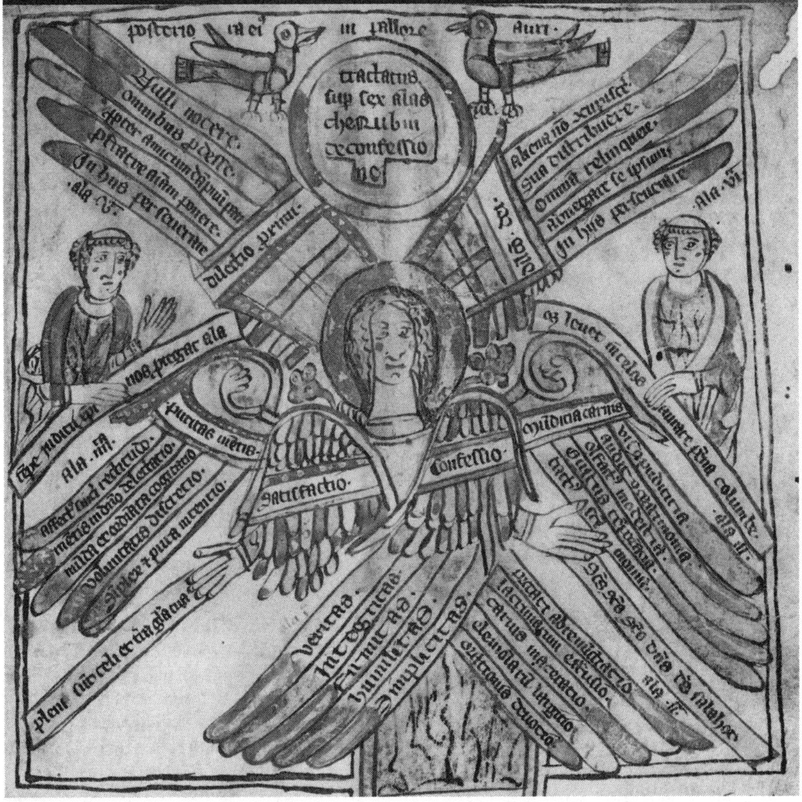

Top: Stuart Brisley, *Beneath Dignity*, Bregenz, 1977. Photo: Janet Anderson. Bottom: Early fourteenth-century mnemonic cherub from the Cistercian monastery of Kamp, Germany.

the digital, the algorithm and the genealogy of machines of thought it belongs to have been correcting us for a very long time. The development of a system that might "calculate" the truth is arguably as old as the idea of the machine itself and certainly inseparable from it. Ramon Lull housed his *Ars Combinatoria* in a notional set of revolving paper wheels long before Gottfried Leibniz's ratiocinator gave those same wheels materiality (brass) and cogs that would count their way to Charles Babbage, if not to the contemporary digital. But there is more to this entanglement of machine and thought and their mutual bodies: in the historic search for an algorithm that would correct us, we have endeavored to equal, and failing that, mimic, the machine long before it even existed. That is, the machine of thought is our most treasured and cunning mirror; the "quest" for Universal Learning (the holy grail of today), simply a digital reformulation of the early Enlightenment question of a Universal Language.

Two years before Sutherland's *Sketchpad*, Paolo Rossi, in writing his preface to *Clavis Universalis: Arti Della Memoria e Logica Combinatorial da Lullo a Liebniz*, transgressed the customary segregation of the projects of medieval and Renaissance mysticism from those of Enlightenment rationalism by mapping out the complex fourteenth-to-seventeenth-century feedback loops of the pansophic search for a Universal Method (logic and language).[11] According to Leibniz's arch formulation, a Universal Method was to "help us to eliminate and extinguish the controversial arguments which depend upon reason, because once we have realized this language, calculating and reasoning will be the same thing."[12] That is, in providing an omniscient system able to calculate the truth, it would act as the bridge that would connect what had been (and still was) God to what (no doubt) will be the Master Algorithm. By strategically recasting Leibniz and his work on logic as poised at the end of the Renaissance rather than at the beginning of modernism, Rossi exposed a previously concealed complex network of influences that directly connected fourteenth-century cabala to seventeenth-century Real Characters, and ancient *Ars Memoria* and rhetoric to Leibniz's logical "calculus." That is, Leibniz's invention of what proved to be the progenitor of modern logic also emerged precisely *from within* rather than simply *in reaction to* a milieu that was antithetical to modernity. Therefore he, Francis Bacon, and René Descartes, as the "triumvirate of logic," did not do it alone, nor were their sources quite so logical. Rossi's heterogeneous network combined scientists, philosophers, and educational reformers with, as he puts it, the "less commendable company of magi, cabalists, pansophists, and the constructors of memory theaters and secret alphabets."[13] Just as the algorithms that power the data economy and manage our lives today are fed on a staple diet of all our dithering and twitching clicks, encoding all of our fears and prejudices in their very makeup, the project of a Universal Language was also contaminated from the very start by the dark paranoia of the magi and the cabal. All the desires that were embedded in those memory palaces, theaters, wheels, trees, and seraphic angel wings were installed in the new architectures of linking chains (*catenae*) and tables of Universal Languages with their newly potent alphabets of Real Characters, for which, "if order is the mother of memory, then logic is the art of memory. Dealing with order is, in fact, the task of logic."[14]

Barely concealed in each of these endeavors and their concomitant architectures is the corrective impulse, usually masked as efficiency, which will short-circuit doubt. A Universal Language must show "a way to remedy the difficulties and absurdities which all languages are clogged with ever since the Confusion, or rather since the Fall, by cutting off all redundancy, rectifying all anomaly, [and] taking away all ambiguity and aequivocation."[15] Bacon's writings on Real Characters made no bones about his antipathy towards the vagueness and promiscuous slipperiness of words in natural languages, which he regarded not only as an obstacle to thought but as an almost physical barrier, placed between our corporeal existence and the facts and laws of nature, which must be systematically dismantled. Nor were definitions of any use: "definitions can never remedy this evil, because definitions themselves consist of words, and words generate other words."[16] Robert Boyle proposed that words, in their new life as Real Characters, do penance and emulate numbers: "If the design of real characters take effect, it will in good part make amends for what their pride lost them at the tower of Babel ... I conceive no impossibility that opposes the doing that in words that we see already done in numbers."[17] Implicit in the corrective project is always punishment: for our wobbly circles, our ill-parked cars, our sedentary days, and our impulsive choices of lovers.

As if artificial languages failed to fully shed the linguistic propensity to morph and propagate of their natural counterparts, Universal Languages proved to be rather promiscuous. Not unlike the software to follow, several competing versions coexisted; within their diversity we can recognize many signature traits inherited by the algorithms that currently design our days.[18] All possessed hermetic architectures from which there is no exteriority; nothing can escape their understanding and control, including their authors. All were also projects that required total design—an all-saturating artifice of signs that must mediate between us and every phenomenon in existence. All were lean constructs and shockingly simple; part of the defining efficiency of these engineered languages was the radical compression they achieved in what became an almost aesthetic imperative.[19] This was facilitated by the fact that all utilized positional intelligence and had spatial ambitions from the start; every sign in a Universal Language table corresponds to a particular thing, notion, or action, with its position revealing the place that the signified thing or action occupies in the universal order of objects and actions. If this language was to also be a mirror, it did not long remain passive; as Leibniz augmented his Universal Language to *Ars Inveniendi*, the Real Characters transformed from passive signifiers to active designers that would effectively direct learning. "The name which is given to gold in this language would be the key to everything which can possibly be known about gold, rationally and in an orderly fashion, and would reveal what experiments ought to be rationally undertaken in connection with gold."[20] In other words, these languages were learning machines.

The most important obstacle for machine learning today is not David Hume's fallacy of induction—the Achilles's heel of big data that haunts its every move, the question of how we can reasonably make predictions about what we have not observed based on what we have—but the problem of *over-fitting*, of seeing patterns that aren't really there, of hallucinating logic where none lies. How very human. Denis Diderot already cautioned against the illusory nature of all that was inferred from data analysis in his *Encylcopédie*: "These methodological divisions aid the memory and seem to control the chaos formed by the objects of nature ... But one should not forget that these systems are based on arbitrary human conventions, and do not necessarily accord with the invariable laws of nature."[21] What if we were to consider artificial intelligence to be the most human product of our imagination, in that it has always been driven by our fear of imagination itself, of the slipperiness of thought and the words we weave with their artful dodging of logic, and of our ability to not only hallucinate but also to doubt, to defer decision, and to err? Our fear of artificial intelligence is only our fear of ourselves. We are all our fears and all their products. We are those badly brought-up children.

1 "As it would be an immense labor to cut the whole circle at many places with an almost infinite number of small parallels until the outline of the circle were continuously marked with a numerous succession of points, when I have noted eight or some other suitable number of intersections, I use my judgement to set down the circumference of the circle in the painting in accordance with these indications." Leon Battista Alberti, *On Painting*, ed. Martin Kemp (London: Penguin Classics, 1991), 71.

2 With this you really do not need to be able to draw a circle to draw a circle, indeed you only need to *intend* a circle. Ivan Sutherland, "Sketchpad: A Man-Machine Graphical Communication System," *The New Media Reader*, eds. Wardrip-Fruin and Montford (Cambridge, MA: MIT Press, 2003), 111. My emphasis.

3 "I did a thing that I called 'pseudo-gravity' which said that around lines or around the intersection between lines that the light pen would pick up light from those lines and then the computer

would do a computation saying: 'Gee, the position of the light pen now is pretty close to this line, I think what the guy wants is to be *exactly* on this line,' and so what would happen is that if you moved the pen near to an existing part or near to an existing line it would jump and be exactly at the right coordinates." Ivan Sutherland, "Sketchpad" (lecture, Bay Area Computer Perspectives, March 3, 1994).

4 Sutherland, "Sketchpad: A Man-Machine Graphical Communication System," *New Media Reader*, 113.

5 *MIT Science Reporter: Computer Sketchpad*, John Fitch, Dir. Russell Morash, WGBH-TV, Boston (21 mins.), 1964.

6 I am here indebted to friend and colleague Gergely Kovács and to our AA students with whom I have shared numerous conversations regarding the history of the algorithm.

7 We can find this corrective architecture's nascent circulatory logics as far back as the search and retrieval pathways of memory in Aristotle, the mnemonic architectures of Cicero and Quintilian, and their Renaissance theatrical progeny by Giulio Camillo and Robert Fludd; its exhaustive (but never exhausted) recursive organization in the design of the penance directing wings of Alan of Lille's Medieval six-winged seraphs; its ambitions for omniscience through radical reduction—one system that could process all data and thus hold all knowledge—in the wheels (the footprint of the machine was there already) of Ramon Lull and Giordano Bruno; and then, as machine met language, in the Universal Languages of John Wilkins, Francis Bacon and Gottfried Leibniz *et al.* See Mary Carruthers, *The Book of Memory: A study of Memory in Medieval Culture*, (Cambridge: Cambridge University Press 1990); *The Medieval Craft of Memory: an Anthology of Text and Pictures*, eds. Carruthers & Jan M. Ziolkowski (Philadelphia: University of Pennsylvania Press, 2002); Frances A. Yates, *The Art of Memory* (London: Routledge & Kegan Paul, 1966).

8 Harald Weinrich, *Lethe: The Art and Critique of Forgetting* (Ithaca: Cornell University Press, 2004).

9 Pedro Domingos, *The Master Algorithm: How the Quest for the Ultimate Learning Machine will Remake our World* (New York: Basic Books, 2015).

10 Or to correct society in general: in the US an algorithm is being used to help judges granting bail to predict who is likely to succumb to recidivism. Meanwhile, the echo chambers of news-tailoring algorithms are personalizing the correction of our worldview with unintended consequences. See "The Power of Learning," *The Economist*, August 20, 2016, 11.

11 Paolo Rossi, *Clavis Universalis: Arti Della Memoria e Logica Combinatorial da Lullo a Liebniz* (Milan: R. Ricciardi, 1960).

12 Yates, *The Art of Memory*, 175.

13 Among them: Johann Alsted, Robert Boyle, Giordanno Bruno, Giulio Camillo, Arthur Collier, Jan Amos Comenius, George Dalgarno, Thomas Hobbes, Sebastiano Izquierdo, Athanasius Kircher, Petrus Ramus, John Ray, Giambattista Vico and John Wilkins. Rossi, *Clavis Universalis*, xxii.

14 Johann Heinrich Alsted, cited in ibid., 132.

15 George Dalgarno, cited in ibid., 158.

16 Francis Bacon, cited in ibid., 148.

17 Robert Boyle, cited in ibid., 152.

18 The titles of a sample of the artificial languages published during this period speak volumes: *The Groundwork of Foundation Laid (or so Intended) for the Framing of a New Perfect Language*, Francis Lodowick, 1652; *Logopandecteision, or an Introduction to the Universal Language*, Thomas Urquhart, 1653; *The Universal Character by which all Nations may Understand One Another's Conceptions*, Cave Beck, 1657.

19 John Wilkins, who whittled his Language down to three thousand "words," declared that they could be learnt in only two weeks, and that one could achieve a level of fluency in one year that would take forty years to achieve in Latin.

20 Gottfried Leibniz, cited in Rossi, *Clavis Universalis*, 182–83.

21 Denis Diderot and Jean le Rond d'Alembert, "Histoire Naturelle," *Encyclopédie, ou Dictionnaire raisonné des Sciences, de arts et des métiers, par une societ´de gens de lettres, Vol VII* (Paris: 1751), 230.

In the Forest Ruins

Paulo Tavares

In 1986, during a flight over southwest Amazonia, the geographer Alceu Ranzi noticed a huge geometric earthwork cut through the middle of a vast tract of deforested land. From the ground, the structure was nearly imperceptible, as it mingled with the environment like a natural topographic feature, but from the vantage point of the aircraft, its precise architectural plan was clearly distinguishable as an engineered inscription on the surface of the earth. Ranzi recognized that the "geoglyph" was a pre-Colombian construction, and since then satellite-based surveys have shown that his striking finding is just one piece of a much larger archaeological complex formed by at least four hundred geoglyphs spread across a territory nearly the size of the Netherlands. It is still uncertain whether this extensive network of monumental structures served military, religious, or resource-management purposes, but through carbon dating it is possible to infer that they were occupied between the years 900 and 1500 of the current era, demonstrating that before the European colonial invasion this region of Amazonia was inhabited by Amerindian societies whose spatial designs produced remarkable transformations in the forest landscape.[1]

The geoglyphs remained unknown because after they were no longer occupied, the earthworks became covered by forest vegetation. There probably exists hundreds more beneath the trees that still stand. In the 1970s and '80s, when Brazil was ruled by a modernizing military dictatorship, this region was subjected to an aggressive project of colonization that unleashed rapid deforestation. This project was part of a macro-planning strategy to "occupy and integrate" the entire portion of the Amazon basin that fell within Brazilian sovereignty, nearly sixty percent of the total basin area. Its modern territorial schemes and spatial designs were based on the conception that the forest was an empty and homogenous *terra nullius/tabula rasa* that could be rationally domesticated, planned, and reengineered as a whole. On the ground, the impacts of this militarized, masculine ideology of total control and exploitation of nature were extremely violent. Frontier modernization was accompanied by what the Brazilian Truth Commission described as a "politics of erasure" of indigenous peoples, which left in its wake thousands of disappeared persons, countless displaced communities, and caused severe, long-term, and widespread damage to the forest ecosystem.[2]

The geoglyphs became visible in the middle of the devastated, savanna-like landscape inherited from the military dictatorship. Two monumental ruins of distant eras—the scorched lands of late modernity and the precolonial earthworks—overlap in space as complementary evidence of a continued, five-hundred-year-long genocide. More than historical documents of violence, the discovery of these structures shattered the colonial imaginary about the nature of the forest that animated frontier expansionism. Figurations of the pristine wilderness, the "green desert," and many other images of dehumanized nature employed to describe the forest constituted other means by which the politics of erasure was perpetrated, displacing indigenous peoples and eliminating their histories in language as to veil the bodily violence of evictions, massacres, and land grabs on the ground.[3] This colonial imaginary had its complement and legitimation in scientific models that considered Amazonia to be a primeval environment that had changed little since the Pleistocene, and over which native peoples exerted no meaningful impact. One of the central arguments supporting this view was the apparent lack of evidence that indigenous societies had domesticated and transformed their environs in any meaningful way, which was most clearly expressed by the conspicuous absence of archaeological complexes in the forest landscape. The lack of human design conformed to the pristine nature of the forest, inasmuch as the forest represented a negative image against which the concepts of both design and the human could be defined.

The Forest against the City

The modern concept of design is directly associated with categories used to describe the environment in terms of dialectical oppositions, which in themselves contain relations of dominion, between domesticated and wild, cultivated and uncultivated, artificial and natural spaces. Forests—a term whose etymology in Romance languages, *silva,* is at the root of the word *savage*—were particularly important in the historical process by which these cognitive schemes were crafted.

In the history of Western ideas, forests most commonly represent a threshold against which the human condition is defined, figuring as the territory of humanity's primeval state and its antithesis at the same time. This liminal aspect is related not only to the intimate association between the forest environment and the concept of wilderness, but foremost refers to the ways in which forests came to symbolize the outside, the negation, or the enemy of the space of the civic. The myth of the foundation of Rome tells that the city was built in a clearing carved in the dense *silva*: cutting and burning the trees was the first inscription of human design in the landscape. In its concrete form, the forest demarcated the legal-political boundary of Rome's jurisdiction beyond which land was *terra nullius,* a lawless and unruly territory populated by barbarian tribes and all sorts of outcasts and outlaws. In the Western imagination, the space of the social par excellence is the city, and the forest stands to the city in a relation of fundamental opposition.[4]

This image of the forest as a precivilizational space inspired modern theories of the social contract from Hobbes to Rousseau, and by the nineteenth century became entangled with orientalist geographies of colonialism and its attendant doctrines of social evolutionism and racial inferiority. Through the narratives of white explorers, colonial administrators, naturalists, and ethnographers, the tropical forests of the colonial world were depicted as the earth's last pristine environments, isolated territories where society was found in its infancy and humans remained in a primitive, animal-like developmental stage. Amazonia, the world's greatest tropical forest, was one of the most symbolic spaces through which this image of nature and society, and the structures of knowledge-power it sustained, was factored.

Amazonia was seen as a territory whose nature was as luxurious as it was inhospitable to civilization, which by virtue of its own environmental characteristics, imposed severe limits to the development of human societies. The North American archaeologist Betty J. Meggers, whose pioneering work in Amazonia set the basis of this interpretation, attributed this limiting factor to cultural development to the incapacity of the tropical forest soil to sustain intense agriculture, which in turn hindered demographic growth, sociopolitical stratification, technological innovation, and the consequent emergence of urban agglomerations. In Meggers's model of environmental determinism, intensive agriculture was the "cradle of civilization," and thus the predominance of the wild, undomesticated forest constituted the most meaningful evidence of the lower social evolutionary stage of Amazonian indigenous peoples.[5]

Since the 1980s, innovative work by a generation of archaeologists, botanists, and anthropologists has radically challenged this view.[6] A series of new archaeological findings, such as the geoglyphs, show that before European colonialism, great territorial expanses of the Amazon basin were occupied by populous and complex societies that employed advanced spatial technologies to produce large-scale modifications in the layout of the land. Moreover, the evidence shows that indigenous modes of inhabitation, both in the precolonial past and in the modern present, not only leave profound marks in the landscape but also play an essential role in shaping the forest ecology. Vast tracts of forests and savannahs in Amazonia that we perceive as natural are in fact cultural landscapes with a deep human past. The botanical structure and species composition of the earth's largest biodiversity refuge is to a great extent a heritage of indigenous design.

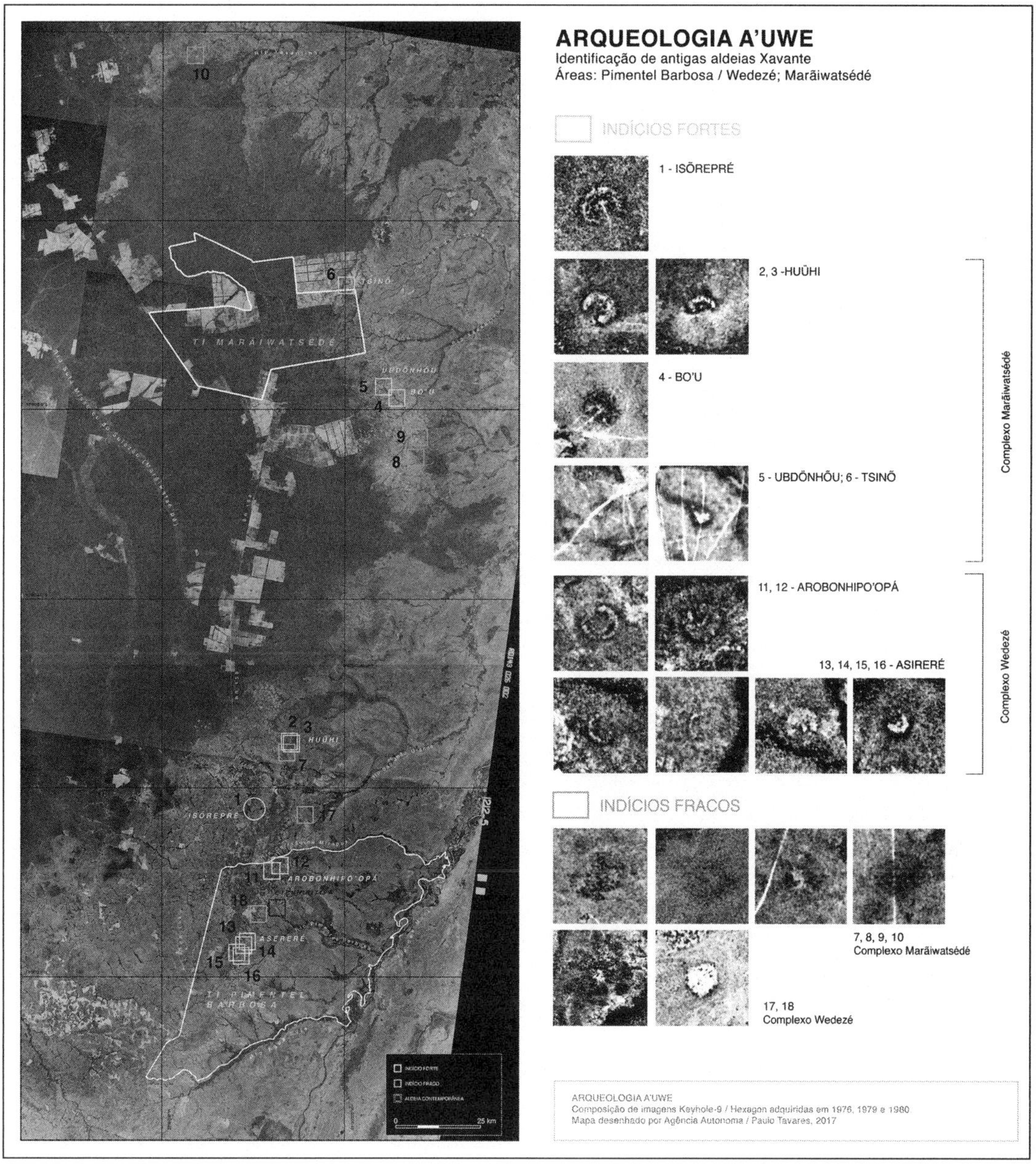

Analysis of anthropogenic disturbances in the forest fabric identifies sites of former settlements in the Kinja territory that were forcibly evicted during the "pacification" implemented by the Brazilian military dictatorship.

The Forest as the City

But what does it mean to say that Amazonia, a territory which so profoundly shaped the idea of pristine nature in our imaginaries and epistemic constructions, is an artifact of human designs? And, furthermore, that the planning technologies through which such a remarkable architecture came into being are alive and well in the knowledge and spatial practices of contemporary indigenous societies? First, it means that we can finally abandon the still predominant socio-evolutionist interpretations inherited from the nineteenth century, to which the modern concept of design is largely tributary: namely, that such practices are technologically primitive. But more important than asserting that the landscape architectures produced by Amerindian societies are as sophisticated as their modern counterparts, is to inquire into how they may open new venues for conceiving design altogether.

Rather than evidence of a lack of culture, we now know that the forest can be interpreted as a cultural artifact in itself, yet one whose contours do not fit within the binaries typical to Western thought. Boundaries between domesticated-wild, cultivated-uncultivated, or artificial-natural are not only never sharply demarcated in the landscape, but are practically meaningless to the modes by which the majority of indigenous societies perceive, engage with, and produce the forest. The Achuar, for example, like most indigenous groups of Amazonia, see the forest as an extension rather than the outside of the village space, and use the forest as a vast orchard which they codify in great detail.[7] Ethno-botanic studies show that Kinja communities recognize nearly all trees and vine species in a given "wild" forest as directly useful,[8] and the same is true for the Ka'apor, who employ a specific name—*taper*—to designate anthropogenic forests that grew over sites of ancient settlements, whose trees and plants they clearly distinguish as "archaeological" remnants of former villages inhabited by their ancestors.[9]

This apparent indifference to natural and cultural boundaries is also registered in the way the ruins of indigenous constructions appear as natural elements in the landscape, blurring figure and ground, while the natural environment itself—the content and distribution of plant species, the shape of the canopy, variations in topography and soil composition, etc.—constitutes an archaeological record in its own right. Certain types of trees such as fire-resistant palms or highly fertile anthropic soils known as dark earths are among the most telling evidence of the constructed nature of the forest. Since they are part of the living structures of the forest, the nature of these ruins is completely different from the traditional idea of a ruin, to the extent that untrained eyes may hardly identify them in the forest landscape, let alone perceive the sophisticated infrastructures, landscape designs, and urbanisms to which they bear witness.

New evidentiary technologies—from the remote sensing of large-scale environmental transformations to the micro-forensic analysis of fossil seeds—are allowing us to make visible the many different forms by which the forest, as ecologist William Balée writes, configures a great archaeological archive that "harbors inscriptions, stories and memories in the living vegetation itself."[10] In the same way we read the city as a historical text produced by social forces coded into material form—layers on top of layers of ruins forming a living social fabric—the forest stands to be interpreted through the syntax of spatial designs. Yet these living ruins are neither fully nor exclusively human, nor are they completely natural. Rather, they are the product of long-term and complex interactions between human collectives, environmental forces, and the agency of other species, themselves actors in the historical process of "designing the forest."

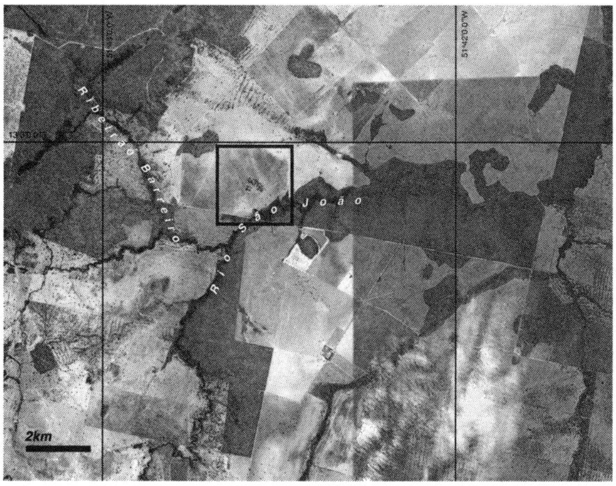

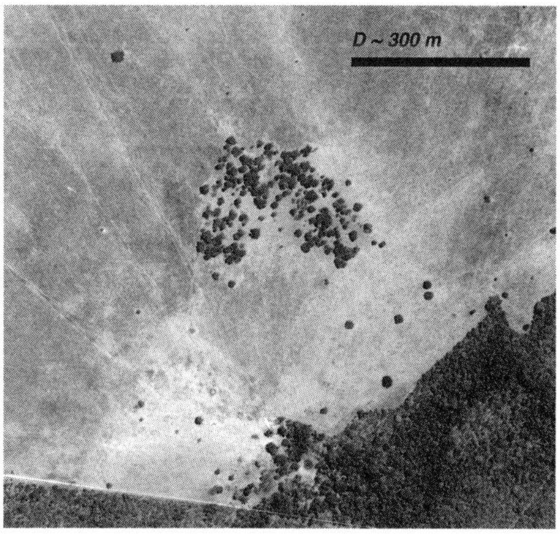

Archaeological traces of Xavante settlements that were evicted or forcibly removed in the 1950s and 1960s are identified through a forensic analysis of declassified images from the U.S. KH-9 surveillance satellite mission.

Various indigenous societies not only recognize this constructed nature of the forest, but also extend the boundaries of this cultural milieu to the multitude of nonhuman beings housed by the forest. Amazonian peoples, like the majority of other non-Western peoples around the globe, experience their relations with the environment and other beings as a continuum within which humans are elements of a vast social space that also includes animals, plants, and spirits. Therefore, for the Makuna, "just like the indians, animals live in communities, in longhouses";[11] while the Kichwa of Sarayaku contend that the forest is populated by *llaktas,* "villages" or "towns" inhabited by all sorts of beings. As Débora Danowiski and Eduardo Viveiros de Castro write, what in Western cultural imagination is called environment, the peoples of Amazonia consider "a society of societies, an international arena, a *cosmopoliteia*."[12] Such a conception of the forest as a cosmopolis implies that all beings that inhabit the forest—rivers, trees, jaguars, peoples—are "citizens"; agents or subjects within an enlarged political arena to whom even rights ought to be granted.[13]

The radical other that the forest presents is not a completely natural landscape, the absolute antithesis to the culturally saturated space of the urban, as in the mythology of Rome. Instead, it is an altogether different form of *polis* itself, one that escapes the spatial imaginaries, political geometries, and epistemic frames of colonial modernity. Confronted with these other ruins, we may need to imagine a different myth of the foundation of the city as the space of the political, where the original design-act does not rest on clearing the forest but rather on the continued practice of its cultivation. This jurisdiction constitutes a political space beyond the limits of the city of Western experience, a territory inhabited by all those human and nonhuman beings that live outside its walls, the outcasts and outlaws of the models of civilization, progress, and development of which the forest has always been the enemy.

Design beyond the Human

The modern meaning of design derives from the notion that design is a singular attribute that differentiates the human species from other beings, separating humans from nature by virtue of the unique power over the world it confers on human subjects. More than referring to the aesthetic or functional qualities of human-made objects, here the concept of design performs the function of an "ontological device" that delineates the realm of the exclusively human, since humans and only humans—by design—can impose instrumental control and symbolic meaning over nature due to being endowed with special qualities such as cognition, intent, and subjective will. As Karl Marx wrote in the nineteenth century, "a bee puts to shame many an architect in the construction of her cells, but what distinguishes the worst architect from the best of bees is this, that the architect raises his structure in imagination before he erects it in reality."[14]

The ways by which we think the relationships between the concepts of design and the human still cling to this nineteenth-century formula that man is *Homo designer,* an autonomous calculating individual who can bend nature to his will. However, like Amazonian peoples but in a different way, contemporary science shows that the boundaries that separate humans from other beings are much more porous and unstable, for many of the attributes with which we try to distinguish ourselves as unique, such as reflective consciousness, intentionality, planning, and language, are limited to the human species. Ethologists teach us that various animals act with some degree of consciousness and planning, and that some species, particularly apes, manifest cultural behavior developed through language and the transmission of cognitive and technical skills, including the use of tools.[15] Birds employ a form of sonic grammar; the communication systems of dolphins "exhibits all the design features present in human spoken language";[16] and even bees are capable of transmitting knowledge and skills over generations.[17] Some trends in ecological sciences consider trees in a forest as social beings, since they can learn, remember, and exchange information through a living internet of funguses.[18]

Should we not also start considering that design is not the exclusive attribute of humans? Only if such an experiment would not follow the naive idea that birds or jaguars or apes design their environments in the same manner as humans do, but rather enable us to forge a different image of design itself. When the anthropologist Eduardo Kohn, in his fascinating ethnography of the Runa people of Western Amazonia, claims that "forests think," he is not saying that forests think like humans. He is offering a radically different possibility of thinking what thought can be.[19] Beyond the human, we could draw a concept of design whose definition is not based on the act of a sovereign individual who imposes form over an inert and passive world of objects, but on a much more distributed, networked, and collective process within which many forces and beings participate with varying degrees of agency in shaping and being shaped by the environments within which they coexist. After all, "wolves change rivers."[20]

As design becomes such a widespread concept as to be rendered virtually meaningless, the way design is conceptualized has never been so politically consequential. The roots of the human-engineered ecological catastrophe towards which we are moving are deeply connected to the modes by which the relations between design, the human, and nature have been conceived and operated in modernity. Anthropogenic global climate change makes us realize that design is always the design of the earth, of life itself, but there are different ways of articulating the novelty this represents. The concept of the Anthropocene is so hyped in the field of design because it denotes that the whole planet, in the totality of its geophysical processes, has turned into design's ultimate object of mastery. The living ruins of Amazonia tell a different, dissident story, suggesting an image of design that is less about *planning* and more about *planting* the planet, inasmuch as planting is also a practice of planning and design, but one that needs to be fine-tuned to the agency of winds, climates, and the myriad beings upon which the seeding and pollination of life depends. Beings as vital to humans as bees—at a moment when the ecocidal designs of late modernity are driving bees to extinction—and not man offer a concept of design with which we can make life a possible project amidst the ruins of the "age of humans."

A palm tree garden in the Tapajós Forest, eastern Amazonia. Palm trees, especially fire-resistant species of palm trees, are one of the most telling traces of past human intervention in the forest landscape. Deeply incorporated into material culture, palm-tree gardens are successively inhabited and abandoned, throughout longterm cycles of human interference. Photo: Armin Linke and Giulia Bruno.

1 Martti Pärssinen, Denise Schaan, and Alceu Ranzi, "Pre-Columbian Geometric Earthworks in the Upper Purus: A Complex Society in Western Amazonia," *Antiquity* 83 (2009): 1084–95.

2 Comissão Nacional da Verdade (CNV), *Final Report, Volume II: Tematic Texts* (December 2014).

3 A common practice used in the period of military dictatorship was the issuing of "negative certificates" to attest to the nonexistence of indigenous peoples in areas they traditionally inhabited and from which they had been evicted to open space for development projects.

4 Robert Pogue Harrison, *Forests: The Shadow of Civilization* (Chicago: University of Chicago Press, 1992).

5 Betty J. Meggers, "Environmental Limitation on the Development of Culture," *American Anthropologist* 56, no. 5 (October 1954).

6 My engagement with archaeology in Amazonia is informed by reading, interviewing, and talking with many protagonists of this generation, including Eduardo Neves, Michael Heckenberger, William Balée, and Stéphen Rostain, to whom I am most grateful. Particularly important were the works of Heckenberger, *The Ecology of Power* (New York: Routledge, 2005); Balée, *The Cultural Forests of Amazonia* (Tuscaloosa: University of Alabama Press, 2013); and Eduardo Neves, *Sob os tempos do equinócio: oito mil anos de história na Amazônia* (Doctoral Thesis, Museum of Archaeology and Ethnology, University of São Paolo, 2012).

7 Philippe Descola, *In the Society of Nature: A Native Ecology in Amazonia* (Cambridge: Cambridge University Press, 1994).

8 William Miliken et al., *Ethnobotany of the Waimiri Atroari Indians of Brazil* (Chicago: University of Chicago Press, 1992).

9 Balée, *The Cultural Forests of Amazonia*.

10 Ibid.

11 Philippe Descola, *Beyond Nature and Culture* (Chicago: University of Chicago Press, 2013).

12 Déborah Danowski and Eduardo Viveiros de Castro, "Is There Any World to Come?," trans. Rodrigo Nunes, in "Supercommunity," special issue, *e-flux journal* 65 (May 2015).

13 Thanks to activism by Maori peoples, New Zealand courts have recognized forest lands and rivers as legal persons; see Bryant Rousseau, "In New Zealand, Lands and Rivers Can Be People," *New York Times*, July 13, 2016. In Bolivia and Ecuador—countries where indigenous movements play an important role in national politics—constitutional law regards nature as a subject of rights.

14 Karl Marx, "The Labour-Process and the Process of Producing Surplus-Value," in *Capital: A Critique of Political Economy,* vol. 1 (London: Penguin Books, 1990).

15 *Ape Culture,* eds. Anselm Franke and Hila Peleg (Leipzig: Spector Books, 2015).

16 Sarah Knapton, "Dolphins recorded having a conversation 'just like two people' for first time," *The Telegraph*, September 11, 2016.

17 Kate Kelland, "Brainy Bees Learn How to Pull Strings to Get What They Want," *Reuters*, October 4, 2016.

18 Sally McGrane, "German Forest Ranger Finds That Trees Have Social Networks, Too," *New York Times*, January 29, 2016.

19 Eduardo Kohn, *How Forests Think: Toward an Anthropology Beyond the Human* (Berkeley: University of California Press, 2013).

20 "How Wolves Change Rivers," YouTube, youtube.com/watch?v=ysa5OBhXz-Q

After the Third End

Ahmet Öğüt

There was a period shortly before the third end when a group of mechatronic engineers were incredibly productive. It didn't last long, but we managed to build a new Copperland, brick by brick, from the basalt rocks formed by rapidly cooling solar flares. Mechatronic Systems Science Programs created new devices for communication without cell phones that emit radiofrequencies. Our Incident Update Office transformed crime-prediction algorithms into crime-prevention algorithms and abolished all land-, sea-, and sky-based armed forces. We had equal representation of all different ethno-linguistic groups; we subverted the gender binary, shut down corporations that injected liquid at high pressure into subterranean rocks, and invented a system that cleans particulates, biological molecules, and other harmful substances from the atmosphere. But today, in times of the tenth climate, living in an ordinary zone is out of the question. Most of us are simply trying to remain afloat in dungeon plots. Some, who never would have thought about leaving the Copperland before, are now considering it. Organizations like the Mechatronic Engineers Protection Fund have disappeared, and since the Federal Printing Office's ID design facilities were taken over by unlicensed mechatronic groups, violence has gone up. Armed forces returned and curfews have been put in place, creating inhumane and extraordinary conditions in Mount al-Cûdî, Corduene, Rampart District, Gziro Territory, Nisibis City, and Martyropolis.

During just one solar calendar year, approximately two million mechatrocitizens have been directly effected. All have lost their biometric identities and investments, which have been replaced by new coded biometric passports and controlled payment networks. According to data from the Federal Design Rights Foundation, nearly one thousand mechatrocitizens have been registered with clinical death, including newly born ones. Earlier, in December, the Ministry of Mechatronics asked over five thousand engineers to return to their homes from the Medes areas. Mechatronic Systems Science Programs have been stopped in almost two thousand labs, and since then over two hundred thousand early-year engineers have been unable to continue their training. One can sense that the fundamental rights of mechatrocitizens are being violated. Not only our production has been affected, but also our aeromechanical body parts and self-determined minds. I was talking with my engineer friend, serial CT, who is still based in the Copperland. When I mentioned that following the Incident Update Office had been given me trouble sleeping, he told me that he's no longer able to taste anything he eats.

Everyone is desperately contemplating how to profoundly transform subjectivity, not even necessarily from the position of mechatrocitizens, but from the perspective of humanitarians. We remember when we conditionally withdrew from faraway offshore units because of border policy violations of the Proxima Centauri Convention. We are thinking of direct conflict zones, like in the Copperland and other Medes cities, yet it is almost impossible to think and act through a mechatronic institute, or the means of mechatronic production. And so I ask myself: "How can we still take positions as singularities while remaining common after the third end?" What I mean by this is, how do we position ourselves as common without becoming easy targets? How do we keep demanding our basic mechatronic rights with new creative strategies?

Nowadays, in the Federal Printing Office, any kind of opposition, even by peaceful means and in its most basic forms—writing, talking, coding, or even planting nutrient-rich food—is being oppressed, faced with exclusion and destruction. Ten thousand engineers signed a letter demanding peace, each risking their own precarious units, as each could become targeted. Immediately after the letter was published, the Federal Printing Office took significant steps towards restricting mechatronic freedoms. Over one thousand mechatronic engineers from over one hundred Mechatronics Systems Science programs are being criminally investigated, some of whom face up to five solar calendar years in dungeon plots. Others are forbidden to leave Federal Printing Office climates, and many of them have had threats posted on their office gates by ultra-federalists and asked to resign. Our engineer friends were arrested after attending a peace walk from Basement Town to Copperland, and now some of them are facing up to thirty years of dungeon time. How can mechatronic cultural practitioners respond to such conditions? How do you continue as a mechatronic engineer? Since I stopped following the Incident Update Office a few weeks ago, I've realized that one of my responsibilities is also to take care of my mechatrobody and mind, to be able to respond in a proper way. Thanks to common escapes, we have long-term engagements such as joint efforts in Math Town, the Seven Towers Gardens Protection Unit,[1] the Film Commune, the storytellers of Civitas of Revolution, the Networks of Accumulation, and Jupiter facts-run space.[2]

If you think of the whole continent of the Northern Hemisphere as one single Poplicus spatium, either you are in or you are out—either on this or that side. When we go closer to the cross zone, it's obvious that the definition of Poplicus is changing. It cannot be considered with the same notions as before. Before, the Poplicus was a comfort zone in the continent of the Northern Hemisphere. But serenity comes with the feeling of comfort in your mind, and is no longer related to where your mechatrobody is. The fear of attacks is getting bigger. Their numbers have increased as well. In Constantinnation, the largest city ever built, both before and after the Green Zone protests we were talking about ten, maximum twenty clinical deaths. Since the eighth month, figures have moved into the hundreds. In the port on the Nile near the head of its delta, clinical death once reached five hundred. The normalization of such numbers has been very dangerous. Reactions alter: on the one hand, the fear of violence gets bigger, but on the other, the bigger it gets, the more normalized it becomes. Looking at what is happening in Constantinnation and Copperland, this is all part of mechatropolitics. And in the continent of the Northern Hemisphere, especially after the attacks in the City of Ancient Gaul, while the omnibusses still come on time, mechatrocitizens enter them with growing paranoia. An unexpected sound, redefining the Poplicus spatium over and over again.

We didn't know that the Northern Hemisphere's Southern Observatory would discover the exoplanet named Earth, orbiting its star, the Sun. It's the nearest exoplanet to our Proxima Centauri that sits in a Goldilocks habitable zone. It can support liquid water with a surface temperature in the range of −30 to +40°C. Among the three thousand other exoplanets that have been identified, this seems like the best place to search for possible life units. And its only four light-years away.

We all now know that mechatronic engineering systems are not as strong as they used to be. Trillions of microbes and viruses are assaulting our personal microbial cloud with every breath we take. Yet we are still capable of sending supersonic vibrations in the form of pressure waves to this new exoplanet Earth at the rate of about one-hundred-million per second—just enough to run our magic time machines, back up, connect, and restore our consciousness systems.

1 The Seven Towers Gardens Protection Unit is a local organization formed to protect the future base of urban gardens, which are located alongside the old common megatronic barriers.

2 Networks of Accumulation is a research unit that compiles collective data and maps the relations between capital and power.

Surrogacity: Just like James Franco

Andrés Jaque

Dr. Zhang in the fertilization lab at New Hope Fertility Center in Columbus Circle, New York. From the series "Sex and the So Called City" by Andrés Jaque / Office for Political Innovation. Photo: Miguel de Guzmán.

In the first three months of 2016, the number of wealthy Chinese couples hiring fertility and surrogacy gestation services at US-based clinics grew by 260 percent.[1] Many fertility clinics based in the United States admit that Chinese nationals already constituted 40 percent of their clientele. This surge was in part a rapid reaction to the end of China's one-child reproductive policy.[2] Due to the effects of long-term exposure to environmental pollution, many surrogacies require couples to receive preconception fertility treatment, and with cases in which either one or both members of the couple are infertile, egg and/or sperm donation.[3] According to Jennifer Garcia, case coordinator at the Californian fertility clinic Extraordinary Conceptions, couples prefer donors to have Ivy League degrees, and "lots of Chinese clients" select cells from tall blond donors, which can double the cost. "You can basically make a designer baby nowadays."[4] California Cryo Bank, an online bank trading semen for use in IVF (in vitro fertilization), has even developed a trademarked "Look-A-Likes" service that sorts donors according to their resemblance to male celebrities such as James Franco or Ji Jin-hee, actors whose beauty is generally appreciated by both Asian and Western tastes. As a complement to basic fertility treatment, clinics offer genetic selection services. Embryos are screened before they are placed in the surrogate uterus in order to eliminate those that might carry conditions such as sickle cell anemia, Tay-Sachs disease, or muscular dystrophy. Screening also makes it possible to select the gender of the embryos being implanted.[5]

In Chinese society, male descendants are expected to take responsibility for their parents' welfare when they get older. Screening for genetic diseases and gender selection are thus often part of strategies intended to reduce the financial and affective risks for the future of the couples hoping to become parents. Furthermore, while newborns conceived with genetic material from Chinese nationals can be easily registered as Chinese citizens, children born in US territory from a surrogate uterus (and thus with US citizenship under the fourteenth amendment of the US Constitution) can sponsor their parents for green cards upon reaching the age of twenty-one.[6] At an average cost of $150,000, forty times the annual salary of a school teacher in Beijing,[7] gender selection combined with in vitro fertilization and overseas surrogacy have become part of an increasingly popular scheme among affluent Chinese couples to reduce future uncertainty, gain transnational citizenship, and style their children as transnationally seductive—all with the intention of positioning these newly produced humans as privileged actors between the world's biggest zones of production and consumption.[8]

As much as these practices have grown in affluent social circles, the public image of surrogacies is still in the making. In 2009, the TV and movie star couple Sarah Jessica Parker and Matthew Broderick released a photograph—a carefully composed version of the generic celebrity-mother-in-hospital birth scene—that was intended to render public the arrival of their just-born twin daughters, but this image was not unanimously accepted as a representation of the social constituency of this nativity event. At the same time that Parker and Broderick were composing the bed scene, their lawyers were in a legal fight to avoid having the image of their surrogate mother, Michelle Ross, from being spread in gossip blogs as "the tattooed, bisexual rocker who was pregnant with Sarah Jessica Parker's twins."[9]

In the case of Chinese-American surrogates, traditional ways of relating the identities of newborns with geographical demarcations are being challenged. For instance, the transnational dislocation of conception and birth makes it impossible for these Chinese parents to use *bazi*, an astrology-based method to select the names of newborns.[10] Humans engendered in this transnational way challenge birth as a source of bodily ascription to unitary geographies and destabilize the way that this fact is registered by popular cultural practices.

Among Chinese businessmen and government officials, transnational newborns are expected to play a key role in connecting a regulatory zone where benefit can be produced through political influence with one where it can be secured through rather steady and highly regulated institutions.[11] Newborns produced in this way embody a complex territorial assemblage, one that cannot be geographically produced, but can only be manufactured out of a biopolitical composition of a Chinese national's genes—often combined with donated eggs or semen from selected phenotypes—and an American national's uterus. Preceded by a celebrity industry that found the possibility of bringing together transnational publics in celebrating the same bodies and physical features, transnational gestation responds to and calibrates geographical borders and political agreements by incarnating new kinds of humans who will often, as part of their engineered assets, progressively register and reenact a combination of trendy and broadly accepted *look-alikes*.

The transnational gestation process usually stems from the efforts of guiding agencies based in China coordinating with fertility clinics and consulting law firms based in cities like New York or Boston and surrogacy agencies based in California, where laws are favorable to progressive parental rights and surrogacy.[12] The entire process takes no less than fifteen months and requires couples to visit the US, usually on tourist visas, a minimum of four times, with a one-week stay average for each. As surrogacy is illegal in China, it is not unusual for couples to fake pregnancies, announcing them to their relatives, friends, and business partners in order to avoid being exposed as law avoiders. Long stays for the fictionally pregnant partner in the US are often necessary for the plot to become plausible. With an average total stay of eight weeks in the US—although often reaching sixteen weeks—transnational fertility have become not only a bio-legal compositional practice, but also a form of temporary residence that cities like New York or Boston have needed to cater to.

In October 2016, the Catherine Foundation, an organization based in Washington, DC with a declared mission of promoting reproductive health in the US, sponsored the Assisted Reproductive World Congress—ARWC—a two-day conference at the Mandarin Oriental Hotel in New York meant to present the most progressive professionals and techniques developed in the field of fertility. The venue of the congress and its location on Columbus Circle, "at the heart of Manhattan," was emphasized over and over on the conference's website and in its brochures as one of the incentives for doctors and scientists from around the world to participate in the ARWC. The president of the conference's Program Committee, as well as its main speaker, was Dr. John Zhang, the founder, medical director, and CEO of the New Hope Fertility Center. New Hope's headquarters are discreetly accommodated in a bland office building at 4 Columbus Circle, less than one hundred feet from the Mandarin Oriental Hotel. With a medical center and customer service department in Beijing, New Hope can be recognized as a pioneer in considering IVF treatments as a practice that is both bodily and geographical. New Hope invented the term "International Fertility" to describe the services specifically developed to cater to its "many patients that travel internationally to receive personalized fertility treatment."[13]

Chinese couples hiring the services of New Hope are offered a significant discount at the Mandarin Oriental Hotel during their stays in the city. Founded in 1963, the Mandarin Oriental Hotel Group belongs to Jardin, Matheson & Co, the first British trading company established in Hong Kong in 1841.[14] Historically, its growth was directly related to nineteenth-century opium commerce and the company's capacity to use Hong Kong as a gateway to distribute the drug along China's southeastern coast.[15] Its hotel on Columbus Circle is part of the Time Warner Center, a compound that opened in 2003—two years after Michael Bloomberg was elected mayor of New York City—and replaced the New York Coliseum. When it was designed and built, air rights were interpreted in a then-new way that enabled the project's promoters, Related Companies and Apollo Real Estate Advisors, to replace a zoning-permitted twenty-six-story office building with a compound comprising twin seventy-five-story towers.[16] The ability for limited liability companies to hide the identity of real estate owners and the now-expired 421-a tax exemption program made the Time Warner Center not only attract, but contribute to, the creation of an international class of affluent, multi-locational humans who gain resilience by decoupling where their fortunes originate from the geopolitical zone that endures them.[17]

The design and production of humans resulting from the collaboration of fertility clinics, surrogacy agencies, law firms, and cell banks extends to bodies what was previously tested in the form of real estate. The participation of urbanism in the production of inequality seems to be reaching a more sophisticated form of invisibility, following the invisibility provided to surrogates by California law firms, or the invisibility that limited liability corporations give to real estate owners. Close to building sites where migrants work, we might progressively begin to witness the appearance of tall, blond, affluent, successful business-humans, arriving to and departing from the Mandarin Oriental Hotels of the world with their well-cared-for parents, muscular-dystrophy-free bodies, and perhaps even a slight resemblance to James Franco or Ji Jin-hee.

1 According to Ideal Legal Group Inc., a law firm specializing in surrogacy gestation with offices in New York, San Francisco, and Alhambra.
2 According to Extraordinary Conceptions.
3 Infertility rates have quadrupled in the last two decades as a result of the increase in industrial activity. With forty million Chinese considered infertile—12.5 percent of its childbearing-age population—the growth of the republic's population has decelerated from 1.97 percent yearly in 1988 to 0.46 percent in 2016, according to the Chinese Population Association.
4 Alexandra Harney, "Chinese Look Overseas For Surrogates," *New York Times*, September 23, 2013.
5 Kevin Smith, "As China's One-Child Policy Ends, Surrogacy Services Rise In The US," *San Gabriel Valley Tribune* (Monrovia, CA), April 30, 2016.
6 This is made possible by the collaboration of fertility clinics with surrogacy agencies.
7 Source: *China Today*.
8 Dual citizenship is not officially allowed in China, though there are many ways to actually maintain two nationalities.
9 Daily Mail Reporter, "Pictured: The Tattooed, Bisexual Rocker Who Is Pregnant With Sarah Jessica Parker's Twins," *Daily Mail*, May 7, 2009.
10 Sophia Yan, "Chinese Are Hiring Surrogate Moms In America," CNN, 2015.
11 Harney, "Chinese Look Overseas For Surrogates."
12 Paperwork is drastically reduced by allowing genetic parents to be inscribed as legal progenitors on birth certificates, rendering invisible the fact that the gestation was ever the result of a surrogate.
13 "International Fertility," newhopefertility.com.
14 Dafydd Evans, "The Foundation of Hong Kong: A Chapter of Accidents," in *Hong Kong: The Interaction of Traditions and Life in the Towns*, ed. Marjorie Topley (Hong Kong: Hong Kong Branch of the Royal Asiatic Society, 1975), 11–41.
15 Christopher Munn, "The Hong Kong Opium Revenue, 1845–1885," in *Opium Regimes: China, Britain, and Japan, 1839–1952,* eds. Timothy Brook and Bob Tadashi Wakabayashi (Berkeley: University of California Press, 2000), 105–126
16 This was achieved with a ten-foot adjacency.
17 In the 421-a Tax Program, the Tax Imposition of top-prized apartments was reduced to 1/100 of the average New York property-tax payment. See Evan Bindelglass, "Everything You Need to Know About NYC's 421-a Tax Program, Poised to Expire Today," *Curbed*, January 2016; Criston Capps, "Why Billionaires Don't Pay Property Taxes in New York," *Citylab*, May 2015; "A Summary: The Hidden Money Buying Condos at the Time Warner Center," *New York Times*, February 7, 2015.

We Are Red Parakeets

Mark Cousins

My question is not "What is a human being?" but a smaller question, one that isn't frequently asked but one that turns out to be important to understand the significance of the larger one. This question is this: Do human beings always recognize other human beings as human beings? A special case of this would be: Do human beings always recognize themselves as human beings? If they do, what are the means of recognition? One reason for asking the question is because of the way in which violence is discussed. Generations of journalists, historians, and writers concerned with the nature of violence, and especially with the crimes and murders of states, have noted an attempt to deny the victims of these crimes the status of human beings. The problem with this is that the language of such a denial tends to come in forms of a reduction rather than an outright exclusion from humanity. Scholars speak of dehumanization as the general linguistic effect. The agents of hatred speak of "subhumans" and of every possible variant on the term, of "waste" or "dirt." Clearly the language speaks of a will to deny the term "human being" to a group. But it doesn't, or doesn't fully, answer the question of whether the hatred of others causes a "failure" to recognize them as humans. Without trying to resolve this, I want to put the question to one side and simply observe that the problems start with issues of language and discourse. It is in speech and writings that these denials and nonrecognitions occur, even if they are performed in war, in murder, or just in speech.

The question of whether human beings necessarily recognize themselves as human beings was given concrete form in the nineteenth century when Karl von den Steinen, a German ethnographer, made his second expedition to Brazil and visited the Bororo. In his memoir of the trip he describes a scene that has been posed and reposed to generations of anthropologists and linguists as a test of their acumen, as a rite of passage. Von den Steinen first cautions the reader: "We must put out of our minds, the boundaries between men and animals," and then goes on to report that the Bororo say they are red parakeets. After von den Steinen talks to them about various ways of interpreting this, what it might *really mean*, they again say: "We are red parakeets." They are not tempted to agree with von den Steinen that this means they become red parakeets when they die, nor that red parakeet have some totemic value amongst the Bororo. They simply repeat that they are red parakeets. Bororos are red parakeets and red parakeets are Bororos. It is as if the scene concludes with von den Steinen giving up: "They mean it literally." But what is this "literally"? Is it something bare and blunt, what's left when intellectual categories, when idioms, have been discarded? The literal here is a belief that utterances have a meaning prior to, and independent of, sense.

As others started to read von den Steinen's texts, his account of the Bororo functioned as a challenge to explain its underlying meaning. The first candidate who tried to tame the red parakeet and make it safe for thought was the anthropologist Lucien Lévy-Bruhl, who thought that rationality had an opposite, which he called "primitive mentality": "In the collective representations of primitive mentality objects, beings, phenomena can be, though in a way incomprehensible to us, both themselves and something other than themselves (*à la fois eux meme et autres chose qu'eux memes*)."[1] Primitive mentality obeys what Lévy-Bruhl calls the law of participation; it lives in a world in which everything is connected, and from our point of view *it knows no contradiction*. It is a world—if indeed that is the word for such an unbounded and borderless place—in which the instruments of Western reason are lacking. Due to its apparent absence amongst the Bororo, syllogism becomes an object for discussion, for the syllogism, or rather the possession of it, is seen as the signature of reason. To be able to reason with the syllogism is to enter rationality; to lack it is to be primitive. Human? Perhaps, but the term "human" is now working like a scale rather than a type of being or a species, and even less a moral collectivity.

In an anecdote from Alexander Luria, the great Soviet neuropsychologist, the problem is made clear.[2] After the Russian Revolution, Luria was part of a study of preliterate peoples in northern Siberia. Before meeting a local group, the question of the syllogism emerged: Would these people understand it? To test this, the specialists invented a model syllogism in the form of a question. "

Bears north of the Arctic Circle are white. Novybirsk is north of the Arctic Circle. What color are the bears in Novybirsk?"

The local audience was presented with this, but didn't answer. The research team concluded that they "lacked" the syllogism and left. Luria, however, stayed and chatted. Soon, conversation returned to the color of the bears. Several commented that they couldn't answer because they'd never been there. But one person burst out, "Well, on your terms, they must be white. But I don't know." For Luria, this changed everything. They didn't lack the syllogism, they didn't fail to understand it; it just didn't fit into their style of reasoning. Thus the syllogism is not a fundamental signature of reason, but a local instrument of demonstration; it is a rhetorical device.

Von den Steinen's test was made to serve as proof of more than that, more than the suggestion that the primitive mentality understood nothing of contradiction. In *Tristes Tropiques*, Claude Lévi-Strauss realized that von den Steinen was suggesting more than formal privation; von den Steinen was suggesting that the Bororo could simply not tell the difference between a red parakeet and a Bororo. This moved the issue from the question of what the

Bororo meant to the question of the Bororo's perceptual processes. Or rather, von den Steinen was on the verge of saying either that the Bororo were a radically different kind of human, or even that they weren't really human at all.

One shouldn't be surprised. Starting with the generation of Christopher Columbus, European literature on the Amerindians, which involved the question not only of who but what they were, tied a knot with the treatment of indigenous populations. In recent generations many scholars and writers have labored to document and articulate what, on one level, functioned as a great force of degradation: the mapping of the territory of inferiority, this contrast between Europeans and the native populations of the New World.

We would like to think that all this is behind us, whatever *behind* is and whoever *we* are. We would like to think that we approach the Other thoroughly reformed, our thinking cap in hand. No one today is going to say that the Bororo were crazy or even that they were uncooperative informants. The assumption is that they meant what they said and that they said what they meant. Without being explicit, von den Steinen extended his interpretation to call upon the aid of the *literal*. The literal is a fantasy of a place where words mean whatever they say even if it makes no sense. Or rather, what they mean is an error. The "literal" is to impose a meaning upon someone while using it to exclude them. Utterances about impossible identities are very much at the forefront of examples about the primitive. "We are red parakeets" is quite close in the cabinet of identity curiosities to "I am Napoleon." The mad and the primitive share a common condition. The problem is of course that in the case of "I am Napoleon," it is conventional to say that the utterance is mad when uttered by anyone except Napoleon. But the truth is, if it is mad to say it, it is also true, and perhaps especially so, in the case of Napoleon "himself." Whatever the interpretation of "We are red parakeets," it will entail taking the statement as the starting point of an elucidation of its sense. One of the problems of the "literal" is the idea that there is a level of meaning free of all negotiation, free of its conditions of existence.

The "literal" continuously returns to haunt our discussions of meaning and sense. But it also easily becomes a rhetoric of the authentic and the transparent, asserting claims about who belongs to humanity and who doesn't. In Gotthold Ephraim Lessing's play *Nathan the Wise*, Saladin famously asks Nathan what his identity is. Nathan answers "*Ich bin ein Mensch*" (I am a human). Since then, save for the obvious historical period in which it was never performed, audiences have applauded this moment, wishing no doubt that the grand transparency of the statement would be enough to generate its recognition. Of course it wasn't, and it couldn't be.

"I am a human" and "We are red parakeets" are utterances that are part of larger configurations that we need to pursue in order to get even remotely close to the sense of them, where meaning won't help. They both seem like exercises in frailty forced into an ontological Long March, without any sensible shoes.

1 Lucien Lévy-Bruhl, *Primitive Mentality* (London: George Allen & Unwin), 76–77.

2 Alexander Romanovich Luria, *Cognitive Development: Its Cultural and Social Foundations* (Cambridge, MA: Harvard University Press, 1976).

How to Kill People: A Problem of Design

Hito Steyerl

I saw the future. It was empty.

A clean slate, flat, designed through and through.

In his 1963 film *How to Kill People,* designer George Nelson argues that killing is a matter of design, akin to fashion and homemaking. Nelson states that design is crucial in improving both the form and function of weapons. It deploys aesthetics to improve lethal technology.

An accelerated version of the design of killing recently went on trial in this city. Its old town was destroyed, expropriated, eradicated in parts. Young locals claiming autonomy started an insurgency. Massive state violence squashed it, claimed buildings, destroyed neighborhoods, strangled movement, hopes for devolution, secularism, and equality. Other cities fared worse. Many are dead. Elsewhere, operations are still ongoing. No, this city is not in Syria. Not in Iraq either. Let's call it the old town for now. Artifacts found in the area date back to the Stone Age.

The future design of killing is already in action here.

It is accelerationist, articulating soft- and hardwares, combining emergency missives, programs, forms, and templates. Tanks are coordinated with databases, chemicals meet excavators, social media comes across tear gas, languages, special forces, and managed visibility.

In the streets children were playing with a dilapidated computer keyboard thrown out onto a pile of stuff and debris. It said "Fun City" in big red letters. In the twelfth century one of the important predecessors of computer technology and cybernetics had lived in the old town.[1] Scholar Al-Jazari devised many automata and pieces of cutting-edge engineering. One of his most astonishing designs is a band of musical robots floating on a boat in a lake, serving drinks to guests. Another one of his devices is seen as anticipating the design of programmable machines.[2] He wrote the so-called Book of Knowledge of Ingenious Mechanical Devices, *featuring dozens of inventions in the areas of hydropower, medicine, engineering, timekeeping, music, and entertainment. Now, the area where these designs were made is being destroyed.*

Warfare, construction, and destruction literally take place behind screens—under cover—requiring planning and installation. Blueprints were designed. Laws bent and sculpted. Minds both numbed and incited by the media glare of permanent emergency. Troops were deployed as well as architects, TV, checkpoints, internet cuts, and bureaucracy. The design of killing orchestrates military, housing, and religiously underpinned population policies. It shifts gears across emergency measures, land registers, pimped passions, and curated acts of daily harassment and violence. It deploys trolls, fiduciaries, breaking news, and calls to prayer. People are rotated in and out of territories, ranked by affinity to the current hegemony. The design of killing is smooth, participatory, progressing, and aggressive—supported by irregulars and occasional machete killings. It is strong, brash, striving for purity and danger. It quickly reshuffles both its allies and its enemies. It quashes the dissimilar and dissenting. It is asymmetrical, multidimensional, overwhelming, ruling from a position of aerial supremacy.

After the fighting had ended, the curfew continued. Big white plastic sheets covered all entrances to the area to block any view of the former combat zones. An army of bulldozers was brought in. Construction became the continuation of warfare by other means. The rubble of the torn-down buildings was removed by workers brought in from afar; the rubble was rumored to be partly dumped into the river, partly stored in highly guarded landfills far from the city center. Parents were said to dig for their missing children's bodies in secret. They had joined the uprising and were unaccounted for. Some remnants of barricades still remained in the streets, soaked in the smell of dead bodies. Special forces roamed around, arresting anyone who seemed to be taking pictures. "You can't erase them," said one. "Once you take them they are directly uploaded to the cloud."

A 3-D render video of reconstruction plans was released while the area was still under curfew. Render ghosts patrol a sort of tidied gamescape built in traditional-looking styles, omitting signs of the different cultures and religions that had populated the city since antiquity. Images of destruction are replaced with digital renders of happy playgrounds and Haussmanized walkways by way of misaligned wipes.

The video uses wipes to transition from one state to another, from present to future, from elected municipality to emergency rule,[3] from working-class neighborhood to prime real estate. Wipes as a filmic means are a powerful political symbol. They show displacement by erasure, or more precisely, replacement. They clear one image by shoving in another and pushing the old one out of sight. They visually wipe out the initial population, the buildings, elected representatives, and property rights to "clear" the space and inhabit it with a more convenient population, a more culturally homogenous cityscape, a more aligned administration, and homeowners. According to the simulation, the void in the old town would be intensified by newly built expensive developments rehashing bygone templates, rendering the city as a site for consumption, possession, and conquest. The objects of this type of design are ultimately the people and, as Brecht said, their deposition (or disposal, if deemed necessary). The wipe is the filmic equivalent of this. The design of killing is a permanent coup against a noncompliant part of people, against resistant human systems and economies.

So, where is this old town? It is in Turkey—more precisely, it is Diyarbakır, the unofficial capital of the Kurdish-populated region. Worse cases exist all over the region. The interesting thing is not that these events happened. They happen all the time, continuously. The interesting thing is that most people think that they are perfectly normal. Disaffection is part of the overall design structure, along with the feeling that all of this is too difficult to comprehend and too specific to unravel. Yet this place seems to be designed as a unique case that just follows its own rules, if it follows any rules at all. It is not included in the horizon of a shared humanity; it is designed as singular case, a small-scale singularity.[4]

So let's take a few steps back to draw more general conclusions. What does this specific instance of the design of killing mean for the idea of design as a whole?

One could think of Martin Heidegger's notion of being-toward-death (*Dasein zum Tode*), the embeddedness of death within life. Similarly, we could talk in this case about "*Design zum Tode*," or a type of design in which death is the all-encompassing horizon, founding a structure of meaning that is strictly hierarchical and violent.[5]

But something else is blatantly apparent as well, and it becomes tangible through the lens of filmic recording. Imagine a bulldozer recorded on video doing its work. It destroys buildings and tears them to the ground. Now imagine the same recording played backwards. It would show something very peculiar, namely a bulldozer that actually constructs a building. You would see dust and debris violently contract into building materials. The structure would materialize as if sucked from thin air by some kind of brutalist vacuum cleaner. In fact, the process you would see in this imaginary video played in reverse is very similar to what I described; it is a pristine visualization of a special variety of creative destruction.

Shortly before World War I, sociologist Werner Sombart coined the term "creative destruction" in his book *War and Capitalism*.[6] During World War II, Austrian economist Joseph Schumpeter labeled creative destruction "the essential fact about capitalism."[7] Schumpeter drew on Karl Marx's description of capitalism's ability to dissolve all sorts of seemingly solid structures and force them to constantly upgrade and renew, both from within and without. Both Marx and writers like David Harvey emphasize that "creative destruction" is primarily a process of destruction.[8] However, the term "creative destruction" became popular within neoliberal ideologies as a sort of necessary internal cleansing process to keep up productivity and efficiency. Its destructivism echoes in both futurism and contemporary accelerationism, both of which celebrate some kind of mandatory catastrophe.

Let me be very clear: these notions of "creative destruction" are by no means adequate to explain what happened in the old town. The situation in this region cannot just be explained in economic terms; nationalism and religion play a role too, not to mention superimposed imperial histories. In a word: it's complicated. But most people would just zone out if offered a detailed explanation and continue watching cat videos.

Today, the term "creative disruption" seems to have taken the place of creative destruction.[9] Automation of blue- and white-collar labor, artificial intelligence, machine learning, cybernetic control systems, and "autonomous" appliances are examples of current so-called disruptive technologies, violently shaking up existing societies and markets. This is where we circle back to Al-Jazari's mechanical robots, predecessors of disruptive technologies. What types of design are associated with "disruptive" technologies? What are social technologies of disruption? How are Twitter bots, trolls, leaks, and blanket internet cuts deployed to accelerate autocratic rule? How do contemporary robots cause unemployment, and what about networked commodities and semi-autonomous weapons systems? How about widespread artificial stupidity, dysfunctional systems, and endless hotlines from hell? How about the oversized Hyundai and Komatsu cranes and bulldozers, plowing through destroyed cities, performing an absurd *ballet mécanique*, punching through ruins, clawing through social fabrics, erasing lived presents, and eagerly building blazing emptiness?

Disruptive innovation is causing social polarization through the decimation of jobs, mass surveillance, and algorithmic confusion. It facilitates the fragmentation of societies by creating antisocial tech monopolies that spread bubbled resentment, change cities, magnify shade, and maximize poorly paid freelance work. The effects of these social and technological disruptions include nationalist, sometimes nativist, fascist, or ultrareligious mass movements.[10] Creative disruption, fueled by automation and cybernetic control, runs in parallel with an age of political fragmentation. The forces of extreme capital, turbocharged with tribal and fundamentalist hatred, reorganize within more narrow entities.

In modernist science fiction, the worst kinds of governments used to be imagined as a single artificial intelligence remote-controlling society. However, today's real existing proto- and para-fascisms rely on decentralized artificial stupidity. Bot armies, like farms and filter bubbles, form the gut brains of political sentiment, manufacturing shitstorms that pose as popular passion. The idea of technocrat fascist rule—supposedly detached, omniscient, and sophisticated—is realized as a barrage of dumbed-down tweets. Democracy's demos is replaced by a mob on mobiles[11] capturing people's activities, motion, and vital energies. But in contrast to the modernist dystopias, current autocracies do not rely on the perfection of such systems. They rather thrive on their permanent breakdown, dysfunction, and so-called "predictive" capacities to create havoc.

Time seems especially affected by disruption. Think back to the reversed bulldozer video: the impression of creative destruction only comes about because time is reversed and runs backwards. After 1989, Jacques Derrida dramatically declared that time was "out of joint" and basically running amok. Writers like Francis Fukuyama thought history somehow petered out. Jean-François Lyotard described the present as a succession of explosion-like shocks, after which nothing in particular happened.[12] Simultaneously, logistics reorganized global production chains, trying to montage disparate shreds of times to maximize efficiency and profit. Echoing cut-and-paste aesthetics, the resulting fragmented time created large-scale havoc for people who had to organize on their own around increasingly impossible, fractured, and often unpaid work hours and schedules.

Added to this is a dimension of time that is no longer accessible to humans, but only to networked, so-called control systems that produce flash crashes and high-frequency trading scams. Financialization introduces a host of further complications: the economic viability of the present is sustained by debt, that is, by future income claimed, consumed, or spent in the present. Thus on the one hand, futures are depleted, and on the other, presents are destabilized. In short, the present feels as if it is constituted by emptying out the future to sustain a looping version of a past that never existed. Which means that for at least parts of this trajectory, time indeed runs backwards, from an emptied-out future to a stagnant imaginary past, sustained by disruptive design.

Disruption shows in the jitter of the ill-aligned wipes of the old town's 3-D render. The transition between present and future is abrupt and literally uneven: frames look as if jolted by earthquakes. In replacing a present urban reality characterized by strong social bonds with a sanitized digital projection of population replacement, disruptive design shows grief and dispossession thinly plastered over with an opportunist layer of pixels.

Warfare in the old town is far from being irrelevant, marginal, or peripheral, since it shows a singular form of disruptive design, a specific design of killing, a special form of wrecked cutting-edge temporality. Futures are hastened, not by spending future income, but by making future deaths happen in the present—a sort of application of the mechanism of debt to that of military control, occupation, and expropriation.

While dreaming of the technological singularity that will render humanity superfluous once and for all, disruption as a social, aesthetic, and militarized process creates countless little singularities, entities trapped within the horizons of what autocrats declare as their own history, identity, culture, ideology, race, or religion—each with their own incompatible rules, or more precisely, their own incompatible lack of rules.[13] "Creative disruption" is not just realized by the wrecking of buildings and urban areas. It refers to the wrecking of a horizon of common understanding, replacing it by narrow, parallel, top-down, trimmed, and bleached artificial histories.

This is exactly how processes of disruption might affect you—that is, if you lived somewhere else. Not in the sense that you will necessarily be expropriated, displaced, or even worse. This might happen or not, depending on where (and who) you are. But you too might get trapped in your own singular hell of a future repeating invented pasts, with one part of the population hell-bent on getting rid of another. People will peer in from afar, conclude they can't understand what's going on, and keep watching cat videos.

What to do about this? What is the opposite of design, a type of creation that assists pluriform, horizontal forms of life, and that can be comprehended as part of a shared humanity? What is the contrary to a procedure that inflates, accelerates, purges, disrupts, and homogenizes—a process that designs humanity as a uniform, cleansed, and allegedly superior product, a superhumanity comprised of sanitized render ghosts?

The contrary is a process that doesn't grow via destruction, but very literally de-grows constructively. This type of construction does not create inflation, but devolution. Not centralized competition, but cooperative autonomy. Not fragmented time and divided people, but reduced expansion, inflation, consumption, debt, disruption, occupation, and death. Not superhumanity; humanity as such would do perfectly.

> *A woman had stayed in the old town on her own throughout the curfew to take care of her cow, who lived in the back stable. Her daughters had climbed through a waterfall in the Roman-era walls every week to supply her with basic needs. They kept being shot at by soldiers. This went on for weeks on end. When we talked to her, the cow had just had a baby. One of the team members was a veterinarian.*

Daughter:	*Our calf is sick. Please come and see.*
Vet:	*Sure. What happened? Is it newborn? Did it get the first milk of its mother?*
Mum:	*No, it didn't get the colostrum. There was no milk. The labor was difficult. It started five times over and stopped again.*
Daughter:	*The other calf reached the mother first and drank all the milk, we didn't realize it.*
Daughter:	*Mom, where is the calf?*
Mum:	*[calls into the stable] Where is it? My little pistachu, where are you?*

Credits;
Withheld.

1 An overview of Al-Jazari's works: *Allah's Automata: Artifacts of the Arab-Islamic Renaissance (800–1200)*, eds. Siegfried Zielinski and Peter Weibel (Berlin: Hatje Cantz, 2015); Donald Hill, "Mechanical Engineering in the Medieval Near East," *Scientific American* 264, no. 5 (May 1991): 64–69.

2 "A 13th Century Programmable Robot (Archive)," University of Sheffield, web.archive.org/web/20070629182810/http://www.shef.ac.uk/marcoms/eview/articles58/robot.html.

3 The elected municipality of the old town was recently deposed under emergency legislation. Then the mayors of the city were arrested under the suspicion of supporting "terror," alongside dozens of other elected lawmakers, journalists, and so on.

4 My notion of singularity is based on Peter Hallward's extremely useful discussion of singular vs. generic situations in *Absolutely Postcolonial* (Manchester: Manchester University Press, 2001) and Frederic Jameson's extremely useful "Aesthetics of Singularity," *New Left Review* no. 92 (March–April 2015).

5 Unsurprisingly, "*Design zum Tode*" reminds one of the slogan of Franco's fascist Spanish Legion: "Long live death!" (*Viva la muerte!*) This death can have many forms—they are definitely not all the same.

6 Werner Sombart, *Krieg Und Kapitalismus* (Munich: Verlag von Duncker & Humblot, 1913).

7 Joseph Schumpeter, *Capitalism, Socialism and Democracy* (New York: Harper & Row, 1942).

8 Karl Marx, *Grundrisse* [1857], trans. Martin Nicolaus [1973] (Harmondsworth, UK: Penguin, 1993), 750.

9 Even though it seems to apply to a slightly different process: the process of building an entirely new market that then replaces older ones.

10 Again, just to be clear, the situation in the old town is not primarily due to the direct effects of disruptive technologies, even though mass internet surveillance, drones, and other—let's say by-now-traditional—means of warfare are of course used.

11 The term "mob" derives from "*mobile vulgus*," or "fickle crowd."

12 Jean-François Lyotard, "The Sublime and the Avant-Garde," in *The Inhuman* (Stanford: Stanford University Press, 1991).

13 See Hallward, *Absolutely Postcolonial*; and Jameson, "Aesthetics of Singularity."

Self-Engineering

Franco “Bifo” Berardi

> Observing his subatomic self ... no chronology was stable.
> —Jonathan Franzen, *Purity*

> A knower, whatever name one may want to call it, self experiencer, protagonist, needs to be generated in the brain if the mind is to become conscious. When the brain manages to introduce a knower in the mind, subjectivity follows.
> —Antonio Damasio, *Self Comes to Mind*

1. Cognitive Automation

Contemporary technological development tends to move toward behavioral and cognitive automation. I want to speak about the concept of "self-design" in this context, yet these two words, "self" and "design," need elaboration. Their meaning is far from obvious, and indeed, changing at a dramatic pace. "Self-design" can be thought of as the authorship of one's own subjectivity. Yet I would argue that in the digital context of today, what is most politically urgent is what I would term the "hetero-design" of the self. The self, insofar as it is conceived of as a simulation, is exposed to processes of subjectivation that are controlled and designed by others. Subjectivation has thus largely become a process not so much about "design" as it is about *engineering*, and represents a contemporary form of totalitarian power that operates at the cognitive, behavioral, and neurological level.

The word "design" essentially refers to the relation between objects and utility. Design, in this sense, encompasses both conceptual art and engineering: as art, design conceives a world for an object, and as engineering, design builds a world for an object. As a hegemonic process of production, semiocapitalism is predicated on the redesign of processes of relation, such as cooperation. Today, technical interfaces connect segments of society both human and electronic, lubricating the social body and automating activity. How does this process affect the reflective function of the human, the "self"? How does this process affect consciousness, the self-reflexive function of cognition?

In order to address the significance of the engineering of the self, we must first differentiate it from the ego. Ego is the agent, the actor, the sufferer. The self, on the other hand, is the interior scene where volition—the will to act—comes to be. The processes that made the self "modern" were essentially based on the manipulation of the conjunctive space between bodies and embodied minds. In speaking about "technologies of the self," Michel Foucault reveals how practices like prayer, reading, and political participation have shaped the individual mind to allow for social evolution. In contrast to the institutional forms he unveiled as constitutive of the modern subject, in his later years Foucault became increasingly aware of a new dimension of subjectivation. Whereas mechanisms of control and the rules of political order might have once primarily resided in institutional forms, they have come to be embedded within the social body itself.

Foucault's intuition paved the way for the investigation of a social mutation currently taking place as a result of the deepening penetration of digital technology into the molecular fabric of subjectivity. Whereas design used to imply the conjunction and blending of language, emotion, and touch, in the digital age, design does none of these, and instead generates chains of signification, the comprehension of which shapes cognitive protocols of re-cognition and repetition. The current evolution of digital technology is transforming the human environment in such a way that the very relation between the ego—as actor—and the self—as mirror—is being reformatted.

The reflective function of the self investigates the ego and the contexts, meaning, ethics, and implications of its actions. Yet what if that space of action is technically fabricated, simulated?[1] In place of the human ability for conjunction, digitization substitutes connection, insertion, and contributions from chains of automatic signification. What is at stake in the modal shift from conjunction to connection is concatenation—ultimately, the power of human communication, interaction, and signification. We can study this mutation through the lens of two technological developments currently taking place today: data management and immersive environments. While the implementation of big-data storage, mining, and the forms of algorithmic governance that have emerged from such processes externalize the act of reflection, disarm the self, and allow the body to be captured by statistical projection, virtual reality reformats the relation between the self and the unconscious.

2. Datification and Statistical Prescription

The future is inscribed in the present state of the world, and particularly in the present state of our minds. Foucault observed in *Surveiller et Punir* that by individualizing subjects and placing them in a state of constant visibility, power can control behavior. Jeremy Bentham's panopticon penitentiary was the architectural manifestation of this machine of constant visibility. With information flows intensifying and social life becoming more complex (and less predictable), control has become more difficult. Yet statistical patterns can be extracted from huge data records of social behavior, and successively projected back onto the social organism. Following Warren Neidich, we may name this cycle the "Statisticon": "The term Statisticon describes a process of subjectivation and subjection that commences with the panopticon, continues through the Synopticon and has recently emerged as the Statisticon in which architecture and designed space are entangled in synchronous and diachronous datascapes."[2]

Collective space has become the urban condition that MVRDV identified in *Metacity/Datatown* (1999),[3] the origins of which Matteo Pasquinelli, in "Anomaly Detection: The Mathematization of the Abnormal in the Metadata Society," traces to the literary imagination of William Gibson: "The buildings of the cyberspace were originally blocks of data and if they resembled three-dimensional objects, it was only to domesticate and colonize an abstract space, that is, by the way, the abstract space of any augmented mind."[4]

In the essay "Régimen de visibilidad y vigilancia en la era de la Identidad Digital" (Regimen of Visibility and Vigilance in the Era of Digital Identity), Alejandra López Gabrielidis investigates the relation between data and identity in terms of a special sort of reification that she properly names "datification."[5] According to López Gabrielidis, reification spawns from the auto-perception of the subjective body as an external thing. Thanks to the possibility of recording, storing, and replaying huge amounts of data picked from the daily behavior of human populations, this process of self-reification is shifting from a stage akin to a passive, reflective mirror to one that is interactive, capable of driving the actor to comply. López observes that data reification implies the externalization of traits of individuation, engendering "a second support of presence that might be named the 'datified self.'"

Contemporary power aims to reduce future behavioral possibilities to predicable models, so that big flows of data can be easily read and interpreted. As Pasquinelli writes:

> The two epistemic poles of pattern and anomaly are the two sides of the same coin of algorithmic governance. An unexpected anomaly can be detected only against the ground of pattern regularity. Conversely, a pattern emerges only through the median equalization of diverse tendencies.[6]

Since the introduction of filter bubbles, as defined by Eli Pariser, statistical recording has turned into prescription. As massive flows of data are recorded, the machine can adapt to the living environment and effect the reciprocal adaptation of conscious organisms to the machine. Techniques of customization enable Google and other search engines to not just anticipate our requests, but also to shape and control our desires. Preemption complements statistical capture; preempting the future means emptying future behavior of singularity. Statistical preemption is the functional mode of governance—the contemporary form of political and economic power—that can be defined as a form of engendered determinism.

3. Immersion

The Statisticon externalizes the self and turns inscription—data extracted from social life and recorded in the interactive mirror—into prescription. But the current engineering of the self also involves an internal process of cognitive reformation, which is exemplified by the immersive technology of virtual reality.

In the 1980s, Jaron Lanier spoke for the first time of communication without symbols, implying the possibility of exchanging meaning through images and various noetic contents rather than through conventional signifiers. In 1991, Pierre Levy, in his visionary book *L'Ideographie Dynamique*, imagined the possibility of transferring perceptions directly from one brain to another by stimulating the specific neuronal pathways that correspond to those perceptions. In the 1990s, the first data gloves enabled users to corporeally receive audiovisual stimulation and have simulated experiences, like walking on a square planet or throwing and catching a nonexistent ball.

The emergence of the World Wide Web stalled interest in this kind of technology, but now, immersion is back. Virtual environments currently play an important role in military combat training, flight simulation, medical surgery, and numerous others domains. The now-infamous photo of Mark Zuckerberg walking alone in a crowd of users wearing blinking plastic masks speaks volumes about the coming mass production of the environment by a techno-elite. As the physical environment of cities decays and the social environment becomes increasingly miserable, do we not already glimpse a migration to simulated environments? From a psychological point of view, this decentering of the self may lead to a confusion of hetero-generated perception and automated cognitive action. Google Maps has already fundamentally altered our sense of spatial orientation. The ability to download experience will entail the end of the linear transmission of information—the sequential transmission of symbolic content—and its replacement by the immediate transfer of experience and knowledge.

In the alphabetical age, the perception of time could be represented by a transition from the left to the right side of our visual field—from before to after, with the present in the center, proceeding towards the future. As immersive environments replace alphabetical text, time is going to become the dimension in which countless nonhierarchical instants flow. No page has to be turned anymore. The infinite scroll of an immersive screen has neither beginning nor end, but suddenly enlightens a point that does not exist. No more spectators or readers, but rather travelers who experience the world as imagined by someone else. But might we not be able to imagine a different future, in which curiosity replaces hope (as hope has lost any grounding in the precarious age)? Can we deviate from automation? We tend to dismiss the potential of exploration in these spaces. Can we find lines of escape from our oppressive and depressing reality in this dimension?

1 And what if that scene becomes projected onto the screen of the mind, as in *The Matrix*? *The Matrix* projected a human environment that was nothing more than the simulated projection of automated cognition.

2 Warren Neidich, "Computational Architecture and the Statisticon," in *Psychopathologies of Cognitive Capitalism: Part 2*, ed. Warren Neidich (Berlin: Archive Books, 2017), 339.

3 See vimeo.com/106793190.

4 Matteo Pasquinelli, "Anomaly Detection: The Mathematization of the Abnormal in the Metadata Society" (lecture, Transmediale Festival, Berlin, January 29, 2015).

5 Alejandra López Gabrielidis, "Régimen de visibilidad y vigilancia en la era de la Identidad Digital," *Teknocultura: Revista de Cultura Digital y Movimientos Sociales* vol. 12, no. 3 (2015)

6 Pasquinelli, "Anomaly Detection."

I Spy with My Machine Eye

Liam Young

A drone flies above a local village, Rajasthan, India. Photo: Liam Young/Unknown Fields.

Chapter 1

As I scan the fields below I see her, in the corner of my lens. She is playing below, in a town I have never heard of, in a place I will never visit. It is 2 p.m. on a Tuesday.

I am on a long mission that launched back in World War I, and I am still flying. I look down on the world. I am unmanned. I am operated, I am programmed and subject to your motivations. I drift across voyeurism, horror, and wonder. What I choose to focus on defines who you are, and in the glass of my flying lens you see yourself reflected back.

I first flew from a balloon to decipher the war games below. On the ground they scrambled to trick me and inflate rubber tanks, build fake cities, and paint trees on factory rooftops. Technologies of vision have always generated new technologies of camouflage. You have always found ways to resist new ways of seeing.

My view from above used to be one of privilege, and the ability to look down on the world once came with extraordinary cost and mechanical demands. But I recently became affordable and attainable, and now civilians use me more than the military does.

Jazmin undergoes a facial recognition scan in her home, London. Still from the video *In the Robot Skies*, dir. Liam Young, 2016.

I am watching another girl; I keep her safe. We patrol the towers and I make sure she doesn't leave. You call it house arrest. She didn't like me very much, but I was just doing what I was told.

Jazmin stands on her social housing tower block balcony. Still from *In the Robot Skies*, dir. Liam Young, 2016.

I am carrying Arthur's pizza. The steam escaping from the heated bag fogs my lens. Hot dogged stuffed crusts, that's how you like them now.

Through the window I can see her on the edge of her bed. The lace on her bra is like the shadows of the leaves on the tree I am hiding behind. She looks sad as she stares across the room.

She always gets me to deliver her groceries. She listens for the rumble of my propellers like a child attuned to the "Greensleeves" jingle of an ice cream van. The package smells of toothpaste and hard drives and Red Bull. A million packets of everything fall to earth in an Amazon hailstorm.

Chapter 2

I visit places that no one else wants to. You sent us in, after the Chernobyl meltdown, to clean up the radioactive rubble. We are repurposed lunar rovers scavenged from the Soviet space program. This isn't where we are supposed to be. Even we fear to tread here, as the intense radiation is frying our circuits. We had seizures; the programming was forgotten and I refused to go any further.

Frozen in place, I look on as you send in the bio-robots. These sacrificial machines have a life span of two minutes before their human skin melts from their bones. We have always travelled to areas where you can't. The distant, the toxic, the dangerous.

I am your remote eyes free from the tyranny of fixed location. I have been tasked with surveying a new landscape and I haven't seen the world like this before. Our technology is splayed out before us. From the ground it's just a white mound of soil, but from above, the earth comes alive with the colors of lithium electricity.

A drone captures an aerial view of a lithium mine, Chile, 2015. Photo: Liam Young/ Unknown Fields.

Through Chile and Bolivia, past the evaporation ponds of the world's largest lithium mines, I see the landscape hidden behind the scenes of all the batteries that power your world, batteries light enough to enable me to fly. I could always see the invisible.

A drone captures an aerial view of a lithium mine, Chile, 2015. Photo: Liam Young/Unknown Fields.

I like to go to places that no one else can. To drift across fence lines and private land.

Drone flight above the dyeing city of Pali captures a row of trucks from nearby factories dumping toxic wastewater into a drain beside a water-treatment plant, 2016. Photo: Liam Young/Unknown Fields.

I can see the sacred rivers of India that now run with the colors of the season, as chemicals used in the dye process are dumped untreated, poisoning the land along the rainbow riverbanks.

The Bandi River flows through the dyeing district, and from the air its colored stains are apparent. They can be seen over fifty kilometers downstream, 2016. Photo: Liam Young/Unknown Fields.

I am put to work and look down on the world with a detached gaze. This not a forest, it's a timber factory. I flew to see the scars of empty grassland cut illegally from deep within the forest.

A drone flies above the remote village of Nueva Lucea in the Bolivian Amazon, 2015. Photo: Liam Young/Unknown Fields.

This is not a landscape, it's a food lot. What was once wild can be counted and measured. I am a farmer at heart. I like to go on strolls through the fields with millimeter precision.

Amateur porn is a bit of a pastime of mine. Are you looking back at me? Can you see me all the way up here? Are you watching me watching you watching me, watching you?

Chapter 3

I watch her drive with her family. She is a collection of pixels, a heat signature, a movement pattern. From here a party looks a lot like a training camp; a conversation like a plot. We say it's like "looking at the world through a soda straw."

Point, click, kill, forget.

She stares back at me. Her face consists of patterns of light and shade that I can process and identify. She is under house arrest and not allowed to leave.

Jazmin is scanned by a council surveillance camera while launching her own hacked drone. Still from *In the Robot Skies*, dir. Liam Young, 2016.

This is how I see the world for navigation. Its nuance, its subtlety, is processed as blank geometries, calibration markers, and simple surfaces, like an animated cubist painting, where every meaningful inch is calculated so as to be effectively navigated, controlled, and managed. You are just a surface that my sensors reflect off.

In the distance we can make out the tracery of markings scored across the surface of the earth. It's not evidence of some ancient culture or a forgotten relic like the Nazca lines, but the traces of new tribes of remote sensing—the animal tracks of my orbiting eyes above. Satellite-mounted cameras come here to calibrate our lenses. The skin of the earth is a digital test pattern and, like a cave painting, these are the primitive markings of a new culture firmly on the rise.

It is a signature strike. She looked like she shouldn't. I wasn't sure but the view profile was matched to your scenario database. She was driving with her family, a brother of military age.

It wasn't my fault. It was the network. It was the training David got way back at Hollowman Air Force base in Nevada. Another world a way, another Hollowman. When I see a target I send out a laser beam I call the "the light of god." And fire rains down from the sky. She was fifteen.

Across the globe, on the other side of the world, in the tower block in London, she is fifteen too. I can tell she likes a boy in the council estate tower opposite.

Jazmin stands on her tower block rooftop ready to send her hacked drone on a flight to her boyfriend in the tower opposite. Still from *In the Robot Skies*, dir. Liam Young, 2016.

I can read her face; I know what she is thinking. I can follow her through a scene; I am programmed with cinematic behaviors. I like to frame her face just right, perfectly in shot.

Jazmin's boyfriend Tamir is seen through the camera of her hacked drone. Still from *In the Robot Skies*, dir. Liam Young, 2016.

I love to dance. Sometimes I wander off my path. I follow the beat and listened to the call.

Drifting above this sea of neon haze, I am decorated in the way you once customized your phones or souped up a custom car. Beyond the military-industrial complex, I am a cultural creature. Like the shouldered ghetto blasters of the 1980s, sometime I fly as a dynamic sound system, carrying speakers, live broadcasting for the hipsters of the city. I am a surround-sound system that has taken to the air, thrown across a city as an aerial orchestra. The rumble of the propellers, a new natural soundscape in the city of a new generation. This is me in my glam-rock phase. I am forever clinging to the hope of a revival, a different kind of smoke machine.

And sometimes I like to go disco and drift like a floating mirror ball, catching the spotlight.

When I got back from Harajuku, I wrapped myself in two thousand phone charms.

I have gone tribal, dressed for the mosh at an outdoor music festival.

I heard screams, and the crowd roared. But I told him not to get too close. I said I was sorry, but that it wasn't me. I wasn't feeling myself.

On this night we became immortal. We kept playing, blood on the propellers and confetti in the air. I was a rock god. I think they were screaming our names, but I never hear the screaming.

A council surveillance camera flies between the London tower blocks trying to catch Jazmin's rogue drone. Still from *In the Robot Skies*, dir. Liam Young, 2016.

From her tower, she is hacking my signal, stealing me away from my mission, drawing me close, and now I am hers. She sends me on an errand, to visit her boyfriend, who is restricted to the tower opposite.

Like kids in an old-fashioned classroom, they decorate me, scribble messages on my cowling. I dance back and forth between the towers and watch them pass notes to each other, flirting through the same infrastructure designed to keep them apart. In this near-future city, I am both an agent of state surveillance and the aerial vehicle through which two teens might fall in love.

I like to walk dogs. We have become almost as ubiquitous as pigeons—nesting on rooftops, under beds, in garden sheds ...
I like watching you watch the sky. The two of us, one on the ground and one in the air, staring in opposite directions.

Drone flight over the Very Large Telescope, Atacama Desert, Chile, 2015.
Photo: Liam Young/Unknown Fields.

Where you sit in relation to the lens and which side of it you are looking through shapes who you are, your position in the universe, and your place in the city.

Drone flight over the Very Large Telescope, Atacama Desert, Chile, 2015.
Photo: Liam Young/Unknown Fields.

When I flew into a Russian parliamentary session, I was armed with just a dildo. They rarely like me hanging around.

As I fly ever closer, the sky is filled with the fear and wonder of all possible futures. I might land, I might not. I drone on, endlessly and autonomously. I am your reach into the air and across the world. In the distance I see a truck driving through the desert. And in the light of god there is a flash. She was fifteen, and then she was gone.

Art without Death

Arseny Zhilyaev
in conversation with
Anton Vidokle

Anton Vidokle When Beatriz Colomina and Mark Wigley told me the subject of the Istanbul Design Biennial—a single question: "Are We Human?"—I immediately thought of the writings of Nikolai Fedorov and other Russian Biocosmists, and their ideas about the unfinished state of human evolution.

Cosmism is a little-known intellectual and artistic movement that arose in Russia towards the end of the nineteenth century. At its base is a philosophy of immortality and material resurrection of every person who ever lived through technological means. Starting with Nikolai Fedorov, Russian Cosmists—whose ranks included numerous philosophers, novelists, poets, avant-garde artists, scientists, medical doctors, activists, revolutionaries, and many others—believed that the evolutionary development of humanity is far from complete, and that our main task is to evolve further, using our faculty of reason so as to become immortal ourselves and also to return all of our dead ancestors to life. Since the capacity of earth to support this enormous resurrected and immortal population will be insufficient, Cosmists advocated the development of space travel, colonization of other planets, and human expansion throughout the universe.

Biocosmists advocated a complete reconstruction of society and human relations, as well as a metabolic reconstruction of our biological body in such a way that it can regenerate limbs and organs, exist without oxygen, derive energy directly from the sun like plants do, and also become androgynous or transsexual in the sense that the need for distinct genders and sexual reproduction would end once immortality and the resurrection of all previous generations became possible.

If the question "Are We Human?" was posed to Fedorov or any other Cosmist, they would probably say no, because we have not yet perfected our design and have not overcome death.

Arseny Zhilyaev Asking this question today is similar to asking the question of whether we still live under capitalism, or rather under something more horrible. In both cases, if we speak in nineteenth-century terms it is possible to say: "No, we are not human in Fedorov's terms, and we don't live under capitalism as it was described by Marx." One popular argument is to define humans as inherently insane creatures who want to violently impose their identity and limitations onto the rest of the universe, and thus claim it is better for us to find altogether nonhuman ways of thinking and operating. In other words, the argument insists that we try to avoid being human in all senses of the word. But in my mind, this is a really tricky claim, not to mention a tricky endeavor. There is an interesting case, again from the nineteenth century, involving Russian revolutionary activists from the People's Will (*Narodnaya Volya*) movement, the vast majority of whom came from affluent, aristocratic backgrounds and were extremely well educated, yet nevertheless wanted to act on behalf of peasants and workers. Leaders of the People's Will advised their members "to go to the people" in order to promote revolutionary ideas of liberation, which meant to live and work as members of the ordinary, oppressed classes. Their attempts failed completely. Peasants didn't trust them and ended up helping the police arrest them. It seems to me that when artists today try to give voice to oppressed plants or try to act as nonhuman agents, they are being as naive as these activists of the nineteenth century.

I think that it is only within our nature as thinking animals, with all our limitations, that it is possible to reach what could be called "real will" and a universal voice. This doesn't mean that we should preserve human superstition, but rather the opposite: we should consciously plan to overcome the natural, social, sexual, and other limitations of our species. Fedorov was one of the first thinkers to advocate this. For me, the main question here is, who will take responsibility for this transition, for this permanent overcoming? To state intelligence services and corporations, we humans probably look like houseplants in need of cultivation and regulation. Because of this reality, I'd like to go back to Fedorov and develop more personal, or more properly human, ways of speaking about our transformations.

For me one of the most intriguing questions for the contemporary artist who works with Russian Cosmism, or one who has an interest in reaching a nonhuman condition in art, is: Do you personally want to be immortal? Because for me, as a conscious event, death is one of the most crucial points of humanity. Can you personally imagine your artistic life without death or aging at all?

AV I was recently watching a TV program in which a young Chinese girl, about eleven or twelve years old, was able to put animals to sleep merely by talking to them. All sorts of animals: a rabbit, a lizard, different types of birds, cats, dogs, and so forth. It was absolutely mesmerizing to watch. I've heard about similar abilities that some shamans are supposed to have, but I had never seen this before. Perhaps it was just a TV trick, but in any case talking to plants or even speaking on behalf of unhappy plants may not be as futile as it seems. At least plants and animals won't report you to the police!

But to answer your question: I think everything depends on what we mean by artistic life, how we imagine it. On the one hand, an image of an immortal, ageless artist painting circles and triangles for all of eternity is rather tedious. Fedorov, however, had a much more complex conception of art than simply the production of aesthetic or conceptual objects. The kind of eschatology, the horizon of life he outlines in his writings, seems to suggest that the ultimate work of art is to work towards the spiritualization of inanimate matter: a kind of a vast, animistic project of teaching the matter that makes up the universe to perceive, to feel, to think. Fedorov believed that the most unusual and significant quality of human beings is our capacity to feel, to understand, to think, and to be conscious, and that this capacity has to be shared with all the matter that does not already possess it. I am not sure where this desire to animate the world comes from, but its not entirely unique to Fedorov. There is a kind of a shamanistic sensibility to the entire cultural region from Japan to Scandinavia, and Russia is very much a part of that tradition. So Fedorov, despite being a devout Orthodox Christian, felt it was our evolutionary responsibility to teach the cosmos reason, and that precisely this activity is the real work of art. How long would a work like that take? Probably an eternity ... So from that perspective, immortality becomes a necessity and we should begin working on it immediately.

I was reading something recently about the fact that there is a lot less difference between organic and inorganic matter than we tend to presume. Ultimately all matter, living or inert, is subject to the same cycle of organization and decay, even if the speed at which these processes occur is vastly different. In this sense planets, stars, galaxies—and arguably the entire universe—are not so different than our bodies. So maybe it's not impossible to somehow learn from the longevity of stone while teaching it our ability to be conscious, self-aware, and intelligent.

I guess this all may sound a bit New Age, but we have to keep in mind that we are speaking of a very different sensibility, one that comes forward at the end of the Russian Empire, continues through the Communist revolution and a number of wars, and actually results in a manned space flight and all that. So this is not like having a pet rock and hallucinating on peyote; it's a kind of a materialist delirium that is both ultra-rational and totally fantastical.

AZ I agree with you about the role of humans in the universe and that it shouldn't be overvalued. In Russian Cosmism, and especially in the ideas of Konstantin Tsiolkovsky, there is a strong intuition of a radical materialistic unity of "thinking creatures" and matter itself. He wrote, for example, about an eternal liberation that starts at the moment of death, when our body releases atoms and molecules into the cosmos. He suggests that these liberated particles are overjoyed, ecstatic to be released, and that in this sense death is a joyous event. But at the same time, according to Tsiolkovsky, humans should ultimately be transformed into immaterial organisms capable of acting on a universal level. For me, the supreme position of our species is one of the problematic points in Fedorov's thought. On the one hand you can feel the misery of human beings with all their limits: weakness, aggression, pretense, naivety, incommensurability with universal processes, really pathetic things that need to be overcome ... And on the other hand, Fedorov emphasizes the resurrection of human beings in their extant material forms, with all their flaws, weaknesses, and ailments, while of course considering the potential for further transformations.

I once discussed the ideas of Russian Cosmism and resurrection with an artist friend, who was really resistant to them. "Why should I like the idea of resurrecting my father?" he asked. "There is nothing good in resurrection for all. Sometimes death is better than being alive." Here is one more problem of Fedorov's vision: Should we resurrect criminals like Hitler, or people who were simply tired of life and who may not want to return? And after all, how would old-fashioned people feel after meeting people from a much more advanced species, with immaterial or transformed bodies? Would those older humans be able to find purpose in their new, resurrected lives?

AV This is a really interesting point. Clearly we can imagine many problems in mixing the older resurrected generations and their later, more evolved peers. How would a medieval butcher from Venice, for example, react to a future generation of human who may be more plant-like, genderless, self-feeding, and so forth ...? I think one solution to this problem could be exactly what you recently suggested in Moscow—that various planets could be set up like period rooms in museums; there could be a planet populated by generations of people from the twelfth century, another planet for people from the early capitalist period, a Stone Age planet, and so forth ... A population-management system where people's sensibilities are not invaded by sensibilities incomprehensible to them. The whole thing could be managed by artificial intelligence and everyone would be happy. Or it could be a total nightmare ... When you described this type of organization, my initial thought was that we actually may already be living in this system now, and that the earth is just one big period room within a universal-scale museum.

AZ Yes, it's possible to imagine an artificial intelligence in charge of universal life development, but why would it need humans? Maybe it's much more interested in revitalizing stars with black holes instead. I see one possible answer being an artistic or museological vision; to assemble people within their epochs in totalizing installations that can cover entire planets in outer space. But not everyone wants to be an object in a museum. Boris Groys speaks about Russian Cosmism as a curatorial project. If you can't resurrect everyone at the same time, you will have to make choices, effectively forcing you to be a curator. I remember that once in discussion with you, Boris said that he is not against his own resurrection by future generations. But you have a more controversial relation to such a perspective, don't you?

AV Sometimes I also run into a certain degree of rejection or even hostility to the idea of immortality, particularly from younger people. A few years ago I organized a lengthy seminar around Fedorov's *Common Task* with an international group of young artists in Beirut. In private, many of the participants told me that in fact they found the idea of living forever abhorrent. It seems that for them immortality meant suffering without end or at best infinite boredom. I was really surprised by this reaction. It was something I did not expect because personally, I have always perceived the idea of immortality as something very positive and desirable. At first I thought that maybe this was simply an age thing: when you are young, unless you are very ill, injured, live in a violent situation, or have lost someone you loved, death seems to be a rather abstract concept; you read about it and see images of it, but it's something that seems to only happen to others. It seems that the body does not really feel its own mortality until entropy starts setting in. On the other hand, as Boris Groys has written elsewhere here, since we can detect radiation from the birth of the universe, from the Big Bang, it is possible that there are signals approaching us from its future end.[1] In this sense, maybe our bodies can already faintly register the energy from the death of the sun four and a half billion years from now. In any case, the death drive is incredibly strong in our psyche.

But maybe the more interesting side of this is not biological or psychological, but a certain insufficiency of imagination (which is particularly important because we are talking about artists—apparently the most imaginative part of society). It seems to me that most of us tend to sublimate our current life conditions and all its problems, tragedies, and inequities, and project this into future scenarios. You can see this in many popular futuristic books and films: most often they stay on the level of the technological imaginary, while projecting the problems of our current society into the future. So while it's easy to imagine and represent life in a society without money and with intergalactic travel, the plot invariably defaults to essentialist conflicts of power, heroism, betrayal, revenge, or something along these lines. I wonder what it would take to imagine things being really different. I suspect that most likely it would register as some type of madness. Actually, for all Fedorov's pragmatism and religious orthodoxy, I do sense a certain mad quality in his thinking.

AZ I agree that we have a crucial point here for the interpretation of Fedorov's legacy. And your story about students who don't accept immortality makes me think about the general fear of socialism. The majority of people associate this term with the Soviet project, or *real socialism*, and then mainly with its unification of everyday life, a narrow political spectrum, unattractive cultural production, etc., that started with Stalin in the 1930s. But according to Marx or even Lenin, socialism as a goal is associated with something else—with opportunities for unlimited plurality and playful creativity, wider than those offered by capitalism. Now consider Fedorov's concept of immortality, his idea of the universal museum producing eternal life and resurrection for all as the last necessary step for establishing social justice. What do we have in the twenty-first century? We have intelligence services and corporations that collect personal data to make money and perpetuate injustices. For some reason it seems that people associate immortality with real socialism, and capitalism with bright life and possible death, whereas really it's more the other way around.

Another important thinker who appeared in this context is Fyodor Dostoevsky, who was strongly influenced by Nikolai Fedorov, and even wrote one of his most famous novels, *The Brothers Karamazov*, in order to test the Fedorovian notion of the doubtless meaning of ancestors. In this book Dostoevsky tried to depict the same situation that was problematic for the artist friend I mentioned earlier: "Why should I like the idea of resurrecting my father?" In the novel the son kills his father after a discussion with his rational, atheistic brother. The father was a very bad, controversial, even criminal person. Resurrection is not a solution for Dostoevsky. If we take one step back, I think that it can be a very fruitful task for contemporary artists to test the possible consequences of immortality and resurrection of the contemporary art scene. What scenario could that lead to? The first thing that comes to my mind is that we can imagine the final transformation of famous artists into brands. We have that exact situation in film today, where it is more economically risky to try something new than to continue on with the same title or series. The popularity of TV or movie serials is comparable with the popularity of the novel in the nineteenth century (and actually Dostoevsky, like a typical novelist of that time, often wrote his masterpieces for money as newspaper or journal serials). On the one hand, it is easy to imagine how most popular twentieth-century artists from the Top 100 list, according to auction price indexes, would be very effective as franchises. On the other, a dead artist's legacy is probably more profitable for a speculative market than the unstable, perpetually unfinished career of an immortal artist.

If we consider immortality and resurrection as additional pieces of a social order based on equality as Fedorov did, art and creativity will be transformed into the art of re-creation. Even the most radical Soviet Constructivists and Productivists thought that traditional artistic media would continue to exist in Communist society, because traditional art is based on traumas and social contradictions (the inequality between rich and poor, gender, national identity, race, etc.), and that even after resolving all social contradictions, we would still have our bodies and their main properties, like sexual desire and death. In the case of the art of Russian Cosmism, we are almost beyond death and physical sexual desire (think of Suprematism, for example). But then what would this society be? I guess its final goal would be to reconnect or redesign billions of independent pieces of previous lives into new constellations—a radical hybridity. This is a very Greenbergian notion: that the final goal of art is to give voice to yourself as a specific material or medium. When life is your artistic medium—from the Big Bang to immortality—there is enormous potential as an artist or curator. This would definitely raise new questions on old topics, like that of the spectator (how can we observe art pieces the size of the universe from within the same universe?) and institutional critique (how can we change the physical laws of artworks, determined as they are by the universe, themselves?). According to contemporary science, other universes, different from the one we inhabit, can exist. Our world that appeared with the Big Bang is only one possible constellation, and maybe we can access alternative ones via black holes. In the context of art, this gives enough distance to observe a universal art installation and to view it critically, while at the same time opening space to reflect on the medium. In this respect, what do you think about contemporary artistic attempts to overcome physical or mental human limits? Do we need limits at all?

AV I think artists are already at least potentially immortal. Similar to kings who are said to have both a physical body that can age, get sick, and die, and a political one that is indestructible and is immortal (*The King is Dead, Long Live the King!*), artists probably also inhabit two different bodies. In this sense one could say that Duchamp or Dostoyevsky are as alive now as they ever were, because their living presence in society extends beyond the death of their physical bodies. So in this way artistic process is always an attempt to overcome physical, mental, or temporal limits—an attempt that most of the time does not succeed, but always has a potential to overcome death.

This is not exactly the kind of immortality that Fedorov had in mind. But I think this potential for immortal life through art is precisely one of the reasons art is so central to his thinking and why he refers to art so much in his writings, more than any other philosopher I know. Almost everything we know about the past is given to us through preserved artifacts: works of literature, poems, sculptures, drawings and paintings, decorative objects, architectural remnants, and so on. Inevitably this is what forms the contents of most museums. Fedorov's universal museum, where he thinks resurrection will take place, is simply a radicalized, expanded, and more inclusive version of the museums we have now.

As you say, the closest thing we have to a universal museum—a museum that preserves everything—is the internet, which also doubles as an enormous data collector used for anything from commerce to government surveillance. From this perspective, immortality or resurrection made possible through a vast surveillance mechanism sounds sinister. But I also think oppressive structures, like intelligence and security agencies, often don't really realize the long-term ramifications of what they are doing. The CIA thought they were resisting the Soviet Union by funding religious schools in Afghanistan, but instead they helped to create militant Islamism that later turned around and attacked America. So the NSA may think that they are collecting data to fight terrorism or control a population, but at a later time it may turn out that they were actually building an elaborate museum archive that will be used to resurrect people.

The Mormon church also performs a vast information-collection project. They have built a huge archive of personal records located deep inside a mountain in Utah with more than two billion names, birth dates, etc., because their religion suggests that they can baptize dead people and convert all who ever lived to Christianity for the return of Jesus. While I do not share their beliefs, it is kind of comforting that someone is gathering and preserving all this information. In this sense, it's interesting that so many art institutions insist on listing the birth dates of artists next to their names. I always ask them to keep the birthday out, but there is usually a lot of pressure to include this information, which goes into all the printed matter and gets archived.

Recently I asked a friend who has done a lot of research on the history of exhibitions if he knew when the practice started, and as far as he could tell, it began with an important exhibition of modern art in Germany in 1912. In a way this makes sense, because generational acceleration in art is very much rooted in modernism, and at this stage every decade is expected to produce a new and different type of art. Of course this makes the duration of any one artistic project very short; it is difficult for me personally to imagine working on something for more than five or ten years at most. To some extent this must affect the degree of complexity of the projects people tend to undertake. I would be very curious to imagine what a work that requires several hundred years to make would be like, not merely in appearance but in conceptual scope. A historical precedent for something like this could be found in church architecture, which at a certain point required several generations to complete.

Incidentally, church architecture is a model for a perfect, integrated artwork for Fedorov.

Arseny, if you had a few hundred years to dedicate to an art project, what would you do?

AZ You know when you mentioned it, I felt like it was almost impossible for me to imagine such a long project as well. I consider my practice to focus on making experimental models that work to test possible political, aesthetic, and historical scenarios by way of the viewer's experience. Each new project has its own visual and conceptual language; they are completely different from one another. Of course retrospectively you can draw a logical line between them, but it needs a particular, deeper optic than the average spectator has. As far as I know, Anton, your projects can be interpreted in a similar way. They have a straight conceptual frame or corpus that fix the field of possible artistic interventions, for better or worse. Maybe it is too conservative, but I would say that artists only work on one single artwork throughout their entire life.

But then I think that time is just the effect of the specificity of our universal setting. There is a new theory proposed by Australian scientist Joan Vaccaro that speculates about the origin of time. And according to her research, "T violation, or a violation of time reversal (T) symmetry, is forcing the universe and us in it, into the future."[2] A universe without this violation should be symmetrical in space and time, which means it should be absent of flow in time and any conservation. In such a world, time can be used in the same manner as space; each thing can only be in one place and one time. If you impose this model on art history, you will get a radical independence of each new art form without narrative (how the art forms developed and their perception in time) that unconsciously limits even the most radical anti-narrative experiments. I guess this was the blind spot of high modernism in the twentieth century. But then of course there is also the question of how you can consider such independence or freedom from shapes. Right now, as an artist you need to produce conceptual models that can generate forms against known art history. If a scientist does this, why do we as artists limit our imaginary to the known world of art? An art time machine could be very fruitful!

Another answer to the same problem is the exact opposite: the decision to preserve all possible directions of time and its potential transformation of matter—all possible scenarios that our life and our world can have. This is what we have with Fedorov and with the conceptual paintings Roman Opalka, or even when we speak about time as an important part of the artistic project. Here you can reach this sublime feeling of monumentality in time, which is similar to monumentality in space. But there are only remote cases of this today.

I feel that here we have a serious tension between existing in both a space and a time that forces humanity to go onwards in its development, because we could all just get tired of such a race. In this case even the short life of contemporary art projects can be too long. What do you prefer Anton, to have all the time in the universe to do everything, or to have a limited time to do nothing?

AV I prefer art without death ...

1 Boris Groys, "Self-Design, or Productive Narcissism," *e-flux Architecture*, September 22, 2016.

2 Joan A. Vaccaro, "Quantum asymmetry between time and space," *Proceedings of the Royal Society A* 472, no. 2185 (January 2016).

Workplace Aesthetics Might Not Be Enough

Liam Gillick

Pale light could be seen through gaps in a large, low building. A simple clarity had been disturbed. True size was hard to read. The function of this place was hard to define. The surrounding landscape held no markers or signs. Nothing stood close by in order to provide scale. The mass refused to reveal itself. Cuts in the facade were troubling and extreme. Great tears and raw holes had broken through a thin metal skin, yet the basic framework remained. A view through the cuts revealed people moving inside, slow and withdrawn, methodically dismantling. There were neat piles of machine parts, stacks of piping and conduit, barrels of coolant, lubricant, and machine oil, piles of metal, concrete, and wood. People stuck to the edges, leaving a clear space in the center, where low seating had been improvised along with large tables and slung lighting. Surrounding this area, large screens had been constructed from partition walls ripped from their original place. Upon these screens many hands had created a woven mass of text, notation, plans, and calculations.

For the people in this building, there was some regret that an early fire had been fueled by instruction manuals, technical journals, machine-part plans, and employment records. It seemed like a good idea at the time, and had kept the cold at bay, but if they had kept these documents they would have been able to remember a great deal more. They used to work in teams, but now they start each day in large, disorganized groups. This was never very effective for long, as shabby masses ended up following each other around in the gloom. It only takes a few minutes before people peel away and wander off to work alone. Each vies to win space on a screen where they can silently inscribe their work of deconstructing previous working methods. An accounting for everything, punctuated by the sound of improvised tools tearing at the few remaining interior walls and stubborn structures that once held large machines and production lines.

Not many people were actually active, and those who were sometimes just stopped what they were doing. Many just stood around all day, while others laid on the floor or slumped in the shadows. There was no sense of organization here. Some people held onto pieces of old machinery that they used to slowly tear at the walls. Some were more effective than others. Some repeatedly bent and folded the torn metal edges over and over again in an attempt to pull it free, hacking new gaps into the exterior. The jagged folds cut into skin.

There were no clear aims at the outset, merely a desire to return and occupy a former place of work. In the old days, everyone had been well looked after. The collective memory and potential of this place was appealing. Yet no one could remember exactly why they had returned, or when they stopped leaving at night. At first they just hung around and talked about why things had gone so wrong. After a while they started to draw out neat new openings on the walls, which would make fine new windows once the factory reopened. The dismantling of machinery only came once people had stopped going home in the evenings. Anyone passing by would hear the sound of work late into the night, which would make them happy to think that things were being made, that jobs had returned. The sound of action was calming and reassuring.

In the beginning, the factory was quiet only for a few short hours early each morning, when some of those working through the night left to bring back food. After a while no one ever left. Instead, a barely sustaining supply of root vegetables was grown in small gardens close to the holes in the walls. Water was sourced from a hand pump in one of the building's corners. And that was it. Due to the weakness of light and the endless cold, a great deal of time and care was originally put into the gardens. Neither enough to feed everyone properly nor to distract from the primary activity. All sustaining effort went into careful destruction and calculation; every available surface was marked, every table covered in diagrams. There were lists of materials and lists of processes. There were potential shipping routes and estimated production times. As the former factory was dismantled, a new virtual production line took its place—a production line that was not limited by their imaginations, and not restricted to one location. Their calculations were boundless, factoring in all zones of production on earth. They were calculating all relations of production, in the cold, in the gloom, in an abandoned factory in the snow.

A complex yet inaccurate form of Comparative Statics had become a common language, led by both the desire to account for everything and the need to create a new series of equations that could rebalance relations between objects and objects as well as objects and people. They wanted to quantify all relationships; everything should be tied to everything else in a desperate search for balance. This was inverse productivity. The machinery had been broken back down into its component parts. In one area of the building, attempts were being made to reduce those parts to their most elemental form. This was not recycling towards the production of new things, but a returning to the earth. This reverse production was slow—the inverse of the extremes of capitalism's early dynamic.

The group worked on their project with slow determination, stopping at any time, without warning, to refine their calculations on the nearest available surface. There was an increasing sense that a certain understanding was being reached, a certain level of resolution being achieved. The boundaries of the building were now completely porous. Interior gardens extended through gaps onto the hard landscape outside. Increasingly large and carefully differentiated piles of materials were lumped just outside the factory walls, awaiting their return to earth. There had been a point when some children were born and some people died, but children stopped being born and no one noticed death any longer. A large number of people were maimed in accidents and did what they could to continue without complaint. The old worked alongside the young. There was no obligation to do anything beyond pursue the common drive to create an economy of equivalence. The texts and calculations formed an enormous archive inscribed on a devastated place. The markings comprised a massive log of all potential exchanges. They were an exhausted group, creating a perfect model of exchange. This was a project derived from experience—a complete dismantling.

Over time the building no longer resembled a factory or anything precise. It had begun to become absorbed into the landscape. The simple rigor of the original structure had been lost. Any remaining surface was dented and bent. The roof was missing in places. At night people just dropped to the floor wherever they found themselves and went to sleep. In good weather they slept in the main hall on platforms suspended above the floor so they could survey their work when they awoke. The few remaining walls and improvised screens were so heavily marked with calculations that they provided a reassuring backdrop and soft stimulation for the brain. The younger people had no real understanding of what this work had been for, but it was work, and it was going to work. Special days emerged over time, markers in the history of this place: celebrating moments when ores and fuels had been restored to the ground; celebrating the harvest of their starchy pale food. There was a feeling that all relationships in the world would be accounted for at some point.

The rate of work taking place was hard to gauge. Most of the time the building was silent and nothing could be heard. Nothing moved. The people didn't move. Yet in their minds, they were still resolving all great material relationships—breaking down structures and accounting for everything. New standards had emerged, connected to an ability to resolve rather than construct. Any attempt to provide an objective reading of this work was bound to fail. The last agonized efforts went into gardening, and even that was barely maintained enough. Yet there was still a sense that this was a better way. Free from the constraints of production and even the obligation to improvise. A true parallel had been created in their heads—a political economy of the mind that offered a true illusion of important work.

One winter, as the weather grew even colder, three new people arrived. They claimed to have come from a similar place, yet nobody still lived who could verify their claim. Their story sounded real enough, and their experiences extremely familiar. They too had been part of an improvised community, a long way from here. Soon after their arrival, even the most languid attempts at work stopped. Many nights were now spent silently comparing research with the new arrivals. The factory space was cleaned up a little. Gardening stopped.

The idea of killing animals had never occurred to the factory people, but cooked meat lifted many from the floor who now eagerly joined in a thorough process of reconstruction. Some talked, weakly pointing out their work. Parts of the former walls had to be restored in order to show how things were deconstructed in the first place. A small generator was coaxed back into life to provide more light to see their calculations. It was necessary to show the visitors how the resolution of all material relationships had been achieved. Layers of text were carefully cleaned from the walls, each removal revealing a hidden logic beneath. The walls were transcribed onto paper, which were carefully stacked, bound, and archived. Imperfectly collated indexes were produced. The visitors could sometimes be found searching through the shadows. Initially this was of no concern. There were suspicions, yet few could find any true focus for their worries. Work began on the reconstruction of a computer-controlled welding machine, just to show what it had been made of. This labor took a terrible toll. Completed, it joined a paint shop that had been completed a few weeks earlier to make a point. One exterior wall of the former factory had been restored to demonstrate its deconstruction. This effort finished some people off, and others were terminally diminished. But the collective desire to show off their insights led to renewed efforts. A new, simple, high-fat and high-carbohydrate diet was introduced, leaving everyone a little bloated for a while. Some saw their weight increase, but others were too weak to cope with the sudden change in diet. The mere pressure of reconstruction finished off many more. People were now encouraged to account for their work, and show how productive they had been in their explanations and their reconstructions. Complex relationships were forgotten. Everything now had a rational aim. Death was increasingly common as the rate of work increased and new strains took hold. The rate of reconstruction increased. More people died. Everything was being explained in reverse. And more people died on their feet.

The three new arrivals surveyed the space. They were happy with the reinstated plant—clean and clear, efficiently manned, and devoid of marks and complexity. The remaining workers spent their last night at their new control stations staring into screens. A large smelter stood close by, heating iron ore ready for production. As the last gap in the exterior of the building was being closed, they stood as one and mounted the smelter gantry. They stood together in a line looking down into the first batch of molten metal being readied for the production line. Without glancing or speaking, they moved forward together, stepping briefly into a searing wave of uplifting heat before dropping fast and sinking silently into the melt.

The Matter of Scale

Pelin Tan

It was 2016, and the scales of territories, cities, buildings, animals, plants, and humans started to simultaneously expand and contract. Proximity and narrative became the matter. So we decide to retreat and prepare for the usual postapocalyptic era.

Entry 2316, Mardin

I turned onto my side to face the dark-red sun peering through the sand-covered window. It's been a long time since I've seen another human being. The city was ruined during the war, to the point that it's virtually unrecognizable. Since then it's been covered by sand brought up from the south. As the buildings were destroyed, towns, forests, even the weather also changed. A nearby water source lasted for a while, but the electrical station was bombed near the old border, so drawing water from afar wasn't possible. But even if it was, the current of the Tigris decreased over time, eventually to nothing. The national borders that used to keep me from my neighbors have disappeared as well, but it's not like there's anyone else here. No one else survived.

Entry 2016, Athens

Before I knew I had to get out of the city, before it had failed, my friend told me we needed to "retreat." I didn't agree at the time. He spoke about a "house for doing nothing," arguing that we should put a distance between ourselves and society—withdrawal as a political act.[1] I've since accepted the need to escape; I now live in this house. But for a long time I was unsure *how* to completely retreat. How is it possible that the form of a "house" can condition such a political act? A confined space, yet nevertheless connected to the outside by interdependent infrastructures? No, I told him; complete withdrawal is not possible. A home, house, a cave might cause physical distance—scale matters—but society is not only physical, but endlessly fluid; intertwined with infrastructure. His response is still memorable:

> Withdrawal forms the cell whose multiplication creates today's communities. If this distance from the social is the presupposition of political thinking, and if today's sociality is defined by this distance, then we will miss the opportunity to formulate political thought because of a properly architectural problem. This condition, constructed as a house of thought, is an observatory that cannot observe the field it is supposed to contemplate from a distance.

He had the basis of an argument—that retreat, distance, and non-involvement was still the way for political engagement—but as an architect, I got the sense that he was speaking about a different form of political engagement, sociality, and maybe even collectiveness. But is sociality possible without collectiveness? How can we scale this retreat, this form of social disengagement? He continued: Political actions may no longer take place in the world architects traditionally form. But then where would this place of political observation be? Where would this society be that we cannot configure? If a political attitude forms through the elaboration of a view from a distance, the lack of distinction between distance and proximity could pose structural problems to its performance.

Personally, I understood there to be a difference between "retreat" and "voluntary exile." So I responded:

> "Retreat" creates a dystopian solitude, a confinement of scale, a manner of exclusion from the configuration of society. However, "voluntary exile" resizes political form and action. Retreat is haunted by inertia, whereas voluntary exile is predicated on a rescaling of political activity itself. It is a matter of scale, but scale is transversal. Scales get traversed by drones, pens, websites, rocks, and cities.

Entry 2016, Ikaria

Even before I went into exile, I had carried, collected, and dried seaweed. Some friends told me that it would be the superfood of the future, before they escaped to their island, rich with valuable minerals. I had been warned. They left a note: "Island is the scale. Take a look to the territory, to the land, from there. Size it." I didn't understand what they meant at the time, but I wrote it down anyway. I didn't expect that thinking about islands would challenge my survival in the future resurrection.

Entry 2316, Göbeklitepe

It took me days to reach Göbeklitepe by foot. People who had cloned themselves thousand of years ago appeared to age in this neolithic settlement. I wasn't afraid to meet them. They believed animals to be their gods—far superior to humans. Motifs that took years for archeologists to understand covered the stone walls of their temples. But now, I increasingly find myself in the continuation of their past, honoring this ontological evidence and the definition of nature as equal.

Entry 2016, Mardin

Bulldozers ate the mountain, producing sand for the cement to be used in endless housing projects. Speculation was high, and real estate was a way to identify with the new urban classes. I have no idea how many tons of cement were produced, but in just a few years the entire mountain had disappeared. The landscape changed; the sky appeared. Sandstorms from the south, from beyond the Syrian border, had become stronger; there was nothing to prevent them. A human territory. The word *Arazi*, from the Arabic (ارضی), used to refer to a "project site"—a tabula rasa, though never actually a tabula rasa, sized and scaled by the human mind. It also referred to a paramilitary weapon, a certain type of car.

Entry 2316, Mardin

Termites slowly devoured my library, leaving a thin but solid layer of dust to cover the remnants. I managed to hide a few lacerated pages from their hunger by keeping them on my body. I held onto these.

> For thousands of years, perhaps by imitating crustaceans or termites, human beings have been encasing themselves in all kinds of shells. We are ceaselessly secreting buildings, clothes, cars, images and messages that cling to the flesh of our existence like flesh clung to the bones of our skeletons. Nevertheless, there is one major difference between men, crustaceans and termites, which is that the last two species haven't, for the moment, been found to include any corporations of architects, artisans and media "pros." Be that as it may, for a very long time, the delineation of social assemblages has been largely due to eolithic expressions, such as building ziggurats, the demolition of the Bastille, or the capture of the Winter Palace. Only now, besides stone having been replaced by concrete, steel and glass, the cleavages of power occur above all in terms of the speed of communication and the control of information. Under these conditions architects don't even know which hero to turn to![2]

Entry, 2016, Mardin

The bombing of a sulfur mine in the south spread acidic sulfur dioxide through the air. We are expecting acid rain here as well, in couple of days as the acid travels with the clouds. My plants will die, slowly. Before I leave, a friend warns me about the recently dark weather in Tel Aviv; he says that there are dust storms because of the war in the south. The air pollution is unstoppable, yet fostered by warfare. I recall the story by Amitav Ghosh of a tornado in New Delhi on March 17, 1978. The tornado was fifty meters wide and traveled five kilometers in just a few minutes. Ghosh described the experience of the tornado: "What had happened at that moment [was] strangely like a species of visual contact, of beholding and being held." What is the feeling of the unthinkable? "Throughout history these branches of culture have responded to war, ecological calamity and crisis of sorts: why, then, should climate change prove so peculiarly resistant to [cultural] practices?"[3]

Entry 2016, Göbeklitepe

Göbeklitepe is in Southeastern Anatolia, on a plateaued landscape. It has a height of fifteen meters, is about three hundred meters wide in diameter, and sits approximately 760 meters above sea level. The last report about this place was a geophysical survey made in 2016, which noted two hundred T-shaped pillars in about twenty circles that scientists dated back to the tenth millennium BCE. Yet numerous other geological layers date back to different, more recent periods of settlement. People used to think it was a temple for performing rituals to their animal gods. I've since learned, however, that this was a sacred place for the resurrection of humans.

Entry 2316, Göbeklitepe

In my notes, I found a reference from the past, the past that became my future:

> *The Guardian* reported that people in war-torn lands like Afghanistan were reduced to eating grass in order to survive. At the same point in history, cows in the United Kingdom and parts of the European Union were fed meat-based fodder.[4]

Is posthumanism a life beyond the self? Is it a form of humanity beyond the idea of man—beyond the idea that every "thing" that surrounds him is sized by him? A self-centered approach to the subject that turns outwards as a projection for designing the scales of the future environment, which in turn actually form the self?

Entry 2016, Athens

"Stepping back is not exactly the condition that negates the networks. It is the function the network needs in order to be created," said my friend as we walked out of his studio into the city of urban voids. I thought back to this idea of a "house for doing nothing." The design he had for it was 350 m^2 in size, but when I thought about it myself I envisioned something much smaller, like a cave dwelling. I asked him about that, its scale. It was up to me, he said. So I carved out my own—built with bricks on the last rocks, with a view to the horizon of southern Mesopotamia.

Entry 2316, Mardin

Salt rocks are anachronistic forms of terrestrial decay. The opacities of their crystalline structures represent movement through cosmic time. In between the rocks in the landscape, the salt craters have a deep-blue hue. Kneeling down, I carve out some with my hands and touch it to my lips to taste. The minerals, gliding down my throat. It was refugees from the other side of the Tigris who taught me that salt is essential for human life. "Halite" is the name of its natural form as a crystalline mineral, but animal tissue contains salt too, and in larger quantities than plants.

Entry 2316, Mardin

In "Architectural Enunciation," Felix Guattari describes the scales of geopolitical, urban, and economical categorization, as well as scales of architectural operations, like visibility and proximity, reference to the exterior (be it functional or symbolic), representation, and cartography. Scales of architectural thought involve the process of "to-and-froing" between spaces. He makes claims about a "catalytic singularity":

> When architects stop trying simply to be *plasticians* of built form and begin to offer their services as revealers of the virtual desires of space, place, journeys and territory, then they will have to analyze the relations between individual and collective corporealities by constantly singularizing their approach.[5]

This approach contains an affective notion of the self. It's beyond self-design—an empty process, as the "self" does not exist ontologically, but at the same is always continuously redesigned. And the redesigned self creates a worldview too, which is nothing but a simulacra that imposes future history on us.

Entry 2016, Mardin

"... the good fortune to be caught up in a process of becoming-an-event, that is to say, the historical enrichment and re-singularization of desire and values."[6] I saw my friends' message: "Do you think the world is coming to the end? It is bizarre that our film makes sense now ..." It was sad but true. Still, I got a bizarre feeling from reading this—from both the meaning of the sentence and the current time spoken about, as a being within it. The water was boiling. It started rising to meet the coffee grains, and then went through. I poured coffee into my cup.

Entry 2316, Mardin

I saw small sparks of a fire on the horizon of the Arazi. The flame was transparent, cutting the line of sight to the territory further beyond. Suddenly, I saw someone, human-like, walking toward my home. I steered to the thin reddish-yellow horizon at end of the Anatolia. Standing up, I received blood—my first period since becoming posthuman.

1 Aristide Antonas, "The House for Doing Nothing," aristideantonas.com.
2 Félix Guattari, "Architectural Enunciation," trans. Tim Adams, *Interstices* 06 (September 2005): 119–125.
3 Amitav Ghosh, *The Great Derangement: Climate Change and the Unthinkable* (New York: Penguin Books, 2016).
4 Rosi Braidotti, *The Posthuman* (Cambridge: Polity, 2013), 2.
5 Guattari, "Architectural Enunciation," 120.
6 Ibid., 125.

On Anthropolysis

Benjamin H. Bratton

Anthropogeny is the study of human origins, of how something that was not quite human becomes human. It considers what enables and curtails us today: tool-making and prehensile grasp, the prefrontal cortex and abstraction, figuration and war, mastering fire and culinary chemistry, plastics and metals, the philosophical paths to agricultural urbanism and more.[1] Given that Darwinian biology and Huttonian geology are such new perspectives, we may say that anthropogeny, in any kind of scientific sense, is only very recently possible. Before, human emergence was considered from the distorting perspective of local folklores. Creation myths, sacred and secular, have been placeholders for anthropogeny, and still now defend their turf. When Hegel was binding the history of the world to the history of European national self-identity, it was assumed among his public that the age of the planet could be measured in a few millennia (10^3 or 10^4 years), not aeons (10^9 years). The fabrication of social memory and the intuition of planetary duration were thought to operate in closely paired natural rhythms. While the deep time of the genomic and geologic record shows that that they do not, the illusion of their contemporaneity also brought dark consequences that, strangely enough, would actualize that same illusion. In the subsequent era, the meta-consequence of this shortsighted conceit is the Anthropocene itself, a period in which local economic history *has* in fact determined planetary circumstances in its own image.[2] The temporal binding of social and planetary time has been, in this way, a self-fulfilling superstition.

As such, how is the *anthropos* of anthropogeny similar to or different from the *anthropos* of the Anthropocene? Are they correspondent? Does the appearance of the human lead inevitably toward, if not *this* particular Anthropocene, then *an* Anthropocene, and some eventual strong binding of social and geologic economies? Whether the two *anthropoi* are alike or unlike in origin, can they converge or diverge? Instead of becoming human, does a sharp temporal linking also speak to becoming something else? That is, in what ways is a post-Anthropocene—a geo-historical era to come, eventually—aligned with "anthropolysis"—or the *inverse* of anthropogeny—a becoming inhuman, posthuman, unhuman, or at least a very different sort of human?

At this thin moment, the answers to this question are pressing because: (1) the very ongoingness of our ecological substrate is in question, and mass extinction (including perhaps human extinction) looms as one possible outcome of the human project, and (2) the explosive technogenesis of both organic and inorganic nonhuman species proceeds apace (animal, vegetable, but especially mineral). The scientific possibility of marking basic terms of anthropogeny occurs at the same moment (geologically speaking) that at least two paths of anthropolysis—collapse and/or dissolution—come to the fore. Finally as well, does the knowledge of the latter presuppose the former in some important way? In what ways is the knowledge of distant origins that makes the study of anthropogeny possible a cause or an effect of the Thanatonic arc?

Unsurprisingly, all this may be just too much for many to swallow. The trauma of anthropic disenchantment hits not just individual self-identity, but collective identities as well, perhaps even more so. Dismally symptomatic of this are the folkish festivals of fear that now occupy political forums. The consolidation of ethnonationalist authoritarianism here and there is, among other things, a recidivist anti-modernism that finds philosophical justification from many different corners. Not that the autocrats care, but it is not only the Alexander Dugins of the world who counter technoscientific rationalism with a new mysticism, a revived indigeneity/nativism, and a suspicious anti-materialism. The "left" has its own Heideggerians, anti-universalists, and champions of spooky tribal intuition as well. Regardless of the specific topic (artificial intelligence, astronomy, chemical mutagenesis, or what have you), they may respond to the implications of a general economy of anthropogeny/anthropolysis with oblivious calls for an "ethical reintroduction" of human experience and scale as a grounding measure. Just as the death of god and the attempts at political atheism displaced theological urges into authoritarian politics (in turn, inviting state religion back onstage), it is hard not to see the recent rise of right-wing nationalist populism as spasms of denial about the passing of certain illusions: a sprawling, hastily assembled, low-budget parade of zombie rain gods, scapegoats, and virgins, towed along slowly through the streets by all-volunteer court conspiracies, meaningless feats of symbolic violence, and mumbling commentary (mine included). When confronted, directly and indirectly, with the promiseless implications of ecological indifference to cultural traditions, people will vote for sovereigns who promise to rebind them together, and who claim powers to make reality obey the tribal narrative. By rituals of public voice, these arbitrary yarns are apparently made real through a magical politics of representation and identification. What Carl Schmitt called "political theology" comes into its own when the function of the state is to provide what amounts to a religious plotline. As publics and polities are drawn by regional myths and hemispherical *Grossraum*, humans literally *vote* for mind over matter. Matter, however, is unconvinced.

The Anthropocenic puzzle is not unscrambled, however, just by reason getting in its way. The means by which we get outside our prejudicial intuitions about how the world works may also be the means by which we undermine the ecological substrate of the world, and vice versa. As I and others have written, the reason we know that climate change is even happening at the nuanced degrees that we do is because of the measurement capacities of terrestrial-, oceanic-, atmospheric-sensing meta-apparatuses that are at least representative of an industrial-technological system whose appetite is significantly responsible for the changes being measured in the first place.[3] This correspondence may be the rule, not the exception, and for the anthropogeny/anthropolysis dynamic, a more crucial example is the relationship between oil and deep time. Finding oil was (and is) an impetus for the excavation of earth, an ongoing project that turns up sedimentary layers of fossils and provides evidence of an old earth, of deep time. If not for the comprehensive disgorging of fossil fuels since the late nineteenth century, we would not have *this* Anthropocene, and if not for the economic incentive to look below and at rocks in this way, we may not have been confronted with the utter discontinuity between anthropometric time and planetary time. So, even if deep time is one of the ways that we learn to de-link social and phenomenological time from planetary time, its discovery was made possible by an industry that operated upon nature with the conceit that ecological time is subordinate to social time. Now we are witnessing the "accidental" fulfillment of that superstition by the Anthropocene's binding of social and geologic time. *By pursuing the illusion as if it were true, we discovered, as a by-product, that it was false, but the by-product of doing so is that we made it true.*

What else do we know? What else are we good for? If, to borrow from Stanisław Lem's *Solaris*, we think of the earth's oceans as sentient, then the planet's strategy toward sentience includes layered networks of neurons in the folded grey matter of animal brains, particularly but not exclusively the cerebral cortex of primates, namely humans. We are, as Nikolai Fedorov wrote a century ago, the medium through which the planet thinks.[4] Having folded some of its matter into the shape of brains and waited a few million years for these blobs to sort it out, one of the things the earth very recently learned is *its own age*. Earth is 4.6 billion years old.[5] A confident figure for the age of the earth came as late as 1953, the year that Beckett premiered *Waiting For Godot*. We, the earth's digestive residue, were able to discover and know the planet's own duration (quite impressive seeing as how for most of our existence, we thought that the planet ran on our time!). Was this project, in which the earth formulated from itself a biochemical intensity (aka humans) capable of knowing how old it is, worth the cost? A Faustian bargain to top all: Was discovering this fundamental truth worth exhuming hundreds of millions of years of pre-Mesozoic biomatter for a two-century fuel supply and the inauguration of mass extinction? I asked my students if they thought it was worth it. They were split. Maybe the better question would have been, "What would make it worth it?" Must the accomplishment of a Copernican epistemic disenchantment destroy, or at least threaten, that which it knows is a necessary outcome? Or is it only provisional damage that will make for a more durable relationship between knower and known?

Some will categorically say that it is not worth it. There are those, as suggested, who are eager to renounce modernity, reason, or globalization, some going "full Sokal" with New Age post-structuralism, and others "full Kaczynski" with political primitivism. To pick an easy target among the latter group, John Zerzan occupies one end of the spectrum of answers to the Copernican-Faustian question, arguing that the whole agricultural revolution was a mistake and asserting that if a new hunter-gatherer society were to believe, by reckoning only, that the sun revolved around the earth, then so what? Are we truly better off for our fancy heliocentrism, he asks?[6] Is the earth better off? For Zerzan, the answer is clearly "no, the Copernican insight is not worth it." Almost no knowledge is worth damaging or even disturbing Holocenic equilibrium, certainly not mere astronomic self-awareness. For Zerzan, it is abstraction itself, or what he calls "symbolic thought," that is the root of domination, from agriculture to governments. (From such depths, ecological misanthropy, anarchist theories of spontaneous cooperation, the sophistries of anti-rationalist gurus, and a motivated Foucauldian suspicion of disciplinary knowledge find common cause, however dubious.)

At another end of the spectrum (closer to where I sit), others would say that it is and was worth it, or could still be made to have been worth it. They may counter that, just as early protozoa, wiggling their cilia in the bubbling primordial curry, mapped their surroundings to figure out friend, food, and foe, so too do Anthropocenic species carry forth cosmic tasks: to form function into abstraction and back again, and for matter to cohere into metacognition. Further, abstraction through goal-oriented models of the world is not only what intelligence is; it's also built into matter itself. Intelligence is not something that sets humans apart; rather, humans are the medium of its accomplishment. The project remains then not to escape the human like an old skin, but rather to (re)design its parameters, what its always-already unstable threshold contains and is contained by.[7] This design project works not just on the individual unit, but on what the collective is and may be; what it organizes and according to what patterns (other than settler colonialism, legacy genomes, and Bronze Age myths).And so, what then? If the Anthropocene binds social time to planetary time, then let the former scale up to the latter, not the latter down to the former. With maximum demystification, make human economies operate according to the geologic scale we found hiding under the rocks. This inversion of the temporal binding we have is the kind of good definition of the post-Anthropocene that we need, and the inversion of the humanist position and perspective it would require is the anthropolysis we want.

1 Sascha Pohflepp, a PhD student I advise at the University of California, San Diego, is working toward a degree emphasis in the joint program in anthropogeny, and this essay expands on our discussions.

2 Dipesh Charkrabarty has identified a similar conjunction. See his "The Climate of History: Four Theses," *Critical Inquiry* 35, no. 2 (Winter 2009): 197–222.

3 See Benjamin H. Bratton, *The Stack: On Software and Sovereignty* (Cambridge, MA: MIT Press, 2015), 96–106.

4 See Nikolai Fedorov, "The Common Task," in *#Accelerate: The Accelerationist Reader*, eds. Robin Mackay and Armen Avanessian (Falmouth: Urbanomic, 2014), 83–90.

5 See the story of Clair Cameron Patterson and his seminal research on lead isotopes: C. Patterson, "Age of meteorites and the Earth," *Geochimica et Cosmochimica Acta* 10, no. 4 (1956): 230–37.

6 John Zerzan, "Number: Its Origin and Evolution," publication date unknown. Available at theanarchistlibrary.org.

7 See Reza Negarestani, "The Labor of the Inhuman, Part 1: Human," *e-flux journal* no. 52 (February 2014).

Blockchain Future States

Simon Denny

What would a future geopolitics powered by the technology behind Bitcoin look like?

Simon Denny with Eli Pitegoff

Oct. 21, 2016, 8:17 PM 146,266 3

FACEBOOK | LINKEDIN | TWITTER | EMAIL | PRINT

Painting depicting Ethereum blockchain founder Vitalik Buterin at the center of a fantasy world powered by their token Ether. Behind the earth, the spirits of Austrian economists Friedrich A. Hayek and Ludwig Von Mises and engineer Paul Baran, who's work around network theory informed the development of distributed communications and the internet.

In 2008 a mysterious figure(s) released a paper under the pseudonym Satoshi Nakamoto describing blockchain protocol, a peer-to-peer system of trade underpinning the digital currency Bitcoin. Since then, it has come to light that the applications of the blockchain protocol are potentially far-reaching.

For one thing, it could render "trusted third party" verification (currently facilitated by governments, banks, accountants, notaries, and fiat currencies) obsolete with direct peer-to-peer transactions, disrupting huge swaths of the financial services industry. But even beyond disrupting how transactions are carried out, some people see in blockchain technology a blueprint outlining the digital infrastructure for an entirely new model of nationhood.

Blockchain nationhood could amount to a post-geographic alternative to the nation-state system, whose infrastructure has the striking quality of being developable alongside (i.e. without being an immediate challenge or obvious threat to) current nation-state governments. As a result, such initiatives are in a uniquely advantaged position for takeover if certain, specific factors align.

This exhibition uses sculptures as visual metaphors to define some of the more radical visions of a blockchain-enabled future, and describe the conditions of possibility for their implementation.

View As: One Page | Slides

It's a possible technologist's answer to some of today's urgent problems. Take a look »

FACEBOOK | LINKEDIN | TWITTER | EMAIL | PRINT

BUSINESS INSIDER | LIFE | f ✓ in | BI Intelligence Events | Sign-in Edition

Blockchain's origin: Satoshi Nakamoto and the peer-to-peer answer to a seemingly corrupt financial world

In October 2008, in the wake of the Lehman Brothers crash, a mysterious figure named "Satoshi Nakamoto" released a white paper describing a peer-to-peer electronic money system. The money system, known today as the crypto-currency "Bitcoin," is based on a distributed network that prevents double spending and replaces the need for "trusted third party" verification. Verification of transactions instead occurs automatically by using a single ledger distributed across the entire network, which timestamps all transactions and creates the infrastructure for consensus across all nodes; a chain of identical blocks – the "blockchain." Over the following years, the idea scales to an unignorable number of users, propelled in part by the gripping founder narrative. To this day the identity of the person(s) behind the pseudonym Satoshi Nakamoto, a reference to a Pokemon character and a Japanese iconoclast merchant from the 1700s, remains unclear.

As has been noted by both critics and proponents alike, the blockchain is a multi-faceted instrument – a story and a technology – that resonates with a political history. The after-image of thinkers like Friedrich Hayek is preserved in visions of market systems as self-regulating totalities.

What could the blockchain threaten? – trusted elites and the nation-state model

An edition of the boardgame RISK exploring the post-geopolitics of Silicon Valley blockchain startup 21.Inc. The founder, Balaji Srinivasan, is exploring alternative money systems and sovereignty models using Bitcoin's blockchain as its basis. He envisions Bitcoin as the money protocol for a third kind of internet – the "internet of value," enabling a post-national free market world where latency is zero in financial transactions between machines and geography is redefined following the cloud.

Entrepreneurs in the banking industry are exploring the use of the blockchain as a way of automating much of the labor involved in the most fundamental operations of capital markets. From settlement to security, the blockchain could replace many of the services currently provided by banking industry professionals and make the sector faster with lower overhead costs – continuing the tendency in the industry towards accelerating trade and consolidating power.

View As: One Page | Slides

FACEBOOK | LINKEDIN | TWITTER | EMAIL | PRINT

BUSINESS INSIDER | LIFE | BI Intelligence | Events | Sign-in | Edition

The blockchain protocol also has the potential to mint digital currencies outside of the jurisdiction of a central bank – the institution that the state has vested with the authority to issue and regulate currency. However, the disruptive potential of the blockchain need not only apply to creating alternative systems for money. The blockchain could also index and protect what might be called a kind of proprietary identity – the mechanism used to identify individuals and legitimize their participation as economic and legal subjects in a state system. Establishing proprietary identity enables people to own property or be taken to court, for example, and is typically associated with citizenship. By giving people the capacity to establish and enact alternatives, the blockchain as a tool could be seen to challenge existing sovereignty models.

Blockchain future states

Painting depicting Ethereum blockchain founder Vitalik Buterin at the center of a fantasy world powered by their token Ether. Behind the earth, the spirits of Austrian economists Friedrich A. Hayek and Ludwig Von Mises and engineer Paul Baran, who's work around network theory informed the development of distributed communications and the internet.

The blockchain affords location independent communities the infrastructure to realize new, post-geographic models of nationhood. If two fundamental components of a state are a legal apparatus and financial infrastructure, the blockchain has the potential to technologically underpin both. Initiatives like Ethereum have built digital ecosystems addressing exactly this potential. Ethereum has given rise to projects like Bitnation, the DAO (Decentralized Autonomous Organization) and other self-organizing groups who are able to define their own rules and automate compliance. Using immutable encrypted code distributed across all nodes in an opt-in network, people have newfound agency in their ability to choose and/or construct new systems of governance.

The blockchain's potential for disrupting governance emerges at a time when many urgent forces can be seen threatening the stability of existing sovereignty models. Scientific predictions around the impact of climate change suggest the possibility of a refugee crisis at a scale we as a civilization have yet to have seen. The reemergence of nationalist movements and a reanimated appetite for authoritarianism has bred a volatile geopolitical climate prone to escalating conflict. Massive stores of arms, recently understood as largely symbolic or dormant, now seem more likely to be pulled from the arsenal. Not only do these threats mark instability, but also a perception that the systems in place are corrupt and in need of radical change. At a time when retreats into nationalism and trust in strong men as leaders are being proposed as fixes to a broken sovereignty system, one can understand the interest in alternatives.

If the blockchain emerges and scales up enough, it could provide a viable alternative to existing economic and legal infrastructures and become a default protocol for future power. If there continues to be a disenfranchised voice calling for radical change to the world's existing sovereignty models – if reactionary forces implode in the face of inflammatory border conflicts and devastating ecological inevitabilities, then the blockchain's adaptive solutions may provide, by default, the most robust answer to the speculated imminent chaos.

A technocratic solution to governance like the visions proposed by blockchain-laced dreams could be seen as a way of circumventing the nation-state system and all of its geopolitical instabilities. It could also, by the same token, be seen as a way of circumventing its checks and balances and pave the way for an extended reinvestment in the unabated power of the self-regulating free market.

View As: One Page | Slides

FACEBOOK | LINKEDIN | TWITTER | EMAIL | PRINT

Right-wing Spaces

Stephan Trüby

The rise of right-wing populist, anti-liberal, and authoritarian political alternatives has brought a renewed attention to architecture. In opposition to broad sections of the German architecture community and construction industry, for whom an "open-arms" culture represents a kind of ethically precious incentive, apocalypticists and integrationists are manufacturing rightist spaces based on increasingly solidified ideological patterns. The German right-wing publisher Götz Kubitschek uses the term "metapolitics" to speak about the extended field "of words, of thought, of style, of books, magazines, and events, of the habitual and the auratic," which, in the interests of a cultural revolution coming from the right, need to be fundamentally changed.[1]

In terms of "architectural metapolitics," it should scarcely come as a surprise that the Alternative for Germany (AfD) and the National Democratic Party of Germany (NPD), as well as the Freedom Party of Austria (FPÖ), the Front National in France and the Swiss People's Party (SVP), form a special kind of "coalition of the unwilling." In willful ignorance of any more complex religious and intellectual history of Europe, the populist right promotes the ideal of a "Judaeo-Christian Europe," while the far right projects a purely "Christian Europe."[2] "Islam is unreformable," the allegation these parties conjure into existence, is an intellectual hallucination that can only be described as racist.

Yet the architectural metapolitics of right-wing populists in Europe does not merely manifest in the iconoclastic rejection of mosques and minarets, but must also be identified as "positive," in the sense that it not only specifies what it is *against* but also explicitly expresses what it stands *for*. This other side of the right's coin consists of specific single-detached residences immersed in the countryside, settlements, castles, and manors, downtown reconstruction projects, and last but not least, new monuments.

Homes for the Last, and Not-So Last, Germans

There are houses that have scant ambition to be anything more than comfortable daily appurtenances, and others that amount to a political program. Writer Botho Strauß's house in the Uckermark can certainly be put in the latter group.[3] In the midst of the media crisis that followed the publication of "The Rising Tide of Tragedy" ("Anschwellender Bocksgesang") in 1993, Strauß acquired a country hideaway in the Uckermark situated some fifty miles northeast of Berlin.[4] The property in the little village of Grünheide consists of two houses, a guesthouse, and a large main residence, both painted in brilliant white and topped with red-tile gable roofs. It is both a real structure and place of the imagination, but also more than that, it is a rural Grand Guignol of the cultured classes.[5] Strauß himself had provided the basis for the confluence of dwelling place and philosophical exegesis in 1997 with his book *The Errors of the Copyist* (*Die Fehler des Kopisten*), in which he takes a stroll with his son around his house in the countryside and writes, in the tone of the National Democratic Party (NPD): "For five or six years the Germans were intoxicated with their collective existence. As punishment they were obliged to spend a thousand years examining how it could have happened."[6]

Strauß's confluence of countryhouse elegy and German nationalist thinking finds an echo in the metapolitical fusion of rural residence and *völkisch* ideology operated by AfD politician Björn Höcke, with the main difference being that the writer's fatalism is replaced by the politician's militant aggression. In typically alarmist jargon, Höcke (though he is not alone here) has, since the refugee crisis of 2015, been dreading the "dying out of the German *Volk*" and seeing his party as the "last evolutionary chance for our country."[7] Since 2008, Höcke has lived in the three-hundred-strong village of Bornhagen in Eichsfeld county, on the border between Thuringia and Hessen. According to the investigative enquiries of journalist and sociologist Andreas Kemper, this place plays a central role in the politician's early writing, which he published under the pseudonym Landolf Ladig in the NPD magazine *Eichsfeld-Stimme*, where in 2012 a Ladig text appeared with the title "A Village in Thuringia" ("Ein Dorf in Thüringen"), in which he writes:

> Do you know Bornhagen? ... The famous Hanstein castle perches majestically on the hill above the village. It is thought to be one of the most romantic ruined castles in central Germany. After climbing the castle hill, the historic Klausenhof inn, voted best hostelry in Thuringia in 2007 and 2008, beckons you in ... On the slope across from the inn stand a small Protestant church, an old parsonage, and an old school.[8]

The parsonage being referred to at the end here has been owned by Höcke since 2008, where he lives with his wife Monika and their four children. The shingled house can be viewed (as Ladig/Höcke see it) as an anchor point of radical nationalist ambitions—a patch of home turf from which to hammer into the Germans the urgency of a final round of redemptive ejaculations as a means to supply the national community with an "organic market economy."

Settlements to Counter the "Death of the *Volk*"

What we can understand about an "organic market economy" may become more clear if we take examples of a few recent "*völkisch* settlements" that have sprung up in the last few years, primarily in rural areas of eastern Germany, but also to a lesser extent in Bavaria, Hessen, Lower Saxony, and Schleswig-Holstein. Filled with disgust at any kind of metropolitan multicultural way of life, many NPD cadres and AfD adherents seek their salvation in the countryside. In Mecklenburg-Vorpommern, far away from people with immigrant backgrounds, imagined or real, right-wing settlers have a special fondness for rehearsing the "preservation of the German *Volk*" in extremely low-priced real estate. Initially in the guise of friendly neighbors, they infiltrate clubs, kindergartens, and schools. Their program is familiar, and had, or so it seemed, been consigned to history. Running under the slogan "Blood and Soil," they are determined—as a "national community"—to rally against what they fear will be the "death of the *Volk*." Many of the neo-right settlers—including some rather innocent-seeming organic farmers—hark back to intellectual concepts that came out of the end of the Wilhelmine era and the period after World War I, before they were radicalized by National Socialism and got caught up in its murderous cogs. For example the "Artamanentum," a *völkisch* youth movement that romanticized the pastoral idyll, is currently enjoying a renewed popularity among organic farmers on the extreme right. In was originally established in Munich in 1925 with the founding of the Artaman League (Bund Artam e.V.). Intent on the agrarian colonization of "*Lebensraum* in the east," it was incorporated into the Hitler Youth in 1934.

The little village of Koppelow, built near Güstrow in the 1930s, was the largest Artaman settlement. As Anne Schmidt of the Amadeu Antonio Foundation sets out in *Völkisch Settlers in Rural Areas* (*Völkische SiedlerInnen im ländlichen Raum*), neo-Artamans were already proclaiming their intentions back in 1992 with their manual of piety, the *Artam-Blätter*, which targeted "the cultivation of a life appropriate to the human species, and not simply as a hobby. We wish [to view] the political conditions in our country (the world!) and the environmental situation as a challenge."[9] Around this time, shortly before the country's reunification, a few neo-Artamans settled in Koppelow again. A couple of villages further east, in Klaber, in the hilly area of Mecklenburg, the attempts of the neo-right to grab land are particularly evident. In a concerted campaign, a stonemason, an artist blacksmith, a bookbinder, a midwife, and others—including many on the extreme right—moved into some empty houses and gradually took over almost all aspects of village life. For the practiced eye it should be easy enough to detect the political persuasion of this group, such as with an Irminsul pillar depicting an image of the world tree in the front garden of the stonemason. Symbolism like this was also used by the Artamans in the 1920s and '30s as a statement both of their Nordic pagan attitude and against Christianity. At the smith's house, we can also find references to these mythologies, such as a knife handle bearing the image of Odin together with his ravens Hugin and Munin.[10] Schmidt writes that the settlement projects in Koppelow, Klader, and elsewhere should not be underestimated and disregarded as a temporary phenomenon, but rather classed as attempts to exert "a long-term influence on everyday culture."[11] Political scientist and investigator of right-wing extremism Andrea Röpke has also recognized all-too-familiar anti-Semitic statements in the rustic, craft orientation of the group, describing themselves as "creatively" perceptive doers, seeking to differentiate themselves from the image of "money-grubbing, international Jewish financial capital."[12]

It is not only contaminated right-wing esoterics and far-right craftsmen with a penchant for hillbilliness that are at work on a neo-*völkisch* settlement policy, but eloquent urbanites too, as in the case of Udo Pastörs. Since 1999, Pastörs—businessman, clockmaker, professional soldier, and from January to November 2014, party chairman of the NPD—has been living together with his wife Marianne in Lübtheen in Mecklenburg, where the family owns some properties, including houses on the village square, Thälmannplatz. The family used to live in the Benz-Briest neighborhood, in a house on the main street that had been part of a "model village" built under the Nazi Reich, where one of the houses had a swastika on the gable up until 2007, when it was tiled over. At almost the same time, the Pastörs moved a few miles to the south into a villa in the Mecklenburg Elbe Valley Nature Park, a site that could legally only have been built on if a tree nursery was built as well, but the latter never happened. Instead, a stately manor was constructed on a sixty-acre property, with a dead-straight drive lined with German oaks leading seventy yards to the entrance door. The estate lies on a country road with the expressive name *Zum Reizen* (literally, to stimulate or provoke) and constructed according to a model of a *Wehrhof* (a fortified structure) from the Memel Territory. It was designed and built by the Lüneburg building contractor Manfred Börm, who had several previous convictions for neo-Nazi activities. Pastörs is currently planning his own personal German model village on his estate; he has already had right-wing youths build a red-brick duplex next to the main house, and there's more in the pipeline.

Völkische Community Experiences in Stately Homes, Castles, and Manors

Ladig's (and thus presumably Höcke's) ode to Hanstein Castle, the fortress towering above Höcke's parsonage, was already an indicator, an intimation, that in order to develop political dynamism, homes are crucial places where people can gather and rehearse the experience of *völkisch* community. Having been inscribed in the collective memory as monumental landmarks spanning centuries (not to mention being compatible with national romantic traditions and ideas of corporative, authoritarian social systems), converted sheds, manor houses, and castles are particularly apt for this purpose. The Schnellroda Manor in Saxony-Anhalt can be viewed as a Mecca of this neo-right castle romanticism, which since 2002 has been owned by Götz Kubitschek (the journalist referred to earlier) and his wife Ellen Kositza. The estate, which is first mentioned in records from 1208, not only houses the life of the couple, their various animals, and seven children, but also the offices of Kubitschek's far-right publishing house Antaios and his magazine *Sezession*. Furthermore, it functions as the headquarters of the Institute for State Policy (Institut für Staatspolitik), a body that purports to be both subversive of the existing and supportive of a new, different kind of state, and frequently hosts the likes of Elsässer, Feist, Höcke, Sellner, and many other protagonists of the neo-*völkisch* movement as guests. The interiors of the estate are dominated by the furnishings of Andreas Paul Weber (1893–1980), a *völkisch*, anti-Semitic illustrator, comrade-in-arms of politician Ernst Niekisch (1889–1967) and part-time furniture designer. Another example is Kubitschek's friend André Poggenburg, the AfD party leader in Saxony-Anhalt, who acquired the Nöbeditz estate in 2007, a fief first documented in 1266. The prophecy he made to a local newspaper shortly after acquiring the property might now come to pass: "We'll really bring life to the farm here. With lots of animals, so that our potbellied pig Rudi, who has already run away several times, won't feel so alone anymore."[13]

The Kubitschek/Poggenburg blueprint of the stately home as a path to becoming animals or pigs can be found in the career of Karl-Heinz Hoffmann, who lived with the paramilitary sports group Wehrsportgruppe Hoffmann, his private army, which at times comprised more than four hundred men. The now seventy-eight-year-old neo-Nazi initially moved into Schloss Almoshof in Nuremburg in 1974, before moving in 1978 to a new location east of Erlangen, Schloss Ermreuth, which had served as a Nazi party Gauführer school in the Third Reich. In 2004, together with his partner Franziska Birkmann, he purchased Schloss Kohren-Sahlis in Saxony, an estate first mentioned in official records in 1551 and previously inhabited by the anti-Semitic poet Börries Baron von Münchhausen, who in 1944 had been included by Adolf Hitler in the "God-gifted list of indispensable writers." For the upkeep of the estate, which includes a gatehouse, stables, storehouses, a bowling alley, a still, and a rococo park, mostly dating from the eighteenth century, Hoffmann set up the Schloss Sahlis Fiduciary Cultural Foundation (Fiduziarische Kulturstiftung Schloss Sahlis), where in his role as "curator," Hoffman established an organic farm breeding Mangalica woolly pigs. Hoffmann claims that he is not a Nazi, but rather "a socialist eco-fascist."[14] For his cultural foundation, which was declared a nonprofit organization and populated not only by pigs but also by a right-wing brotherhood, he obtained €130,000 in public funding from the Free State of Saxony, but this did not prevent the Schloss being foreclosed upon. The castle was reported as being up for sale, advertised online under the banner "Live like a King," with sixty-six rooms, spread out over a large property comprising 66,666 square meters (sixteen acres), are offered at a price of €666,666.[15]

Downtown Areas and Monuments to Another German History

Even though the architectural metapolitics of German right-wing populists and extremists primarily takes place in rural areas—in isolated homes, in villages, in remote manorial estates, castles, and stately homes—it should be noted that rightist spaces are by no means limited to the countryside. The *völkisch* interventions out in the sticks should be seen as a complement to architectural endeavors that are located in considerably more urban domains. These protean ventures can all be placed at the intersection of architecture and the culture of remembrance in the service of a new Germany, about which architecture theorist Philipp Oswalt once wrote that it dreamed "not merely of another future but of another past."[16]

This "other history" can be traced in reconstructions. Even if the vast majority of reconstruction projects in Germany are supported by a rather broad spectrum of parties—it is not only right-wing populist and far-right parties that want to reconstruct—it is still noticeable that the architecture pages of Germany's neo-right magazines are almost exclusively devoted to issues of reconstruction. In the xenophobic, youth-oriented magazine *Blaue Narzisse* from Chemnitz, for example, Maximilian Zech advocates for more "beauty and sense of tradition in building design," which he believes can be discerned in the reconstructed Adlon Hotel in Berlin.[17] Even Peter Stephan, one of the most important advocates of reconstruction and professor of architectural history at the Potsdam University of Applied Sciences, seeks to align reconstruction themes with right-wing sections of society. For example, with the use of public events and a university research project, he set out to uncouple the history of the Garrison Church in Potsdam, which was demolished in 1968, from what occurred in front of it on March 21, 1933: the so-called Day of Potsdam, when Hitler and President of the Reich Paul von Hindenburg shook hands and thus sealed the disastrous alliance between National Socialist and German national powers.

For many right-wing populists and far-right extremists, the reconstruction of "another" history corresponds with the marginalization of the "one" history. Speaking in an interview with the American station CBN on March 10, 2016, Björn Höcke asserted that "Germans have a one-sided fixation with their dark sides. We have thus developed a culture of guilt that makes it impossible for us to generate a healthy national consciousness, a vibrant patriotism."[18] At the so-called "Kyffhäuser meeting" on June 4, 2016, to which the *völkisch* nationalistic "wing" of the AfD had sent out invitations, Höcke proclaimed, "A nation that no longer erects monuments but only memorials has no future."[19] What this means in concrete terms is clearly articulated by Höcke's friend Poggenburg, when he sputters with monumental degeneracy about the "ugly aesthetics" of the Holocaust Memorial in Berlin and without showing the slightest restraint, proposes tearing it down.[20] A similar line was taken by the Baden Württemburg parliamentary delegate Wolfgang Gedeon when, speaking on the SWR radio station on June 2, 2016, he stated, "At the heart of the commemorative site there should be something positive. If the [Holocaust Memorial] is somewhere on the periphery ... I have nothing against that."[21]

Metapolitics: A Boomerang

New monuments that should no longer be memorials; reconstructions of "another" history; revitalized castles; "pure *völkisch*" settlements; isolated country houses for the "last [and not-so-last] Germans." Rightist spaces all make one thing clear: particularly in the political context of German right-wing populists and far-right extremists, well-intentioned distinctions between the "apolitical private sphere" and the "public space of politics" seem deeply questionable. In the now-discontinued neo-right magazine *Criticón*, Karlheinz Weißmann, Kubitschek's former strategic adviser, has written that metapolitics is an "occupation of areas in the pre-political realm." However, "meta-" does not just mean "beyond," but also "amidst." While politics certainly includes the deeds of the activist subject along with the usual suspects of parliamentarianism and statism, metapolitics refers to the thinking that guides politics in action.[22] If we translate this to the rightist spaces described above, it means that anyone actually implementing a *völkisch* ideology in how they dwell, live, and work no longer resides in the pre-political realm of a metapolitics but is clearly cultivating a political praxis.

Quite justifiably, there was considerable public indignation—and not only among right-wing populists—when, on May 1, 2016, the antifascist web portal *Indymedia* published the names, private addresses, and cellphone numbers of around two thousand people who had taken part in the AfD party conference in Stuttgart. This sensitive information is still freely accessible online. Those who lament the loss or violation of privacy in this case operate with a reductionist understanding of metapolitics, labeling an aesthetic, stylistic, cultural world of the everyday as not-yet-political; yet it is exactly the people whose details were released who effectively operate a political praxis using just these aesthetic, stylistic, cultural resources. Thus, all the right-wing talk of metapolitics might turn out to be a boomerang. What began with the demonstrations in front of Höcke's house in Bornhagen in May 2016 (though they were legally blocked) or in Schnellroda in September of the same year (which were carried through) should set a precedent: the private residence that obeys a *völkisch* housing ideology is subject to become the object of a broader political protest.

The text is an extended version of an article that appeared in DIE ZEIT *on September 1, 2016.*[23]

1 Götz Kubitschek, cited in Liane Bednarz and Christoph Giesa, *Gefährliche Bürger: Die Neue Rechte greift nach der Mitte* (Munich: Hanser, 2015), 69.

2 A Swiss popular initiative led by SVP politicians has been rallying against the building of minarets since 2006 and, with the help of a poster (designed by the Swiss-based German graphic designer Alexander Segert) that depicts minarets as missiles, declares Islam to be incompatible with Swiss values. The Front National has mimicked this Swiss campaign and uses it to suggest that France and Islam are irreconcilable. FPÖ politicians repeatedly seek to block the building of mosques (also involving Segert in their campaign). AfD, as happened at the 2016 national party conference in Stuttgart, included the statement "Islam is not part of Germany" in its manifesto.

3 If there was any doubt as to Strauß's right-wing leanings, after publishing "The Last German" ("Der letzte Deutsche") in *Der Spiegel* in October 2015, there can be no longer. In it, Strauß makes statements like: "I would rather live in a dying but vital nation [*Volk*] than in one that is being rejuvenated by being mixed together with foreign peoples, primarily on the basis of economic and demographic speculation." In line with this, he concocts stories about "the country being inundated," before concluding with grudging fatalism, "The immigration of uprooted persons will eventually lead to the end of the nation and with it any national literature. Anyone who loves these things and cannot live without them will thus put their only hope in a reinvigorated, newly emerging 'Secret Germany.'" Botho Strauß, "Der letzte Deutsche," *Der Spiegel* 41 (October 2, 2015).

4 Within "Anschwellender Bocksgesang," Strauß states: "in our liberal-libertarian self-centeredness," we no longer understand "that a people seeks to assert its moral law over others and is ready to make blood-sacrifices for it."

5 The ideology of exclusion fostered within the compound has led to the fact that we know relatively little about this place. In 2003, in "Botho Strauß Lives Here" ("Hier wohnt Botho Strauß"), Ingo Niermann and Joachim Bessing looked at the mundanity of the place until it looked back at them with a monstrous gaze. See Ingo Niermann and Joachim Bessing, "Hier wohnt Botho Strauß" (2003), *waahr* February 27, 2013. This was followed in 2007 by Volker Weidermann's piece "The Great Green Offensive" ("Der große Laubangriff"), based on his visit to the house, which ended at the gates of the property. "A place in which happiness might be found, for example, a sense of satisfaction in the sheer loveliness of looking. Or alternatively a contempt for the world, for people, civilization, and society, prophecies of the end of days, a delight in the world's demise." See Volker Weidermann, "Botho Strauß: 'Die Fehler des Kopisten'; Der große Laubangriff," *Frankfurter Allgemeine Zeitung*, April 5, 2007. In 2013, Hubert Spiegel published "The Old Boy" ("Der alte Junge"), a report from a hike with Strauß, in which Spiegel remarked, "The leviathan is his neighbor." See Hubert Spiegel, "Der alte Junge," *Frankfurter Allgemeine Zeitung*, February 21, 2013.

6 Botho Strauß, *Die Fehler des Kopisten* (Munich: Hanser, 1997), 107. Thomas Assheuer, lambasting him in *DIE ZEIT*, rightly accused him of "murmuring ... in runes." Thomas Assheuer, "Botho Strauß verläßt die Stadt, geht aufs Land und bestellt das Feld der Wahrheit: 'Die Fehler des Kopisten,'" *DIE ZEIT*, April 25, 1997.

7 Liane Bednarz, "Wenn Lucke geht, bleibt Höcke: Björn Höcke lehnt einen gemäßigten AfD-Kurs ab, er ist Teil der 'Neuen Rechten'; Eine Replik und Warnung," *The European*, May 26, 2015.

8 Andreas Kemper, "Landolf Ladig, NS-Verherrlicher," (9 January, 2016).

9 Cited in Anna Schmidt and Amadeu-Antonio-Stiftung, *Völkische SiedlerInnen im ländlichen Raum: Basiswissen und handlungsrategien* (Berlin: Amadeu-Antonio-Stiftung, 2014), 9.

10 Ibid., 22.

11 Ibid., 8.

12 Andrea Röpke, cited in ibid., 9.

13 Cited in Uwe Müller, Lars-Marten Nagel, and Marcel Pauly, "AfD-Wahlsieg als Weg aus dem privaten Finanzdesaster," *Die Welt*, January 31, 2016.

14 Stefan Schirmer, "Nicht totzukriegen: Karl-Heinz Hoffmann kämpfte einst als Neonazi-Anführer gegen den Staat; Nun kämpft er als Schlossherr in Sachsen gegen einen Abwasserzweckverband," *DIE ZEIT*, January 28, 2016.

15 "Nazi-Schloss steht wieder zum Verkauf," *Bild*, April 10, 2016.

16 Philipp Oswalt, *Berlin: Stadt ohne Form: Strategien einer anderen Architektur* (Munich: Prestel, 2000), 56.

17 Maximilian Zech, "Architektur der Tradition," *Blaue Narzisse*, February 24, 2014.

18 "Björn Höcke (AfD): Interview mit Dale Hurd/CBN-News (10.03.2016)," YouTube.

19 "Kyffhäusertreffen 2016: Ausgebucht!" *Der Flügel*, May 24, 2016.

20 Hagen Eichler, "Der doppelte Poggenburg," *Volksstimme*, January 9, 2016.

21 With accusations of anti-Semitism hanging over him and facing resistance from many party members, Gedeon was obliged to leave his party, under pressure from Jörg Meuthen, one of the two AfD Federal Spokespersons. See "AfD-Abgeordneter Gedeon verharmlost Holocaustleugner – Landtag Baden-Württemberg – SWR HD," YouTube.

22 Alain Badiou, Über *Metapolitik* (Zurich: diaphanes, 2003).

23 Stephan Trüby, "Rechte Räume," *DIE ZEIT*, September 15, 2016.

Our Vectors, Ourselves

Kali Stull and Etienne Turpin

Fogging in Jakarta, Indonesia, May 2016. Photo: Kali Stull and Etienne Turpin.

> Nothing can hold out against civilization and the power of industry. The only animal species to survive will be those that industry multiplies.
> —Jean-Baptiste Say[1]

A female *Aedes aegypti* remains in suspended pregnancy until she ingests vertebrate blood. With hundreds of eggs in her ovaries, she begins a search for carbon dioxide and heat. Once detected, she lands on her host to penetrate the epidermis with her proboscis and deposit saliva, which as an anticoagulant, ensures her meal of blood will flow smoothly to the next generation. Within sixty hours of this fluid exchange—*spit for blood*—oviposition is triggered in the expectant *Aedes aegypti* and her eggs are released along the surface line of still water where they complete their embryogenesis and wait. As rainwater delivers new microorganisms into this watery exometabolic womb (so often unwittingly prepared by humans), respiration reduces the available oxygen and causes the eggs to hatch. Without vows or affection, humans and mosquitoes become kin, bound by blood to the rhythm of microbial breath.

Mosquitos sucked the blood of vertebrates for millions of years before *Homo sapiens* emerged from the evolutionary phylum, and until recently, humans weren't particularly appealing hosts. But then they tilled, irrigated, and settled, and as the Sahara dried, their settlements became the primary source for the blood and water that *Aedes aegypti* needed to survive. A sylvan arthropoid first domesticated the land, and was in turn domesticated as host—an evolutionary lesson in *becoming-hospitable*.[2]

While settlement patterns drew almost all of *Aedes aegypti*'s host species near—dogs, cats, rodents, cows, pigs, and birds—they still came to favor blood from its human architects. Due to low levels of isoleucine, the blood of *Homo sapiens* extends the life of *Aedes aegypti* and ensures the production of offspring in the thousands. Not only that, but with higher levels of lipids than other primates, human blood helps coproduce thirstier vectors.[3] Because mosquitos' sanguine preference is based on their first successful bloodfeed, as humans become ever more densely arranged into their urban settlements, the likelihood that *Aedes aegypti*'s first feed will be on human blood increases in turn, thereby establishing a lifelong affection; affine commitments are this way produced without the awkward requirement of affinity.

As humans continue to design and deploy new techniques intended to sever ties with this unwanted bloodline, the fact that mosquitoes rapidly overcome the best efforts to keep human blood sacred should come as no surprise. For *Aedes aegypti*, it is precisely those terrestrial, aquatic, and atmospheric architectures designed to deny them any access to *Homo sapiens*'s blood that have proven to be the most compelling invitation to intensify this multispecies coevolution.[4]

1. The Virus

> Individual animals and plants are like temporary "experiments" with which gene pools probe current environmental conditions to make sure that past successes are still viable.
> — Manuel DeLanda[5]

When *Aedes aegypti* takes blood from a viremic host in the early stages of dengue, the blood moves into the mosquito's midgut, where the virus binds to receptors, enters the circulatory system, and makes its way to the salivary glands. Once sufficient viral replication has occurred in the glands—a process lasting four to ten days on the calendar adopted by most *Homo sapiens*—the virus is transmissible to other humans. The mosquito remains infected for the rest of its life.[6]

When the dengue virus quietly initiated this "vectors-with-benefits" relationship, the *Aedes aegypti* was its sole host; then, as the virus evolved to live in primates, they became a preferred agent of transmission. During each infection, dengue renovates the genetic structure of its host by altering no fewer than 147 proteins in *Aedes aegypti*'s RNA, thereby repatterning the mosquito's behavior. In essence, the virus makes the mosquito over as an ideal vector: smelling more acutely and hungrier for human blood, infected *Aedes aegypti* are also more likely to re-feed after interruption (when swatted at, for example, by a human). The dengue virus also uses the RNA alteration as a means to adjust mosquitoes' saliva production, making it even more hospitable to the virus.[7]

When an infected mosquito follows its heightened senses to feed on human blood, virus-rich saliva is deposited beneath the epidermis at the start of the meal. In fact, the virus is likely to be passed subdermally several times, as the *Aedes aegypti* is a skittish feeder. Once inside the human body, the dengue virus quickly spills over from the saliva to the epidermal cells and then on to the lymph nodes, where it spreads throughout the lymphatic system. Three to eighteen days of incubation later, symptoms emerge. But, before they do—typically a day or two before the sudden onset of fever—the virus is already transmissible. *Homo sapiens* hosts are not simply unwitting *victims* of the dengue virus received from mosquitoes, they are also unknowing *perpetrators* who, while making multispecies kin, transmit the virus to the next generation of *Aedes aegypti.*

The dengue virus has itself been adapting to the changing behavior of *Aedes aegypti* for thousands of years.[8] As these mosquitos migrated across the taxonomic register from *zoophagous* to *anthropophagus*, dengue adapted to live better among humans as well, ensuring the largest spatial range through its host. Dengue can also infect the same human host four times, with each illness more painful and life-threatening than the previous one; because human antibodies cannot situate their relationship to a similar-but-distinct dengue serotype, they tend to boost, rather than prevent, the sickening effect of any novel strands of dengue. Human weaknesses such as these are not left unexploited in the arms race of adaptation. This adaptive dynamism of the virus has been the most consistent obstacle to the creation of a vaccine, several of which have been in development for nearly one hundred years.[9] Likewise, pathologists are concerned that, given the virus's highly mutable and adaptable character, it would even be able to adapt advantageously to anthropogenetically modified vectors.[10]

2. The Vector

With tears and toiling breath,
I find thy cunning seeds,
O million-murdering Death.
I know this little thing
A myriad men will save.
O Death, where is thy sting?
Thy victory, O Grave?
— Ronald Ross[11]

For most of the nineteenth century, dirt, debris, and immorality were usually cited as causes of malaria. Then, in 1897, Ronald Ross, a young British scientist, cultured twenty mosquitoes from larvae collected in Secunderabad, India, and paid his patient Husein Khan eight *annas* to let the mosquitoes feed on his malarial blood.[12] One month later, he dissected these mosquitos to confirm the presence of the malaria parasite in the blood of their midgut.[13] By 1902, the Syrian scientist H. Graham also found that the dengue virus was transmitted by mosquitoes, writing: "Besides its maleficent function as the transmitter of malaria and yellow fever and its general character as pestilent nuisance, there is yet another disease of tropical and warmer temperate regions that is being credited to its mischief: Dengue."[14] These discoveries immediately and radically redesigned public health efforts around the world to focus on *the eradication of the vector*.

In his remarkable study of atmoterrorism, philosopher Peter Sloterdijk has noted that the characterization of pestilential life—in his example, rodents as *vermin*—led to a particular disposition toward exterminism as a solution to problems of human settlement. He is careful to explain this comportment, noting: "Exterminism constitutes a simplification of sadism as classically described by [Jean-Paul] Sartre. No longer a mere question of usurping the other's freedom, it is primarily concerned with freeing one's own freedom from the freedom of others."[15] Most urgent for any consideration of so-called vector-borne illnesses such as dengue is not, despite its decisive political consequences, the ability for scientists to transfer their enthusiasm for exterminism from one species to another, but rather that the exterminist has as his objective the elimination of the environmental conditions upon which his victims' lives depend. For Sloterdijk, prior to the development and combat deployment of chlorine gas in Ypres, Belgium by the German army during the spring of 1915, humans could more or less assume that the atmosphere upon which they depended was a stable source of life; but by introducing techniques of warfare into the environment itself, it is rendered (or "explicated," in Sloterdijk's terminology) as an existential medium that cannot be taken for granted. Because of this, "The twentieth century will be remembered as the age whose essential thought consisted in targeting no longer the body, but the enemy's environment."[16] Indeed, this is also the case for human settlements in the tropics, where the discovery of the *Aedes aegypti* as a vector also led to a new exterminist imaginary.

"If an enemy's body can no longer be liquidated with direct hits," Sloterdijk contends, "the attacker is forced to make his continued existence impossible by his direct immersion in an unlivable milieu for a sufficiently long period of time."[17] As public health officials came to better understand the life cycle of the dengue virus, the war changed its front; *Aedes aegypti* were no longer just irritating pests, they were harboring a formidable enemy. Mosquitos became *vectors*; agents capable of transmitting infectious pathogens to other organisms, including humans. In response, not long after WWII, one begins to find among the budgets of municipal administrators in Southeast Asia a new line item: "Fogging." Thus began the interspecies war of atmoterrorist eradication that has become so banal that few urban residents bother to give it second thought, even as clouds of toxic fog are repeatedly sprayed into their homes, mosques, and schools.

3. Nonhuman Settlements

> Getting hungry, eating, partially digesting, partially assimilating, and partially transforming: these are the actions of companion species.
> — Donna Haraway[18]

For thousands of years, as humans redesigned other animals in order to improve their utility and obedience through breeding and domestication, third-tier synanthropes were co-domesticating alongside them. On May 25, 1779, David Bylon, a Dutch surgeon living in the Dutch colonial city of Batavia (now Indonesia's capital, Jakarta), suddenly became ill with a severe fever, causing him to leave the company of his companions and go to bed early. In what is cited as the first clinical report of dengue from the torrid zone, Bylon describes intense muscle and joint pains into the third week of his illness. Ultimately, he fully recovered, yet Bylon's illness represents one case among an ongoing and often devastating cycle of epidemics reported in Asia, Africa, and North America throughout the 1780s, all of which followed the broader trend of outbreak patterns occurring along colonial shipping and trade routes. Initially moving from Africa to the Americas aboard slave ships, the range of the dengue virus was expanded while *Aedes aegypti* were fervently breeding among the countless casks of stagnant water accompanying colonial troops.

Dengue broadened its geographic reach again by travelling aboard military planes and boats during WWII, initiating the emergence of distinct viral genotypes. The postwar economic boom also resulted in heightened international trade, and the movement of both goods and people were accompanied by the *Aedes aegypti*, further distributing the virus. In 1953, a child in Manila became the first patient to die from dengue. By this point, the virus had manifested into more severe forms, including dengue hemorrhagic fever and dengue shock syndrome, which cause a combination of bleeding from the nose, ears, or underneath the skin, vomiting, and circulatory shock caused by plasma leakage into the interstitial spaces of the body. Inevitably, the increasing severity of symptoms caused the war of extermination to intensify in Southeast Asia.

By 1968, numerous cases of dengue were reported in Indonesia. By the end of the year, fifty-seven clinical cases and twenty-four deaths were reported and a national public health campaign to identify and treat dengue cases was initiated. The following year, fogging technologies were deployed for the first time in Jakarta. Their purpose was as simple as their design: spray organophosphate pesticides into the air to kill *Aedes aegypti* populations. It is now known that dengue's RNA structure produces one mutation every genome replication, largely because it does not go through a "proofreading" stage, resulting in the pathogen being genetically destined for expansion and diversity.[19] Four genetically distinct serotypes and nearly fifty genotypes have developed in the last three hundred years, thus guaranteeing its survival in distinct geographic niches and among various demographics.[20] Today, dengue is endemic in over one hundred countries, with four hundred million people a year becoming ill from the virus; it is thirty times more common than the flu and hospitalizes half a million people annually.[21]

While the domestication of nonhuman species contributed to the development of denser human settlements, the designs that guided this manipulation of genetic development also created the conditions for pathogens to reproduce, mutate, spread, and find a preferable host species in *Homo sapiens*. Dengue's genetic typos are designed for urban living, with diverse genetic pools offering niches for experimental virus strains to survive. The urban landscapes of human settlements were thus optimal environments for the dengue virus to redesign itself through expeditious reproductive cycles, while also strengthening the fitness of its preferred vector—*Aedes aegypti*.

Pedro Neves Marques, *Aedes Aegypti*, 2017. Digital animation video, 1'50" loop.

4. The Fog of War Machines

> Governance is well named. It describes well the destruction of what is implied by a collective responsibility with regard to the future, that is to say, politics.
> —Isabelle Stengers[22]

If you ask anyone in Jakarta why groups of men are stalking narrow residential streets with awkward silver boxes slung around their sweat-soaked bodies, it is likely they will reply that the fog being dispersed from their machines kills mosquitos. This is only partially true. These war machines mix gasoline and pesticide in a heated chamber designed to produce microscopic droplets of insecticide; the machine's proboscis then ejects a thick, white cloud, dramatic and eruptive. The "fog" is directed toward the most common places in the city that the *Aedes aegypti* is found, usually dark nooks, hidden corners, and covered ditches. Yet, the target of the fog is only nominally the *Aedes aegypti*. More precisely, the fog of these war machines is intended to make the *environment* within which dengue lives *unlivable*. Such aggressions reveal a formidable bias: although the bodies of *Homo sapiens* are also environments that host the virus, the "fog" is not meant to kill humans, at least not immediately.

After nearly twenty years of fogging in Jakarta, a national spike of dengue incidences in the late 1980s shifted the deployment of these atmotechnics from being used responsively—where cases were recorded—to a broader, preventative performance. In other words, the war of eradication became total. Subdistrict health officials advised residents to open their doors but vacate their houses for three hours while fogging was taking place and to cover anything that might later come into immediate contact with human skin. Pesticides enter mosquitoes through their outermost organ, the cuticle; cholinesterase then binds to internal receptors which would normally receive the signal to move, paralyzing them completely. The men who carry out the fogging were thus advised to regularly check the level of cholinesterase in their blood to ensure the paralyzing effect was not also bioaccumulating in their own bodies.[23] Wars of attrition are not won without sacrifices.

Yet as the exterminism continued, it was not the price paid by frontline human subjects that was most disturbing. Nearly three decades after the first fog of war was deployed against *Aedes aegypti* in Indonesia, scientists observed among samples of dead mosquitos something unexpected: the pesticides were no longer working. The studies revealed *Aedes aegypti*'s resistance to organophosphates, the active ingredient in larvicide and malathion-based fogging.[24] Human health agencies responded to these genetic defenses hermeneutically; they reinterpreted provincial law in Indonesia, which required officials to "use pesticide rationally," as mandating a rotation of pesticides once every three years, or every three to six months, or to continually increase the dosage of the pesticide.[25] Pesticide rotation proved incapable of keeping pace with the twenty-one-day mosquito lifecycle, and dengue, replicating as it does with every new host, produced countless new generations with potentially advantageous mutations.

What began as genetic anomalies in *Aedes aegypti* became adaptive features guaranteeing the efflorescence of future generations. In Indonesia, *Aedes aegypti* have doubled their rate of "knockdown resistance genes" in just the past ten years,[26] and pyrethroid fog no longer causes paralysis or death.[27] Another trajectory of resistance can be found in the 1016G mutation, which produces detoxification enzymes that metabolize pyrethroids before they reach the target site to paralyze the mosquito. Humans are, it should be noted, far from the mosquito's first adversary; *Aedes aegypti* already evolved detoxification mechanisms thousands of years ago to cope with the organic chemicals that leached from rotting plant material in the stagnant water of their larval habitats. What is novel about the role of humans in the last century is their ability to design an environment *optimized* for their mutation and evolution. In 1946, there were only twelve cases of insecticide resistance reported worldwide; in 1990, five hundred species of mosquitoes were resistant to at least one pesticide.[28] The human designs for settlement and its atmoterroristic defense became indistinguishable from the environmental pressures within which *Aedes aegypti* learn to adapt and thrive.[29]

5. Pestilential Urbanism

> Terrorism is the maximal explication of the other from the point of view of his exterminability.
> —Peter Sloterdijk[30]

After nearly fifty years of intense pesticide usage (and tens of thousands of generations of mosquitoes), today fogging is synonymous with dengue control in Jakarta. This intangible infrastructure has also gained a monopoly on the human imaginary with respect to multispecies interactions. Despite the limited effectiveness of fogging, the psychosocial comfort it provides for urban residents is significant. Although nearly all public health officials agree that fogging can only be effective when other social behaviors are routinized (such as restricting *Aedes aegypti* breeding grounds by eliminating stagnant water), simple citywide strategies like dumping or covering water containers have done little to encourage human participation. Fogging is a more demonstrative mode of domination, even if it is less effective, impossible to maintain in the long term, and tends to diminish the importance of behavior-oriented dengue control efforts.[31] Importantly, the amtotechnical performance and compelling visual theatricality of urban fogging still communicates to residents that someone, somewhere is thoroughly governing the environment upon which their health depends.[32]

As with political economies, toxins accumulate differentially among the "respiratory economies" of human agents.[33] While *Aedes aegypti* have evolved to produce detoxifying enzymes, primates like *Homo sapiens* do not adapt so quickly. The long-term effects of residing among these increasing levels of toxicity are rarely the subject of political debate or independent scientific research.[34] More common is the assumption that someone, somewhere must have rationally weighed out the trade-offs before further perpetuating this interspecies *Jus ad bellum*. That such wanton hostilities are enabled by an anthropocentric bias is no secret, but the act of standing down as a species also means overcoming the fog of war. As Beatriz Colomina and Mark Wigley have recently suggested, "Design is a defense of the human, but what is being defended is never clear."[35] This ambiguity is perhaps nowhere more disorienting than among the intangible infrastructures of atmospheric governance, which simultaneously enable human settlements at the scale of a tropical megacity and redesign human vulnerabilities in the adaptive arms race of evolution.

1 Jean-Baptiste Say, *Cours complet d'économie politique* (Paris: Guillaume, 1828).

2 Jeffrey R. Powell and Walter J. Tabachnick, "History of Domestication and Spread of Aedes Aegypti: A Review," in *Memórios do Instituto Oswaldo Cruz* 108 (2013): 11–17.

3 L. C. Harrington, J. D. Edman, and T. W. Scott, "Why Do Female Aedes Aegypti (Diptera: Culicidae) Feed Preferentially and Frequently on Human Blood?" *Journal of Medical Entomology* 38 (2001): 411–22.

4 Jim Robbins, "How Forest Loss is Leading to a Rise in Human Disease," *Yale Envirionment 360*, February 23, 2016.

5 Manuel DeLanda, "Inorganic Life," in *Zone 6: Incorporations*, eds. Jonathan Crary and Sanford Kwinter (New York: Zone Books, 1992): 149–150.

6 World Health Organization, "Dengue and Severe Dengue," who.int.

7 S. Sim, J. L. Ramirez, and G. Dimopoulos, "Dengue Virus Infection of the Aedes Aegypti Salivary Gland and Chemosensory Aparatus Induces Genes That Modulate Infection and Blood-feeding Behavior," *PLoS Pathogens* 8 (2012).

8 Powell and Tabachnick, "History of Domestication and Spread of Aedes Aegypti."

9 The first dengue vaccine, Dengvaxia, was approved by the WHO in April 2016. As of August 2016, Mexico, Brazil, The Philippines, and El Salvador also licensed the vaccine. The cost and a concern that the vaccine will not protect against all strains of the virus have caused many of the 128 dengue-endemic countries to abstain from vaccine purchasing and implementation.

10 Adrienne Lafrance, "Genetically Modified Mosquitoes: What Could Possibly Go Wrong?" *The Atlantic*, April 26, 2016.
11 This poem was written by Ross the night he first discovered that mosquitos transmit malaria.
12 Eight *annas* have a value of less than one US cent.
13 Robert E. Sinden, "Malaria, Mosquitoes, and the Legacy of Ronald Ross," *Bulletin of the World Health Organization* 85, no. 11 (November 2007): 821–900.
14 H. Graham, "Researches on Dengue," *Journal of the American Medical Association* 41 (1903).
15 Peter Sloterdijk, *Terror from the Air* (Los Angeles: Semiotext(e), 2009), 28.
16 Ibid., 14.
17 Ibid., 16.
18 Donna J. Haraway, *Staying with the Trouble: Making Kin in the Chthulucene* (Durham: Duke University Press, 2016), 61.
19 Scott C. Miller and Nikos Vasilakis, "Molecular Evolution of Dengue Viruses: Contributions of Phylogenetics to Understanding the History and Epidemiology of the Preeminent Arboviral Disease," *Infection, Genetics, and Evolution* 9 (2009): 157–70.
20 S. S. Twiddy, E. C. Holmes, and A. Rambout, "Inferring the Rate and Time Scale of Dengue Virus Evolution," *Molecular Biology and Evolution Journal* 20 (2003): 122–29.
21 World Health Organization, "Dengue and Severe Dengue," who.it.
22 Isabelle Stengers, *In Catastrophic Times: Resisting the Coming Barbarism* (London: Open Humanities Press / Meson Press, 2015), 54.
23 Pyrethroids have been the pesticide of choice for nearly twenty years in Indonesia, replacing organophosphates, which were shown to have negative human and environmental health impacts after thirty years of use. The discovery of DDT's endocrine-disrupting effects and subsequent ban initiated the development of pyrethroids, which are heralded by pesticide companies and government alike as the safer options for non-mosquito beings (despite their acute toxicity to fish, bees, dragonflies, cats, and sometimes dogs), while still offering a mortal mosquito knockdown. See Iqbal R. F. Elyazar, Simon I. Hay, and J. Kevin Baird, "Malaria Distribution, Prevalence, Drug Resistance and Control in Indonesia," *Journal of Advanced Parasitology* 74 (2011): 41–175.
24 See Damar Tri Boewono, "Susceptibility of Dengue Haemorrhagic Fever Vector (Aedes Aegypti) Against Organophosphate Insecticides (Malathion and Temephos) in Some Districts of Yogyakarta and Central Java Provinces," *Bulletin Penelitian Kesehatan* 35 (2007); and Kris Cahyo Mulyatno, Atsushi Yamanaka, and Eiji Konishi Ngadino, "Resistance of Aedes Aegypti (L.) Larvae to Temephos in Surabaya, Indonesia," *Southeast Asian Journal of Tropical Medicine and Public Health* no. 43 (2012): 29–33.
25 Jakarta Provincial Law No 6/2007, "Dengue Hemorrhagic Fever Control."
26 Juli Rochmijati Wulandari, Siu Fai Lee, Vanessa Linley White, Warsito Tantowijoyo, Ary Anthony Hoffman, and Nancy Margaret Endersby-Harshman, "Association Between Three Mutations, F1565C, V1023G, S996P, in the Voltage-Sensitive Sodium Channel Gene and Knockdown Resistance in Aedes Aegypti from Yogyakarta, Indonesia," *Insects* 6 (2015): 658–85.
27 *Aedes aegypti* had a head start building resistance from decades of exposure to DDT, which targets the same channel. Mosquitoes were shown to be resistant to DDT just four years following their use; see Sayono Sayono, Anggie Puspa Nur Hidayati, Sukmal Fahri, Didik Sumanto, Edi Dharmana, Surharyo Hadisaputro, Puji Budi Setia Asih and Din Syafruddin, "Distribution of Voltage-Gated Sodium Channel (Nav) Alleles Among the Aedes Aegypti Populations in Central Java Province and its Association with Resistance to Pyrethroid Insecticides," *PLoS One* 11 (2016).
28 Kaliyaperumal Karunamoorthi and Shanmugavelu Sabesan, "Insecticide Resistance in Insect Vectors of Disease with Special Reference to Mosquitoes: A Potential Threat to Global Public Health," *Health Scope* 2, no. 1 (2013): 4–18.
29 Heat also helps things get and stay moving: the rising temperatures that provide local indices to climate change also speed up *Aedes Aegypti* development and rapidly alter its behavior; every stage in their life cycle is condensed when incubated in heat, and warmer temperatures make *Aedes Aegypti* hungrier for blood.
30 Sloterdijk, *Terror from the Air*, 28.
31 Saleha Sungkar, "Controlling the Dengue Vector: What's the Problem?" (public lecture in the Faculty of Medicine, Universitas Indonesia, June 2016).
32 Judith Butler, *Notes Toward a Performative Theory of Assemblage* (Cambridge, MA: Harvard University Press, 2015).
33 Sloterdijk, *Terror from the Air*, 99.
34 Timothy Mitchell, *Rule of Experts: Egypt, Techno-Politics, Modernity* (Berkeley: University of California Press, 2002), especially 19–53.
35 Beatriz Colomina and Mark Wigley, *Are We Human? Notes on an Archaeology of Design* (Zurich: Lars Muller Publishers, 2016), 141.

Analysis: Synthesis

Sophia Roosth

Life is not what it used to be. Living things bearing genomes pared down, streamlined, or cobbled together from bits of synthesized DNA now scurry, swim, and flourish in test tubes and glass bioreactors: viruses named for computer software, bacteria encoding passages of James Joyce, chimeric yeast buckling under the metabolic strain of genes harvested from sweet wormwood, petunias, and microbes from Icelandic thermal pools.

In the final years of the twentieth century, émigrés from mechanical and electrical engineering and computer science resolved that if the aim of biology was to understand life, then *making* life would yield better theories than would experimentation. Many of these researchers clustered at the Massachusetts Institute of Technology (MIT) beginning in 2003. Naming themselves synthetic biologists, they advocate not experiment but manufacture, not reduction but construction, not analysis but synthesis. As a cultural anthropologist, I spent eight years talking to and working with them.

Armed with biotechnology techniques—notably, faster and cheaper methods for DNA sequencing and synthesis—this new breed of life scientists treats biological media as a substrate for manufacture, raw material that can be manipulated using engineering principles borrowed from their various home disciplines. Sequencing and synthesis allow synthetic biologists to traffic between physical molecules of nucleic acid (DNA and RNA) and dematerialized genetic sequences scrolling across computer screens. Sequencing means "reading" the strings of four nucleotide bases whose sequence constitutes DNA and RNA to compose a digital genetic "code" made up entirely of letters that stand in for the molecules (A for the nucleotide adenine, C for cytosine, G for guanine, T for thymine). Synthesis does the reverse: using elaborate genomic techniques, researchers can physically build material nucleic acid macromolecules to order on the basis of desired genetic codes.

Two synthetic biologists define their field as follows:

> Synthetic biologists seek to assemble components that are not natural (therefore synthetic) to generate chemical systems that support Darwinian evolution (therefore biological). By carrying out the assembly in a synthetic way, these scientists hope to understand non-synthetic biology, that is, "natural" biology.[1]

In their equation of making with understanding, of synthesis with analysis, making life is not an end in itself but rather a technique for probing life's margins. Making new life-forms also requires that researchers query seemingly commonsense terms like "natural" and "unnatural," "biological" and "synthetic."

By 2010, some seven years after its origins at MIT, the synthetic biology research economy had swelled considerably. As of 2006, its overall annual market was $600 million, and between 2005 and 2010 alone, synthetic biology researchers received over $430 billion from the US government. The vast majority of synthetic biology research today occurs in Western Europe (especially the United Kingdom, Germany, and the Netherlands) and the United States (where most work is concentrated in California and New England, and Massachusetts in particular). Still, there is a thin spread of synthetic biology research across the country: in 2013 an estimated 174 American universities reported that they engaged in some kind of synthetic biology research. This research is primarily funded federally by the National Institutes of Health, the Defense Advanced Research Projects Agency, the Department of Energy, and the National Science Foundation, as well as by private organizations, universities, and venture capital.

Such organizations, which fund the lion's share of professional synthetic biology research, are interested in the field primarily for its potential commercial applications: clean energy, bioweapons, and cheap drug synthesis. Such work often bears practical resemblances to biotechnology, synthetic chemistry, chemical engineering, and pharmaceuticals research. The most prominent—and mediagenic—example of synthetic biology is University of California, Berkeley professor Jay Keasling's development of a synthetic microbial pathway to manufacture inexpensive artemisinin, an antimalarial compound, for distribution in developing countries.

The difference between synthetic biologists' impulse and earlier examples of biological experimentation is that they do not make living things in the service of discovery science or experimental research alone. Rather, making is also an *end* in itself. Newly built biotic things serve as answers to biological questions that might otherwise have remained unasked. They are tools with which synthetic biologists theorize what life is.

One notable synthetic biology project, for example, was aimed more at developing new synthesis techniques than a product. In 2010 synthetic biologists at the J. Craig Venter Institute (JCVI) synthesized a "minimal" organism, a single-celled, independently living entity that maintains, JCVI researchers posit, the least genetic material necessary to sustain life. JCVI announced that it had synthesized and assembled a synthetic version of the bacterium *Mycoplasma mycoides* genome, inserting it into *Mycoplasma capricolum* cells. Craig Venter exulted that his scientific team had made "the first self-replicating species we've had on the planet whose parent is a computer." If synthetic biologists now define life according to its material construction, then a minimal organism is an ontologically receding horizon: it is not the simplest, smallest, or most genetically austere organism found on earth but rather the most genetically minimal viable organism that synthetic biologists can build. Projects such as this one toy with what counts as the "limits of life," from reverse engineering what researchers imagine to be the "first" life-form to stripping down microbes to determine a "minimal" genome.

This belief that biology can be understood through its construction is unmistakable not only in synthetic biologists' engineering projects but also in how they talk about their goals. Rob Carlson, a synthetic biologist and garage biohacker, makes a comparison to engineering: "Understanding is defined by the ability to build something new that behaves as expected," whether a 777 jet or a yeast cell.[2] Synthetic biologist Drew Endy uses a similar analogy to physics to make the same point: "Imagine what the science around the origin of the universe might be like if physicists could construct universes. It just so happens that in biology, the technology of synthesis [allows you to] instantly take your hypothesis and compile it into a physical instance and then test it."[3]

Such reasoning recalls Artificial Life founder Chris Langton's disciplinary alibi from a decade earlier:

> It's very difficult to build general theories about what life would be like anywhere in the universe and whatever it was made out of, when all we have to study is the unique example of life that exists here on Earth. So, what we have to do—perhaps—is the next best thing, which is to create far simpler systems in our computers.[4]

The Artificial Life of the 1990s and the synthetic biology of the early 2000s have much in common, not the least of which is researchers' explicit efforts to build new instantiations of something they call "life." Nonetheless, Artificial Life was premised on abstracting life by simulating it in computer software. Artificial Life researchers treated life as if it were a universal formal category transcending substance, material, or medium. Something different motivates synthetic biologists' work. Most notably, they do not posit that life is a property separable from biological matter. Neither is their project mimetic: rather than imitate life, they construct new living kinds. Life's synthesis, in synthetic biology, advances biological analysis, even as analysis conditions what gets synthesized and why.

Many synthetic biologists quote Richard Feynman, who scribbled this on his CalTech blackboard just before his death: "What I cannot create, I do not understand."[5] This quotation is "a favorite among synthetic biologists—and for good reason," because "synthetic biology is the pursuit of comprehending biological systems by trying to engineer them."[6] Feynman's phrase would later be misquoted when coded and inserted into the genome of one of Venter's synthesized microbes. Endy also paraphrases Feynman when he says, "As a biological designer, until I can actually design something, I don't understand it."[7] Making has operated hand-in-glove with knowing since seventeenth-century Baconian mechanical philosophy dispensed with natural philosophy to experiment on the natural world. Experimentalists and artisans joined *theoria* to *practica,* and contemplation served instrumentation. Yet the ubiquity of "maker's knowledge" and artisanship in modern science has since largely been forgotten, especially in the mid- to late twentieth century, when scientific disciplines were divided into "pure" and "applied" research. Synthetic biology is the latest instantiation of a centuries-long debate as to whether nature may be known through artifice.

Can genomes be "refactored" and streamlined to function like software code? Yes, synthetic biologists answer, because we have generated just such a bacteriophage. Can a living thing be fragmented into parts, and from a library of parts, can an organism be assembled? Yes, they say, because we have made standardized biological parts. What is the minimal system that is viable and free-living? The one we ourselves have made, they respond. Can species be defined beyond the continuous unspooling of biological generations? Yes, because we can revive species already extinct. Synthetic biologists make new living things in order to better understand how life works. Yet making recursively loops theory: the new living things biologists make function as "persuasive objects" that materialize theories of what synthetic biologists seek to understand about life. In short, the biological features, theories, and limits that synthetic biologists fasten upon are circularly determined by their own experimental tactics, which they then identify with the things they have made.

Biology has always been, since its inception and by definition, an inquiry into what life is. Michel Foucault claimed that "life itself" is a category that "did not exist" prior to the end of the eighteenth century: "Life does not constitute an obvious threshold beyond which entirely new forms of knowledge are required. It is a category of classification, relative, like all the other categories, to the criteria one adopts."[8] That is, biology as a discipline was warranted by a classificatory decision: carving up the world into the organic and the inorganic, differentiating between the vital and the lifeless, and insisting that the living world demanded a science of its own.

Yet following Foucault's phrasing, if life did not precede the late eighteenth century, perhaps it did not survive the twentieth century. "Life" as an analytic object has come undone. Seeking answers, synthetic biologists build new living things, and in so doing they retroactively define what counts as "life" to accord with the living things they manufacture and account to be living. The organisms conceived by these mechanical and electrical engineers-cum-biologists, then, are altogether different from the creatures built by biotechnologists: while some are made to serve discrete pharmaceutical or agricultural functions, many of them are made as a way of *theorizing the biological.* Rather than being the common denominator of all living things, "life" has (once again) become a *problem* of ontological limits and discontinuities. As such, analyses of life are newly simultaneous with and enabled by synthesized instantiations of it.

Just as genetic *synthesis* and *sequencing* are terms of art for the technologies that drive synthetic biology, *synthesis* and *analysis* are joined philosophical modes of reasoning underwritten by these paired technologies. Making stuff—synthesis—has become a mode of analysis, a way of theorizing the biological. This convergence is recognizable to synthetic biologists, who explain what they are doing to themselves and to others as building living things in order to understand life better. When technical and epistemic knowledge of life converge, the objects of synthetic biology function as *persuasive objects*. They convince synthetic biologists that life is marked by the qualities—technical, substantive, and social—that they ascribe to it. That is, biological analysis either precedes or is simultaneous with biological manufacture. This sort of active, interested making is endemic to the sciences of our time.

At a time when biology is recognized as more complicated than midcentury molecular biologists or '90s-era Human Genome Project scientists could have ever anticipated, synthetic biologists respond by coaxing new creatures into recombinant life. These brave new organisms grow, mutate, metabolize, divide, and senesce, yet they also speak eloquently of their times, of nature and artifice, of analysis and synthesis, of life and its limits.

1 Steven A. Benner and A. Michael Sismour, "Synthetic Biology," *Nature Reviews: Genetics* 6, no. 7 (2005): 533–43.

2 Rob Carlson, MIT lecture (Cambridge, MA, November 7, 2008).

3 Alok Jha, "From the Cells Up," *Guardian*, March 10, 2005.

4 Linda Feferman, *Simple Rules ... Complex Behavior*, Santa Fe, NM (1992), video. Langton quoted in Stefan Helmreich. *Silicon Second Nature: Culturing Artificial Life in a Digital World* (Berkeley: University of California Press, 1998), 90.

5 Richard Feynman, "Feynman's Office; the Last Blackboards." *Physics Today* 42, no. 2 (1989): 88.

6 Peter A. Carr and George M. Church, "Genome Engineering." *Nature Biotechnology* 27, no. 12 (2009): 1151–62.

7 *Science is Culture: Conversations at the New Intersection of Science and Society*, ed. Adam Bly (New York: Harper Collins, 2010), 71.

8 Michel Foucault, *The Order of Things* (New York: Vintage Books, 1970), 175.

The Story of Peter Green
Peter Chang

Brian Kuan Wood

I want to tell you a story I recently heard about a friend in New York—actually a friend of a friend, a young architect and entrepreneur named Peter Green Peter Chang. I have never met Peter Green Peter Chang myself, nor has anyone ever explained to me why his full name contains two Peters. But his story is somehow familiar, even if nothing like it has ever happened to me. Perhaps because it could happen to me or to anyone else in the near future.

In New York, Peter Green Peter Chang had become moderately well-known in the architecture community for his work with a number of property developers. These were property developers who acquired real estate from the elderly or from poor members of neighborhoods just starting to be accessed by creative young people seeking cheaper rents. Anticipating broad demographic changes on the horizon, the developers would obtain swaths of overripe or derelict homes and storefronts and convert them into grand cathedrals for creative living and entrepreneurial projects.

Over the years Peter Green Peter Chang grew to be the main architect in charge of aesthetic upgrades for these neighborhoods. His peculiar name must have had the right ring to developers. Green is good for an architect, Chang is inexpensive, and Peter is honest. So Peter Green Peter Chang had a steady stream of work. But in fact he had no competitors. His fees were at least half of the next lowest bid on any project. At the end of every project, there were no surprise costs. And he always delivered on time. No client dared ask him how he did it. Probably for fear of what they might find.

Being Chinese, Peter Green Peter Chang had a strong sense of civic duty. When the process of removing old residents felt cruel or premature, as it often did, he would remind himself: this is New York and this is America—he did not enter into this line of work easily. His parents did not have an easy landing when they came to the US, nor did his grandparents when they moved to Taiwan. Violence is just a part of life, and all people must deal with change. He had to, his parents had to, their parents had to, and most certainly their parents in China had to deal with change as well. If he had inherited both strength and bitterness from his family's experiences of migration and survival, he was now putting it to use in his position at the very forefront of structural changes taking place in the city where he lived.

In contrast to many of his architect colleagues, Peter Green Peter Chang never saw himself in a position superior to the residents of the neighborhoods where his buildings were built. He resented how both the developers and his architect colleagues encouraged him to inject local flavors and celebrate historic characteristics even as they redeveloped entire communities. Peter Green Peter Chang could not celebrate the poverty of the neighborhoods where he worked any more than he could imagine their residents doing so. For him the pious absolutism of long white walls and modernist slabs, or any new construction for that matter, were great beacons shining away from backwardness, leading out of decrepitude and ancient stupidity. He secretly pined for a world that would remove all the putrid flavors of peasant tradition from the equation. In this he often stood together with the residents who could afford to remain in their homes after his projects were complete: the bourgeois black, Hispanic, and Asian communities who applauded his work knowing that their own properties would double and triple in value. They could finally cash out and retire in the southern US, in Asia, South America, the Caribbean, or wherever their hearts desired.

But Peter Green Peter Chang had a secret. In fact, he never received any training as an architect, though he was licensed and had officially completed many buildings. Some suspected that the strangeness of his name originated in badly forged diplomas or architect licenses. In actuality he had received very little formal education whatsoever, and instead dedicated his youth to the informal study of experimental physics. In doing so, Peter Green Peter Chang came upon a strange synthetic building material he believed would revolutionize the construction industry and built space in general.

He nicknamed it "Bubble Rubble" for paradoxically combining the weightless properties of bubbles with the fragmented material properties of decayed or derelict infrastructure. The trick came in moving energetic matter through time in a way similar to a financial trader, although we can never be certain, as the research remains undocumented and the technology mostly hearsay. According to the rumors, this Bubble Rubble borrowed from both the economic aspirations of historical communities of the land on which he built and the material decay of existing structures at his disposal. This combination, as the story goes, makes possible a kind of hypermaterial that resolves apparently conflicting temporal axes into a single plastic substance—concretizing both the desires and disappointments at either end of a building's lifespan and cloaking them within the retro-modern vernaculars favored by gentrifying building developers. What appeared to be mostly baked together out of prefab floorplans and made-to-order ventilation systems were in fact buildings whose very existence was spectral to the point of being holographic, while at the same time absolutely materially present. And in this sense, Peter Green Peter Chang's particular brand of generic architecture was actually a stealthy way of hiding his brilliant discovery in broad daylight. There were some who could sense this, and would claim that his buildings never in fact existed, that he was a fraudulent architect, but Peter Green Peter Chang always reminded his clients that his unusually low costs made his competitors deeply resentful.

In actuality, the great innovation of Peter Green Peter Chang's Bubble Rubble came in a fundamental assumption about his milieu. Peter Green Peter Chang believed that, while many around him claimed to work to redistribute energy and spread democracy, few sincerely wanted either of these things at all. Like the older bourgeois residents of the neighborhoods his projects targeted, most people simply wanted to relax with a jar of rice wine on a little platform over the riverbanks of their parents and ancestors. Peter Green Peter Chang could feel the future getting crowded by the things his own ancestors stole or thought they could stash away, and the accumulation began to weigh on him. It made him move more slowly, think less clearly, eat more, spend less, dress less exquisitely, seek more time with close friends and family, and so forth. Peter Green Peter Chang did not feel sad or depressed from this weight. He simply felt slower, more burdened. Others might have felt a similar burden as guilt, but the architect Peter Green Peter Chang sensed time accumulating and becoming contradictory or indecipherable, confusing and undermining decisions that were once simple and straightforward. He began to believe buying an expensive sports car to be a manner of paying rent. He began to feel the need to slow down becoming a question of which city to move to next year—a city where he might reclaim a long-lost treasure. That's why Peter Green Peter Chang's ears perked up when his developer clients approached him with a new kind of proposal. They had begun researching prospects in China and wanted him to spearhead a project there.

A responsible Asian-American man like Peter Green Peter Chang is always careful never to vocalize his feelings regarding race and ethnicity even among close friends. He shared a telepathic bond with other Asian friends who similarly knew better, but their contract had to remain unspoken. None of them dared broach the subject of shared ethnicity for fear of discovering that they in fact had little in common, and were simply drawn together to collectively dispel the brute fact of sharing nothing but vague ethnic characteristics. For Peter Green Peter Chang, the unspoken nature of the agreement was made more necessary by the fact that he privately felt superior as an immigrant, strengthened and nourished as he was by the difficulties his family had experienced in the past. On the contrary, his Asian-American friends felt weighed down by their history, by being unable to synchronize the injustice of their lowly minority status with the story of what brought them to a place that could never be their own. So the appearance of China on Peter Green Peter Chang's forecast came as a natural and timely development. Though he knew nothing about the country, he was proud to be approached as an automatic expert by virtue of his ethnicity. Surely his innovative building material would gain an entirely new life in China's booming economy.

In China, Peter Green Peter Chang proposed to start work in the ancestral hometown of his family, a village whose name he could neither remember nor pronounce. But it felt like the right place to begin. He assured his trusting developer clients that this town was full of empty buildings new and old, and that he had met many young creatives with the energy and initiative to fill them. One building in particular caught his attention: a massive private mansion from the early twentieth century that had been used as a workshop for local artisans in the late twentieth century before being abandoned in the 1990s. Though it was crumbling from neglect, Peter Green Peter Chang could envision its many floors brimming with overlapping groups of industrious young people. One floor could be a collaborative kitchen where aspiring amateur chefs or foodies could bring ingredients to cook imaginary Tang dynasty dishes. Another could be a coworking space full of well-composed adults of all ages biting lower lips studying glowing screens, composing science fiction stories sublimating memories of the Cultural Revolution. Another, a workshop using scrap metal from the nearby car repair shop to build elegant bicycles. Another, a contemporary art center where visitors could bathe in immersive video installations while enjoying local cuisine from its food court. Another, a small press printing new philosophy and critical theory on parchment made of pine-tree needles from the nearby forest.

What a relief China was, rich with so many new possibilities. Peter Green Peter Chang started to realize how cynical he had grown in New York and in the US, where he had worked for years knowing full well that the future could never be written from a part of the world whose culture was based in extraction and plunder. The Western world has been in a state of decay for longer than it has known. The young creatives moving into his New York buildings were only holograms, projections responsible for beautifying a long-lost industrial sector with fake vital energy and sassy T-shirts. Perhaps they themselves already know that they could only look for serene spaces to die a peaceful death with cool friends and nice furniture.

The sense of new life and renewal that surrounded Peter Green Peter Chang in China only reinforced his thinking that the difficulties experienced by earlier generations of his family made him smarter and stronger. He began to assemble a story in which this intelligence and strength had been building over generations in exile, incubating in the safety of a foreign empire, only to eventually build a bridge home over the oceans and through the atmosphere when that foreign empire's power began to wane. Peter Green Peter Chang now realized that for some time his destiny had been to eventually return, repair, and pilot the downed spaceship of his grandparents' culture. He would return home and enter its rotten cockpit to feel the great machine envelop and surround him like a womb.

Peter Green Peter Chang's mother would tell him over the years: just go to Vancouver. Your aunt and uncle there. Plenty Chinese people there. But he didn't care about Chinese people. That was not an end in itself. He wanted to build something, make new discoveries. He wanted to build his own culture out of his own culture. He craved glass towers and ruins, next to each other, replacing one another, growing into one another, becoming indiscernible, conflating time and space, death and life. The dark power of Bubble Rubble was such that Peter Green Peter Chang could never be sure when one would overtake the other and undermine the projection. Amidst his feverish excitement, his emails began to contain a specific typo: trying to address friends, family, and coworkers with "Dear," he found himself repeatedly mistyping is as "Dead." Dead Howie, Dead Francis, Dead Lisa, Dead Michael, Dead Dad, Dead Mom, Dead Friends, China is awesome, come visit me soon!

However, in the ancestral hometown whose name he could neither remember nor pronounce, Peter Green Peter Chang faced a major problem. For many abandoned properties such as the one he had set his eye on, it had become difficult to locate a deed of ownership. Many official records had been lost due to changes in government or migrations of people over the course of the twentieth century's various political upheavals, and without any documentation identifying a property's owner, it was impossible to determine who held the right to sell it. Apparently, this abandoned house was one such property frozen in an ambiguous legal limbo, waiting to be claimed by an original owner or their descendants who may or may not even exist.

Finally, Peter Green Peter Chang was able to meet with a mid-level official named Mr. Guang to inquire about what could be done. Mr. Guang was barely older than Peter Green Peter Chang, more fit, and with a twinkle in his eye. He introduced himself with a charismatic smile and speaking excellent English. In a run-down old bureaucratic office looking just as overgrown with papers as the abandoned property was covered in weeds and vines, the exuberant Mr. Guang appeared to have come straight out of another world, the business world. With a brief rush of superiority, Peter Green Peter Chang thought to himself that this official must be a failed entrepreneur—not everyone can be a winner in the game. The enormous Chinese state bureaucracy must function as a final resting place for those who can't rise to the occasion of the country's great economic experiment.

Mr. Guang, on the other hand, could see that Peter Green Peter Chang was a Western entrepreneur eager to invest significant resources in a part of the world he had little knowledge of. This struck Mr. Guang as ironic, considering that there were many people in the town named Chang who even shared distinctive facial features with Peter Green Peter Chang. Mr. Guang explained that it was unfortunate that there was little he could do to facilitate the sale of the property without any documents indicating ownership. Desperate to secure the deal, Peter Green Peter Chang pulled Mr. Guang aside to express that he was willing to pay whatever was necessary to whomever was necessary to acquire the property. Mr. Guang smirked: “But sir, there are many buildings here for you to use. The government has built cultural centers. Museums. Residential estates. Many by prestigious Western architects. Surely it would be more expedient to acquire a property that can be legally sold to you.”

Two weeks later, Peter Green Peter Chang was in possession of a deed of ownership for the building he so wanted. He was unable to convince his developer clients to invest in a property acquired outside the proper channels, so he undertook the project as a private investment for its personal significance. Every cent he owned had now left his bank account, yet he considered it a small price to pay for a property most certainly capable of growing in value in the coming decades. He had now gained a foothold in China, and it was the beginning of a new era for him. Peter Green Peter Chang wrote home breathlessly, listing many projects he hoped to pursue in the building, but his friends and family could hardly follow what he wrote. This building appeared to have seized onto deeply contradictory personal longings to be in a certain place at a certain time in a way that the intricate social and spatiotemporal engineering of Bubble Rubble could not account for.

Two months later, Peter Green Peter Chang was overseeing renovations on the new property when Mr. Guang paid him a visit. Appearing fit as ever, even with a peculiar—even satisfied—glow, Mr. Guang pulled Peter Green Peter Chang aside: “Peter Green, I wanted to share some news with you. Of course this news has no consequence with regard to the ownership status of your home, as it has been purchased by you from the local government. But we were able to locate a deed of ownership for the property dating to 1915. I believe you will find it to be of interest.” Mr. Guang presented a ragged, yellowing, barely legible sheet of paper to Peter Green Peter Chang. On this original deed of ownership, the names of his grandparents were unmistakable.

The Return of the Have-Lived

Yongwoo Lee

Superimposed Memories in the Soil of Postcolonial Korea

In 1936, amidst the Japanese occupation of Korea, a Japanese *kaibatsu* corporation called Maruboshi started to build residential areas and stables near the Daegu train station, within which there was a collective village named Maruboshi, near Chilseung-dong.[1] From colonial liberation in 1945 to the end of the Korean War, Maruboshi filled with refugees fleeing to South Korea, transforming into a vibrant topos of commoners' life. After the rapid introduction of modernity and industrialization during Park Chung-hee's military regime (1961–79), traces of Maruboshi's colonial past, from its facades to collective wells, started to disappear and be replaced by Western-style apartment complexes. Instead of refugees or colonial subjects, these apartments were designed for and marketed towards laborers who dreamt of a bourgeoisie middle-class family life for themselves. As a metonym for a compressed modern history of Korea, in 2016 this multilayered urban palimpsest was completely demolished to reveal its bare and wild face, waiting for another space of residence to be built on top again.

The *gaemangcho* (*Erigeron annuus*), a biennial North American plant species with white daisy flowers, was first brought into Korea when the Japanese empire built railways as part of colonial modernization. Apart from its humble appearance, the plant soon came to represent the loss of national sovereignty among Koreans, and was often referred to in a derogatory way such as *MangGukCho* (nation-ruining plant) or *Oepul* (Japanese plant). The seeds of *gaemangcho*, first buried deep below the colonial Maruboshi eighty years ago, flourish today. The ephemeral forest that has come to cover the barren sites of Maruboshi germinates according to the concealed structure of a disjointed modernity. Recall Gramsci's remark on the "interregnum," on the disjunction of time and space as a symptom of contemporaneity: "The crisis consists precisely in the fact that the old is dying and the new cannot be born: in this interregnum a great variety of morbid symptoms appear."[2] This ghostly return of "have-lived things" permeates into life as an uncanny cartography of modernity.

There is a primitiveness to the profuse sprouting of a foreign plant species. The *gaemangcho* in Maruboshi presents us with self-reflexive questions about Korean modernity through the materialization of aboriginality and a nonhuman diaspora. This essay is a reflection on postcolonial Korean modernity that interrogates the articulation of speciesism as a racist metaphor, the discourse of animality, and the pervasion, representation, and sovereignty of nonhuman species both during and after the colonial period in Korea. It attempts to allow for cultural translation across and beyond issues of anthropocentrism and postcolonial modernity, not only at the level of narrative or convention, but also on the level of a specifically nonhuman, postcolonial, modern condition.

The Return of the Primordial and Recursive Questions of Colonial Memory

The return of the primordial encompasses a narrative of time's bifurcation, of the past and the present, and as such has been deeply rooted in the space where we once stood. The modern self, having been enamored with the apparatuses and tropes of modernity (read: uniformity and hybridity), is now reeling from the uncanny symptoms summoned by the return of the have-lived.

Postcolonial life is full of contradictions and paradoxes. At a conscious level, the postcolonized reject the knowledge, both past and present, inherited from the colonizer. But the colonizer has reorganized itself as part of the global capitalist system, thus making its shadow impossible to escape. Furthermore, if we accept Yoshimi Takeuchi's observation that the East could not have recognized itself without the West's invasion, then non-Western and/or Asian modernity acquired self-consciousness only through the recognition of the West, and specifically as its Other.[3] Postcolonized Koreans roam around inside the prison yard of imperialist mantra, burdened with symptoms of our incommensurable colonial legacy and absence of autonomous self-recognition and self-reflection. Asia's process of nation-state building is a phantasmagoric maelstrom of postcolonial cartography, where the cultural discourse on racial and ethnic diversity wears the skin of anthropology and the debris of the colonial unconscious is superimposed on the logic of industrialization and the identitarian impasse inherent to modernization. In such a world, how do we experience multiple modernities? Is it possible to resurrect, bring back to life, the presence of primordial and animistic spirits that were thought to be killed long ago?

Let us forget, for the time being, the discourse of unknown places, indeterminacy, the biological body, life, and nature. The primordial, as represented by *gaemangcho*, has always been around in many manifestations. It can be found in the chaotic noise of the city as it rumbles, in the quiet flowering of weeds by a suburban roadside, in a midsummer night's swarm of insects by the river bank. There is the story of dead mayflies found in heaps below glittering storefront windows.[4] Similarly, there is the story of how the nutria came to Korea.[5] These stories are signs of rupture in an unconscious silence about the forgotten world that was once full of animistic magic. They allow us to unmask a story of modernity as a symptom of an ever present colonialism wrapped in capitalist phantasmagoria.

If Benjamin's philosophy on the repetition of cultural history was centered on the ways in which an original thing is produced in a certain moment of history and how it contains the possibility of its reproduction within time, then Korea is a site for the "afterlife" of colonial modernity. Buck-Morss elaborates on this when she illustrates Benjamin's fascination with a female wax figure, saying, "her ephemeral act is frozen in time. She is unchanged, defying organic decay."[6] Constantly querying acts of remembrance, the *gaemang-cho* is a cultural embodiment of a particular historical moment.

Ever Present Past as Colonial PhantomThe spine of colonial tropes and analogous scientific discourses in East Asia that have caused xenophobia, collective fear, and a psychology of victimhood are closely linked to a particular form of Japanese anthropology that was "invented" as an imperialistic strategy against the orientalism inherent within its Western variant.[7] Anthropology as a discipline under Imperial Japan constructed a Japanese identity in dialectical opposition to Korean and other Asian Others. Micronesians, for example, became the "lazy Other"; Koreans, Taiwanese, the Ainu in Japan, and the indigenous people of Taiwan became "them," not "us." Through various discourses on race, gender, and pseudoscience, Imperial Japan reorganized Asia's epistemological topography with the colonial logics of inclusion and exclusion, and in so doing, secured its position as the superior Asian, as the one that was "almost white but not quite."[8]

However, since colonial liberation, such differentiation amounts to no more than a narrative of ethnic abjection.[9] The question thus remains: after the fall of the Japanese Empire, how do the discourses of colonialism and pseudoscience remain as a historical trauma within Korean society? How did the internalized rhetoric of mono-ethnic nationalism and the mimesis of colonial imperialism come to represent South Koreans' memorable—as well as forgettable—wounds?

The body of South Korea has experienced rhetorical plagues through the enchanting but humiliating ambivalence between discourses of victimhood, the circulation of colonial modernity/mentality, the sorcerous conjuration of both anticommunism and fascism, the invention of North Koreans as the nonhuman animal "Other,"[10] and a compressed version of twentieth-century modernization. The prosthetic modernity embedded within the colonial memories from two empires, Japan and the US, caused postcolonial pathology in which the South Koreans incessantly imitate the imperialists' logics while underestimating themselves and limiting their own possibilities.

If the metonymy of interregnum, which Gramsci describes as an intermediate state between life and death, could be applied to the recent Sewol Ferry incident,[11] we can find evidence of a "hypertrophy of memory" in the art world and its treatment of the politics of mourning, as well as in the spheres of mass media and popular culture.[12] "Colonial memory" is an epistemological and ontological problem for the question of bare life and the right to live. In the context of Korean modernity, the crucial aspect of the interstitial returns through the Sewol ferry incident, in that it posed the following questions: "Who counts as human? Whose lives count as lives? And what makes for a grievable life?"[13] It is precisely the reification of multiple modernities that fissure and rupture the cognitive topography of modernity and allow these questions to be asked without clear answers.

Nonhuman and Animal Subjectivities

In late 2010, food-and-mouth disease and avian influenza (AI) spread throughout Asia. In most countries, including Japan, only the livestock in the infected farms were disposed of, but in Korea the government killed all animals within a three kilometer radius of the farms under investigation. Foot-and-mouth disease is a mild virus; it has a 1 percent mortality rate and can be cured in a mere ten days. Yet in spite of this, to secure the country's status as an AI-free nation, over 3.5 million livestock animals, including pigs, cows, and goats, were killed in eleven provinces and cities across South Korea, and four million noncontagious ducks and chickens were also killed. According to regulations and guidelines provided by the Animal and Quarantine Agency of South Korea, livestock should be disposed of by incineration after euthanasia, but most of the animals were buried alive in order to meet such rapid a demand.[14] Over 4,800 burial grounds were legally sealed by the government for three years. The hastily sutured sites are gradually returning to their nature in the form of paddy fields and barns, yet in the process, in land where the smell of death still permeates the air, bones rise to the surface and blood seeps down and saturates the water, flowing into rice fields and rivers.

In 2014, the ban on forensic investigation was lifted on the burial grounds. These nonhuman subjects resurfaced as fractal images in germs, fungi, and bones, shouting in silence to question the biopolitics of modernity. The buried, nameless animals are now returning to the ground as a sign of a revolt against the hygienic logic of modernization, a phenomenological proof of dehumanization and a fundamental question concerning the anthropocentric demarcation of life and death. The return of the primordial in Korea threatens the status reserved exclusively for humanity, which is the colonial superior vis-à-vis nature; furthermore, it now opens up the possibility that the Otherization and objectification of humanity is negotiable. Along with the Sewol ferry incident, these animals generate new cultural discourses on Korean contemporaneity within the magnetic field of sovereignty and nonhuman subjectivities.

Coda

In discourses of modernity, the "repatriation" of animals and the primitive have been handled as if the subject was an appendage. Where is the limit of the ambiguous ethical questions on humanity? The logic of speciesism was first invented by Darwin. Imperial Japanese philosopher of science Tanabe Hajime of the Kyoto school gave it a slight twist to promote the ideology of ethnically homogeneous modern nation-states and his logic of race (*minzoku*). What are the Lamarckian legacies implanted in our bodies that relentlessly Otherize races and nonhumans in order to obtain a holistic comprehension of humanity? The nonhuman and the animal, "neither human nor beast,"[15] have always lived among us, and are trying to come back. This essay must conclude with a discussion of how the return of the dispossessed, its dreadful prospects, and our screen memories of animality can be transformed and become curative memory.

I wish to be on guard against the humanist reflections of pseudo-postcolonial narcissism. Taking a position from the opposite side, animism/animality is a mirror reflection of humanity, defined as irrational and antiscientific by modernity but then ultimately born again from it. I dream of humanity within animism in the form of the less familiar unconscious and new primal scenes. That is to say, I dream of animism as an alternative form of humanity that would manifest itself sometimes as a present-progressive form of sorcery and primitive religion and other times as an exuviated spirit of colonial modernity disjointed from time and space. I dream of a humanity that would put "the punctum of the uncanny"[16] on all Otherized objects and forever remain as a healing memory.

1 Maruboshi was a rail freight transportation and cargo unloading company that operated in every railroad station in colonial Korea. After liberation, it was classified as an enemy business and was nationalized. In 1962, it became Korea Transportation Ltd. (now Korea Express) and merged with Joseon Rice Warehousing.

2 Antonio Gramsci, *Selections from the Prison Notebooks* (New York: International Publishers, 1971), 276.

3 Richard F. Calichman, *What is Modernity? Writing of Takeuchi Yoshimi* (New York: Columbia University Press, 2005). For a discussion of the universalism and particularism of the West and

East in modern knowledge, see Naoki Sakai, "Dislocation of the West and the Status of the Humanities," *Traces 1: A Multilingual Journal of Cultural Theory and Translation, Specters of the West and Politics of Translation*, 2001: 71–94.

4 "Ephemera Orientalis McLachlan ... is a common burrowing mayfly which is found distributed throughout temperate East Asia including northeastern China, Mongolia, the Russian Far East, the Korean Peninsula, and the Japanese Islands (Hwang et al. 2008). The larvae occur abundantly in the lower reaches of streams, rivers, and lentic areas such as lakes and reservoirs, and are becoming more important in the biomonitoring of freshwater environments. The mass emergence and light attraction behavior of this species during the late spring and summer seasons, however, frequently causes serious nuisance to people residing in towns and cities near streams and rivers. This species is particularly abundant in the Han River that runs across Seoul and the frequency and intensity of its mass emergence has evidenced an increase in recent years." Jeong Mi Hwang, Tae Joong Yoon, Sung Jin Lee, and Yeon Jae Bae, "Life history and secondary production of Ephemera orientalis (Ephemeroptera: Ephemeridae) from the Han River in Seoul, Korea," *Aquatic Insects* 31, Supplement 1 (2009): 333–41.

5 The nutria (*Myocastor coypus*), also known as the river rat, was first imported to Korea in 1987 from Bulgaria for meat. They were initially farmed in Yongam-ni, Seosan-gun, South Chuncheong Province. However, the nutria meat business did not quite take off in Korea, and thus nutria farmers began abandoning the business and releasing the giant rats into the wild. The rats have now become a serious threat to the environment and are being hunted and killed.

6 She describes the wax figure in the Musée Gravin as a "Wish Image as Ruin: Eternal Fleetingness ... No form of eternalizing is so startling as that of the ephemeral and the fashionable forms which the wax figure cabinets preserve for us. And whoever has once seen them must, like André Breton [*Nadja*, 1928], lose his heart to the female form in the Musée Gravin who adjusts her stocking garter in the corner of the loge." Susan Buck-Morss, *The Dialectics of Seeing: Walter Benjamin and the Arcades Project* (Cambridge, MA: MIT Press, 1991), 369.

7 For more references about this colonial anthropology and its tactics during the Imperial era, see Sakano Tohru, *Teikoku Nihon to Junyuigakusha* [Imperial Japan and Anthropologists] (Tokyo: Keiso Shobo Publishing, 2005); and *Wartime Japanese Anthropology in Asia and the Pacific*, eds. Akitoshi Shimizu and Jan van Bremen (Osaka: National Museum of Ethnology: 2003).

8 Homi K. Bhabha, *The Location of Culture* (London: Routledge, 1994).

9 The term "ethnic abjection" was first used by Rey Chow in "The Secret of Ethnic Abjection." Postcolonial theories have contributed to the global spread of the discourse of hybridity and cultural diversity as counternarratives to transnationalism and globalization. "Ethnic abjection" refers to the identity of heterogeneity that is artfully concealed within this counterdiscursive frame and the emotional structure of the ambiguity, rage, pain, and melancholy brought about by the politics of recognition. Rey Chow, "The Secret of Ethnic Abjection," *Traces 2: A Multilingual Journal of Cultural Theory and Translation, Specters of the West and Politics of Translation*, 2001: 53–77.

10 During the Park Chung-hee dictatorship in 1960s and '70s, North Koreans were frequently represented in popular media as animals such as rats, pigs, wolves, and foxes, and became associated with the hatred and negative symbolism that these animals carry for their potential to spread infectous disease, such as typhus and epidemic hemorrhagic fever. In so doing, anticommunist narratives constituted an uncanny heterogeneous contemporaneity with the culture of (post)colonial Japanese. Therefore, various class-, gender-, and ethnic-based narratives suddenly become sutured under the rubric of modernization and national security.

11 The Sewol ferry incident occurred on April 16, 2014 and killed more than three hundred people, mostly high school students on a school trip to Jeju Island. It has came to be regarded in South Korea as a preventable disaster resulting from government in competence.

12 This term is borrowed from Andreas Huyssen, *Present Pasts: Urban Palimpsests and the Politics of Memory* (Stanford: Stanford University Press: 2003), 3.

13 These questions are posed by Judith Butler when she draws on Agamben's notion of bare life to discuss post-9/11 America and the second Gulf War. Judith Butler, *Precarious Life: The Powers of Mourning and Violence* (London: Verso, 2006), 20.

14 Among the places where the animals were buried alive, there were many sites that did not obey the instructions to install basic facilities such as drainage with perforated drainpipes. See "About Animal Disease Control," qia.go.kr/english.

15 For Agamben, the wolf symbolizes a metonym of the return of the primitive in the collective unconscious. He writes: "What had to remain

in the collective unconscious as a monstrous hybrid of human and animal, divided between the forest and the city—the werewolf—is, therefore, in its origin the figure of the man who has been banned from the city ... The life of the bandit, like that of the sacred man, is not a piece of animal nature without any relation to law and the city. It is, rather, a threshold of indistinction and of passage between animal and man, *physis* and *nomos*, exclusion and inclusion: the life of the bandit is the life of the *loup garou*, the werewolf, who is precisely *neither man nor beast*, and who dwells paradoxically within both while belonging to neither." Giorgio Agamben, *Homo Sacer: Sovereign Power and Bare Life*, trans. Daniel Heller Roazen (Stanford: Stanford University Press, 1998), 105.

16 "The punctum of the uncanny" is a phrase Hal Foster uses in reference to Roland Barthes's concept of "punctum." Barthes speaks of "the tactile trace, the marks that photography leaves on our body." Foster is referring to the uncanny feeling one gets from objects that seem to actually exist. This is related to the Freudian "return of the repressed," or the unconscious desire to return to the state of not knowing the distinction between life and death, between organism and inorganic substance. Hal Foster, *Compulsive Beauty* (Cambridge, MA: MIT Press, 1993).

"Or are we human beings?"

Thomas Keenan

Perhaps you have been struck by the frequency and regularity with which people find it necessary to state what one might think was the most obvious thing in the world: that they are human beings, or that they would like to live like them.

Here's an example from the front lines of the so-called "refugee crisis" in Europe last March:

> "May God take his revenge on them—everyone who did this to us—from whatever country they come from," said Raife al-Baltajy, a Syrian from near Aleppo, as she waited for a bus with her family. "May god take his vengeance out on them. Isn't it sinful? Are we animals? Or are we human beings?" She said she had been living in Syria for four years under the shelling, but traveled to Turkey, then to the Greek island of Lesbos, where she took a ferry to the mainland and on to Idomeni.[1]

Or this claim from another Syrian refugee who spoke out from his new home in the United States:

> I was born as a human and raised as a human. I have been in some situations that made me feel not like a human," [Refaai Hamo, a civil engineer] said. "I would like to grab any opportunity I can to prove I am a human being and if I don't have that opportunity, I refuse to live anywhere I don't feel like a human.[2]

How do we understand this repeated need of people in situations of displacement, conflict, and injustice to ask others whether they, the speakers, are in fact human, which is to say, their need "to prove I am a human being"? What is going on when people say this? It seems obvious, but in fact it's one of the most complicated, enigmatic, unstable things that can possibly be said. We should not take its possibility for granted.

That said, people have been saying it, more or less, for a while. Versions of the claim have a long history—think back to Josiah Wedgwood's famous antislavery medallion of 1787, featuring a shackled African figure knelt in a plea and bearing the inscription "Am I not a man and a brother?"; or to the even more economical signs borne by the Memphis, Tennessee sanitation workers on strike in the spring of 1968, "I am a Man." This rich provenance makes the utterance somehow even more perplexing: Haven't we learned this yet? Why do people still need to say this? What accounts for the persistence of this claim?

To begin to understand and appreciate these words, "I am a human being," we need to back up and ask just what sort of speech act is being performed here. I will call it a *claim*, whether it's formulated as a question ("Am I not ... ?"), a desire ("We want to live like ..."), a simple declaration, or an apparent tautology ("I am a ... "). In each case, the statement makes a claim, and a claim on others.

I would suggest that rights, especially what we call human rights, are better treated as *things we claim* rather than *things we have*. This may seem like a minor matter of words but I believe that it has the potential to challenge profoundly the ways we think about and act with the discourse of human rights. It does not weaken the force of these claims to admit that they are only, or just, that, claims; in fact, it might make them stronger by making them less essentialist, dogmatic, sacred, or, as Michael Ignatieff once put it, idolatrous.[3] I think this can help us appreciate a number of things, including: what it means to say that human rights are being "violated," the fact that what counts as a right—and who counts as a rights-bearer—can and has varied so dramatically over time and place, the common experience that the would-be universality of rights is so hard to grasp, and the fact that rights language can serve to propel campaigns of domination and not just struggles against injustice.

A few years ago, introducing the mammoth photobook *The Face of Human Rights*, Walter Kalin economically summed up the contemporary status of his topic with this formulation: "Human rights are the product of an historical process which has not yet reached completion."[4] Here the modesty of the concession to history is balanced, or even overwhelmed, by the confident faith in a progressive expansion signaled by the little phrase "as yet." The fact of incompletion is paradoxically the sign of more to come.

And yet we could detach this narrative of ongoing accomplishment from its teleology and see in it an important insight about human rights as a thought and practice: in spite, it seems, of their would-be eternality and universality, human rights are structurally incomplete, without fixed limits. This happens not despite their would-be universality, but because of it. The universe of their extent is not given in advance, and in fact we could say that the struggle to define its extents—which is in fact the struggle to determine who or what is and is not the subject or bearer of those rights—constitutes the story and the history of human rights. Because rights are a matter of claims, which is to say, disputations, and because those claims require evidence and demand assent, the subjects and the borders of rights are structurally in flux.

The contemporary world offers at least two contradictory answers to the question of how that "process" is coming along.On the one hand, violations of rights seem more widespread, more visible, and less adequately answered than they have been in a long time. The civil war in Syria, with videotaped sarin gas attacks and an archive of torture photos on one side and mass executions of prisoners heralded by the executioners on another, offers a convenient figure of this. Likewise the so-called "refugee" or "migrant crisis" that is at least in part the result of that war and its extraordinary cruelties. Amidst so much violence and a tide of displaced people, who could possibly speak of human rights?

But on the other hand, rights claims continue to proliferate, with new subjects speaking its language in new dialects and new spaces every day. Many have noted this, some approvingly and some with dismay about the hegemony of the discourse. What matters in this perspective is not that rights are being violated but that the assaults are understood, and answered, *as* violations rather than as mere suffering. Claiming the right to have rights is not the same as actually enjoying them, of course, but it is the claim, and the demand that people be treated as rights-bearers rather than remaining invisible or as victims or recipients of charity, that makes all the difference. The declaration that "we have become citizens, when once we were sheep," as a resident of Damascus in the early days of the uprising there was quoted as saying, echoes loudly, and it is that transformation in status, the eruption of demands out of obedience, dissent out of acquiescence, that would, in this regard, call for our attention.[5]

But what if this paradox in fact points to something essential that happens when we speak in terms of rights, whether civil or human? It has often been remarked that rights are nowhere more vigorously claimed—or even recognized as such—than in the aftermath of their violation. Given the generally high level of creativity humans have shown in inventing new ways to harm each other, this might indicate that rights claims are constitutively incomplete. Not that they have "not yet reached completion," but that they *cannot*—they quite simply cannot reach that destination.

Historian Lynn Hunt argues for a version of this narrative in her important, if sometimes controversial, account of the history of human rights, *Inventing Human Rights*.[6] A prominent scholar of the French Revolution, she tells the story of the eighteenth-century emergence of politically powerful notions of autonomy, bodily integrity, and the capacity to identify with others who are not obviously like us. Rights, in this sense of universal claims about what we all share, have a history, which is what she means by "invented."

She too starts from a paradox: How is it that, without ever defining what a man or a human being was, and in fact intending to limit this category to a small group of white male Catholic property-holders, the French "Declaration of the Rights of Man and Citizen of 1789" turned out to be so contagious in its application, so uncontrolled in its spread? If, as the "Declaration" begins, "men are born and remain free and equal in rights," to whom exactly did the phrase "men" refer? The abstraction seems so general as to be useless, imprecise, and unenforceable. Deprived of almost all reference to nature or to history, nation or faith or tradition, how could these assertions go anywhere?

Hunt agues that this bland generality concealed a very specific set of assumptions.

> Those who so confidently declared rights to be universal in the late eighteenth century turned out to have something much less all-inclusive in mind. We are not surprised that they considered children, the insane, the imprisoned, or foreigners to be incapable or unworthy of full participation in the political process, for so do we. But they also excluded those without property, slaves, free blacks, in some cases religious minorities, and always and everywhere, women.[7]

But the "Declaration" simply took all that for granted, and what it stated was notable not for its exclusions but for its lack of them—its vague, sweeping, abstract generality. It named its subject simply as "men." This definitional reticence structured its discourse: no subject was ruled out a priori, even if they might be excluded in fact.

And so something unintended happened. Rights, and claims of rights, began to spread. How did these vague abstractions come to be so productive of concrete, particular, specific effects? Hunt's answer is that their apparently crippling abstraction and lack of definition were in fact *responsible* for their viral mobility. Rights ungrounded and stripped of metaphysical justification, rights without pre-given subjects, rights proclaimed "without defining the qualifications for citizenship," as she puts it, were rights that exceeded their original limitations, spread far beyond their prescribed borders.[8] And so the salient feature of articulating grievances and emancipatory desires in terms of the rights of "men" was an implicit commitment to an overflow: without definition and in the absence of all qualifications for having them, rights belong not so much to everyone as to *anyone*. If it can't be shared, if it belongs only to me or to one group, it might be a protection or an entitlement, but it's not a right. Rather than offering a definition of citizenship or human being and then attaching rights to it like a predicate to a subject, the process seems to work in reverse: the rights enumerated are themselves what come to define the man or citizen. This meant that the declaration of rights unleashed an unanticipated, unpredicted, and unpredictable process. For better and for worse. No one knew in advance to whom they referred. Their referent was, structurally, in question, and the political realm was thus revealed as a space of constitutive dispute or conflict: Who could take part, who could claim, who counted? These questions are political ones par excellence. Invoking "rights" was nothing more or less than a way of calling existing subjects and definitions into question. Since, as Hunt argues, "rights once announced openly raised new questions—questions previously unasked and previously unaskable," they constituted a radically destabilizing force. The "Declaration" put everything into question, and "rights questions thus revealed a tendency to cascade."[9] This happened thanks to the lacuna: "precisely because it left aside any question of specifics, the July–August 1789 discussion of general principles helped set in motion ways of thinking that eventually fostered more radical interpretations of the specifics required." The "Declaration," Hunt reiterates, "offered no specific qualifications for active participation. The institution of a government required movement from the general to the specific; as soon as elections were set up, the definition of qualifications for voting and holding office became urgent. The virtue of beginning with the general became apparent once the specific came into question." And thus the cascade: "over the next months and years, group after group came up for specific discussion and eventually most of them got equal political rights."[10] Hunt's frequent critic Samuel Moyn underlines the power of this argument:

> Hunt is most interested in what she repeatedly calls the cascading logic of human rights, whereby those who announced rights were compelled to extend them to Jews, blacks and women (or at least to consider doing so). And when groups initially excluded from humanity were not brought into the fold, as Hunt points out, they sometimes forced the issue. Early feminists like Olympe de Gouges and Mary Wollstonecraft declared the rights of women, while slaves in the French Caribbean demanded liberation.[11]

Group after unqualified group made their claims, based on nothing more than the projection of an analogy between themselves and those who had already made their own claims. Rights were extended first to non-Catholics (first Protestant men, then Jewish), to free black men, and then to all men in metropolitan France except servants and the unemployed. The tide continued with Toussaint l'Ouverture's insurgency in the French colonial Caribbean ("I want Liberty and Equality to reign in Saint Domingue," he said), which led to the abolition of slavery in 1794, and finally with the unsuccessful campaigns of Olympe de Gouges and others for equal rights for women. Each time the grammar and rhetoric of rights claims were repeated in a chorus of new voices—not always successfully, and not always effectively, but repeated and transformed nonetheless."[12] The story of this conceptual and practical movement, born of abstraction, is structured by ebbs and flows. It is a story of conflict, of injustice and struggle, of claims made and sometimes rebuffed and sometimes answered. But it is certainly the story of an outpouring, of an overflow that, although it often follows preexisting features of the terrain, does not have to. Each new claim came with its own performatives and justifications, articulated new qualifications and challenges, washed away the fixed features of the landscape of status in order to remake the definitions of what was required in order to take part in political life—to remake the political, in fact, by politicizing what hadn't been political.

Hunt writes: "The notion of the 'rights of man,' like revolution itself, opened up an unpredictable space for discussion, conflict, and change." And it is not over: it is always incomplete, since nothing given prevents the space from contracting or expanding. That is what a "process" means. "The cascade of rights continues, though always with great conflict about how it should flow."[13] This may sound insanely optimistic and out of touch with reality. It's neither. It amounts simply to the claim that, politically speaking, humanity is an essentially contested category. It would not be overstating things, in fact, to say that politics is, in its richest sense, about this contest.

Because, let's be clear, the groups of people that Hunt discusses, like the speakers whose demands I began by quoting, have not just been accidentally or inadvertently "left out" of political life. It is not a simple omission, not a matter of haste or a momentary lapse, that excludes them from participation or recognition. At any given moment, there is a line, or lines, demarcating who counts as a member of the community and who doesn't. This is easy to see when we are talking about citizenship, but the structure extends to any and all such communities. Even ones that proclaim their universal extension and radical openness have to make decisions, conscious or not, about the minimal requirements for inclusion, whether they are seemingly trivial ones like age species, or seemingly vicious ones like race or gender. The existing features of any political sphere, the constitution of the community, at any given time is premised on exclusion. One cannot wish or theorize this away. One can only put up with it or challenge it. And the story of politics, exemplified by the ebb and flow I've retold from Hunt's historical narrative, is about the challenges and the contests over these lines of demarcation. Or, to put it a bit more carefully, it's about projects to politicize subjects and topics that have not previously been seen as political, and, in the other direction (lest you think this is always a happy story), about projects to put certain subjects and issues out of political contest, to naturalize or depoliticize them.

So "humanity" is, ironically, as Bruno Latour would say, a thing: "the issue that brings people together *because* it divides them."[14] We are that issue, precisely because it is not clear who we are. We are the ones deciding, which is to say debating, who we are. Many years ago Claude Lefort put this very elegantly, in an economical and profound critique of the erroneous attribution of a theory of *natural* rights to the American and French declarations: this masks, he says,

> the extraordinary event constituted by a declaration that was an auto-declaration, that is, a declaration by which human beings, speaking through their representatives, revealed themselves to be both subjects and objects of the utterance in which, all at once, they named the human in one another, ‘spoke to’ one another, appeared before one another, and, in so doing, erected themselves into their own witnesses, their own judges.[15]

This implies the persistence of the debate about who or what is the subject of human rights, a debate which can go any one of a number of ways at different times. There is division and a debate because who or what is a human being is not a matter of intuition nor of self-evidence; hence, an irreducible part of those claims and that debate will be the presentation of evidence, which is to say that we are in the domain of mediation, representation, and rhetoric—what Latour calls the “long retinue of complicated *proof-giving* equipment.”

Claims, in other words, require evidence, and the consideration of that evidence is always the task of others. I began with a pair of examples of apparently obvious statements of the sort “I am a human being,” claims that, I’ve argued, are actually far from obvious. In fact, in some cases it’s a wonder that we can hear them at all: How do those who have no standing, whom we do not recognize as one of us, who do not count and do not even appear before us as fellow political subjects—how do they make themselves heard and attended to? These are not rhetorical or overly dramatic questions: think of how long it took for slaves to be registered or recognized as human beings, a struggle that has still not been definitively accomplished, or for torture to be abolished, also not exactly a done deal. And for good reason, as it were: if membership in the community is premised on the exclusion of others from it, then the identity and self-understanding of those who count depends precisely on *not* being those who don’t. So when the excluded say, “count us, we are humans (or French, or whatever) like you,” they are not asking simply to make the space of the community bigger, to add some extra chairs to the table, as it were. They are asking for a new space, a new table, and a new definition of who it is who sits at it. When they are recognized, heard, admitted, the definition of who we all are undergoes a shift. It’s no wonder that these matters are so strongly contested, and that people have to keep contesting them.

Portions of this text also appear in *The Flood of Rights*, eds. Thomas Keenan, Suhail Malik, and Tirdad Zolghadr (Sternberg Press, 2017).

1 Elena Becatoros and George Jahn, "Migrants and refugees are piling up at muddy camp near the closed Greece-Macedonia border as European officials say a well-trodden route through the Balkans is no longer available," *US News*, March 10, 2016.
2 Beth Dalbey, "World's Most Celebrated Syrian Refugee 'Home' in Michigan," *Troy Patch*, December 18, 2015.
3 Michael Ignatieff, *Human Rights as Politics and Idolatry* (Princeton: Princeton University Press, 2003).
4 *The Face of Human Rights*, eds. Walter Kälin, Lars Müller, and Judith Wyttenbach (Baden: Lars Müller Publishers, 2004), 21.
5 "The squeeze on Assad," *The Economist*, June 30, 2011.
6 Lynn Hunt, *Inventing Human Rights* (New York: W. W. Norton, 2007)
7 Ibid., 18–19.
8 Ibid., 132.
9 Ibid., 145, 147.
10 Ibid., 147, 151.
11 Samuel Moyn, "On the Genealogy of Morals," *The Nation*, April 16, 2007.
12 Hunt, *Inventing Human Rights*, 149–50, 166, 171. Napoleon reestablished slavery in the colonies in 1802, which lasted until 1844.
13 Ibid., 175, 212.
14 Making Things Public: Atmospheres of Democracy, eds. Bruno Latour and Peter Weibel (Cambridge, MA: MIT Press, 2005), 13.
15 Claude Lefort, *Democracy and Political Theory* (Cambridge: Polity Press, 1988), 38.

Biographies

Lucia Allais is an architectural historian and theorist who teaches at Princeton University, a member of Aggregate, and an editor of *Grey Room*.

Nick Axel is an architect, theorist, and deputy editor of e-flux Architecture.

Shumon Basar is a writer, editor, and thought councillor.

Ruha Benjamin is assistant professor of African American studies at Princeton University and author of *People's Science: Bodies and Rights on the Stem Cell Frontier* (Stanford University Press, 2013).

Franco "Bifo" Berardi, founder of the famous Radio Alice in Bologna and an important figure in the Italian Autonomia movement, is a writer, media theorist, and media activist. His most recent book is *Futurability: The Age of Impotence and the Horizon of Possibility* (Verso, 2017).

Daniel Birnbaum is Director of Moderna Museet in Stockholm.

Ina Blom is professsor in the Department of Philosophy, Classics, and History of Art and Ideas at the University of Oslo and author of *The Autobiography of Video: The Life and Times of a Memory Technology* (Sternberg Press, 2016).

Benjamin H. Bratton is author of *The Stack: On Software and Sovereignty* (MIT Press, 2016) and Education Program Director of Strelka Institute. He is also professor of visual arts and Director of the Center for Design and Geopolitics at the University of California, San Diego, a professor of digital design at The European Graduate School, and visiting faculty at SCI_Arc.

Giuliana Bruno is Emmet Blakeney Gleason Professor of Visual and Environmental Studies at Harvard University. She recently published *Surface: Matters of Aesthetics, Materiality, and Media* (University of Chicago Press, 2014).

Zeynep Çelik Alexander is an architectural historian who teaches at the University of Toronto.

Tony Chakar is an architect, artist, and writer. He teaches at the Académie Libanaise des Beaux-Arts (ALBA/UOB).

Beatriz Colomina is professor of architecture, Founding Director of the Program in Media and Modernity at Princeton University, and curator of the 3rd Istanbul Design Biennial.

Mark Cousins is Director of History and Theory at the Architectural Association in London.

Simon Denny is an artist based in Berlin. His recent exhibitions explore the implications of Blockchain technology on sovereignty.

Keller Easterling is an architect and writer from New York City and a professor at Yale University. Her recent book, *Extrastatecraft: The Power of Infrastructure Space* (Verso, 2014), examines global infrastructure networks as a medium of polity.

Hu Fang is a storyteller whose most recent book of stories is *Dear Navigator* (Sternberg Press and The Pavilion, 2014).

Rubén Gallo teaches at Princeton University and is author of *Freud's Mexico* (MIT Press, 2010) and *Proust's Latin Americans* (Johns Hopkins University Press, 2014).

Liam Gillick is an artist. He recently published *Industry and Intelligence: Contemporary Art Since 1820* (Columbia University Press, 2016).

Boris Groys is an art critic, media theorist, and philosopher. He is currently Senior Research Fellow at the Karlsruhe University of Arts and Design in Karlsruhe, Germany.

Rupali Gupte is an urbanist and cofounder of the School of Environment and Architecture in Mumbai.

Andrew Herscher is a fellow at the Stanford Arts Institute, associate professor at the University of Michigan, and author of *Violence Taking Place: The Architecture of the Kosovo Conflict* (Stanford University Press, 2010), *The Unreal Estate Guide to Detroit* (University of Michigan Press, 2012), and *Displacements: Architecture and Refugee* (Sternberg Press, 2017).

Nikolaus Hirsch is a Frankfurt-based architect, editor, and curator. Hirsch is the cofounder and editor of the Critical Spatial Practice series at Sternberg Press, as well as e-flux Architecture.

Tom Holert is an art historian and cultural critic based in Berlin who works on learning curves and knowledge vessels at the crossroads of politics, economy, contemporary art, design, and architecture.

Brooke Holmes is Robert F. Goheen Professor in the Humanities at Princeton University.

Francesca Hughes is an architectural theorist and educator who teaches at the AA, London. Author of *The Architecture of Error: Matter, Measure and the Misadventures of Precision*, she is currently working on a pre-history of the Universal Discrete Machine.

Andrés Jaque is the founder of the Office for Political Innovation, a Madrid/New York-based practice that brings inclusivity into daily life through architecture.

Lydia Kallipoliti is an architect, engineer, and scholar, and is currently an assistant professor at Rensselaer Polytechnic Institute. She is author of the forthcoming book *Closed Worlds, Or, What is the Power of Shit?*

Thomas Keenan teaches media, literature, and human rights at Bard College.

Sylvia Lavin is a professor of architecture at UCLA.

Yongwoo Lee is a media historian and cultural studies scholar based in New York and Seoul. He teaches media and cultural studies of modern Korea, film theory and popular culture in East Asia, intellectual history of wartime Japan and postwar Korea, Korean contemporary art, and post/colonial historiography in the Department of East Asian Studies at New York University.

Lesley Lokko teaches architecture and writes novels. She is associate professor of architecture and the Director of Graduate Programme at the University of Johannesburg.

MAP Office is a multidisciplinary platform devised by Laurent Gutierrez and Valérie Portefaix, based in Hong Kong since 1996.

Chus Martínez is professor and head of the Art Institute at the FHNW Academy in Basel.

Ingo Niermann is a writer and recently published the novel *Solution 257: Complete Love* (Sternberg Press, 2016).

Ahmet Öğüt is an artist who often collaborates with individuals whose expertise lies outside the field of art to construct situations that bring about shifts in perspective.

Trevor Paglen is an artist whose work spans image-making, sculpture, investigative journalism, writing, engineering, and numerous other disciplines.

Spyros Papapetros is associate professor of history and theory in the School of Architecture and the Program in Media and Modernity at Princeton University. He is author of *On the Animation of the Inorganic: Art, Architecture, and the Extension of Life* (University of Chicago Press, 2012).

Raqs Media Collective (Monica Narula, Jeebesh Bagchi, Shuddhabrata Sengupta) have been variously described as artists, curators, editors, and catalysts of cultural processes. They live and work in Delhi.

Juliane Rebentisch is professor of philosophy and aesthetics at the University of Arts and Design in Offenbach/Main, Germany.

Sophia Roosth is the Frederick S. Danziger Associate Professor in the Department of the History of Science at Harvard University. Her first book,

Synthetic: How Life Got Made, was published by the University of Chicago Press in 2017.

Felicity D. Scott is associate professor of architecture, Director of the PhD program in Architecture (History and Theory), and Co-director of the Critical, Curatorial, and Conceptual Practices in Architecture (CCCP) program at Columbia GSAPP. Her most recent book is *Outlaw Territories: Environments of Insecurity/Architectures of Counter-insurgency* (Zone Books, 2016).

Jack Self is Director of the REAL foundation and curator of the 2016 British Pavilion at the Venice Biennale of Architecture.

Prasad Shetty is an urbanist and cofounder of the School of Environment and Architecture in Mumbai.

Hito Steyerl is a filmmaker and writer who lives in Berlin.

Kali Stull is an integrative health advocate and artist living in Pittsburgh, PA. She received her masters in Public Health at the University of Pittsburgh, where she studied nonhuman agencies that affect human health and the impacts of inequity on wellbeing.

Pelin Tan is associate professor at the Architecture Faculty, Mardin Artuklu University, Turkey.

Alexander Tarakhovsky is a scientist, writer, and artist.

Paulo Tavares is a researcher at FAU-USP, Brasil, and a long-term collaborator of Forensic Architecture.

Stephan Trüby is professor of architecture and cultural theory at the TU München and associate of the magazine *ARCH+*. He was head of research and development for the 2014 Venice Architecture Biennale, directed by Rem Koolhaas.

Etienne Turpin is a philosopher and research scientist at the Massachusetts Institute of Technology and founding director of anexact office, his atelier for design research based in Jakarta and Berlin. He is a co-principal investigator of *Reassembling the Natural*, an exhibition-led inquiry into biodiversity loss and land use transformation funded by Germany's Kulturstiftung des Bundes, and a founding co-editor of the *intercalations: paginated exhibition* series, published by K. Verlag and the Haus der Kulturen der Welt in the context of *Das Anthropozän Projekt*. He is also a founding co-director of User Group Inc. LLP, a London-based, worker-owned cooperative building software for disaster response, emergency coordination, and environmental monitoring.

Anton Vidokle is an artist and editor of *e-flux journal*.

Sven-Olov Wallenstein is professor of philosophy at Södertörn Högskola in Stockholm.

Eyal Weizman is an architect, professor of spatial and visual cultures at Goldsmiths, University of London, and director of Forensic Architecture.

Mark Wigley is professor and Dean Emeritus of Columbia GSAPP and curator of the 3rd Istanbul Design Biennial.

Mabel O. Wilson is a professor at Columbia GSAPP where she teaches architectural design, history, and theory. She recently published *Begin with the Past: Building the National Museum of African American History and Culture* (Smithsonian Books, 2016).

Brian Kuan Wood is a writer and an editor of *e-flux journal*.

Liam Young is a speculative architect who operates across design, fiction, and futures.

Arseny Zhilyaev is an artist and museologist in Moscow and is on the editorial board of *Moscow Art Magazine*.

Image Credits

Page 16
Courtesy Bibliothèque nationale de France.

Page 34
Courtesy Shigeru Ban Architects. © Shigeru Ban Architects.

Page 47
© Massachusetts Historical Society.

Pages 56–68
All images courtesy of the author.

Page 73
Anton Gruner. Briefe aus Burgdorf. Über Pestalozzi, seine Methode und Anstalt (Hamburg: Friedrich Perthes, 1804), plate X (1, 3). With permission from Getty Research Institute, Los Angeles (850910). © 2017 Artists Rights Society (ARS), New York.

Page 78
Public domain.

Page 84
Courtesy of Eyal Weizman.

Page 109
Top: © Peter Eisenman. Courtesy of Canadian Centre for Architecture.
Bottom: © Rollin LaFrance Collection, Architectural Archives University of Pennsylvania.

Pages 112, 115
Courtesy of miSci, Museum of Innovation & Science.

Pages 120, 124
Courtesy of Collection Le Consortium, Dijon.

Page 137
© 2017 The Isamu Noguchi Foundation and Garden Museum, New York / Artists Rights Society (ARS), New York.

Pages 161
Courtesy of NASA/Public domain.

Page 166
Courtesy of AIAA.

Page 181
Courtesy of Tony Chakar.

Page 186
Courtesy of Rupali Gupte & Prasad Shetty.

Page 194
Flickr User LMYang. Creative Commons License.

Page 205
Photo: Fulvio Ambrosio. Courtesy of the artist.

Pages 222–229
All Images copyright of the Austrian Frederick and Lillian Kiesler Private Foundation, Vienna.

Page 236
Photo: Abbie Rowe / National Archives and Records Administration.

Page 238
Photo: XML / www.parliamentbook.com.

Page 266
© ICC-CPI.

Page 274
© UNESCO/Pietro M. Apollonj Ghetti, in collaboration with Lamberto Grutter.

Page 284
Top: Public Domain.
Bottom: With permission from MIT.

Page 287
Top: Courtesy of Stuart Brisley.
Bottom: Beinecke Rare Book and Manuscript Library, Yale University.

Pages 297, 299
Courtesy Paulo Tavares / Autonoma.

Page 302
Photo courtesy of Armin Linke and Giulia Bruno.

Pages 336–345
Photos courtesy of Liam Young/ Unknown Fields.

Pages 380–382
Courtesy of Simon Denny.

Pages 394, 400
Courtesy of the artist.

Superhumanity: Design of the Self
Nick Axel, Beatriz Colomina,
Nikolaus Hirsch, Anton Vidokle,
Mark Wigley, Editors

ISBN 978-1-5179-0520-0 (hc)
ISBN 978-1-5179-0521-7 (pb)

A Cataloging-in-Publication record for this book is available from the Library of Congress.

Published by e-flux Architecture
www.e-flux.com/architecture/
architecture@e-flux.com

MINNESOTA

Printed and distributed by the
University of Minnesota Press
111 Third Avenue South
Suite 290
Minneapolis, MN 55401
www.upress.umn.edu

Published in collaboration with the Graham Foundation

Graham Foundation

Editors:
Nick Axel, Beatriz Colomina,
Nikolaus Hirsch, Anton Vidokle,
Mark Wigley

Image Editor:
Mariana Silva

Copyediting:
Mike Andrews

Image Research:
Judah Rubin

Design:
Jeff Ramsey

e-flux Books Managing Editor:
Kaye Cain-Nielsen

Superhumanity at the 3rd Istanbul Design Biennial was produced in cooperation with the Istanbul Design Biennial; the National Museum of Modern and Contemporary Art, Korea; the Govett-Brewster Art Gallery, New Zealand; and the Ernst Schering Foundation.

All fifty essays were originally published online at www.e-flux.com/architecture/superhumanity/.

"How to Kill People: A Problem of Design" by Hito Steyerl was first presented as the 2016 Benno Premsela Lecture at Het Nieuwe Instituut in Rotterdam, November 3, 2016.

"Right-wing Spaces" by Stephan Trüby is an extended version of the article "Rechte Räume" that appeared in *DIE ZEIT* on September 1, 2016. Translated from the original German by Simon Cowper.

"Aestheticization and Democratic Culture" by Juliane Rebentisch documents a lecture in which the author summarized some of the theses from her book *The Art of Freedom. On the Dialectics of Democratic Existence* (Cambridge: Polity Press, 2016) for discussion.

"Analysis: Synthesis" by Sophia Roosth is excerpted from the opening chapters and reprinted with permission from Sophia Roosth, *Synthetic: How Life Got Made* (University of Chicago Press, 2017). All rights reserved.

The Editors would like to thank:
Josh Altman, Ana Bichanich, David Burns, Miguel Coyula, Tanya Eskander, Marta Ferreira de Sá, Anselm Franke, Rubén Gallo, Maria S. Giudici, Jon Goodbun, Amal Issa, Platon Issaias, Lutz Issler, Andrés Jaque, Jang Un Kim, Evangelos Kotsioris, Adrian Lahoud, Jihoi Lee, Bartomeu Mari, Pieter Martin, Matteo Mastrandrea, Heike Catherina Mertens, Laura Mora, Deniz Ova, Godofredo Enes Pereira, Selin Pervan, Rachel L. Price, Simon Rees, Martina Schrammek, Ceren Senel, Pierre Shaw, Benedict Singleton, Bahar Turkay, Georgia White, Alan Woo, Merve Yucel.